JAMES JOYCE
AND
THE POLITICS OF DESIRE

Can Joyce be reclaimed for feminism?

James Joyce and the Politics of Desire offers the first feminist/ psychoanalytic reassessment of the Joycean canon in the wake of Freud, Lacan, and Kristeva.

Suzette Henke writes as a "resisting reader," centering her discussion of *Ulysses*, *Dubliners*, *A Portrait of the Artist*, *Finnegans Wake*, and *Exiles* around questions of desire and language and the politics of sexual difference.

Discussing *Dubliners* and *A Portrait of the Artist*, Henke argues that Joyce invokes gender stereotypes only to mock and subvert traditional notions of masculine aggression and feminine passivity. She interprets *Exiles* as a turning point in Joyce's developing sexual politics, and her analysis of *Ulysses* focuses on constructions of the gendered subject, as well as textual resonances of androgyny, bisexual fantasy, maternal abjection, and Lacanian masquerade. Henke's analysis of Molly Bloom's monologue relates her polyphonic soliloquy to Bakhtin's theories of dialogism in language, and shows how Molly's Penelopean discourse is steeped in the languages of Edwardian pornography and Victorian sentimental fiction.

Finally, Henke suggests that *Finnegans Wake* contains a female story which appropriates the textual authority of the male master narrative, thereby deconstructing the linguistic codes which underpin western patriarchal culture.

Suzette Henke's radical "re-vision" of Joyce's work is a striking example of the crucial role feminist theory can play in contemporary evaluation of canonical texts. As such it will be welcomed by feminists and Joyceans alike.

JAMES JOYCE
AND
THE POLITICS OF DESIRE

SUZETTE A. HENKE

ROUTLEDGE

NEW YORK AND LONDON

First published 1990
by Routledge
11 New Fetter Lane, London EC4P 4EE

Simultaneously published in the USA and Canada
by Routledge
a division of Routledge, Chapman and Hall, Inc.
29 West 35th Street, New York, NY 10001

© 1990 Suzette A. Henke

Printed in Great Britain by
Richard Clay Ltd, Bungay, Suffolk

British Library Cataloguing in Publication Data

Henke, Suzette A.
James Joyce and the politics of desire.
1. Fiction in English. Joyce, James 1882–1941
I. Title
823'.912
ISBN 0 415 01056 X HB
0 415 01057 8 Pbk

Library of Congress Cataloging in Publication Data

Henke, Suzette A.
James Joyce and the politics of desire / Suzette Henke.
p. cm.
Bibliography: p.
Includes index.
ISBN 0 415 01056 X. – ISBN 0 415 01057 8 (pbk.)
1. Joyce, James, 1882–1941 – Criticism and interpretation.
2. Psychoanalysis and literature. 3. Feminism and literature.
4. Desire in literature. I. Title
PR6019.09Z5815 1990
823'.912 – dc20 89-10075 CIP

For Elizabeth Kish Henke
and
In Memory of Allen James Henke

CONTENTS

ACKNOWLEDGEMENTS

The present examination of James Joyce's slippery and elusive politics of desire was inaugurated shortly after the 1982 publication of *Women in Joyce*, a collection of feminist essays co-edited with Elaine Unkeless. While exploring Joyce's controversial canon these past several years, I have had cherished support from friends, colleagues, students, and feminist sympathizers – all of whom cannot here be mentioned, but who should rest assured of my warm appreciation. I owe a large debt of gratitude to Bonnie Kime Scott of the University of Delaware, whose careful reading of the manuscript and salient criticisms gave force and direction to both textual formation and ideological revision. Professors Morris Beja, Michael Groden, Margot Norris, and R. B. Kershner read earlier versions of this book at various stages of production and provided helpful suggestions for improvement. My erstwhile graduate mentors, Professors Robert Polhemus, David Halliburton, and Albert Guerard of Stanford University, have remained trusted academic associates. A number of colleagues at SUNY-Binghamton have greatly enriched my professional life these past several years, and I wish to thank, in particular, Professors Richard McLain, Jean Quataert, and Bernard Rosenthal, three chairpersons who have done much to make working conditions at SUNY amenable to scholarship. For a grant that allowed me to spend the spring of 1985 reading French feminism on the Mediterranean coast, I am indebted to the Camargo Foundation of Cassis, France. For a research semester that enabled me to complete work on this project in Spring 1988, I am grateful to the State University of New York at Binghamton. I can only begin to thank Janice Price, the Routledge editor whose encouragement and unflagging patience made this book possible.

ACKNOWLEDGEMENTS

Because the past decade has been happily punctuated with guest professorships and peripatetic scholarship, my list of personal acknowledgements reads like an academic atlas. Nonetheless, I will "murmur name upon name" in gratitude to those friends who have done much to improve the life of a wandering professor and to facilitate scholarship in far-away places. For collegiality in a cold climate, I thank fellow faculty-members at the University of Aarhus and, in particular, Per Serritslev and Torben Kisbye. For aesthetic companionship in Denmark, Lise and Mogens Skjoth. For hospitality in Israel in 1983 – 4, my extraordinary colleagues at Haifa University. For enriching life in the middle east, Barbara Golan, Marion Hiller, Mary Khyatt, and Fischlers on both sides of the Atlantic. For welcoming me to India on a lecture tour in 1984, the United States Information Service and the faculty of Jadavpur and Delhi Universities. For openness in Australia, the faculty of Melbourne and Deakin Universities. For assistance and affability in London, Peter and Sybil Hunot, Adrian Williams, Deborah Philips, and Norman Bacrac. For hospitality in New York City and environs during stints at the New York Public Library, Dorchen Leidholdt and Elizabeth Tenenbaum. For a great deal of feminist inspiration, Jane Marcus of the City University of New York. For scintillating conversations on various parts of the planet, Professors Patricia Clements and Robert Rawdon Wilson of the University of Alberta. For friendship in wondrous places, Mary Faith Bonney and James Francis Rooney. For editorial assistance at the eleventh hour, Mary Le Donne and Michael Pavese. For familial support, I fondly acknowledge all of the Henkes, Kovacs, and Fiersts, as well as the Kishes and the Gishes – the latter of whom, in true Joycean fashion, have doubled their Austro-Hungarian signatures. As always, I owe continuing gratitude to Elizabeth Kish Henke, warmest friend.

Portions of this text have appeared in earlier, somewhat different, incarnations. Sections of the introduction were included in "James Joyce and Women: The Matriarchal Muse" in *Work in Progress: Joyce Centenary Essays*, ed. Richard F. Peterson, Alan M. Cohn, and Edmund L. Epstein and brought out by Southern Illinois University Press in 1982. Chapter 1 was first published as "Through a Cracked Looking-glass: Sex-Role Stereotypes in *Dubliners*" in *International Perspectives on James Joyce*, ed. Gottlieb Gaiser, 1986, and is reprinted by permission of the Whitston Publishing Company. An earlier version of Chapter 2 came out as "Stephen Dedalus and Women: A Portrait of the Artist as a Young Misogynist" in *Women in Joyce*, ed. Suzette Henke and Elaine Unkeless, 1982. A section of Chapter 5 originally appeared as "Speculum of the Other Molly: A Feminist/Psychoanalytic Inquiry into James Joyce's Politics of Desire" in *Mosaic*, Special Issue on *CONTEXTS*, 21/2–3 (Spring/Summer 1988). Some of the material in Chapter 6 formed part of "Anna the Allmaziful," published in *James Joyce and His Contemporaries*, ed. Diana A. Ben-Merre and Maureen Murphy (Westport, CT: Greenwood Press, 1989). All have been reprinted with permission of the publishers.

ABBREVIATIONS

CW   Joyce, James. *The Critical Writings of James Joyce*, ed. Ellsworth Mason and Richard Ellmann. New York: Viking Press, 1959.

D   Joyce, James. *Dubliners*, ed. Robert Scholes and A. Walton Litz. New York: Viking Press, 1969.

E   Joyce, James. *Exiles*. New York: Viking Press, 1951.

FW   Joyce, James. *Finnegans Wake*. New York: Viking Press, 1939; London: Faber & Faber, 1939.

GJ   Joyce, James. *Giacomo Joyce*, ed. Richard Ellmann. New York: Viking Press, 1968.

JJ   Ellmann, Richard. *James Joyce*. 1959; rpt New York: Oxford University Press, 1982.

JJA   *The James Joyce Archive*, ed. Michael Groden *et al*. New York and London: Garland Publishing, 1978.

JJQ   *James Joyce Quarterly*.

Letters I, II, III   Joyce, James. *Letters of James Joyce*. Vol. I, ed. Stuart Gilbert. New York: Viking Press, 1957; reissued with corrections 1966. Vols II and III, ed. Richard Ellmann. New York: Viking Press, 1966.

P   Joyce, James. *A Portrait of the Artist as a Young Man*, ed. Chester G. Anderson. New York: Viking Press, 1968.

SH   Joyce, James. *Stephen Hero*, ed. John J. Slocum and Herbert Cahoon. New York: New Directions, 1944, 1963.

SL   Joyce, James. *Selected Letters of James Joyce*, ed.
Richard Ellmann. New York: Viking Press,
1975.

U   + episode and line. Joyce, James. *Ulysses*, ed.
Hans Walter Gabler *et al.* New York and
London: Garland Publishing, 1984; rpt New
York: Random House and Harmondsworth:
Penguin, 1986.

INTRODUCTION
Defusing the Patriarchal Can(n)on

How can a feminist begin to approach the writings of James Joyce? A number of contemporary critics have indicted Joyce as a chauvinist author singularly devoted to projects of male linguistic mastery and to a celebration of what Jacques Lacan calls the primordial "signifier of signifiers," the Freudian phallus. If one accepts Lacan's psychoanalytic definition of the phallus as Logos – presence revealed in speech – then, metaphorically at least, Joyce would seem to occupy an exalted place in the logocentric and phallocentric pantheon of twentieth-century writers. Like most modernists, he longed to write himself into the body of the text – to transform world into word, life into Logos, in a magnificent aesthetic couvade that would re-create the cosmos in his own mental image.

Love melded with lust, desire, fantasy, scopophilia, infantile need, incestuous longing, vulnerability, and fear – such is the awesome figure of male/female desire informing Joyce's decentered and vertiginous universe. Women are constantly foregrounded in his texts as the focal point of Ulyssean wanderings and Dedalian aesthetic contemplation. Figures of love or loathing, worship or disdain, they emerge as emblems of that sacred coupling the author thought essential to art. Alone, Joyce's artist is insufferably narcissistic, a logocentric creator awash in a free play of signifiers ultimately signifying nothing. For inspiration and, indeed, for aesthetic grounding, he must turn to woman as both virgin and mother, creator of life and symbolic emotional savior. The female becomes in Joyce's writing a redemptive model of altruism and fertility, regenerative strength and matriarchal power. In the guise of phallic mother, she inaugurates a dream of psychoanalytic satisfaction, a center for that complex "dialectic of fantasies which takes the maternal body as its imaginary field."[1]

It would probably be a serious misprision to identify Joyce with his misogynist alter ego, Stephen Dedalus, or to label the author of *A Portrait* and *Ulysses* an "enemy of woman." Throughout his life, Joyce caricatured *machismo* notions of manly behavior and expressed horror at the Catholic doctrine of conjugal appropriation of the female body in marriage. In conversation with Arthur Power about Ibsen's drama, the mature Joyce championed what he termed the contemporary "revolt of women against the idea that they are the mere instruments of men" and defended the "emancipation of women," which he described as "the greatest revolution in our time in the most important relationship there is – that between men and women."[2] Nevertheless, Joyce's own attitude toward feminine desire always remained highly ambivalent. The dichotomy in his mind was not, apparently, between virgin and whore, but between narcissistic virgin and phallic mother – between the untouched and untouchable *ingénue* and the experienced maternal female. In the role of Dublin coquette, the Virgin Mary of Catholicism became a nubile temptress, coyly flirting with adult sexuality. At the same time, Joyce was fascinated by the Circean image of a voluptuous enchantress who could nurture or destroy the male enthralled by her charms.

In much of his early work, Joyce adopts what Julia Kristeva would describe as a theological stance. He transfers the transcendental, univocal value of phallic presence to woman as archetypal Other – the omnipotent mother and angelic muse who functions as "a pseudo-center, a mystifying center . . . to permit those making up the Same to identify with it" by a process of negation. Because the idealized female offers a Lacanian mirror image of fictive coherence, she evolves into a permutative symbol of radical otherness. On the basis of sexual difference, the "network to be deciphered" in Joyce's fiction "seems to be split in half. *Desire*, where the subject is implicated (body and history), and *symbolic order*, reason, intelligibility."[3]

In Joyce's canon, woman is both desirable object and subject of desire – the incomparable Other who remains mysterious and enigmatic. His female characters frequently embody that imaginary maternal presence that the unconscious constructs as a corollary to the pleasure principle of infantile need. A fantasmatic figure of satisfaction and plenitude, woman, as Lacanian "symptom," proves defiant of either knowledge or appropriation. Her physiological

2

blood-flow symbolizes the magical process of gestation and a curious sacramental alterity. She is mother, *mater*, matter, and *materia* – the symbolic ground of being from which all life flows. But she appears, simultaneously, as a threatening and perplexing *imago*, a chimera of fantasized phallic power that might, at any moment, overwhelm, engulf, and castrate the male. The figure of woman is perpetually abducted from a mimetic frame and framed by the sexual differences imposed by an idealized, matrifocal text.

Woman emerges in Joyce's work as virgin or whore, madonna or temptress, but usually within a problematic context of maternity. A "woman's love," Joyce declared, "is always maternal and egoistic" (*Letters* II, 912). Even the temptress is implicitly portrayed as a potential mother in training. Driven by the unconscious life-force of the species, she becomes a pawn to the instinctual drives of racial propagation. From her Oedipal role as "Papa's little bedpal. Lump of love" (*U* 3: 88), the adolescent girl learns to weave a web of romantic entrapment. Socialized in ritual patterns of seductive behavior, she practices alluring tricks to tempt the ingenuous suitor by acting on the knowledge that her body is her sole commodity, the one good that she can trade for the illusory security of marriage. For the most part, Joyce's Irish virgins are detached from both desire and personal will and skilled in a selfish manipulation of altruism. The intact virgin keeps herself aloof and unattainable; her chastity is a visible sign of invisible virtue as she remains, whole and unspoiled, a commodity available only at the price of life-long marital commitment. Refusing the scar of penetration or experience, she clings to moral values determined by the economy of libidinal exchange on a restricted sexual market.

Traditionally, readers have either praised Joyce for his intimate knowledge of the female psyche or condemned his view of women as stereotyped and reductive. As Simone de Beauvoir would remind us, it is not a very great leap from the celebration of woman as archetype to a denigration of her as stereotype. The idealized goddess can be just as debasing as a negative representation: "To say that Woman is Flesh, to say that the Flesh is Night and Death, or that it is the splendor of the Cosmos, is to abandon terrestrial truth. . . . Woman is not merely a carnal object. . . . To assimilate her to Nature is simply to act from prejudice."[4] Karen Horney is more candid in her assertion that "always, everywhere, the man strives to rid himself of his dread of women by objectifying it. . . .

3

May not this be one of the principal roots of the whole masculine impulse to creative work – the never-ending conflict between the man's longing for the woman and his dread of her?''[5]

There is, however, another side to Joyce's canon – a more ironic and compassionate dimension evident to the reader who applies a judicious, parallactic perspective to his work. In *Feminist Literary Criticism*, Cheri Register praises art that promotes a new social order founded on anti-patriarchal values, some of which have been perceived as traditionally female.[6] It is at this point that Joyce's writing might be placed within a more recognizable feminist context. Joyce clearly eschews the literary fraternity that Shulamith Firestone labels "Virility, Inc." when he challenges an authoritarian power-structure and satirizes patriarchal privilege. By comically deflating sex-role stereotypes of masculine prowess and feminine passivity, Joyce tends to advocate more enlightened principles of androgynous behavior in the complex politics of desire that govern sexual transactions.

In *Dubliners*, for instance, he tacitly acknowledges the undercurrents of anger, frustration, and helplessness that pervade Irish life. His short stories suggest that marriage is the primary profession open to young girls in turn-of-the-century Ireland and that most would rather choose a loveless match than none at all. The women of *Dubliners* are frequently trapped in limited domestic situations prescribed by the Catholic Church, by nineteenth-century moral training, and by Irish puritanical values. When they behave like shrews or termagants, they often are responding to a kind of sex-role enculturation that forces them to cling to the only shards of personal power accessible to their grasp. Ignatius Gallaher can make his way in the wide world, but women like Eveline Hill and Polly Mooney have only one option for survival – success on the marriage market, preferably in a match that promises upward social mobility. Many, Joyce implies, take the path of Annie Chandler, who reacts to marital frustration by bullying her timorous husband and doting excessively on her infant son. Both Catholic piety and Celtic sentimental attitudes cloak repressed sexual hostilities that adhere to the dark underside of Irish life.

The female characters in *Stephen Hero* and in *A Portrait of the Artist as a Young Man* are thinly sketched and fairly two-dimensional. Seen through the eyes of a self-consciously rebellious young man, women are perceived as threatening or enchanting, seductive or aloof. Their fictional portraits are largely contingent on Stephen's narcissistic projections and misogynist frame of mind. The shadowy Mercedes of *A Portrait* becomes the romantic object of Stephen's prepubescent fantasies, just as the Virgin Mary later appeals to his ascetic, monkish mentality. Once at university, Stephen rejects Irish puritanical values and the mores of bourgeois society. In *Stephen Hero*, he presents the ingenuous Emma with a startling proposition: "Just to live one night together, Emma, and then to say goodbye in the morning and never to see each other again! There is no such thing as love in the world: only people are young" (*SH* 198). Emma is understandably shocked by her suitor's outrageous suggestion and, unacquainted with the ideas of Ibsen or with *fin de siècle* notions of free love, she dismisses the bohemian artist as nothing less than mad. Stephen, in turn, rationalizes his rejection "by anathemising . . . Emma as the most deceptive and cowardly of marsupials. He discovered that it was a menial fear and no spirit of chastity which had prevented her from granting his request" (*SH* 210).

Both *Stephen Hero* and *A Portrait of the Artist* might be seen as extended delineations of Stephen's "flight from woman," first in the guise of a maternal authority figure, then as a Circean temptress.[7] Raised in a repressive Catholic environment, Stephen tends to reduce all women to threatening emblems of the flesh allied with the chaos of nature. Terrified of a fantasized temptress and haunted by fears of erotic compulsion, he seeks Freudian mastery over the "eternal feminine" through the "spiritual-heroic refrigerating apparatus" of art (*P* 252). As a poet, he can transcend physical excitation by consigning the temptress to a refrigerated world of aesthetic stasis and transforming her into a disembodied muse, an *objet d'art* controlled by the male imagination. The phantom subject of Stephen's villanelle appears to be a further projection of E— C— in still another poetic emanation. The young woman whose "simple and wilful heart" (*P* 216) eludes the suffering adolescent is here celebrated as a voluptuous object of masturbatory inspiration – naked, yielding, "odorous and lavish-limbed" (*P* 223). As seductress and autoerotic muse, she can be possessed in a moment of sublime ecstasy that offers both sensuous and imaginative gratification.

The protagonist of Joyce's *Exiles*, Richard Rowan, shares a number of Stephen's misogynist propensities. Joyce warns us in a note that "Richard must not appear as a champion of woman's rights. His language at times must be nearer to that of Schopenhauer against women and he must show at times a deep contempt for the long-haired, short-legged sex" (*E* 120). In *Exiles*, all the world is a stage, and Rowan assumes the role of author-director in the drama of his own betrayal. Horrified by the prospect of cuckoldry, he wants to plunge into the void of incertitude and freely offer his common-law wife to her suitor, Robert Hand. Paradoxically, Richard plays the benevolent patriarch by assuming that Bertha is a conjugal possession – that she is his to give away, like a cow or a piece of movable property. Acting as a puppet-master behind the scenes, he haughtily organizes Bertha's sexual temptation, as well as his own elaborate drama of self-conscious renunciation. Much to her credit, Bertha maintains a combination of dignity and naturalness throughout the play. She proves to be a fiery, autonomous individual who rebels against Richard's arrogant manipulations and demands recognition in her own right as a central and centrally heroic figure in the play.[8]

Throughout *Ulysses*, Joyce deliberately problematizes gender and interrogates sexual practice. The novel unfolds as a radical exploration of different forms of psychic mobility. Sexual identity is at once ambiguous and polymorphous, a state to be achieved through the textual exploration of a series of ostensibly perverse psychological drives. Characters are radically decentered by erotic fantasy and attempt to uncover new identities latent in residual needs that overflow the boundaries of sex-role expectations. Polymorphous perversity, translated into the bisexual drives of the unconscious, yields a curious and perplexed dissemination of sexual signifiers that challenge culturally embedded scripts of Oedipal triangulation.[9]

In the "Penelope" episode, Molly Bloom emerges as the *clou* of Joyce's novel (*Letters* I, 170) – a clue to the male-dominated, anti-heroic modern epic and a nail in the coffin of bourgeois, sentimental literature. Her world-view is gynocentric, and her monologue "turns like the huge earth ball slowly surely and evenly round and round spinning, its four cardinal points being the female breasts, arse, womb and [cunt] . . . expressed by the words *because, bottom, . . . woman, yes*" (*Letters* I, 170). Since the publication of *Ulysses* in 1922, readers have tended to see Molly either as an archetypal representation of Joyce's "eternal feminine" or as a debased stereotype of female eroticism. Carl Jung, for instance, praised Joyce for revealing a dimension of female psychology heretofore obscured in psychoanalysis. He described "Penelope" as a "string of veritable psychological peaches. I suppose the devil's grandmother knows so much about the real psychology of a woman. I didn't" (*Letters* III, 253). Philip Toynbee qualified Jung's assertion by suggesting that Molly represents not the "female mind" but "the *anima*, the female image in the mind of the male, sensual, intuitive, submarine." She embodies "womanhood in its sexual aspect" (*JJ* 295) as envisioned by "a feminate (androgynous) male."[10]

Although Leopold Bloom may see his wife as a figurative earth-mother and the reader may attribute to her an idealized, mythic stature, the mimetic Molly is emotionally frustrated and trapped in narrow, inhibiting female roles.[11] She nonetheless succeeds in spinning, through logorrheic iterations, a web of imaginative possibilities that allow her psychologically to inscribe herself in a complex polymorphous and polyphonic discourse of desire. Molly's great talent, apparently, is neither song nor sex, but dream and amorous reverie. She proves, in her own right, to be a poet of the imagination whose final soliloquy elevates *Ulysses* to the heights of lyrical discourse. By virtue of her capacious monologue, Molly can be envisaged as both goddess and whore, Dublin housewife and archetypal precursor to Anna Livia Plurabelle, the great mother/lover of *Finnegans Wake*.

Nowhere is Joyce's anti-patriarchal obsession more evident than in his final *magnum opus*. A number of recent interpretations of the *Wake* have proposed a feminist, post-structuralist analysis of this most radical and deracinated of texts.[12] Julia Kristeva, for instance, praises Joyce on the grounds that *Finnegans Wake* challenges paternal authority "not only ideologically, but in the workings of language itself, by a return to [pre-Oedipal] semiotic rhythms connotatively maternal."[13] Kristeva convincingly argues that Joyce attacks in the *Wake* the ideological code of patriarchy indigenous to domestic, religious, and political myths in western society, as much as he subverts the linguistic code basic to the structure of a logocentric culture.[14] She implicitly suggests that Anna Livia Plurabelle embodies what Lacan terms *le vréel* – the "she-truth" of female *jouissance* and the ultimate limit of any discourse articulated by man.[15]

In all his work, Joyce portrays human civilization enacting a continual dialectic between Logos and Eros, between male and female principles, between symbolic discourse and semiotic process.

Women represent for him the opulence, the chaos, and the naturalness of maternal passion, in opposition to the masculine impulse toward phallocentric domination and aggressive control. In the interests of racial survival, he implies, male authority must continually be subverted by vital amalgamation with the semiotic pulsions of feminine desire. In *Finnegans Wake*, a male master narrative gives way to a fluid female story in a linguistic bricolage that valorizes non-mastery and explodes the perpetual western preoccupation with a Nietzschean will to power.

In the *Wake*, the earth-mother Gea-Tellus has been overwhelmed by the more primal forces of flowing water symbolic of a mysterious, protean unconscious. As womb of the world, Anna Livia Plurabelle absorbs both squalor and sentiment, reality and dream. She is the archetypal river-woman, flowing out of the depths of the earth and carrying the leaves, flowers, and sediment of life in the wake of her shifting shoreline. Whereas the principal male persona, Humphrey Chimpden Earwicker, is identified in terms of an ancient Irish giant buried in the rocks of Howth and Chapelizod, Anna Livia embodies a fertile but ever-elusive reality. She captures the Heraclitean flux that fascinated her creator, and she forever changes in the context of a changeless biological cycle. Even more than Molly Bloom, Anna Livia articulates the rhythms of a capacious unconscious, as her fluid, fragmentary discourse irrupts in the elusive iterations of *écriture féminine*. She is open and forever yea-saying to the rushing torrents of temporal phenomena that characterize the "given" moment of cosmic experience.

Biographical evidence suggests that James Joyce eventually came to terms with the kind of adolescent misogyny earlier exhibited by his fictional surrogate Stephen Dedalus. Through Nora Barnacle, he found the madonna and muse who could both inspire his art and satisfy his arcane sexual desires.[16] Nora was the imaginary mother/wife whose exuberant sexuality finally released the inhibitions, both artistic and sexual, that once had stifled her shy, but willing son/lover, Jimmy Joyce. In a passionate invocation, Joyce wrote to her: "Guide me, my saint, my angel. Lead me forward. *Everything* that is noble and exalted and deep and true and moving in what I write comes, I believe, from you. O take me into your soul of souls and then I will become indeed the poet of my race" (*Letters* II, 248). He also exclaimed, in a fantasy of infantile regression: "O that I could nestle in your womb like a child born of your

8

flesh and blood, be fed by your blood, sleep in the warm secret gloom of your body!'' (*SL* 169).

I will not risk a defense of Joyce as "protofeminist" or attempt to recast his image as Woolfishly androgynous. A great deal of biographical evidence can be marshaled to press charges against him for narcissism, egotism, lewdness, and ostensible misogyny. Nonetheless, the historical Joyce seems eventually to have outgrown the kind of Daedalian/Dedalian narcissism he draws so boldly in *Stephen Hero* and in *A Portrait of the Artist*. The young man emerging from this ironic *Künstlerroman* has yet to learn the word of love "known to all men" and thoroughly inscribed (on the margins, to be sure) of Joyce's infamous "blue book of Eccles," as well as in the iconoclastic fabulations of *Finnegans Wake*.

In the course of the past several years, traditional feminist and psychoanalytic paradigms have given way to the influence of revolutionary critical voices. Issues of desire have proven ever more perplexing, despite (or because of) their current scholarly proliferation. One might begin with Plato and Aristotle, perhaps, in distinguishing desire from appetite, emotional affect from physical concupiscence. René Girard provides a useful schema in *Deceit, Desire and the Novel*. But otherwise, the territory of desire has largely been appropriated by modern psychoanalysis. Freud analyzed psychic longing in terms of physical need and emotional demand, mapping an economy of drives and satisfactions that still forms the skeleton of contemporary theory.[17] Jacques Lacan both refined and mystified Freudian hypotheses by introducing theories to explain the mirror stage of development, "splitting," the enunciation of the subject, psychological inscription into the register of paternal law and language, the phallus as transcendental signifier, and the Other as an imaginary construction of the infantile psyche that refuses to acknowledge the self as a fragmented *corps morcelé*.[18] Julia Kristeva further elaborated on Lacan's celebration of sexual *jouissance* and emphasized radical psychic and aesthetic differences between the logocentric, symbolic register of the father and pre-Oedipal, semiotic attachment to the mother. The last distinction is crucial to this study, since I have suggested that, for Joyce, the locus of psychic desire is often matrifocal and that the absence of primordial maternal bonding evinces a state of infantile abjection necessarily carried over into adult life.

In the following study I make use of a feminist/psychoanalytic methodology that draws freely on the theories of Jacques Lacan and Julia Kristeva, while not excluding other psychological and critical models. Re-visioning Joyce's work from the perspectives of radical feminism, I refer to the writings of Sigmund Freud, Luce Irigaray, and Jane Gallop, as well as to the object-relations psychology of Nancy Chodorow and the schizoanalytic positions of Gilles Deleuze and Félix Guattari. I use the term "politics" in the context of "sexual politics" to delineate those struggles and maneuvers involved in the psychosocial construction of gender. Kate Millett, in her ground-breaking book *Sexual Politics*, was the first American theorist to point out that the personal is the political – that issues of power and domination unconsciously determine sex-role stereotypes that have historically oppressed and disempowered women. For neo-feminists like Luce Irigaray, Hélène Cixous, Alice Jardine, and Toril Moi, patriarchal ideology is contingent on the humanist notion of a "seamlessly unified self . . . which is commonly called 'Man,'" but which is "in fact a phallic self, constructed on the model of the self-contained, powerful phallus."[19] Hélène Cixous believes that non-phallogocentric "feminine writing" can challenge the political dominance of the law and the word of the Father. And Julia Kristeva, who similarly identifies the symbolic order as patriarchal, suggests that the "text is a practice that could be compared to political revolution" – that any writer who responds to the semiotic pulsions of the unconscious is engaged in an act of revolt against a phallogocentric hegemony.[20] One of the purposes of this study is to show how Joyce, in the course of his career, became such a revolutionary writer, forging new psychosexual subject-positions in a controversial discourse of desire.

The parameters of this project have necessarily dictated a discussion closely focused on issues of desire and language, the politics of sexual difference, and the imbrication of gender stereotypes in twentieth-century aesthetics. The first two chapters, "Through a Cracked Looking-glass: Desire and Frustration in *Dubliners*" and "Stephen Dedalus and Women: A Portrait of the Artist as a Young Narcissist," examine *Dubliners* and *A Portrait of the Artist* with an eye to the analysis of Joyce's ironic framing of woman as specular object. Chapter 3, "Interpreting Exiles: The Aesthetics of Unconsummated Desire," sees this unique dramatic work as a turning-point, a pivotal text in which Richard Rowan, the artist/protagonist, is determined to take spiritual possession of his mother/lover/muse, but eventually capitulates to the intuitive matrix of feminine desire embodied in Bertha, the heroine of the play. The discussion of Leopold Bloom in Chapter 4, "Uncoupling *Ulysses*: Joyce's New Womanly Man," has been restricted to a critique of the novel's fictional representation of androgyny, bisexual fantasy, and psychic construction of the gendered subject. In Chapter 5, "Molly Bloom: The Woman's Story," the intriguing figure of Joyce's modern Penelope introduces the issue of feminine desire elaborated in the context of maternal abjection. Chapter 6, "Reading *Finnegans Wake*: The Feminiairity Which Breathes Content," alters reading strategies and draws on Jungian archetypal perspectives to elicit a feminist portrait of the enigmatic ALP, whose fluid iterations shape the polyglottic discourse of Joyce's most farraginous text. A concluding "Ricorso" then circles back to a discussion of figuration, language, and *écriture féminine* in the *Wake*.

Despite the fact that Joyce has earned a notoriously ambivalent reputation among feminist scholars, I have taken as my premiss the assumption that a reader sensitized to contemporary issues of sexual politics can successfully insinuate her/himself into this particular author's fictional microcosm both as sympathetic narratee and as skeptical respondent.[21] One can be what Judith Fetterley calls a "resisting reader" and, simultaneously, an appreciative one.[22] The polymorphous resonances of Joyce's experimental canon everywhere mock his sex-stereotyped portraits and exhibit a pervasive anti-patriarchal bias. His writing introduces a lexical play-field that challenges the assumptions of traditional culture, including phallo-centric authority and logocentric discourse. Doing both male and female characters in the many voices of carnivalesque play, Joyce subverts the name and the law of the Father and delights in the subvocal utterances of "gramma's grammar," that fluid and elusive *semiotexte* that wends its way through the final "Lps" of *Finnegans Wake* and brings us back, by a "commodius vicus of recirculation" (*FW* 3. 2), to a lyrical riverrun of aesthetic *jouissance* defusing the patriarchal can(n)on.

1

THROUGH A CRACKED
LOOKING-GLASS

Desire and Frustration in Dubliners

Virgin veers into Virago. . . . No body,
no belly, no breasts, just tongue.
(Hélène Cixous, ''Sorties'')

At the time he was composing *Dubliners*, Joyce was fond of envisaging himself as an Irish Zola (*Letters* II, 137) and, in a 1904 letter to Constantine Curran, declared that his short-story collection would ''betray the soul of that hemiplegia or paralysis which many consider a city'' (*Letters* I, 55). It would hold up to his fellow citizens a ''nicely polished looking-glass'' of moral opprobrium and offer a caustic, multi-dimensional mimesis of Irish decadence.[1] If one reads Joyce's indictment of Dublin's ''hemiplegia'' from a psychoanalytic perspective, then Irish paralysis might be diagnosed as a Freudian symptom of psychic hysteria – the neurotic displacement of aggression, anger, or frustrated libidinal desire played, replayed, and played out in the text of *Dubliners* through a pervasive leitmotif of collective repression and social decenteredness. In Joyce's city at the turn of the century, men and women are continually pitted against one another in patterns of anxiety and hostility, with each sex perversely demanding mythic satisfactions of imaginary presence and psychic integration that the other cannot possibly provide.[2]

Women and children have been relegated to the margins of discourse in a culture that is male-centered and woman-avoidant. Barred from communal iteration, they cannot articulate desire, communicate feeling, or valorize emotional need. Males, in turn, adopt a speech that strips language of affect and represses erotic expression, until masculine sexuality erupts as a manifestation of phallic urgency – an instinctual yielding to dark, secret, and inarticulate drives. Eros is enacted on a stage of overt danger and covert pleasure, so that the model for heterosexual coupling becomes one of antagonism and conquest – a battle for power won by such gay lotharios as Corley and Gallagher and lost by confused, unimaginative spirits like Little Chandler and Bob Doran. In relationships between the sexes, the central specter is always envisaged in terms of male desire blocked by the perversities of an arbitrary and tyrannical female will.

Joyce incorporates into the text of *Dubliners* an anatomy of male hysteria over the paralytic fear of being feminized – a terror of Mother Church and Mother Ireland that gives rise to the psychological need for coldness, detachment, and logocentric control. Unconsciously emulating their English masters, the Irish assert a specious manhood through blustering claims to patriarchal privilege, making infantile demands that frustrate and feminize those already demeaned by colonial subjugation. The citizens of Dublin are tormented by insatiable desires endlessly replayed on the body of Mother Ireland – a body defiled, raped, and adulterated by British authority. The body of the mother has been usurped by English impostors, but the Irish refuse to enact a national Oedipal rebellion. Kathleen ni Houlihan has been reconstituted in fantasy as an infinitely desirable female, an imaginary presence and center of psychic integration whose possession is always-already deferred by the intervention of paternal antagonism.

Abject, and cast off from the maternal body, Irish males search for symbols of replacement everywhere in their environment. Mimicking the father, they make themselves into concretized fetishes and identify with the child-phallus that could, in fantasy, satisfy and fully possess the alienated maternal figure. Ireland becomes a text replicating the repressed Gaelic unconscious, and the citizens articulate the letter of the unconscious by inscribing themselves in language as the "child-phallus who wishes to penetrate his mother's body. . . . Exhausted in its course, desire ultimately becomes its own object."[3]

CHILDHOOD AND INITIATION

The beginning of *Dubliners* is oddly sterile and womanless. Joyce depicts a desiccated Garden of Eden inhabited by a fallen race whose imaginary maternal center has been erased, lost to memory, and eradicated from the mind of the child-narrator who appears in the text as a self-generating character. Maternal separation is the background of his emerging consciousness, the wound or scar of abjection that unmans him even before he has developed a sense of mature individuation. The perpetual gap in the narrative is the unnamed loss of a mother never mentioned – a symbolic absence at the heart of a barren world. It is indicated only in the interstices of the text and evoked, perhaps, by the child's comforting recollection of the familial warmth of Christmas, a pre-Oedipal fantasy that gives refuge from the "vicious region" of paternal nightmare.

Joyce's inaugural story, "The Sisters," is dominated by the shadow of a phallic lawgiver whose physical deterioration and mental paralysis were abruptly terminated by a fatal stroke. The boy in the tale has apparently been captivated by the name of the Father, so that his impressionable mind resembles an Aristotelian *tabula rasa* inscribed by an impotent pedagogue. Barred from self-defining utterance, the child writhes in a world of silence and isolation: he does not speak, but ponders with curiosity the contradictory grown-up voices that appropriate the powers of language. Baffled and mute, the enraged boy tries to sublimate passion in futile, animal gestures: "I crammed my mouth with stirabout for fear I might give utterance to my anger" (*D* 11). Incapable of naming the father who has died and betrayed him, he reverts to a semiotic system of bodily maneuvers while pondering the ellipses of adult discourse that obscure the identity of a failed Father-God.[4] "I puzzled my head to extract meaning from his [Cotter's] unfinished sentences" (*D* 11), the boy tells us.

Apparently orphaned (or, like Nora Barnacle, sent out to fosterage with relatives), the child, in search of a paternal surrogate, submits to rigorous training in the kind of logocentric discourse that eventually destroys his tutor, Father Flynn. Yet it is the boy who functions as confessor to the drooling prelate in a dream that identifies the priest as a virtual "simoniac" guilty of foisting outmoded ecclesiastical offices onto his vulnerable charge. Although the pedagogue can mimic the most august of Catholic theologians, he has evidently lost faith in the Jansenist dogma he preaches. His stance is hypocritical, his tutelage a game. He becomes hebephrenic and hysterical when the womb/chalice of Mother Church cracks and is rent asunder by his own megalomanic and specular gaze. With his faith in sacramental authority shattered, Father Flynn can no longer atone for the religious doubts that finally drive him mad. His desire for faith and spiritual *jouissance* flows back upon itself in frustrated torrents that flood the soul with guilt and deny satisfaction to an unquenchable passion for hermetic power.

As in traditional myth, the impotent patriarch must be killed in order that the young – and the simple – may survive. Joyce calls attention to Father Flynn's sisters in the title of the story, despite their seemingly peripheral role in the narrative. Nannie and Eliza are ignorant and ill-educated, naïve, and somewhat fatuous. They employ malapropisms, talk about "rheumatic wheels" and the *Freeman's General*, and superstitiously proclaim that James's "life was, you might say, crossed" (*D* 17). Although barred from the dominant discourse, they express gentle sympathy for a brother whom they tried to protect from the assaults of a perilous world. "We wouldn't see him want anything while he was in it" (*D* 16), they proclaim. In the first version of "The Sisters," Joyce is more explicit about the priest's phallocratic arrogance: "He had an egoistic contempt for all women-folk and suffered all their services to him in polite silence" (*D* 247). It is the sisters, however, who provide an incisive, epigrammatic diagnosis of James's malady: "He was too scrupulous always" (*D* 17). Oblivious of the Draconian complexities that tormented their brother, Nannie and Eliza minister to his needs without succumbing to dementia. They respond to the priest's truculence with beef-tea and conversation; and they survive, like Anna Livia in *Finnegans Wake*, to serve a communion of sherry and crackers at his wake.

When females in the story attempt to speak, their words are usually reduced to vacuous gibberish. Unable to master patriarchal discourse, they function as servants to the cultural imperatives that circumscribe their lives. Feminine utterances belong to the little language of social banter and polite conversation – a *parole* that tends to be euphemistic and evasive. Poor deaf Nannie has been "wore out" from catering to the exigencies of her brother's illness and, like a classical fate or a figure out of Dante, mutely points upwards and beckons to the terrified child. Her mutterings and elocutionary failures veil the reality of death and distract the boy from direct confrontation with the spectral body laid out before him. As he expresses silent contempt for the shabby old woman who summons him to ritual mourning, the child-narrator, mirroring his mentor, already exhibits a dangerous penchant toward intellectual arrogance and self-conscious scrupulosity.

It is significant that the boy's aunt cannot bring herself to utter the word "die" and cloaks the event in dramatic mystery: "Did he . . . peacefully?" she asks. Death is obscured by euphemistic language until the horror has been sanitized and fades into a static verbal icon. The vocabulary of prettiness and tidiness reduces the priest to an aesthetic object, a decorous and decorative artifact – little more than a "beautiful corpse" (D 15). St Thomas Aquinas's definition of beauty as "that which, when seen, pleases," illumines the sisters' repressed emotional relief at their brother's recent demise. Freed from the intrusions of imperious male authority, the survivors celebrate a wake that releases them from deepseated hostility and allows them to admire the priest as a safely crystallized visual spectacle in a non-threatening, photographic tableau. The dead – essentialized, objectified, and mentally displaced – become the malleable property of the living who mold the memory of the deceased in the image of their own projected fantasies.

If Nannie and Eliza are contemporary versions of the New Testament figures Martha and Mary, their brother is portrayed as a parodic Lazarus with little potential for resurrection. The moribund Father Flynn could hardly be aroused from sedentary torpor and, in the last years of his life, seemed only to respond to the stimulus of *High Toast* snuff. Death comes as a climax to protracted paralysis – a condition that might, ironically, have been symptomatic of tertiary syphilis.[5] At the end of the story, Father Flynn's body is exhibited as a stiff phallic rod, a visible sign of masculine authority mentally ossified long before *rigor mortis* sets in. "There he lay, solemn and copious, vested as for the altar, his large hands loosely retaining a chalice. His face was very truculent, grey and massive, with black cavernous nostrils and circled by a scanty white fur" (D 14). The savage and threatening nostrils, surrounded by tufts of animal hair, possibly suggest an unconscious screen-image of the threat of genital invagination.

The verbal puzzles initially announced in "The Sisters" by the words "gnomon," "simony," and "paralysis" are eventually revealed not as riddles, but as indeterminate symbols that haunt the textual unconscious of the narrative. The priest's potential *siglum* proves to be the incomplete angular or phallic formation of a parallelogram stripped of a diminutive, filial corner. "Without a doubt," says Cotter in the original version, the "upper storey . . . was gone" (D 244). Similarly, the story (or storey) is rife with examples of both physical and spiritual paralysis, as well as simoniacal practices that barter ecclesiastical offices purchased at too high a price.[6]

Two genuine riddles or aporias in the tale – the mystery of

Persia and the mysterious chalice – both evoke repressed symbols of ritual wholeness and imaginary plenitude. In response to Cotter's "unfinished sentences," the boy recollects a dream set in the sensual ambiance of "long velvet curtains and a swinging lamp of antique fashion. I felt that I had been very far away, in some land where the customs were strange – in Persia, I thought" (D 13–14). The reference to Persia alludes to an Oriental Other, an exotic vista projected by the fragmented male consciousness and fantasmatically associated with harems, licentiousness, and voluptuous female flesh. The Catholic priest's western asceticism is challenged by the boy's unconscious through inverted images of tantalizing desire. The "grey paralytic" is imaginatively represented as a greedy simoniac eager to exchange ecclesiastical knowledge for a disciple's unwitting troth. The death of this stern father-figure, who lives by the letter of the law, exchanges *règles* for *jeux* in the boy's psychic economy through a movement of carnivalesque pleasure. The child becomes the priest's confessor, and traditional authority is up-ended in magical, exotic charade. When the word-master dies, the narrator acknowledges a sudden surge of psychosomatic release: "I felt even annoyed at discovering in myself a sensation of freedom as if I had been freed from something by his death" (D 12). The boy's unconscious knows what his waking mind cannot admit: that this "great friend" was guilty of sins of pederastic desire deflected into a demand for psychic appropriation. The older man's "great wish" for the child was a powerful projection of his own need for psychological mastery – a desire to gain control of the boy under the aegis of pedagogical insemination and to mold this docile disciple into a spiritual replica of himself. It is not surprising, then, that the protagonist confronts his erstwhile guru in a land whose voluptuous topography subverts the older man's pretensions toward asceticism and logocentric control. His indeterminate fantasy lacks both closure and accessible intellectual meaning. "I could not remember the end of the dream," the narrator confesses (D 14).

According to the symbol-system of the Oriental Tarot, the chalice or cup designates a female fertility principle – the womb/body/invaginated mother worshiped as pre-Christian goddess. Catholic ritual appropriates the sacred cup for purposes of symbolic couvade in the Mass – a ritual that re-enacts Christ's "last supper" and his nurturance of the twelve apostles with the bread/host of his own sacrificial body. By virtue of ecclesiastical authority, Father Flynn

17

could mimic the creative function of the mother by pronouncing words that evoke the living presence of Christ in "body and blood, soul and divinity." The law and authority of the father supplants the pre-symbolic, uterine magic of the fertilized mother. The body of Christ becomes a maternal, nurturant host, and the words of the priestly father summon the sacramental rebirth of a divine, incarnate Son. The metaphorical rite, however, is suspended over the void by perpetual acts of faith. If belief in the ritual should fail and the body of the surrogate womb/chalice crack, then the priest will be stripped of his theological center and "castrated" of the rights/rites of phallic mastery. The demented prelate is powerless to recuperate an integrated image of himself without faith in the specular projections of a mirroring maternal chalice. In compensation for the loss of mystical contact with an imaginary and valorizing maternal field, he turns to a young disciple in search of an/Other to replicate his schizophrenically split subjectivity.[7]

The priest attempts to seduce the young boy through Lacanian movements of mesmerizing speech. He consigns a fragmented self-image to the care of the other, whose admiring gaze, reflected back in the eyes and consciousness of the subject (*je*), will offer an ideologically unified, if illusory vision of the self (*moi*). It is only through the *regard* of the other (the look, gaze, or mirror of approval) that the fragmented subject is able to construct a fictive self-image – an image which, for all its apparent integrity, is a myth contingent on deliberate misprision. The child performs for the priest a function that the chalice of Mother Church could not. He provides a Lacanian mirror for the debilitated prelate and, by doggedly re-enacting the priest's ecclesiastical obsessions, sutures an implied wound of psychic castration.[8]

Father Flynn, in turn, shields his naïve disciple from acknowledging a split in human subjectivity by acting as a psychological mirror that displaces the repressed figure of a pre-Oedipal mother and inscribes (or indoctrinates) the child into the symbolic order and law of the Father. The priest perpetuates a myth of subjective cohesion accessible through complex strategies of intellectual and linguistic mastery. The boy-disciple has recourse to patriarchal assurances of personal initiation into a superior world of masculine knowledge, power, privilege, and satisfaction. In the original story, the child naïvely speculates: "Of course neither of his sisters was very intelligent. . . . Perhaps he found me more intelligent and honoured me with words for that reason" (*D* 247).

The "queer old josser" of "An Encounter" casts still another shadow of the menacing patriarch who tries to lure an ingenuous youth to religious or physical perversion. Fired by a "cowboy and Indian" notion of heroic prowess, the narrator and his friend Mahony go off to seek adventure at the mysterious Dublin Pigeon House, a topography that assumes tropological status as a locus of mysterious desire and forbidden sexual pleasure. Their experiment with adult freedom is frustrated by a disturbing encounter with a would-be pederast. Circling discursively around obsessional fetishes of "white hands" and "beautiful soft hair," the man conjures up hypnotic images of virginal nymphettes, then rises to the occasion by going off to masturbate. When he leers at the children and ostensibly exhibits an engorged phallus, the boys witness titillating *machismo* degenerate into homoerotic perversion and the wild sensations of youth give way to the lurid obsessions of senility. At some level, both the narrator and his companion recognize but never fully acknowledge that an aggressive code of masculine prowess can be perverted, by way of frustrated desire, into the emotional chaos of sexual dementia. Libidinous fantasy spins in ever-fixed patterns of deferred homosexual arousal – a physical replica of the need displayed by Father Flynn to penetrate the mind of his child-disciple and implant seminal knowledge spewed forth from ecclesiastical tradition. As Jane Gallop speculates, there is "a certain pederasty implicit in pedagogy. A greater man penetrates a lesser man with his knowledge."[9] Both Flynn and the josser take sadistic pleasure in catechetical lessons demonstrative of invidious phallic manipulation.

The adolescent protagonist of "Araby" turns from the inchoate desires of latency to overtly heterosexual longings. Emotionally, ontogeny recapitulates phylogeny, as the child re-enacts courtship rituals of medieval worship and sacramental obeisance to a distant, unattainable icon. Perched precariously on the brink of erotic expression, he sublimates burgeoning sexual drives to sentimental fantasies of an ideal, chivalric love. The boy's *inamorata*, simply identified as "Mangan's sister," is portrayed as an idolized romantic heroine. Shadowy and elusive, she plays the role of seductive temptress, with swinging dress and a "soft rope" of hair suggestive of fetishistic entrapment. Her appearance inspires Wordsworthian rapture, though she is little more than the shadow of a dream – a "brown figure" peered at in specular fashion from behind the blinds of a shabby tenement in North Richmond Street. The young woman becomes a goddess shrouded in mystery, and her adored replica is detached from the real world to be kept safe from mundane defilement. It soon becomes clear that the protagonist is enamored not of Mangan's sister, but of her sanctified presence as an emblem of psychic integrity, a figure that mirrors back the boy's own inflated dreams of heroic valor. In the tradition of courtly love, this modern-day knight has been entranced by an "older woman," an eroticized virgin who becomes the focal point of sacerdotal worship. Like Sir Galahad, he cherishes a chaste ideal of masculine gallantry and proudly bears his chalice of platonic devotion "safely through a throng of foes" (D 31).

In all the ardor and confusion of adolescent attraction, the boy-narrator fails to recognize symptoms of erotic obsession disguised by ritual homage. Shyly, he admits: "my body was like a harp and her words and gestures were like fingers running upon the wires"(D 31). The musical simile, borrowed from Coleridge's "Aeolian Harp," represses a veiled but displaced longing for tactile stimulation – for the wires of the boy's newly awakened phallic consciousness to be fondled by the delicate white hands of his beloved. The protagonist yearns for sensuous contact, and his language is saturated with Freudian *double entendre* when he imagines "fine incessant needles" of rain impinging on the earth's sodden labial beds (D 31). But like a monk struggling for dignity and self-control, he finds ritual solace in a litany of ejaculations repeated like a mantra evocative of his beloved.

When the distant object of his affection finally speaks to him, the protagonist is understandably confused and disoriented. Mangan's sister twists a silver bracelet "round and round her wrist," unconsciously engaged in gestures of hypnotic seduction. Trained in the body language of feminine flirtation, she unwittingly tempts and taunts her would-be suitor. The boy, in turn, focuses not on her face but on fetishistic projections of her figure – the "white curve of her neck," her illumined hair, a hand clutching the spike of a railing, and the "white border of a petticoat" (D 32). Luxuriating in eastern enchantment, he excitedly promises, like a knight of old, to bring back a trophy from the oriental bazaar. As the girl vanishes from sight, she remains perpetually other – a wistful, "brown-clad figure" inscribed in the young man's consciousness as a fetishistic supplement to male subjectivity.

20

When Joyce's Arthurian knight, in search of the Holy Grail, finally reaches the Chapel Perilous, he discovers a deserted gallery bereft of eastern splendor. The stall attendant flirting with two English gentlemen exposes the vulgar side of eroticism, and the boy is forced to acknowledge the profane reality of his own emotional infatuation: "I saw myself as a creature driven and derided by vanity; and my eyes burned with anguish and anger" (*D* 35). The vanity he bemoans evinces a futile desire to appropriate the beloved as an ideal, mystifying center and dubious mirror-image of coherent subjectivity. Once again, the individual unsuccessfully appeals to an/Other for the psychological reification of a unified, idealized self. Earlier, he had imagined himself an heroic priest of love, secretly bearing his chalice of devotion through a venal, commercialized world. As the lights go out in Araby, the narrator, "blinded" by infatuation, sees himself clearly for the first time and is shocked by the realization that he, too, is one of the vulgar. Try as he might, he cannot detach himself from the human comedy of sexual experience, and he chafes at the powerful illusions perpetuated through culturally inscribed romantic myths.

The disillusioned adolescent suddenly understands that he has been socialized into feudal and archaic codes of chivalric behavior incongruent with the commercial exchange of sexual favors on the nineteenth-century marriage market. Overwhelmed by the veiled mystery of the female body, he sublimates the physical demands of adolescent sexuality to a ritualized discourse of courtly love. Only at the end of the story does he begin to acknowledge, in a moment of epiphany, repressed torrents of sexual desire swirling beneath artificial cultural codes. A tawdry shopgirl reluctantly fends off the advances of two randy Englishmen seeking a bit of fun to enliven their Irish holiday. The boy knows that his own platonic love affair is motivated by a similar agenda. He would like to bed down with Mangan's sister, but is forbidden even to contemplate the satisfactions of erotic contact with a figure as inaccessible as the Virgin Mary. Spiritual obsession has obscured the emotional urgency of his quest and dammed the course of sexual drives rendered futile by the prohibitions of contemporary Catholic mores.

Joyce reverses the narrative of "Araby" in his tale of Eveline Hill, whose dreams of escape and amorous salvation are imbued with all the exotic trappings characteristic of the kind of popular fiction published in late nineteenth-century ladies' magazines.

Eveline sees her suitor Frank as a bronze-faced prince who promises personal redemption and a future of wedded bliss. Caught up in the excitement of "having a fellow," this Dublin Desdemona floats on illusion until, in her rife imagination, the "kind, manly, open-hearted Frank" takes on heroic stature. Absorbing the figures of Odysseus and Sir Galahad, he becomes just as unreal as the tales of the "terrible Patagonians" with which he amuses, and possibly manipulates, his enthralled and exploitable beloved.[10]

If Eveline is bewitched by Frank's stories of adventure, she feels equally moved by "the pitiful vision of her mother's life," a nightmare that lays its "spell on the very quick of her being" (D 40). Eveline determines to avoid her mother's battered servitude: "She would not be treated as her mother had been" (D 37). But those haunting words, "Derevaun Seraun!," uttered in meaningless madness, call Eveline to a vocation of spectral dissolution. Self-sacrifice to the point of dementia will be the ghost's sole benefice. Wresting a solemn promise from her docile daughter, the dying mother seals Eveline's bonds of incestuous entrapment. The girl, torn between a childhood pledge of filial duty and an exotic fantasy of personal happiness, conducts both sides of a mental debate whose outcome has already been determined. The motif of "home" resounds like a metronome throughout the story, suggesting the moral compulsions that hypnotize consciousness and preclude the possibility of meaningful change. In this trial of the soul, Eveline serves as both prosecutor and defendant, analyst and spiritual analysand. As she weighs emotion and romantic fantasy against the judgmental voice of conscience, she engages in an exercise of deliberate misprision that sacrifices free will to those Irish gods of hearth and home she has been taught to worship from infancy. Abandoned by her mother and bereft of nurturant care, Eveline succumbs to a compulsive need to *become* the mother sacrificed on the altar of Dublin domesticity. She must fetishize her body and offer herself as sexual and social victim to a demanding patriarch who threatens incestuous entrapment.

Altruism and self-effacement are the edicts inscribed on the young girl's unconscious, and, by the end of the story, she lets her mind switch to automatic pilot. Begging God to show her "her duty," Eveline reverts to a simple rhetoric of docility and obedience echoing the Virgin Mary's response at the Annunciation: "Be it done unto me according to thy word." Resolute in her paralysis, she stares

22

vacantly, almost catatonically, at her departing suitor. Nausea and bodily distress indicate mounting sexual anxiety, as Eveline dimly begins to perceive that elopement with Frank would mean, in realistic terms, a commitment to an intimate physical union that has never come within the purview of her disembodied dreams. The wound of sexual penetration evinces the kind of psychic violation she associates with marriage, servitude, and relentless domestic battering. In a moment of Freudian terror, she imagines replicating her mother's story and drowning in the "seas of the world," an oceanic symbol that provokes sudden hysteria at the thought of physical defloration. Conflating Frank with the father who "would drown her," the young woman holds her ground "like a helpless animal" – trapped, panicked, and frozen in a stance of neurotic immobility. Visions of engulfing seas accost her with uncanny (*unheimlich*, unwombly) resonance, as sex threatens to impinge on a tightly sealed world of romantic illusion. Eveline longs to escape from adult libidinal drives and return to an infantile fantasy of pre-Oedipal bliss, a womb-like passivity in which she would be nurtured and protected by a warm and loving maternal caretaker. But her desire for embryonic security and connection to the body of the mother forces her back into the arms of Mother Church and into lifelong servitude to an unsolicitous male parent who forever prohibits access to the unauthorized phallus of the husband/engenderer.

Bound from childhood to a negative self-image, Eveline can never extricate herself from the web of words woven around the sacrosanct authority of the patriarchal Irish father. In this asphyxiating world of psychic imprisonment, the daughter becomes surrogate spouse to her tyrannical "Da." Clearly, Eveline is destined to repeat the sado-masochistic patterns of her mother's life – "that life of common-place sacrifices closing in final craziness" (*D* 40). "Derevaun Seraun" apparently means, in demotic Irish, that "the end of pleasure is pain." As Jane Gallop observes, "the daughter's obligation to reproduce the mother, the mother's story – is a more difficult obstacle than even the Father's law."[11]

Eveline's catatonic silence at the end of the tale merely confirms the shadowy silence she has always inhabited both at home and in the Stores. She has been inscribed into a male register of need and desire, of authority and irascibility characteristic of Irish parental models. Her exclusion from the dominant discourse is doubled by an enigmatic portrait of another male, the aged priest (now in

Melbourne) whose photograph constitutes a specular shrine to absent authority. Unable to question the mysteries of male bonding, Eveline dusts the photo but never demands a fuller portrait of the Irish prelate who has disappeared "down under," to the antipodes of geography and consciousness, beyond the reach of concupiscence. His picture serves as a fetishistic reminder of ecclesiastical power – a patriarchal authority contingent on the law of phallic veiling and a self-conscious, ascetic renunciation of women.

As in "The Sisters," females are excluded from male discourse and consigned to the realm of silence, gibberish, and babble. Once Eveline's mother breaks out of her prison of verbal constraint, she speaks the truth in demented utterances that defer meaning along with linguistic closure. Hysteria, given voice, shrieks in tones of warning and fatuity, casting a lugubrious spell over the perplexed auditors who try to interpret encoded deathbed commands. Babble flows like a turgid excrescence of womb and consciousness, the misshapen effluvia of unbearable oppression. The mother murmurs a private idiolect that bequeathes to her female child the weight of iniquity and misprision. Caught between semiotic dementia and catatonic silence, Eveline predictably chooses the latter.

Young Jimmy Doyle in "After the Race" is portrayed as an inverted replica of the naïve Eveline. He has attended a "big Catholic college" in England and "been sent to Cambridge to see a little life" (D 43). His father, an erstwhile Kingstown butcher, has amassed sufficient wealth to be touted in the papers as a "merchant prince" and to support his son in the style of civilized leisure to which the young man has happily become accustomed. The ingenuous Jimmy entertains fantasies of commercial power and aristocratic privilege bolstered by *nouveau riche* aspirations toward upward social mobility. Desirous of psychological valorization from a group of surrogate fathers, he toadies to European playboys who force him to grovel ignominiously for scraps of male camaraderie. In awe of continental culture but pathetically bereft of *savoir-faire*, Jimmy makes a fetish of his body and sacrifices a large chunk of his bankroll in a desperate attempt to act like "one of the boys" and be initiated, metaphorically, into an exclusive, upper-class men's club. The Irish subaltern is feminized and symbolically castrated by a crowd of arrogant foreigners who ruthlessly exploit Mother Ireland and dupe her vulnerable farrow for the sake of an evening's entertainment. In this land of the gratefully oppressed, aspiring subordinates willingly squander their lives and their substance to win spurious approval from insouciant (fatherly) oppressors. Significantly, Jimmy the Irishman and Farley the American are left "heaviest losers" in this demeaning game of cultural colonization.

COURTSHIP AND MARRIAGE

"Two Gallants," "The Boarding House," and "A Little Cloud" form a courtship-and-marriage trilogy in which Joyce deals with various stages of adult sexual repression acted out in scenarios of hostility and exploitation. In a spiritually desiccated Ireland, the frustrated Dubliner typically turns his own failure or pent-up rage against those who are even more oppressed, socially or economically, than he. The sexes assume an adversary relationship, with each trying to take advantage of the other's weakness and vulnerability until romance becomes a tawdry ritual debased by greed, deception, and invidious moral simony.

The woman of "Two Gallants" is thinly sketched, but nonetheless pitiable in her gullible naïveté. A country lass who, like Nora Barnacle, came to the city to work as a "slavey," the young girl is buxom and ingenuous to the point of ridiculous caricature. "Frank rude health glowed in her face, on her fat red cheeks and in her unabashed blue eyes. Her features were blunt. She had broad nostrils, a straggling mouth which lay open in a contented leer, and two projecting front teeth" (D 55–6). The girl's porcine nostrils and "contented leer" suggest simple-mindedness, if not retardation. In contrast to the rude dairyman who once courted this country lass, the sweat-laden Corley seems an attractive suitor, despite his "large, globular and oily" head (D 51). Impressed by this Dublin Don Juan, the young woman brings her lover cigarettes and fine cigars, eagerly provides him with Sunday sex, and, at the end of the evening, pays a sovereign to retain his favor.

Corley proves to be an absurdly pedestrian gigolo bragging of his exploits as the bold conqueror of servant girls: "She doesn't know my name. . . . But she thinks I'm a bit of class, you know. . . . She's a bit gone on me" (D 51–2). He takes pride in having driven a former paramour to the turf of prostitution, while "philosophically" disclaiming: "There was others at her before me" (D 53). All women, he implies, resemble race-horses, whom males bet on to win or lose; and, in most of Dublin society, women are definitely the losers, since even the lowest man in the hierarchy of Ireland's capital can at least give thanks that he was not created female.

Lenehan, for his part, derives voyeuristic satisfaction from Corley's adventures and, while downing a plate of peas, fantasizes about his friend's triumphant sexploitation of this gullible country lass. Substituting food for sex, the impoverished Lenehan takes keen pleasure in mentally reconstructing the scenario of masculine conquest and, at the same time, alleviates his own depression through Cinderfella dreams of redemption by a rich woman: "He might yet be able to settle down in some snug corner and live happily if he could only come across some good simple-minded girl with a little of the ready" (D 58). This down-and-out disciple has been feminized by Corley and plays, with tinges of irony and self-indulgent mockery, the role of sexual other, the fictive mirror demanded by his friend's bloated ego. Feminine functions of nurturance and stroking are displaced onto the epicene Lenehan, who courts Corley's favor with a poor man's Wildean wit and punctuates the boaster's monologue with repeated iterations of homoerotic approval:

"Of all the good ones ever I heard, . . . that emphatically takes the biscuit.". . .

"You're what I call a gay Lothario," said Lenehan. "And the proper kind of a Lothario, too!"

A shade of mockery relieved the servility of his manner. To save himself he had the habit of leaving his flattery open to the interpretation of raillery. But Corley had not a subtle mind. . . .

"Ecod! Corley, you know how to take them," he said.

"I'm up to all their little tricks," Corley confessed. (D 51 – 3).

Cheered on by the sycophantic Lenehan, Corley manages to extort a small gold coin from the pathetic slavey whom he sweet-talks or bullies into financial patronage. Of Joyce's two gallants, one triumphs in fantasy, the other in actuality, over an ignorant, licentious, lower-class female. Enthralled by her suitor's urban sophistication and exploited by every stratum of Dublin society, this downtrodden maid-of-all-work looks forward to an even bleaker and more oppressed future than either of her mean-minded predators.[12]

In "The Boarding House," as in "Two Gallants," Joyce exposes Dublin courtship as little more than organized prostitution. Predatory roles are reversed in this tale, as two women connive in the conquest of a vulnerable and timorous male. Mrs Mooney, a calculating and determined woman who deals with moral problems "as a cleaver deals with meat" (D 63), is hardly more attractive than Corley. Imagery of meat, execution, and cannibalism pervades the story, as Mrs Mooney, the butcher's daughter, is on the prowl for a "staggering bob" or sacrificial calf. Doran is led like a calf or lamb to the slaughter, despite an instinct that "urged him to remain free. . . . Once you are married you are done for, it said" (D 66). But instinct proves less powerful than the amorphous sexual drives that swirl beneath the surface of his well-regulated life and traduce his aspirations toward a carefully modulated asceticism.

Scheming to ensnare an eligible bachelor, pretty Polly, a little "perverse Madonna," enjoys the sanction of her mother's approval and, though given "the run of the young men," does not "wish it to be thought that in her wise innocence she had divined the intention behind her mother's tolerance" (D 63–4). Polly, like Doran, perceives herself the victim of limited circumstances. Forced to choose between an ill-paid career as a typist and the comforts of middle-class marriage, she knows that her conjugal fate depends on a random selection of down-and-out boarders, only one of whom appears naïve enough to rescue her from a life of clerical drudgery. Joyce satirically portrays cages within cages of repression and unhappiness. In the game of chance that determines her future, Polly's sole playing-card is her body, and claims of despoiled virginity and possible pregnancy are the trumps she uses to win her man in the sexual sweepstakes.

The intimidated Doran is far too weak and pusillanimous to challenge the "weight of social opinion": "What could he do now but marry her or run away? He could not brazen it out. The affair would be sure to be talked of and his employer would be certain to hear of it. Dublin is such a small city: everyone knows everyone else's business" (D 65–6). Tormented by guilt and cowed by moral platitudes, Doran feels he must make both spiritual and financial reparation for stolen sexual pleasures. Meekly, he yields to the threat of Dublin gossip and ecclesiastical censure, though bitterly resentful of his about-to-be-betrothed for her bad grammar, loose reputation, and lower-class origins: "She *was* a little vulgar; some times she said 'I seen' and 'If I had've known.' But what would grammar matter if he really loved her?" (D 66). The irony, of course, is that Bob does *not* love Polly, or even like her. He feels that he has been seduced by a virginal vamp, wrenched from the security of monkish celibacy, and forced to endure an ignominious liaison in punishment for a few moments of so-called "delirium." "He had a notion that he was being had. . . . He could not make up his mind whether to like her or despise her for what she had done. Of course he had done it too" (D 66).

> It was not altogether his fault that it had happened. He remembered well, with the curious patient memory of the celibate, the first casual caresses her dress, her breath, her fingers had given him. Then late one night as he was undressing for bed she had tapped at his door, timidly. She wanted to relight her candle at his for hers had been blown out by a gust. It was her bath night. . . . From her hands and wrists too as she lit and steadied her candle a faint perfume arose. (D 67)

Like so many of Joyce's Dubliners, Doran suffers from inveterate timidity and a curiously limited imagination. He unwittingly colludes in his own victimization and, like Eveline before him, refuses to extricate himself from a situation of emotional entrapment. He is finally vanquished not so much by the Madam as by a deepseated fear of societal ostracism and an obsessive need for bourgeois respectability. The victim of puritanical repression, Doran mentally yields to those same moral sanctions Mrs Mooney planned to invoke in dissembled outrage. Fearful and passive, he cannot initiate autonomous action and takes refuge, instead, in implausible fantasies of literal flight: "He longed to ascend through the roof and fly away to another country where he would never hear again of his trouble" (D 67–8). His dilemma is further exacerbated by a peripheral awareness of Jack Mooney's pugilist skills and savage threats that "if any fellow tried that sort of a game on with *his* sister he'd bloody well put his teeth down his throat" (D 68).

The hunting of Doran unfolds with such ritual regularity that pretty Polly, after threatening to "put an end to herself" for being undone, doffs her mask of distress and almost forgets to wait for Bob's marriage proposal. All have acted their parts in a nineteenth-century melodrama of wounded honor and virginal violation. Mrs Mooney succeeds in getting her daughter off her hands with a dowry of threats and coercion, but never realizes that she is virtually condemning her offspring to the same cycle of anxiety and frustration that characterized her own disastrous marriage. Polly has evidently chosen a gullible mate in the image of dear old Dad. As we later learn in *Ulysses*, Doran will be a henpecked, irascible, and alcoholic spouse, portrayed on 16 June 1904 indulging in one of his periodical binges of drinking and whoring to escape connubial dreariness. Through guileful seduction, Polly wins the prize of a bitter, resentful groom and, under the direction of a conniving matriarch, manipulates herself and her suitor into a lifelong misalliance. But who is to say which will be unhappier, predator or victim? Once again, Joyce depicts a domestic cage housing luckless moral counterparts.[13]

"A Little Cloud" goes on to portray the kind of conjugal frustration that proves emotionally stultifying for both partners. Little Chandler is an Irish Walter Mitty, a diminutive figure who "gave one the idea of being a little man" (*D* 70), playing the role of henpecked husband to an aggressive, domineering spouse. There is more than a touch of self-indulgence in the melancholic temperament of this Irish poetaster, for whom Ignatius Gallaher and Lord Byron both serve as imaginary alter egos.

Chandler's own literary perceptions are filtered through the cloying, exaggerated tropes that clutter the mind of a would-be aesthete. He envisages himself as the sentimental Irish poet that Joyce refused to be – a sedulous imitator of Yeats and Douglas Hyde, a Celtic bard who would ignore the suffering of his people and transform contemporary Ireland into a landscape of fairy dreams. Despite his metaphorical mind and sporadic epiphanies, T. Malone Chandler will never be able to extricate himself from a murky rhetoric of romantic cliché because he lives in the clouds and lacks the unclouded eye necessary to interpret the seering realities of Irish indigence. He prefers to admire "alarmed Atalantas" or to pity "poor stunted houses" huddled together like "a band of tramps . . . waiting for the first chill of night to bid them arise" than to sympathize with a pack of squalid youngsters squatting "like mice upon the thresholds . . . of the gaunt spectral mansions in which the old nobility of Dublin had roystered." (*D* 71 – 3). Lost in a haze of narcissism and self-deception, he plans to pipe the Celtic note in lofty purple prose crafted to impress the British intelligentsia. "The English critics, perhaps, would recognise him as one of the Celtic school by reason of the melancholy tone of his poems; besides that, he would put in allusions" (*D* 74).

Chandler proves all the more fatuous in his sycophantic admiration of Ignatius Gallaher, an expatriate journalist who defines manly prowess and personal success largely in terms of drinking, smoking, and chasing loose women: "He summarised the vices of many capitals and seemed inclined to award the palm to Berlin" (*D* 78). Monogamy, Gallaher claims, is boring and unsatisfying, as he expresses his own misogyny by comparing wedlock to the "black sack" of sensual oblivion that precedes the hangman's noose. He treats women like "spicy bits," sensuous morsels to be tasted and devoured, or victims to be exploited in gigolo liaisons. "I mean to marry money," he brags, observing that commitment to one woman "must get a bit stale" in comparison to the rich feast of sensations available to the womanizing male. Like Corley, Gallaher will demand payment for sexual services: he is determined to appropriate "the woman and the cash" by picking an ideal spouse from "thousands of rich Germans and Jews, rotten with money" (*D* 81).

Little Chandler, returning to the prison-house of his marriage, is tormented by feelings of envy and self-pity. From Annie's point of view, however, this dreamy poet must seem a thoughtless and wayward spouse who arrives late for tea and forgets even to purchase a requested package of coffee. Joyce's story implicitly evokes sympathy for Annie, though the narrative never penetrates her consciousness. She is domestically incarcerated with a demanding infant and, relieved of child-care only two hours a day, has few social contacts other than the company provided by her younger sister, Monica. Chandler can drink whisky and smoke with the boys, foster dreams of literary eminence, and luxuriate in reveries of Celtic melancholy. But Annie, who must stay indoors, cook, clean, and tend her baby, is even more trapped and beleaguered than her timorous mate. With little adult stimulation and no extra-marital outlets, the young woman focuses her attention on an over-protected son who becomes her sole source of emotional gratification.

Since the story is told from Chandler's point of view, Annie is perceived entirely through her husband's narcissistic perspective. Coldly staring at his wife's photograph, he imagines piercing, defiant eyes that irritate and repel him; and he futilely searches for the kind of rhapsodic mystery that might be discerned in the "dark Oriental eyes" of those Jewesses so intriguing to Gallaher. Chandler longs for the piquancy of Eastern enchantment, but his demands on reality clearly exceed the possibilities of his timid character and circumscribed domestic situation. Inept and impractical, he is totally dependent on Annie's care, even if the life she arranges is a "prim and pretty" model of middle-class respectability.[14]

Chandler is, nonetheless, tied to his wife in a pathological relationship of Oedipal dependency. Childlike and helpless, he agrees to play the role of son-husband to a tyrannical spouse who offers him both domestic security and tacit emotional bondage. According to Freud, a marriage will not be entirely "secure until the wife has succeeded in making her husband her child as well and in acting as a mother to him."[15] But Annie, reducing her immature consort to infantile status, turns all her female affection and solicitude to the boy-baby who has symbolically displaced his impotent father. When she refuses to continue acting as a mother toward Chandler, he feels cast off, disappointed, and suddenly bereft. Having bartered personal freedom for female nurture, he inevitably harbors resentment and sibling rivalry against the child entrusted to his care. This new-born son has clearly usurped its father's place in Annie's heart. Chandler characteristically tries to ignore the baby, whom he identifies solely in terms of the objective pronoun "it" – never "him" or "my son." In a moment of terror, he is frightened of what would happen "if it died" (D 84); but his anxiety is founded more on a fear of his wife's imagined wrath than on the potential loss of a child who threatens him with Oedipal ascendancy.

Chandler has sought the security of a bourgeois household, complete with furniture purchased on the hire system and a screaming baby. Having created a domestic nest that turns out to be a prison, he balks with envy at Gallaher's bachelor freedom. "Was it too late for him to try to live bravely like Gallaher?" he wonders (D 83). Ironically, it has *always* been too late for Chandler to escape the paralysis of Ireland. Ill-equipped to deal with the real world, he perpetually takes refuge in romantic fantasies of Oriental adventure. Reading Byron's lyric "On the Death of a Young Lady," he identifies with the grief-stricken poet mourning a woman's untimely demise. Chandler implicitly prefers a lifeless corpse to a living spouse: reduced to a lump of decaying flesh, Annie would cease to threaten his imperilled virility. Unconsciously, he wants to defuse his wife's spousal authority by invoking the "narrow cell" of death. But the doleful association merely reminds him of his own powerlessness in a marriage that has made him a "prisoner for life." Chandler, it seems, can only deal with women as passionate firebrands or wistfully idealized corpses.[16]

And what about Annie? Is she no less a prisoner? Does her competence and realistic adaptation shelter her from emotional pain? The hatred in her eyes may, in fact, be a reflection of angry disillusionment with the impotent man she has married. Bound to a helpless, ineffectual dreamer, she transfers both spousal and maternal love to the "little mannie" she worships as a miniature Christ, "Mamma's little lamb of the world" (D 85). Marital frustration erupts in shrewish bullying, and romantic love gives way to a mother's idolization of her infant son.[17]

MATURITY AND ADULTHOOD

In "Counterparts," Joyce peripherally depicts a Dublin marriage at a later stage of entrapment, when conjugal coexistence has ossified into a mutual reign of terror. Ada Farrington is described as "a little, sharp-faced woman who bullied her husband when he was sober and was bullied by him when he was drunk" (D 97). From the evidence of the story, one might assume that Farrington is drunk much of the time. Caught in a dead-end job as a copy-clerk, a kind of human Xerox-machine, Farrington buries his anger in alcoholism and domestic violence. He perceives his employer Mr Alleyne as a castrating phallocratic figure, an Anglo-Irish boss whose breed has raped Mother Ireland and continues to hold her sons hostage to capitalistic production and alienated, feminized labor.

If Chandler feels frustrated by the inequities of life, Farrington is moved to fantasies of explosive brutality: "He felt strong enough to clear out the whole office singlehanded. His body ached to do something, to rush out and revel in violence" (D 90). When subjected to a tirade of abuse by the authoritarian Alleyne, Farrington cannot resist making a fool of this "manikin" in the presence of Miss Delacour, "a stout amiable person" who wryly smiles in tacit approval. Farrington knows that he will be forced to pay dearly for his impertinence toward the bully who treats him like a petulant child, but he revels in the momentary triumph of an exhibitionist display. Having played to the hilt the juvenile role of a sassy son challenging patriarchal authority, he recoils from reproach with "savage and thirsty and revengeful" feelings, "annoyed with himself and with everyone else" (D 92).

Both at work and at play, the brutish Farrington is trapped by a compulsive need to assert physical strength, priority of wit, and a narrowly conceived masculine prowess. Drinking the dregs of his earnings from a pawned watch, he stares lasciviously at a woman in the bar – a voluptuous, exotic music-hall artiste dressed in peacock-blue muslin. Pretending that she notices him and answers his gaze, he imagines mutual attraction, then suffers disappointment when she makes a precipitous exit and bursts the bubble of his sexual fantasy. Even this faint erotic snub is sufficient to move Farrington to flex his biceps before the company, but an arm-wrestling contest with the British stripling Weathers ends in further humiliation. Having failed on all counts to prove his manhood, the defeated clerk returns home "full of smouldering anger and revengefulness" (*D* 96). The climactic scene offers a classic example of aggression-frustration displacement. All the rage and disappointments of the day are paid for by Farrington's son Tom, the only object against whom this humiliated and sadistic man can legitimately vent his atavistic fury.

If marriage has its pitfalls in *Dubliners*, celibacy seems to offer a more dangerous trap of physical and spiritual isolation in a landscape of scrupulous meanness. "Clay" and "A Painful Case" give us mirror-images of a contented spinster and a tormented bachelor, respectively. When Joyce finally allows us in "Clay" to explore the consciousness of a woman, he exposes a sensibility oppressed by loneliness but eager to adapt to cloistered and diminished circumstances. From the tone of the narrative, one might surmise that Maria is a bit childlike and simple-minded – or perhaps infantilized by her subservient position in the *Dublin by Lamplight* laundry. Small and wizened, she is described in the language of folklore or fairytale as "a very, very small person indeed but she had a very long nose and a very long chin" (*D* 99), characteristics suggestive of witch-like proclivities.[18]

Having nursed the two brothers Joe and Alphy through an uneasy adolescence, Maria served as maternal surrogate well into her prime, then found herself unmarriageable and took refuge as a paid laborer in a shelter for reformed prostitutes. As Joyce declares in a letter to Stanislaus, the institution "is a wicked place full of wicked and lost women whom a kindly committee gathers together for the good work of washing my dirty shirts" (*Letters* II, 192). It resembles a prison where Maria is virtually incarcerated and must ask permission even to spend an evening out. Although she assures herself that she likes her work, Maria has few sources of emotional gratification – a word of praise from the "genteel" matron and occasional opportunities to play maiden aunt to Joe's impish progeny. Insisting that "she didn't want any ring or man either," the lady protests too much to conceal her "disappointed shyness" (*D* 101). Her proud self-sufficiency is clearly a subterfuge bred of illusion and psychological repression, but imperative for survival in a bleak and hostile environment.

A victim of inveterate timidity, Maria proves just as ineffectual as Little Chandler in dealing with the outer world, but she does not have a conventional spouse to take up the slack and compensate for the gaps produced by her glaring ineptitude. Dublin seems to her a labyrinthine metropolis, and shopping for plum-cake becomes a major expedition for which she must summon all her courage and resources. Maria is so unused to contact with the opposite sex that some casual remarks by an inebriate codger in the Drumcondra tram throw her into total confusion. Befuddled by his startling address, she leaves her cake behind (perhaps as an unconscious offering to the "gentleman") in a gesture that evokes "shame and vexation and disappointment" (*D* 103 – 4).

Trained in a life of perpetual self-effacement, this "very small" person tries to diminish herself even further in social situations, though she is characteristically naïve and bumbling in her childlike efforts to please. A "veritable peacemaker," she manages to make herself unwelcome at the family party by putting in a good word for the estranged Alphy, then clumsily offering apologies to her discomfited host. Maria is the only adult to participate in the children's Halloween game, as the others look on with an air of bemused indulgence. The clay she touches may be a portent of her death – or of the death-in-life that characterizes her service in the Protestant shelter, where she is trapped in life-denying celibacy without the spiritual consolations of religious commitment.

Joyce leads us to suspect that Maria's aspirations are more amorous and worldly than she cares to admit as, blushing with modesty, she celebrates in song the aristocratic life of feudal elegance for which she secretly pines. Art gives her the nobility that life denies and allows temporary escape into fantasies of love and betrothal, wealth and imaginary romance. Not surprisingly, Maria forgets the second verse of Balfe's lyric. Her own pedestrian fate is so unlike that of the Bohemian girl Arline that she cannot bring herself to evoke a medley of suitors vying for her favor or the consummation of love promised by conjugal devotion. Her omission seems a tacit acknowledgement of future isolation. This Irish Cinderella will never be seduced by a Dublin Prince Charming. No suitors will seek the spinster's trembling hand; no knight will attempt to storm the fortified castle of her maiden heart. No one – not even Joe or Alphy – will "love her still the same" as they did when they were children. Singing of marble halls and ancient palaces, Maria knows she is destined to return to the steam-laden halls of institutional vassalage and will never be rescued by the mythic suitor she longs to summon from the landscape of romantic fantasy.[19]

If Maria is humble in her celibacy, James Duffy self-consciously clings to an Irish version of Nietzschean exile. "A Painful Case" presents two contrasting figures of psychological impotence – a woman trapped in a stultified marriage and a man insistent on self-imposed alienation. One of the more sympathetic females portrayed in *Dubliners*, Emily Sinico is a sensitive, passionate, and defiant figure who might well be expected to question the puritanical prac- tices of "dear dirty Dublin." It is remarkable that this unconven- tional woman exhibits a temperament of such "great sensibility" that she manages to penetrate the carapace of Duffy's bachelor reserve and to touch a man so resolutely disdainful of social relation- ship. "He had neither companions nor friends, church nor creed" (*D* 109). Mrs Sinico becomes mother and confessor to Duffy, who gradually bares his saturnine soul to her: "Her companionship was like a warm soil about an exotic. . . . This union exalted him, wore away the rough edges of his character, emotionalised his mental life" (*D* 111).

Because the narcissistic Duffy wants a matriarchal muse rather than a flesh-and-blood lover, he strategically represses the amorous dimensions of their simmering liaison. He adopts a stance of deliberate obliquity by replicating his own mirror image in Emily's adoring gaze. "Little by little he entangled his thoughts with hers. He lent her books, provided her with ideas, shared his intellectual life with her. She listened to all" (*D* 110). Emily's silent audition and laconic responses are open, it seems, to interpretive ambivalence and male misprision. Speaking little, she functions as a Lacanian mirror – an echo, a *heimlich* womb of mental warmth whose hothouse heart encourages Duffy's shrivelled soul to sprout

35

tendrils and gradually blossom. "With almost maternal solicitude she urged him to let his nature open to the full: she became his confessor. . . . He thought that in her eyes he would ascend to an angelical stature" (*D* 110–11). Drawing nourishment obliquely from Duffy's filial affections, Emily finally traduces her own iconic role as imaginary, mystifying center and disillusions her suitor. Through semiotic gestures of feminine desire, she subverts his egocentric fantasies of fictive coherence. "The end of these discourses was that one night during which she had shown every sign of unusual excitement, Mrs Sinico caught up his hand passionately and pressed it to her cheek" (*D* 111). Living always "at a little distance from his body, " the monkish Duffy responds to this effusive gesture with an attitude of shock and stoic rejection. Terrified by the prospect of physical intimacy with the untouchable body of the mother, he breaks off social intercourse and retreats into prudish propriety. A would-be "superman," Duffy chooses an austere, moralistic world of Nietzschean isolation, paradoxically illumined by such potentially revolutionary texts as *The Gay Science* and *Thus Spake Zarathustra*.

Fearing castration, Duffy has few compunctions about castrating his partner's hopes for the future. The desolate Emily, denied speech and contact, uses her body as a fetishistic symbol of passionate appeal. Abusing the carnal flesh that once desired Duffy, the woman, heartbroken and mute, dies like a pedestrian Anna Karenina on the tracks of a suburban tramline. Her body is reduced to the symbolic status of a reparatory fetish to be destroyed and punished – by drink, despair, carelessness, and failure of the heart. Death shatters her ignominious silence but, like Eveline's dying parent, Emily gestures in a semiotic game open to disruption, misprision, and flagrant misinterpretation. Even the body's spectral textuality cannot communicate with the errant son who denies meaningful speech first to a disembodied mother/goddess/muse, then to her mirror image as fallen, desecrated Eve.

Duffy initially reacts to the "painful case" of Emily's death with a stance of ludicrous self-righteousness: "He saw the squalid tract of vice, miserable and malodorous. . . . Evidently she had been unfit to live" (*D* 115). Because he had once aspired to Oedipal union with her idealized figure, he now feels horror and repulsion at the thought of shameful incestuous congress. The lurid nature of her accident ostensibly justifies a role-reversal that makes him into a judgmental patriarch condemning her violation of a presumed code of honor, a transgression to be sutured by masculine moral law. As priest and confessor, he callously denies absolution to Emily's ghost. Woman, for Duffy, functions as the wound in a torn social fabric, the glaring gap that threatens to invalidate male philosophical postures of intellectual mastery and spiritual transcendence.

Only gradually does this alienated bachelor begin to acknowledge personal responsibility for his friend's inebriate self-destruction, as he comes to realize that he has driven Emily to drink and despair, while condemning himself to an empty, meaningless existence. "Why had he withheld life from her? Why had he sentenced her to death? . . . One human being had seemed to love him and he had denied her life and happiness: he had sentenced her to ignominy, a death of shame" (D 117). Has Duffy experienced a genuine eipiphany – a true exposure of the wretchedness and cruelty of his behavior? Or is this attitude of exaggerated self-abasement, in which he imagines himself a failed savior and virtual executioner, simply another egotistical pose? As he moves from a stance of arrogant detachment to one of maudlin remorse, he never seems to escape an invidious circle of infantile self-absorption. Having refused Emily's maternal gifts, he uses her spurned sexuality to appropriate the tragic dimensions of her frustrated desire for love and emotional satisfaction. He plagiarizes her story and steals her suffering by converting melodrama into high tragedy – by assuming that he, like a modern-day Hamlet, might have saved the good Queen Gertrude from an unfortunate demise. The son, unable to rescue the mother who abandons him, takes on the burden of her death through a drama of self-condemnation. Emily's pain has become his own, her despair a visible sign of masochistic recrimination.

Like an abject and abandoned child, Duffy complains that: "No one wanted him; he was outcast from life's feast" (D 117). Having resolutely refused communion with others, he now discovers that Nietzsche's "feast of pure reason" provides the soul with carrion comfort. Gnawing on the bone of moral rectitude, he envies those "venal and furtive" lovers who celebrate the joys of unselfconscious union. Duffy ends by acknowledging his own chronic emotional starvation: "He felt that he was alone" (D 117). Stripped of pompous rhetoric and purple prose, he at last confronts the reality of existential isolation, and his words have the force of both psychological revelation and painful social prophecy.[20]

PUBLIC LIFE

In Joyce's three tales of public life, women are conspicuous either for their absence or for their helplessness in relation to the dominant society. They are excluded from participation in Irish political discourse, a language cloaking the kind of apathy and corruption exposed in "Ivy Day in the Committee Room." In Edwardian Ireland, republican fervor has apparently gone to seed, and Dublin politics proves little more than an excuse for male camaraderie, idle talk, and endless rounds of stout. Imperialistic repression sublimates currents of anger and hostility reflected in ubiquitous domestic violence. At the beginning of the story, old Jack, the caretaker, boasts of his paterfamilial power over a truculent, boozing son: "Only I'm an old man now I'd change his tune for him. I'd take a stick to his back and beat him while I could stand over him – as I done many a time before. The mother, you know, she cocks him up" (D 120). Lines of antagonism have been drawn between obstreperous sons and arrogant fathers, powerless progeny and hypocritical authority figures. The savage politics of family confrontation set the stage for explosive violence in the larger world of Irish colonial subjugation.

Now that Parnell, the impudent son who dared challenge British patriarchy, is "dead and gone," the men who betrayed him feel free to sanctify his memory with sentimental legends and nostalgic reminiscences. The Irish welcome a visit from King Edward VII, whose patronage will mean an influx of money for a beleaguered colonial economy: "The citizens of Dublin will benefit by it. . . . It's capital we want" (D 131). Despite compunctions about "kowtowing to a foreign king" (D 122), they are willing to embrace the monarch as "a jolly fine decent fellow" and turn a blind eye toward his lascivious reputation as a philanderer and "a bit of a rake" (D 132). Only Mr Lyons takes note of the paradox when he reminds his uncomfortable cronies that Parnell, Ireland's uncrowned king, was deposed by a "fell gang of modern hypocrites" (D 134) because of his adulterous liaison with Kitty O'Shea. "What I mean . . . is we have our ideals. . . . Do you think now after what he did Parnell was a fit man to lead us? And why, then, would we do it for Edward the Seventh?" (D 132).

Joe Hynes's puerile but ingenuous elegy, based on Joyce's own juvenile composition "*Et tu, Healy?*", betrays a naïve misprision of

Irish political life. The sentimental tribute exposes the anachronistic machinery operative in Dublin, where provincial power-struggles reduce an election to a petty drama of tribal hostilities. Squabbling in isolated factions, in an atmosphere rife with deceit and suspicion, the Dubliners lack either the moral vision or the heroic imagination necessary for the collective struggle that would free them from British rule. The sons fight among themselves to divert revolutionary energies away from patriarchal authority and bolster a foreign king whose despotism is demystified by way of *ad hominem* arguments. Good old Eddie, they insist, is really just a feckless chap who likes the odd glass of grog, a "mama's boy" who never outgrew an adolescent weakness for the pleasures of the flesh. Transferring British political oppression to the innocuous register of sexual potency, the Dubliners symbolically connive with the forces of imperialism by acknowledging King Edward as a soul-brother – a "good sportsman" in games of both sexual prowess and territorial expansion. "Damn it, can't we Irish play fair?" (*D* 132) asks Henchy. Joyce's polemical tale inverts the query: on a world stage of national alliances, will the British prove fair to their Irish subjects? And is the quest for national autonomy and self-determination merely a ludic enterprise?

It is clear from the story "Grace" that no woman need apply to the deity for commercial salvation, either in this life or in the next. Mrs Kernan is described as an "active, practical woman" who "believed steadily in the Sacred Heart . . . and approved of the sacraments. Her faith was bounded by her kitchen, but, if she was put to it, she could believe also in the banshee and in the Holy Ghost" (*D* 158). For the Irish housewife, religion is a mixture of domestic faith and fairy superstition. She has automatically been excluded from the male coterie that wields ecclesiastical power and from an institution that celebrates the strategies of mercantile success. At the retreat sermon, a caricatured and venal prelate betrays the spiritual ideals of Irish Catholicism by describing the deity as a great accountant in the sky and exhorting his parishioners to be "straight and manly with God" (*D* 174). Misreading the biblical parable of the unjust steward (Luke 16), Father Purdon compares the historical Jesus to a compromising businessman eager to bargain with the mammon of iniquity. For the preacher and his audience, Catholicism is an affair of male bonding, and religious observance has little to do with Christian charity, tolerance, or compassion. Cunningham proclaims that "our religion is *the* religion, the old, original faith" (*D* 166). And the Dubliners arrogantly indict the convert Harford "as an Irish Jew and an illiterate" even though "he had never embraced more than the Jewish ethical code" (*D* 159) – a code implicitly superior, it would seem, to the mercantile philosophy set forth for Christian emulation. The Church has all the trappings of an exclusive men's club, a social organization that covertly sanctions racial bigotry and clings to atavistic tribal sentiments.

Perhaps the most pathetic example of a woman trying to break into a male-dominated power structure occurs in the story "A Mother." Mrs Kearney, the protagonist of the tale, is a stubborn, self-willed matriarch who tries to live vicariously through her timid daughter Kathleen. The matron had remained chilly and aloof when young, repressing her "romantic desires by eating a great deal of Turkish Delight in secret" (*D* 136–7). On the brink of spinster-hood, she chose to marry a bootmaker whose humble and steady qualities would "wear better" than those of a "romantic person" (*D* 137). "She respected her husband in the same way as she respected the General Post Office, as something large, secure and fixed; and though she knew the small number of his talents she appreciated his abstract value as a male" (*D* 141). The frustrated mother has by now managed to displace her own secret romantic aspirations onto the lives of her docile daughters – at least one of whom, as a singer of Irish airs, is sure to cash in on the nascent Celtic Revival.

Although Mrs Kearney initially ingratiates herself with Hoppy Holohan, the scatterbrained secretary of the *Eire Abu* society, her façade of graciousness and gentility quickly dissolves the moment she fears that her daughter might be cheated of her just financial deserts. Standing on principle, she repeatedly insists that the girl "won't go on. She must get her eight guineas. . . . She won't go on without her money" (*D* 146). As self-appointed spokesperson for a timorous *ingénue*, Mrs Kearney confuses her daughter's desires with her own and ends by claiming, intransigently, "I'm asking for my rights" (*D* 148), with little consideration for Kathleen's welfare. This strong-willed mother mistakenly assumes that the tyrannical tactics she uses to manipulate a henpecked husband will prove successful in the dominant world of patriarchal politics. She cannot imagine the value of co-operative strategies or the kind of team spirit in which her male adversaries have tacitly been schooled. Trained exclusively in the art of domestic bullying, she lapses into bizarre and ineffectual torrents of invective in response to frustration and powerlessness. Infuriated, she acts bull-headedly, asserting herself "like a man." As O'Madden Burke grimly predicts, her "scandalous exhibition" will put an end to "Miss Kathleen Kearney's musical career . . . in Dublin" (D 147). "They wouldn't have dared to have treated her like that if she had been a man" (D 148), Mrs Kearney charges. And she is right. The baritone, asked to comment on the heated controversy, "did not like to say anything. He had been paid his money and wished to be at peace with men" (D 147).

A *petit bourgeois* Dublin impresario has the power to ruin both Kathleen and her mother, and he has the backing of a large array of mutilated, but influential cronies. Holohan's final reprimand is delivered in a tone of condescension and disdain: "I thought you were a lady" (D 149). Almost all the men present censure Mrs Kearney's irrational outburst as decidedly unladylike and a shocking breach of feminine decorum. "I'm done with you" (D 149), says Holohan triumphantly. His abrupt retort seems to imply that the Irish Revival has finished with (and done enough to) the hapless Kathleen, as well. Women who dare to step out of line and transgress sex-stereotyped codes of behavior are inevitably doomed to suffer harsh consequences for challenging an obdurate patriarchy. "That's a nice lady!" squeals Holohan. "O, she's a nice lady!" (D 149). The defeated matron, "haggard with rage," is left "arguing with her husband and daughter, gesticulating with them" at the stage door, evidently at odds with the constituency she purports to represent (D 149).

The irony of the story is double-edged. The bourgeois impresarios who control Dublin culture are a sorry lot indeed, and it is not surprising that they immediately ostracize a brash matriarch who fails to keep her place. Mrs Kearney, in turn, is so obsessively motivated by greed and financial ambition that she compromises her daughter's musical career for the sake of bolstering her own ego and maintaining a self-righteous principle. In an atmosphere of backbiting and petty-mindedness, the noble ideals of the Celtic Renaissance envisaged by William Butler Yeats, John Millington Synge, and Lady Augusta Gregory are shockingly absent from Irish cultural practice.

"THE DEAD" – AN EPILOGUE

In his portrait of Gretta Conroy in "The Dead," Joyce fashioned for the first time in his fiction the image of a passionate, nurturant, and life-giving woman whose rich, intuitive consciousness was modeled on the confessions of Nora Barnacle. "The Dead," Richard Ellmann tells us, comprises "one of Joyce's several tributes to his wife's artless integrity. Nora Barnacle, in spite of her defects of education, was independent, unselfconscious, instinctively right. Gabriel acknowledges the same coherence in his own wife, and he recognizes in the west of Ireland, in Michael Furey, a passion he has himself always lacked" (*JJ* 249).

Gabriel Conroy is, at least in part, a figure of the kind of Irish pedant Joyce might have become had he remained in his native country. A writer of book reviews and after-dinner speeches, Gabriel prides himself on his continental perspective and feels a bit ashamed of the Galway wife his mother once described as "country cute." He compulsively protects his family from the hazards of nature by insistent recourse to galoshes, green shades, dumb bells, and stirabout. As a minion of modern civilization, he betrays a deep-seated, almost neurotic fear of exposure to the perilous fluidity of life symbolized in the ruggedness of a western terrain "beyond the pale" of urban amenities.

A Joycean surrogate, Conroy takes refuge in a logocentric and dangerously repressive world of verbal mastery cut off from unconscious drives and explosive libidinal desires. With a mixture of nostalgia and condescension, he contemplates pictures of "the balcony scene in *Romeo and Juliet*" and of the "murdered princes in the Tower which Aunt Julia had worked in red, blue and brown wools when she was a girl" (*D* 186) as artful embroideries that transform Renaissance tragedy into a casual comedy of the nineteenth-century drawing room. Sanitized, and robbed of cathartic effect, the scenes become part of a Victorian memorial to the necrophiliac eruptions of Shakespearean drama. Though contemptuous of his aunts' naïve and ladylike sensibilities, Gabriel proves just as guilty as they of consigning both subversive heroism and *l'amour fou* to the controlled and static frame of aesthetic appropriation. By framing the ineffable and taming the disruptive agents of love and violence, the artist diminishes their phallic force and castrates the figures, who become specular objects to be devoured by the observer's enveloping gaze.

Similarly, in the register of language and social discourse, Gabriel is intent on constructing a phallocentric fortress of masterful rhetoric to protect his vulnerable ego. Despite the benefits of erudition, training, and intellectual sophistication, he treats every personal encounter as a contest for psychological dominance. Caught between an arrogant cultural pose and hidden feelings of self-doubt, Gabriel makes the social world into a narcissistic stage for dramas of continual self-assertion. Habitually condescending toward women, he dares not "risk a grandiose phrase" with the annoying Molly Ivors, but challenges her nonetheless with the incendiary remark that "I'm sick of my own country, sick of it!" (D 189). Such a confession might well deserve the charge of "West Briton" which Gabriel finds egregiously offensive. Instead of expressing his agitation openly, however, and fighting it out with Miss Ivors, he indulges in petty, mean-minded exercises in self-vindication: "Of course the girl or woman, or whatever she was, was an enthusiast but there was a time for all things. Perhaps he ought not to have answered her like that. But she had no right to call him a West Briton before people, even in joke. She had tried to make him ridiculous before people, heckling him and staring at him with her rabbit's eyes" (D 190). In this unconscious appeal to male privilege, Gabriel dismisses his opponent as a childish female whose audacious demeanor has so unsexed her that she seems to belong to a third, unnamable gender. In his mind, the rabid patriot is rhetorically transformed into a heckling rabbit hopping about in irrational frenzy.

Imitating a petulant child, Gabriel saves his final thrust for last. His pedantic postprandial speech tacitly condemns Miss Ivors as a member of the "new and very serious and hypereducated generation" that betrays traditional Irish hospitality (D 192). "Very good," he thinks smugly, "that was one for Miss Ivors. What did he care that his aunts were only two ignorant old women?" (D 192). Gabriel is eager to put down one woman by elevating two others who serve as pawns to balance the scales of masculine indignation and soothe his wounded ego. His indictment of a skeptical and thought-tormented age is largely an act of psychological projection, since Gabriel himself emerges as the most self-conscious figure in the story. Although the speaker mourns the loss of a more spacious era "gone beyond recall," he is ill-prepared to cherish the memory of an Irishman whose fame his wife Gretta cannot "willingly let die" (D 203).

Like Torvald Helmer in Ibsen's *Doll's House*, Gabriel sees his spouse not as an individual with feelings and needs of her own but as a static symbol feeding his creative imagination.[21] "He asked himself what is a woman standing on the stairs in the shadow, listening to distant music, a symbol of. If he were a painter he would paint her in that attitude. . . . *Distant Music* he would call the picture" (*D* 210). Shrouded in grace and mystery, Gretta becomes a model of feminine tranquillity, a romantic image of blue and bronze, blurred in a setting of vague nostalgia. Her feelings are framed and appropriated, her passions castrated and erased. Although *The Lass of Aughrim* has auditory impact on his wife, Gabriel refuses to acknowledge the world of memory and desire stirred by Gretta's response to the Irish ballad. Instead, he translates her meditative mood into a vapid visual impression. Lost in a Whistleresque fantasy, he deliberately distances himself from the emotive qualities of the music and from a tragic sexual narrative rooted in Celtic associations.[22] Like Stephen Dedalus in *A Portrait*, he freezes the moment of experience and imposes the "spiritual-heroic refrigerating apparatus" of art onto a pallid, sentimental figure constructed by his self-absorbed imagination. To facilitate the project, Gabriel misinterprets Gretta's body language and fails to sense the emotional currents of her silence – of thoughts cast out like lyrical fragments that demand a reading of present nostalgia through a history of love and loss. Framing his wife as a specular object, he ignores the context of smoldering passion that evinces her melancholic posture. Feminine desire is subject to amorous misprision, as the gaps and wounds of Gretta's past experience are replicated in her consciousness by mimetic shapes of idealized longing.

About to project his own desire for a "yielding mood" onto his wife's vulnerable figure, Gabriel muses: "She seemed to him so frail that he longed to defend her against something and then to be alone with her. Moments of their secret life together burst like stars upon his memory. . . . He longed to recall to her those moments, to make her forget the years of their dull existence together and remember only their moments of ecstasy. For the years, he felt, had not quenched his soul or hers" (*D* 213–14). Gabriel's surge of conjugal tenderness is entirely focused on private memories filtered through a nostalgic vision of himself as a fiery cavalier. He revels in feelings of spousal possession associated with the couple's dancing earlier that night: "He had felt proud and happy then, happy that she was his, proud of her grace and wifely carriage" (*D* 215). Romantically idealizing Gretta's presence, Gabriel constructs an image of her as an exotic mistress whose mysterious demeanor harbors promises of ecstatic flight: "Under cover of her silence . . . he felt that they had escaped from their lives and duties, escaped from home and friends and run away together with wild and radiant hearts to a new adventure" (*D* 215).

Gretta, however, remains mute. It is Gabriel who speaks for her in this emotionally charged fantasy, and it is he who defines their adventure with the same kind of *naïveté* that characterized the futile aspirations of the young boy in "Araby." His dream of recapturing the thrill of their honeymoon recollects the first days of conjugal life as a model for the kind of integrity, joy, and emotional satisfaction associated with pre-Oedipal bliss. Bourgeois marriage has meant a fall from paradisal union with the beloved, whose erstwhile desirability acts as a spur to the recrudescence of urgent, if insatiable, erotic need.

Once at the Gresham Hotel, Gabriel's thoughts circle obsessively around male dominance and female submission until, on the brink of sexual frenzy, he feels a keen pang of lust and an overwhelming urge to seize, crush, and "overmaster" his wife. "He could have flung his arms about her hips and held her still, for his arms were trembling with desire to seize her and only the stress of his nails against the palms of his hands held the wild impulse of his body in check" (*D* 215). Ironically, he contemplates a kind of emotional (and possibly physical) rape at the very moment when Gretta is most fully absorbed in reminiscences of Michael Furey, a lover whose passion took the form of sacrificial tragedy. This Irish suitor who died for love acted the melodramatic role of a legendary knight who, in good chivalric fashion, laid at the feet of his courtly lady the ultimate gift of his life. By sacrificing all for Gretta, he took permanent possession of her heart. Symbolically, the martyred Furey became a contemporary Christ figure, a mythic hero whose death makes Gretta into an eternal replica of the Virgin Mary as *Pietà*. She is forever an emblem of the *magna mater*, the mother/lover bearing a transfigured godhead in bereft maternal arms.[23]

Lost in a trance of mourning for Michael, Gretta idolizes the boy as an always-already-absent object of desire, forever longed for and pined after until the tantalizing fact of inaccessibility becomes an aphrodisiac of the spirit. Psychological drives that are dammed and sublimated circle back in rich profusion, as death fetishizes the body of the beloved and makes unattainable physical presence a sexual spur in a world of amorous denial. The absent lover torments the dreaming mind until pain piques erotic appetite to the point of libidinal despair. Melodrama prohibits the comedy of physical collusion, the joyous game of "laugh and lie down" that cannot be played among corpses. Pleasure is masked in self-indulgent longing, physical attraction idealized through tears and sentimental yearning. "I want" is echoed back as "I love," Eros disguised in the mimesis of perfect passion for an impotent lover who can no longer touch, threaten, penetrate, wound, or inseminate the female body. The scar of loss, invaginating consciousness, metaphorically reproduces the vaginal gap yearning for prohibited phallic presence. The mind, rent by melancholia, seals up the lover's replica like an embryo in a womb, an encrypted and forever-powerful image of the unattainable lost one. "I was great with him at that time," says Gretta (*D* 220), recalling a phrase descriptive of pregnancy, as well as of girlish infatuation. Gestating in the heart, the once-beloved object is resuscitated and made real, his absence become a presence through a life-giving process that celebrates the dead son/god/lover resurrected by the mythopoesis of feminine desire.

The ghost of inaccessible *jouissance* flows into the present and reduces Gabriel's dream of sexual possession to a futile, impotent fantasy. Cuckolded by a dead man, the husband is overcome with rage, then assaulted by pitiable confusion. Stripped of the conjugal assumptions that have always sustained an illusory faith in his own integrity, he begins to confront the pettiness of his egocentric vision:

> Gabriel felt humiliated by the failure of his irony and by the evocation of this figure from the dead, a boy in the gasworks. [The irony of his mood soured into sarcasm.] While he had been full of memories of their secret life together, full of tenderness and joy and desire, she had been comparing him in her mind with another. A shameful consciousness of his own person assailed him. He saw himself as a ludicrous figure, acting as a pennyboy for his aunts, a nervous, well-meaning sentimentalist, orating to vulgarians and idealising his own clownish lusts. (*D* 219–20; *JJA* 5: 303)[24]

Humiliated by the ashes of burnt-out lust, Gabriel is shocked to encounter an incontestable opponent – a dead man now elevated to the status of a slain deity whose love once flared with consummate ecstasy. The tale of this meteoric devotion sparks the dying embers of Gabriel's passionate commitment to his wife; and the narrative inaugurates a familiar Joycean pattern of triangulated desire, as Michael becomes the spiritual mediator of Gabriel's affection for Gretta.[25] Longing to appropriate and emotionally fuse with the *imago* of a beneficent mother/wife, Gabriel is forced to acknowledge the utter inaccessibility of an/Other's subjectivity. The opaque and rounded character of an imaginary center, a knowable and fully illuminated symbol (or symptom) of womanhood, is suddenly shattered by the startling revelation of a secret love perpetually reconstituted through rites of amorous frustration.[26] Unable to reproduce his subjective self-image in the mirror of an/Other, Gabriel is thrust onto the margins of conjugal doubt and forced to re-integrate his ego through splintered reflections of a recollected past, a plethora of emotional fragments that defy mental coherence. Relinquishing his longing for self-valorization through a totalizing vision of the female, he surrenders himself to the unsettling pulsions of a buried, semiotic life that offers the promise of psychic regeneration. By the end of the story, both Gabriel and Michael have been successfully resurrected – one from the paralysis of death-in-life, the other from a legend of life-in-death.

Touched by the spectral presence of Furey, Gabriel begins to cast off his shell of egotistical self-absorption.[27] He feels his identity "fading out into a grey impalpable world; the solid world itself . . . was dissolving and dwindling. . . . The time had come for him to set out on his journey westward. . . . His soul swooned slowly as he heard the snow falling faintly through the universe and faintly falling, like the descent of their last end, upon all the living and the dead" (*D* 223–4). The ending of Joyce's tale is finely ambiguous. We have learned from the author's ironic sensibility in stories such as "Araby" and "A Painful Case" to distrust swooning souls and self-deceptive epiphanies – especially when, as in this case, the pre-Raphaelite swoon is embedded in a Christological ambiance of crooked crosses, spears, and "barren thorns" (*D* 224). Imitating the Christ-like role of Michael Furey, Gabriel may well be trapped in a self-indulgent replication of romantic asceticism. If so, he has been swept up in the illusory discourse of fealty and courtly love, which Jacques Lacan describes as "an altogether refined way of making up for the absence of sexual relation by pretending that it is we who put an obstacle to it."[28]

In Richard Ellmann's view, Gabriel has achieved a genuine sense of maturity and authentic connection with all the living and the dead, a salutary understanding of the "mutual dependency" and "interrelationship" that links the whole of humankind (*JJ* 252). At the conclusion of "The Dead," the logocentric consciousness of the masculine subject dissolves into a will-less dream of semiotic process where birth and growth are balanced by their binary opposites, decay and death. Gabriel appears to sink into the primitive, repressed world of the unconscious and at last to stand open to those self-effacing dimensions of love and solicitude heretofore denied by a willful, narcissistic ego.[29]

Gretta Conroy, like Anna Livia Plurabelle, has miraculously resuscitated the shade of a dead man as a living, potent spirit. And like Molly Bloom celebrating her sexual initiation on Howth, she draws the past into the present in the mode of impassioned memory. Revitalizing the ghost of her long-dead lover, Gretta gives mythic stature to a man whose life ended in tragic consummation; and, in contrast to the casual comedy enacted by the Dubliners, her act succeeds in endowing Ireland with a kind of legendary grandeur. Through a poetics of absence contingent on desire indefinitely deferred and *inter-dit* (spoken through or between the gaps of frustrated longing), she makes possible the spiritual redemption of Gabriel, whose aesthetic pretensions have degenerated into the fatuities of *l'homme moyen sensuel*. It is, in the end, Gretta who proves to be the true artist of the tale, a woman whose imagination regenerates the past and gives birth to a sustaining narrative that provides a supplement to fading marital affection and inspires the final epiphany of the story. She successfully revitalizes the revolutionary and subversive world of love and violence domesticated by her aunts and puritanically refrigerated by her prurient spouse.

By offering a vivid myth of salutary passion, Gretta rejuvenates the moribund spirit of her husband and, as mother and lover to both Michael and Gabriel, emerges as the first of Joyce's extraordinary female characters. Her emotional vitality will inform subsequent portraits of women who usurp the last word of the paternal text and refuse to allow it narrative closure. In touch with the semiotic rhythms of maternal love and erotic bonding, Gretta articulates a spiritually redemptive aesthetics of desire that subverts the logocentric world of patriarchal discourse and presages the future textual victories of Bertha Rowan in *Exiles*, Molly Bloom in *Ulysses*, and Anna Livia Plurabelle at the end (or beginning) of *Finnegans Wake*.

2

STEPHEN DEDALUS AND WOMEN
A Portrait of the Artist as a Young Narcissist

A boy's journey is the return to the native land, the
Heimweh Freud speaks of, the nostalgia that makes
man a being who tends to come back to the point
of departure to appropriate it for himself.

(Hélène Cixous, "Sorties")

Nircississies are as the doaters of inversion.

(*FW* 526. 34 – 5)

MOTHER AND CHILD

Female characters are present everywhere and nowhere in *A Portrait of the Artist as a Young Man*. They pervade the novel, yet remain elusive. Their sensuous figures haunt the developing consciousness of Stephen Dedalus and provide a foil against which he defines himself as both man and artist. Like everything else in *A Portrait*, women are portrayed almost exclusively from Stephen's point of view. Seen through his eyes and colored by his psychological fantasies, they often appear as one-dimensional projections of a narcissistic imagination and emerge as forceful antagonists in the novel's dialectical structure. Demonized by Stephen's childhood sense of abjection, they stand as powerful emblems of the flesh – frightening reminders of sexual temptation, the process of genera-tion, and the inevitability of bodily decay.

At the dawn of infantile consciousness, Stephen interprets the external world in terms of complementary pairs: male and female, father and mother, politics and religion, Davitt and Parnell. Baby Stephen's cosmos is organized in binary structures that set the stage for a dialectic of personal development. He perceives his father as a primordial storyteller who inaugurates the linguistic apprenticeship that inscribes the boy into the symbolic order of patriarchal authority. Simon Dedalus, like Father Flynn in "The Sisters," is a bearer of the law and the word, instruments of the will that promise psychological mastery over a hostile material environment. The male parent appeals to Stephen's imagination, awakening him to a sense of individual identity at the moment of *Spaltung* or splitting when language necessarily establishes a gap between subjective desire and self-representation in discourse.[1]

> Once upon a time and a very good time it was there was a moocow coming down along the road and this moocow that was coming down along the road met a nicens little boy named baby tuckoo. . . .
> His father told him that story: his father looked at him through a glass: he had a hairy face.
> He was baby tuckoo. . . .
> *O, the wild rose blossoms*
> *On the little green place.*
> He sang that song. That was his song. (*P* 7)

By virtue of receiving a forename, Stephen is able to enunciate himself as a subject of discourse and to gain access to the symbolic order of narrative representation. Inscribed into the linguistic circuit of exchange by Simon Dedalus, he identifies himself in terms of the dominant culture's signifying practices. The nominal referent "baby tuckoo" functions as an inaugural fabulation evocative of the child's dawning powers of self-creation. It also serves as a linguistic mirror whose double "o" sounds replicate the Irish and folkloric "moocow" – a fantasy projection subliminally associated with images of fertility, nurture, and imaginary plenitude.[2]

At the significant psychological juncture between pre-Oedipal attachment and Oedipal separation, Stephen perceives his mother as a powerful and beneficent source of physical pleasure. She ministers to her son's corporal needs, changes the oil-sheet, and encourages his artistic expression by playing the piano.[3] This sweet-smelling guardian is more directly responsive than the father to Stephen's infantile emotional demands and more closely associated with the pleasures of sensuous comfort and bodily joy:

> When you wet the bed first it is warm then it gets cold. His mother put on the oilsheet. That had a queer smell.
> His mother had a nicer smell than his father. She played on the piano the sailor's hornpipe for him to dance. He danced.
>
> (*P* 7)

It is the "nice" mother, however, whom Stephen recognizes as one of the women principally responsible for introducing him to a hostile external world and to the repressive strictures of middle-class morality. The first of the many imperatives that thwart the boy's ego, "apologise," is associated in his mind and vivid imagination with matriarchal threats:

> He hid under the table. His mother said:
> – O, Stephen will apologise.
> Dante said:
> – O, if not, the eagles will come and pull out his eyes. (*P* 8)

Dante and Mrs Dedalus both represent the inhibitions of an ominous reality principle that begins, at this point, to take precedence over the polymorphously perverse gratifications of infantile narcissism. The two women mutually demand the sublimation and repression of pleasurable libidinal drives and the rigorous conquest of the id in favor of a disciplined social ego.[4] As Dorothy Dinnerstein explains in *The Mermaid and the Minotaur*, it is usually a woman who serves as "every infant's first love, first witness and first boss. . . . The initial experience of dependence on a largely uncontrollable outside source of good is focused on a woman, and so is the earliest experience of vulnerability to disappointment and pain."[5] Nancy Chodorow, in her work on object relations, observes that this "preoedipal mother, simply as a result of her omnipotence and activity, causes a 'narcissistic wound.' . . . Children of both sexes . . . will maintain a fearsome unconscious maternal image as a result of projecting upon it the hostility derived from their own feelings of impotence."[6]

According to Freudian theory, the primordial conflict between male and female takes root in the infant's early encounter with a world alien to its sensibilities and antagonistic to the demands of an omnipotent will. As the child (either male or female) begins to distinguish between ego and environment, between self and other, it suddenly becomes aware of a dangerous threat to the struggle for individuation. In a process of transference, the developing ego symbolically equates the mother or a mother-surrogate with the enemy that frustrates libidinal desire and threatens to engulf a newly acquired and fragile sense of self. The female figure takes on extraordinary and mysterious powers. Though a goddess in terms of parental authority, she is unconsciously identified by the child with the hated flesh that eludes infantile control. In compensation for the loss of felt continuity with the mother, the child attempts to console itself by acquiring physical and mental skills that will allow personal affirmation of mastery and self-sufficiency in the outer world. Various modes of creative production function as an enabling symbolic discourse permitting the assertion of an aggressive, sometimes violent "will to power" that defies the rigorous circumscriptions imposed by female authority.[7]

As Simone de Beauvoir explains in *The Second Sex*, the male child, in particular, unconsciously associates his mother, and consequently all women everywhere, with viscosity and immanence – with the inexorable forces of a chaotic, uncontrollable world of physicality, process, and unsatisfied desire. He develops a conviction that women are ineluctably bound by the generative demands of the species, and the presence of his own mother becomes a dreaded reminder of human contingency – the shame of his animal nature and the remorseless threat of personal extinction. "The uncleanness of birth is reflected upon the mother. . . . And if the little boy remains in early childhood sensually attached to the maternal flesh, when he grows older, becomes socialized, and takes note of his individual existence, this same flesh frightens him . . . calls him back to those realms of immanence whence he would fly."[8]

"Reproduction is the beginning of death" (*P* 231) argued Hegel, and so argues Stephen's friend Temple. The Manichaean dichotomy between flesh and spirit, body and mind, has long been allied in the writings of male philosophers with the basic (fantasized) polarity between the sexes and the linguistic construction of sexual difference. Stephen vies with Nietzsche and with Schopenhauer when, in *Stephen Hero*, he proposes a misogynist "theory of dualism which would symbolise the twin eternities of spirit and nature in the twin eternities of male and female" (*SH* 210). According to Simone de Beauvoir, man's symbolic association of woman with the flesh reflects an embedded infantile disdain for human corporality and anarchic libidinal drives. The male identifies himself as spirit by virtue of his own subjective consciousness; he then perceives the female as "the Other, who limits and denies him."[9] In rebelling against woman, "man is in revolt against his carnal state; he sees himself as a fallen god. . . . He would be inevitable, like a pure Idea, like the One, the All, the absolute Spirit; and he finds himself shut up in a body of limited powers, in a place and time he never chose. . . . Man feels horror at having been engendered; . . .

through the fact of his birth murderous Nature has a hold upon him.''[10]

The antagonism of these "twin eternities" is impressed on Stephen at an early age. He disdains his mother's feminine vulnerability and thinks that she is "not nice" when she bursts into tears. Like most young boys, Stephen begins to interpret his relationship with his mother as an embarrassment and an annoying obstacle to more grown-up affiliations with members of his own sex. Armed with ten shillings and his father's injunction toward a code of masculine loyalty, he enters the competitive joust of life at Clongowes determined to adopt an ethic of manly stoicism: "his father had told him . . . whatever he did, never to peach on a fellow" (P 9).

In a world of social Darwinism where only the ruthless survive, Stephen defines himself as both literally and figuratively marginal. Small, frail, and feeling very much like an outsider in this thundering herd of pugnacious schoolboys, he mentally takes refuge in artistic evocations of the family hearth protected by beneficent female spirits – Mother, Dante, and the servant Brigid. As he relives the horror of being shouldered into a rat-infested urinal ditch by the bully Wells, Stephen projects himself beyond the vermin and the scum to an apparently dissociated reverie. He recalls his mother sitting by the fire in hot "jewelly slippers" that exude a "lovely warm smell" (P 10). Alienated from a brutal male environment, Stephen longs to return to his mother and, in true Oedipal fashion, focuses on the fetishistic symbols of her warm feet, sexual totems that offer both kinaesthetic and olfactory satisfaction in compensation for the stench and the slimy touch of the chilling water. Incarcerated in the infirmary, Stephen recalls the funeral of Little, then hallucinates his own death and burial. He also reverts to pre-Oedipal attachment and imagines writing a letter begging his mother to come and rescue him from this alien environment. He desires female comfort and longs "to be at home and lay his head on his mother's lap" (P 13), but distinguishes between this maternal sanctuary and foreboding memories of "his father's house," "cold and dark under the seawall" (P 17).

The incident of Stephen's humiliating plunge into the Clongowes cesspool sparks off a number of subtle associations that weave a web of symbolism around the child's repressed anger at Wells's brutality. The square ditch, Stephen believes, is infested with rats that swim in the scum and feed on human excrement. "And how cold and slimy the water had been! And a fellow had once seen a big rat jump plop into the scum" (*P* 14). Later, when Stephen feels sick in his breadbasket and has an attack of the "collywobbles," he identifies his malady as an illness of the heart similar to the French term for nausea, *mal au coeur*. "He thought that he was sick in his heart if you could be sick in that place" (*P* 13).

Recognizing in his fever and chills a vertiginous reeling between hot and cold, like the spigots of water in the Wicklow lavatory, the boy draws a discomforting analogy between his illness and the "slimy and damp and cold" sensations of vermin. As he associates his flu with the rat-infested cesspool, Stephen tries to analyze his feelings of anger and vulnerability by a lugubrious meditation on the mortality of mice. He first imagines the lurid creatures with "sleek slimy coats, little little feet tucked up to jump, black shiny eyes to look out of. . . . But the minds of rats could not understand trigonometry," he assures himself (*P* 22). Through a process of logical deduction, he concludes that rats, unlike human beings, are mortal – merely desiccated blobs of flesh who "lay on their sides" and are "only dead things" when they die (*P* 22). Echoing the traditional syllogism about Socrates, men, and mortality, Stephen substitutes a rat for Socrates. His implicit conclusion is that men, unlike rats, enjoy the gift of immortality after death.

Unwittingly, Stephen has set the stage for future psychological identification with the political scapegoat Parnell. In the infirmary, the feverish child contemplates Little's funeral, then imagines his own death and burial. But it is not Stephen who dies; it is Parnell, whose demise is reported by Brother Michael and imaginatively represented in an epiphanic reverie that haunts Stephen's consciousness:

—— He is dead. We saw him lying upon the catafalque.
A wail of sorrow went up from the people.
—— Parnell! Parnell! He is dead!
They fell upon their knees, moaning in sorrow.
And he saw Dante in a maroon velvet dress and with a green velvet mantle hanging from her shoulders walking proudly and silently past the people who knelt by the waters' edge. (*P* 27)

It is the rat, finally, that brings the innocent child and his political hero together in symbolic contiguity. At the Christmas dinner,

Simon Dedalus angrily indicts those "sons of bitches" who betrayed Parnell: "When he was down they turned on him to betray him and rend him like rats in a sewer. Lowlived dogs!" (P 34). Both Stephen and Parnell have been betrayed – thrust into a cesspool (one literal, the other figurative) and rent by the rats of a bullying Irish populace. Unjustly punished, brokenhearted (or sick in the heart), and ill with flu or pneumonia, both will emerge from the cesspool victorious and rise like phoenixes to be celebrated by a band of laudatory disciples.

In a confused way, the young Stephen Dedalus continues to deliberate on the inscrutable mysteries of Oedipal desire for an idealized mother whose sexual difference is a source of repressed masculine anxiety.[11] He is unable to distinguish between filial and erotic love and feels hopelessly perplexed when Wells unites the two in a sexual conundrum: "Tell us, Dedalus, do you kiss your mother before you go to bed?" (P 14). Stephen desires the soft wetness of his mother's lips, but is baffled by the moral implications of a riddle that would challenge the saintliness of Aloysius Gonzaga. Later, in Chapter Five, when Cranly asks Stephen whether or not he loves his mother, the young man is still unable to respond. "I don't know what your words mean" (P 240), he replies.

As the curious boy stumbles toward manhood, he feels compelled to cast off every sort of allegiance to maternal figures.[12] His childhood educator Dante, "a clever woman and a wellread woman" who teaches him geography and lunar lore, is supplanted by male instructors: "Father Arnall knew more that Dante because he was a priest" (P 11). The Jesuit masters at Clongowes invite Stephen to ponder the mysteries of religion, death, canker, and cancer. They introduce him to a system of male authority and discipline, to a pedagogical regimen that will insure his correct training and proper socialization. Through examinations that pit red roses against white, Yorks against Lancastrians, they make education an aggressive game of simulated warfare in which the students, like soldiers, are depersonalized through institutional surveillance.[13]

By the time Stephen is old enough to join his parents' table at Christmas, his mother can no longer protect him from the world of masculine aggression or the turbulence of Irish politics. At the holiday meal, Stephen assimilates the knowledge that rabid women like Dante Riordan support ecclesiastical authority in the name of moral righteousness. Like the old sow that eats her farrow, Dante is willing to sacrifice Parnell as a political scapegoat to the prelates of Irish Catholicism. In the face of Mr Casey's Fenianism and Simon's contemptuous snorting, she labels the Catholic clergy "the apple of God's eye. *Touch them not*, says Christ, *for they are the apple of My eye*" (*P* 38). As Ireland's perverted Eve, Dante defends this ecclesiastical apple against an adulterous republican leader, a scandalous sinner crushed by an irate populace. Her impassioned ravings, bred of puritanical self-righteousness, suggest a formidable alliance between the Catholic Church and the inflexible ideals of bourgeois morality guarded by a Scyllan horde of devout Irishwomen. "God and morality and religion come first," shrieks Dante (*P* 38). Mr Casey counters with his own incendiary slogan: "Very well, then, . . . if it comes to that, no God for Ireland!" (*P* 39). "Devil out of hell!" Dante retorts. "We won! We crushed him to death! Fiend!" (*P* 39).

In the battle between male and female, Mother Church emerges as a bastion of sexual repression defended by hysterical women. Dante's own credibility is socially diminished by her age, gender, and involuntary celibacy. Stephen "had heard his father say that she was a spoiled nun and that she had come out of the convent in the Alleghanies when her brother had got the money from the savages for the trinkets and the chainies" (*P* 35). Stephen's male role-models, Simon Dedalus and John Casey, boldly assert masculine prowess through republican fervor directed against dissenting countrymen rather than against their imperial masters. In this mock scenario of political self-assertion, women and children are fair game. Hence Casey's braggadocio in recounting his triumph over the hag who screamed "whore": "I had my mouth full of tobacco juice. I bent down to her and *Phth*! says I to her like that . . . right into her eye" (*P* 36 – 7). The bombastic narrative makes a hero of Casey for conquering the malevolent crone – the folkloric witch, hag, or mother-in-law who caricatures female dementia. Spitting in her eye, he symbolically achieves a talismanic victory through sexual violation of the threatening phallic mother. As Simon's own eyes fill with tears in sentimental tribute to Parnell, his behavior must seem confusing and unmanly to the impressionable child.

When Stephen again returns to Clongowes, he realizes that his peacemaking mother, a mollifying agent of social arbitration, cannot offer a viable sanctuary from the male-dominated power structure that controls the outer world. He must learn to survive in a society that protects bullies like Wells and sadists like Father Dolan, that condones brutality, and that takes advantage of the weak and the helpless. The pandybat incident at the end of Chapter One symbolically reinforces the rites of objectification characteristic of Jesuit training. Father Dolan's authority is absolute and unquestioned, since he relies on patriarchal privilege associated with what Foucault would term "panoptical vision": "Father Dolan will be in to see you every day" (*P* 49). Branded as a "lazy little schemer," Stephen must endure the ignominy of being abused, misnamed, and maltreated by the lower-class disciplinarian. Appealing to aristocratic pretension, he thinks disdainfully: "Dolan: it was like the name of a woman that washed clothes" (*P* 55).

The child is being socialized into what Philip Slater identifies in *The Glory of Hera* as a culture of masculine narcissism. According to Slater, single-sex education and the separation of male children from the emotional refuge of close domestic configurations promotes misogyny, narcissism, and a residual terror of the female. Little boys suffer from an "unconscious fear of being feminine, which leads to 'protest masculinity,' exaggeration of the difference between men and women." Once the child is deprived of maternal affection, he "seeks compensation through self-aggrandizement – renouncing love for admiration – and in this he is encouraged by the achievement pressure placed upon him, and presumably by the myriad narcissistic role-models he finds around him. He becomes vain, hypersensitive, invidious, ambitious, . . . boastful, and exhibitionistic."[14]

Stephen's brash appeal to the rector Father Conmee is motivated not only by optimistic faith in a male-controlled world, but by personal vanity and a tendency toward exhibitionism. With an absurdly Panglossian view of the world, he feels assured of ethical exoneration the moment he presents his case before a seemingly impartial judge. Self-righteous in his rectitude, the trembling boy makes a symbolic rite of passage through the primordial chambers of racial and ecclesiastical history in order to confront the Jesuit rector who will surely "make right" (rectify) his stinging sense of injustice. "The prefect of studies was a priest but that was cruel and unfair" (*P* 52), he insists. Stephen courageously rebels against Dolan's totalitarian power and is unanimously acclaimed a revolutionary hero by "the Senate and the Roman people." But the child, apparently triumphant, later discovers an ironic sequel to his victory: Dolan and Conmee, in smug condescension, treated the incident as a rip-roaring joke. Stephen has unwittingly played the ingenuous fool at the court of his Jesuit masters and, in a bold attempt to assert his budding manhood, has merely served as a feminized object of wry patriarchal amusement. *"Manly little chap!"* remarks Conmee, as he confides to Simon Dedalus: "Father Dolan and I had a great laugh over it. *You better mind yourself, Father Dolan, . . . or young Dedalus will send you up for twice nine.* We had a famous laugh together over it. Ha! Ha! Ha!" (*P* 72).

VIRGIN AND WHORE

In Chapter Five of *A Portrait*, Cranly asks Stephen if he would take particular sexual pleasure in the defloration of a virgin. His companion replies by posing another half-mocking query: "is that not the ambition of most young gentlemen?" (*P* 246). Figuratively, it is Stephen's ambition throughout the novel to "deflower" the Blessed Virgin of Catholicism and to supplant the adored Italian Madonna with a profane surrogate – a voluptuous Irish muse rooted in the joys of sensuous reality.

In Chapter Two, Stephen vainly searches for the romantic figure of a woman who will mediate his artistic transfiguration. Identifying with the Count of Monte Cristo, he conjures up adolescent fantasies of a beautiful Mercedes, whom he stalks in the suburbs of Blackrock. He longs "to meet in the real world the unsubstantial image which his soul so constantly beheld. . . . They would meet quietly as if they had known each other and had made their tryst. . . . He would fade into something impalpable under her eyes and then in a moment, he would be transfigured. Weakness and timidity and inexperience would fall from him in that magic moment" (*P* 65). It is essential to him that the figure of Mercedes be unsubstantial and free of physical dross, for this contemporary Eve must obliterate any palpable connection with the corporeal prison of the body. The semi-religious scene he imagines suggests beatific transformation in the darkness and silence of a moonlit garden when the romantic heroine, releasing her lover from the shackles of inexperience, blesses him with nothing less than the power of refusal. In spiritualizing his life, the woman once guilty of colluding with his enemies facilitates his dreams of revenge: paradoxically, she endows her erstwhile lover with sufficient spiritual grace to turn away from her tantalizing figure and reject the temptations of sexual desire.

When Stephen dreams of himself as Edmond Dantes, he identifies with a man betrayed by his friends and his mistress, unjustly exiled and imprisoned, but eventually able to wreak vengeance on those who failed him. Monte Cristo's adventures culminate in a "sadly proud gesture of refusal": "Madam, I never eat muscatel grapes" (*P* 63). Mercedes proves to be an untouchable mistress tainted by unwitting collaboration with those who betrayed her youthful fiancé. Stephen admires the proud self-sufficiency of Dantes, an isolated hero who eventually conquers the woman he loves through a complex process of phallic veiling that inhibits his amorous desire for her body.

In a different, more realistic setting, the Dublin family ménage provides an unsalubrious environment for those smiling soubrettes whose delicate features grace the evening papers and capture the attention of Stephen's aunt and cousins. "The beautiful Mabel Hunter" of pantomime fame stares from a newspaper photograph with "demurely taunting eyes" (*P* 67). This "exquisite creature" intrudes on the squalor of Irish life to provide a popular, though elusive model of seductive femininity. Stephen's ringletted cousin admires the music-hall *artiste* with the same kind of devotion she might offer to the Blessed Virgin Mary. The popular press has constructed an icon of girlish charm for her to worship and to emulate, a figure of the female body as desirable (and coyly inaccessible) market commodity. The price of such fetishistic commodification of women is reflected in the aggressive behavior of Stephen's unidentified male relative, a boy growing up in an atmosphere of boorish insensitivity. Like a voracious animal, he mauls the edges of the paper with blackened hands and roughly pushes his sister aside to get a glimpse of Mabel's photograph. Greedy and whining, he tries to claim this tempting pin-up for his own lascivious enjoyment.

The enigmatic scene is superseded by a grotesque epiphany of the wizened and gnomish Ellen, a "feeble creature like a monkey" who laughs in senile dementia. The Janus image of the pantomime star is this sexless, simian specter, whose presence intrudes on Stephen's imagination like a decapitated death's head or *memento mori*. Gradually, a human voice begins to taunt the boy with androgynous associations: "I thought you were Josephine, Stephen" (*P* 68). In the Kafkaesque world of Dublin, adolescent males metamorphose into aged women, and cackling crones shuffle around like mobile skeletons.

Art alone promises to provide a refuge from reality and to invest Stephen with the powers of both priest and shaman – the ability to confront the beauty and mystery of creation while tasting the joy of loneliness. Before the tantalizing face of Emma cowled in nun's veiling, Stephen forces himself to remain calm and controlled. Like the boy in "Araby," he is tormented by pubescent eruptions of sexual desire. He hides "the feverish agitation of his blood" and characteristically projects his own erotic vulnerability onto the female he believes to be "flattering, taunting, searching, exciting his heart" (P 68 – 9). Emma, donning a traditional Irish shawl, appears in the guise of Kathleen ni Houlihan, a Celtic figure inviting Stephen to romantic initiation in the peaceful stillness of a moonlit evening. Depersonalized, and seen through the haze of mythic reverie, she emerges as a shadowy emblem out of the unconscious, a symbol of the eternal temptress. For the poet, she becomes a nubile siren – Mercedes in Dublin garb, Eve in nun's habit.

> His heart danced upon her movements like a cork upon a tide. He heard what her eyes said to him from beneath their cowl and knew that in some dim past, whether in life or in revery, he had heard their tale before. He saw her urge her vanities, her fine dress and sash and long black stockings, and knew that he had yielded to them a thousand times. Yet a voice within him spoke above the noise of his dancing heart, asking him would he take her gift to which he had only to stretch out his hand. (P 69)

In an adolescent replication of Freud's *Fort/Da* game, Stephen gains symbolic mastery over Emma's erratic movements by assuming that he can, at will, catch hold of her darting figure. Focusing on fetishes of stockings and dress, he casts her in the incongruous role of taunting seductress. Emma's gift is Eve's apple of sexuality, though in this case, the amorous exchange would entail little more than a chaste adolescent kiss. On the verge of losing his composure, Stephen, like his hero Edmond Dantes, refuses to yield to Emma's ostensible temptation. His thoughts suddenly shift to an earlier incident in the company of Eileen – to a scene whose phallic flagpole and barking terriers evoke subliminal recollections of emotional vulnerability. Stephen fears that the seductive female, mocking and elusive, might at any moment humiliate him with peals of taunting laughter. After all, Eileen put her hands of ivory into his pockets and tempted him, then ran away. Afraid of sexual disappointment, he adopts a pose of isolation and detachment, "seemingly a tranquil watcher of the scene before him" (*P* 69). For a single moment, he contemplates the delights of a furtive embrace: "I could easily catch hold of her when she comes up to my step: I could hold her and kiss her." But, we are told, "he did neither" (*P* 70).

To the reader, the ingenuous Emma is hardly a Circean figure. She seems shy, naïve, and gaily flirtatious. Like Stephen, she probably feels confused by the excitations of a budding sexuality, but her coy gestures of affection are limited to the subtle patterns of cautious courtship available in nineteenth-century Ireland to a young woman fully aware of cultural injunctions to remain chaste and respectable and, above all, to preserve her virginity as a commodity of exchange on the competitive Dublin marriage market.

Like the Count of Monte Cristo, Stephen turns away from Emma in proud abnegation, determined to possess his mistress wholly through art. Blurring the figures of himself and his beloved in the womb of his artistic imagination, he is able in a moment of tranquility to give cathartic expression to the pain of loss associated with unacted desire. Byronic verses written to E— C— consummate the memory of romantic intimacy, as Stephen imagines that "the kiss, which had been withheld by one, was given by both" (*P* 71). Poetry offers the timorous lover aesthetic compensation for frustrated physical desire, and the stirrings of adolescent sexuality are deftly sublimated through an exercise in lyrical fulfillment. The artist's mind is cold, chaste, and detached, like that of the virginal muse Diana, as his disciplined verses statically embalm the experience of romantic epiphany. The scene has been purged of reality and naturalistic detail, the participants vaguely depersonalized: "There remained no trace of the tram itself nor of the trammen nor of the horses: nor did he and she appear vividly. The verses told only of the night and the balmy breeze and the maiden lustre of the moon" (*P* 70). Emotional mutuality has been restricted to art: Stephen feels fulfilled, but Emma is left to pine in her nun-like cowl. Her desires are safely crystallized in Byronic verses framed by two Jesuit mottoes.[15]

The kiss exchanged lyrically, but not in fact, veils Emma's amorous desirability and offers Stephen psychological protection against the phallic threat hidden beneath the innocent demeanor of her burgeoning sexual ripeness. By prodding the young girl's flirtation, then spurning her desire and refusing to unveil the piquant visibility of feminine difference, Stephen elicits a barred aesthetic signature. Emma's invaginated otherness is thrust onto the margins of a poetic text. The artist must paradoxically renounce the flesh-and-blood female in order to free the spur of desirability from the dangers of possible satisfaction. Spurning the beloved, he re-creates her as a figure of imaginary but unattainable satisfaction, a mirror image of his own pressing need to deny psychological fragmentation and assert a sense of phallic coherence. The spurned mistress leaves in her wake perpetual traces of sexual longing that will, through a poetics of erotic absence, spur the poet to nostalgic, compensatory creation.[16]

Resolutely refusing to communicate his passion, Stephen mediates libidinal desire through mimetic language and nineteenth-century literary convention. Emma, inscribed in the body of a lyrical text, relinquishes the threatening aspect of genital invagination and doubles as an archaic ideal of the inaccessible courtly lady. Poetic utterance re-creates her figure as a specular image appropriated by the symbolic order of the Father. Stephen chooses a deviant poet as his artistic predecessor and, taking Daddy Byron as master, succeeds in mastering the young woman who would otherwise be mistress of his heart. The poem that he pens provides an emotional circuit of substitution that short-circuits libidinal drive and sublimates Eros to the symbolic order of Daedalus/Byron/Stephen/Father/Joyce.[17]

On the night of the Whitsuntide play two years later, Stephen remembers the touch of Emma's hand and the sight of dark eyes that "invited and unnerved him" (P 82). "All day he had thought of nothing but their leavetaking on the steps of the tram at Harold's Cross" (P 77). Despite the lapse in time, he continues to feel tormented by the "stream of moody emotions" that hurt him into poetry, as he imagines a tender reunion and a second chance to rewrite the scene with a different ending. Overwhelmed by torrential passions that can find no outlet, the adolescent is drowning in pent-up floods of lascivious desire that swirl "in dark courses and eddies, wearying him in the end" (P 77). Although he congratulates himself for remaining detached from human emotion and from the "fierce love and hatred" he has "met in books" (P 82), Stephen feels an invisible wave of feverish arousal stirred by the memory of Emma's touch. After the performance, when his prey once again eludes him, vaporous emotions infiltrate his mind and, from the crushed and bitter herbs of sexual disappointment, give rise to a sacerdotal incense of "wounded pride and fallen hope and baffled desire" (*P* 86). Clothing his frustration in a tapestry of lyrical effects, Stephen is able to defuse the seminal eruptions of repressed physicality through psychological strategies of erotic displacement.

Dashing to an alley behind the Dublin morgue, he soberly takes comfort in the "good odour" of "horse piss and rotted straw" (*P* 86), mortifying the flesh in a repulsive atmosphere chosen to vent his residual contempt for the female body. The imaginary phallic mother, a tainted source of physical generation, serves as an ominous reminder of contact with those genital functions of menstruation and gestation that must be exorcised from the "clean and proper self" of the narcissistic subject. Urine and ordure symbolically cling to the archaic memory of an inaccessible maternal body always lost to the ego's field of insatiable demands.[18] Stephen's morbid sentiments are Thomistic and medieval, reminiscent of religious triptychs that portray a female figure first at the height of vanity and sensuous beauty, then aged and wrinkled, and finally as a skeleton draped in richly embroidered grave-clothes. Accosted by the immanence of his carnal connection with the world, Stephen, like the medieval Fathers of the Church, rebels against mortality by renouncing the fires of lust. As Saint Augustine wryly noted, "we are born between feces and urine" [*Inter faeces et urinam nascimur*]. Joyce's artist is well on his way to developing a similar excremental vision of sex. Birth and death are so closely linked to physical nature that they are easily allied in the misogynist mind.[19] Rotting bodies in the morgue and rotting straw convince Stephen that "reproduction is the beginning of death" (*P* 231).

Simon Dedalus nostalgically believes in the lyrics of the ballad he sings: " '*Tis youth and folly/Makes young men marry*" (*P* 88). But Stephen, freed of his father's naïve assumptions about youthful innocence, confines his own sexual activities to a series of monstrous pornographic reveries – wild orgies of the imagination in which the voluptuous temptress is robbed of her power and reduced to a specular object of erotic fantasy. He feels horrified at seeing the word *Foetus* scrawled on a desk – perhaps because it suggests frustrated sexuality and the souls "impossibilised" by his onanistic rites; or perhaps because the clinical term links him with the rude, lascivious males of his father's unselfconscious generation. "It shocked him to find in the outer world a trace of what he had deemed till then a brutish and individual malady of his own mind.

. . . The letters . . . stared upon him, mocking his bodily weakness and futile enthusiasms and making him loathe himself for his own mad and filthy orgies'' (*P* 90 – 1).

Like many an Irish Catholic adolescent before him, Stephen feels convinced that he has invented masturbation: ''By his monstrous way of life he seemed to have put himself beyond the limits of reality. Nothing moved him or spoke to him from the real world unless he heard in it an echo of the infuriated cries within him'' (*P* 92). ''Nothing stirred within his soul but a cold and cruel and loveless lust'' (*P* 96). His nocturnal fantasies are motivated not by love or tenderness, but by a narcissistic need to defile the invaginated other, to inscribe the hymeneal folds of the virginal body/text with a male signature of conquest and impregnation. The foetus serves as a visible sign of phallic prowess, of a masculine genetic code imprinted with seminal ink onto the resistant folds of female uterine tissue. The father/engenderer authors a potential child that will replicate and (re)produce its progenitor's image in the outer world. Stephen longs to humiliate the virgin-lover of his orgiastic reveries, to colonize her body, and simultaneously to become the filial foetus blissfully nurtured in her *heimlich* womb.

The image of Mercedes traverses the background of Stephen's memory, but the transfiguration he once sought through her romantic presence is consummated in the embrace of a Dublin whore. Stephen no longer seeks to emulate the Count of Monte Cristo when this ''holy encounter'' occurs. He finds himself stalking a prostitute as if she were an animal in a dark, foreboding jungle. ''His blood was in revolt. . . . He moaned to himself like some baffled prowling beast'' (*P* 99). His search is motivated by a perverse desire for temporary communion, as he seeks release from his own imprisoned ego: ''He wanted to sin with another of his kind, to force another being to sin with him and to exult with her in sin'' (*P* 99 – 100). The sexual imagery at the end of Chapter Two is ironically inverted. As Stephen feels the dark shadow of a streetwalker ''moving irresistibly upon him'' in penumbrous alleyways, he figuratively suffers the ''agony of its penetration'' and surrenders to a ''murmurous flood'' of physical excitation. The fusion of erotic and romantic imagery degenerates into a vague rite of sexual initiation that reverses traditional symbolism. Stephen envisages himself in the role of a deflowered virgin, raped by a phallic figure and flooded with seminal streams. His ''cry for an iniquitous abandonment'' again evokes an excremental vision of sex, as his moans reverberate with "the echo of an obscene scrawl which he had read on the oozing wall of a urinal" (*P* 100).[20]

When Stephen/Icarus, wandering through a Daedalian "maze of narrow and dirty streets," steps before a phantasmal altar illumined by "yellow gasflames . . . against the vapoury sky" (*P* 100), he resembles both a sacrificial victim and a child about to "burst into hysterical weeping." The perfumed female who takes him in her arms recalls his "nice-smelling" mother at the same time that she functions as high priestess or vestal virgin in a contemporary phallic cult. Clothed in a long pink gown, she leads the boy into a womb-like chamber, "warm and lightsome," tousles his hair, calls him "little rascal," and embraces him with a vaguely maternal caress. "Tears of joy and relief shone in his delighted eyes and his lips parted though they would not speak" (*P* 101). "Give me a kiss," the whore instructs her charge. Soothed like a baby or a foetus by the "warm calm rise and fall of her breast," Stephen retreats into kinaesthetic sensation and momentarily retrieves an illusion of infant satiety:

> He wanted to be held firmly in her arms, to be caressed slowly, slowly, slowly. In her arms he felt that he had suddenly become strong and fearless and sure of himself. . . . He closed his eyes, surrendering himself to her, body and mind, conscious of nothing in the world but the dark pressure of her softly parting lips.
> They pressed upon his brain as upon his lips as though they were the vehicle of a vague speech; and between them he felt an unknown and timid pressure, darker than the swoon of sin, softer than sound or odour. (*P* 101).

In this oral-regressive encounter, the prostitute becomes mistress of Stephen's lips and, through a lingual kiss that inaugurates a fantasy of pre-Oedipal bliss, temporarily appropriates the highly guarded powers of artistic speech.[21] Inarticulate and swooning, the boy feels reduced to a lavish, infantile dependency that leaves him childlike and passive, penetrated by a foreign phallic tongue, but gloriously centered in the mystified presence of an imaginary figure of wholeness and coherence. Stephen feels that he has at last realized his dream of spiritual transfiguration: "He was in another world: he had awakened from a slumber of centuries" into a sybaritic, pagan sanctuary (*P* 100).

Stephen's adolescent vision of the female remains ambiguous and curiously perplexed. The traditional dichotomy between virgin and whore, madonna and temptress, tends to break down in the young man's imagination until the categories blur, and all women seem to oscillate between contradictory poles of purity and danger, seduction and solicitude. Females are, by turn, unpredictably authoritarian, nurturant, demanding, and altruistic – sporadically aloof, then sexually receptive. Emma tempted Stephen on the tram and fled, only to be transformed into a lyrical muse, then to be rejected in a cathartic scene of ascetic renunciation after the Whitsuntide play. At the end of Chapter Two, the prostitute functions as an ambivalent figure of masculine aggression and feminine nurturance. Eliciting the forbidden kiss earlier withheld from the mother and from Emma, she demands erotic surrender, yet shelters her adolescent client in a tender, provocative embrace. In the arms of this maternal surrogate, Stephen feels himself born into the manly world of adult heterosexual knowledge. But his sexual initiation is disastrously premature and leads, in the next chapter, to a panicky retreat into the security of Catholic law and patriarchal protection.[22]

THE CATHOLIC VIRGIN

The notion of damnation that Stephen gleans from the priest's retreat sermon in Chapter Three capitalizes on a puritanical hatred of the body and a medieval disdain for human corporality. The five senses become doors to the perverse religious imagination, and each is systematically attacked by metaphors of filth, decay, obscenity, and putrefaction. The priest warns that in the bowels of hell, the souls of the damned will be overwhelmed by a "sickening stench": "All the filth of the world, all the offal and scum of the world, we are told, shall run there as to a vast and reeking sewer. . . . And then imagine . . . a huge and rotting human fungus" (*P* 120). The body is itself obscene, a thing of dirt and filth that will one day decompose into noxious offal. For the Catholic prelate, physicality is the curse of postlapsarian man and sexuality the vehicle of degeneracy.

At the outset of the chapter, we are plunged, once again, into the heart of the brothel district, the squalid quarter now familiar to Stephen. He approaches its forbidden pleasures almost ritualistically, pursuing a devious course among back streets and alleys until surprised by the sudden joy of soft, perfumed flesh. Wallowing in the pleasures of a physicality that has always repelled him, he listens to the counsel of his belly and the cravings of bodily sensation. The chapter begins with fantasies of a greasy, carnivorous feast of "fat mutton pieces to be ladled out in thick peppered flour fattened sauce" (P 102). With a mixture of disdain and pride, Stephen delights in a riot of sensuality. His defiant sexual practices mesmerize consciousness until he imagines himself gifted with hermetic powers. A mathematical equation expands before his eyes into a "widening tail, eyed and starred like a peacock's" (P 103). Watched by a thousand flickering cosmic eyes, Stephen's weary mind is transported into a "vast cycle of starry life" that gives him the illusion of privileged access to the secret music of the spheres. Isolated, and wandering companionless like Shelley's melancholic moon, he envisions a Luciferian fall into the chaos of primordial matter and the cold darkness of Dante's innermost circle of hell.

With Satanic pride, Stephen creates the cosmic drama of his own sinfulness, as his soul goes forth to encounter experience, "unfolding itself sin by sin, spreading abroad the balefire of its burning stars, . . . quenching its own lights and fires" (P 103), just as Lucifer, the light-bearer, descended into darkness after his biblical fall from grace. Stephen imagines his soul creating and destroying the universe, exploding in the heavens with meteoric intensity after every mortal sin. Initially having feared a loss of identity at the moment of orgasm, the young man is astonished by a resurgence of energy through sexual release. A dark peace unites body and soul, as he gains access to "a cold indifferent knowledge of himself," the knowledge of good and evil promised Adam and Eve by the serpent in the Garden of Eden. Unlike these legendary parents, Stephen achieves the illusion of mysterious, godlike powers. But in his fallen state, he is condemned, like Satan, to chaos and darkness; and, like the serpent, he must crawl on his belly, prey to the admonitions of primitive sensual needs.

A childish devotion to patriarchal authority has been displaced by Stephen's amorous wooing of the Blessed Virgin: "The glories of Mary held his soul captive" (P 104). The adolescent boy is, indeed, captivated by the fetishes he associates with the "cultus" of the Madonna – rich garments, perfumed incense, and embroidered emblems of adoration. The religious symbols of Mariolatry offer promises of aesthetic delight through the sensuous music of the Holy Office, a lyrical paean to sacred womanhood. As prefect of the Sodality of the Blessed Virgin, Stephen chants Mary's praise in an act of proud dissimulation. "His sin, which had covered him from the sight of God, had led him nearer to the refuge of sinners" (*P* 105). The Virgin becomes for him an object of courtly devotion whose holiness radiates a strange light that gives her frail flesh a translucent glow. Desirous of serving as her knight and courtier, Stephen prostrates himself in sacerdotal obeisance before his vision of the adored female figure. He worships the flesh of an icon that seems an object of both veneration and desire. A sanctuary of heavenly peace after the fervor of sexual frenzy, the Virgin becomes a post-coital Madonna offering refuge from the turmoil of hormonal agitation. The unrepentant sinner takes perverse satisfaction in "befouling" her image by reciting the Holy Office with "lips whereon there still lingered foul and shameful words, the savour itself of a lewd kiss" (*P* 105). Later in the episode, Stephen will offer a panicked prayer to Mary, whom he invokes in the guise of a beneficent mother. Repentant of his fall from grace, he no longer imagines her as a frail-fleshed virgin but appeals to the powerful *magna mater* whose beauty is *"not like earthly beauty, dangerous to look upon, but like the morning star"* (*P* 139). The Holy Mother will be raised once again in Stephen's mind to the sanctified niche of courtly devotion.

As the "jeweleyed harlots" of lascivious transgression dance before the boy's fevered imagination, "squeaking like mice in their terror and huddled under a mane of hair," (*P* 115), he feels horrified by the realization that he has besmirched the icon of his beloved Emma by making her the object of masturbatory fantasy: "The image of Emma appeared before him and, under her eyes, the flood of shame rushed forth anew from his heart. If she knew to what his mind had subjected her or how his brutelike lust had torn and trampled upon her innocence! Was that boyish love? Was that chivalry? Was that poetry? The sordid details of his orgies stank under his very nostrils" (*P* 115). He feels that he has violated both Emma's honor and his own code of chivalry – not to mention the rigorous ethic of purity enforced by Irish Catholicism. Emma, he decides, shall serve as his envoy to the Blessed Mother. "God and the Blessed Virgin were too far from him: God was too great and stern and the Blessed Virgin too pure and holy. But he imagined that he stood near Emma in a wide land and, humbly and in tears, bent and kissed the elbow of her sleeve" (*P* 116). Stephen fantasizes a scene of heavenly confrontation with the Catholic Madonna, who enjoins the couple to "take hands. . . . You have erred but you are always my children. It is one heart that loves another heart. Take hands together, my dear children, and you will be happy together and your hearts will love each other" (*P* 116). With the help of the virginal Emma, Stephen plans to recoup his spiritual losses and embark on a Miltonic journey toward forgiveness and salvation. Like a new Adam and Eve, the boy and his beloved will be redeemed by the promises of Christ and his sinless mother. But the scenario of their salvation is enacted in a sentimental landscape of romantic dream. Stephen's clouded vision generates a fragile aesthetic reverie imbued with the lunar light of his Shelleyan imagination, as well as a pallid green sky that seems to challenge Fleming's earlier maroon cosmogony.

Without the innocent Emma to serve as a surrogate Beatrice, Stephen feels as "helpless and hopeless" as the souls of the damned in Dante's hell (*P* 123). He hallucinates a vision of the libidinous inferno prepared especially for him: "That was his hell. God had allowed him to see the hell reserved for his sins: stinking, bestial, malignant, a hell of lecherous goatish fiends. For him! For him!" (*P* 138). These "goatish creatures with human faces, hornybrowed, lightly bearded and grey as indiarubber" (*P* 137) are demonic satyrs who mimic the goat-god Pan but whose dry, spittle-less lips are incapable of communicative utterance. This is the artist's nightmare: a hell in which language has been deracinated from meaning, articulation is torturous, and spoken sounds echo in waves of vacuous gibberish. The language of hell proves to be a circular, hypnotic discourse. When the infernal voices *do* speak to Stephen, their perverted injunctions parody medieval Church Latin and the archaic edicts of ecclesiastical authority: "We knew perfectly well of course that although it was bound to come to the light he would find considerable difficulty in endeavouring to try to induce himself to try to endeavour to ascertain the spiritual plenipotentiary . . ." (*P* 136). Like Beckettian oracles, the fiendish voices are trapped in a lewd, mocking, sonorous rhetoric, and their jeers against spiritual irresolution are couched in a senseless, circumlocutory monologue. Awash amid floating signifiers, they sail on a tide of meaningless iteration that engulfs the dreaming artist and thrusts him into a landscape of visual and auditory nightmare.[23]

To escape the threat of verbal castration, Stephen must be willing to purge himself of impure thoughts that stimulate lascivious desire. He must discard "the sootcoated packet of pictures which he had hidden in the flue of the fireplace and in the presence of whose shameless or bashful wantonness he lay for hours sinning in thought and deed"; he must exorcise "monstrous dreams, peopled by apelike creatures and by harlots with gleaming jewel eyes"; and he must repent of those "foul long letters . . . written in the joy of guilty confession" and thrust into some public place where they might be found by some innocent girl. "Mad! Mad! Was it possible he had done these things?" (*P* 115–16).

Terrified not only of women but of the body and its sexual urgency, Stephen is moved simultaneously to renounce Satan, the female, and his own genitalia. Nineteenth-century Irish Catholicism demands that he psychologically castrate himself by consenting to a grotesque dissociation of ego and id. In order to free himself from a demeaning vasselage to involuntary erection, he feels compelled to assert moral superiority over an antagonistic penis that seems to operate with a will of its own: "Was that then he or an inhuman thing moved by a lower soul than his soul? His soul sickened at the thought of a torpid snaky life feeding itself out of the tender marrow of his life and fattening upon the slime of lust" (*P* 140). Like the confused adolescent boy described by Simone de Beauvoir in *The Second Sex*, Stephen feels "possessed by a magic not of himself. . . . That organ by which he thought to assert himself does not obey him; heavy with unsatisfied desires, unexpectedly becoming erect, . . . it manifests a suspicious and capricious vitality."[24]

In order to confess his sins against the sixth and ninth commandments, Stephen must self-consciously revert to a state of childhood innocence and amend his life for the sake of atonement with the Christian community that has marginalized the adult and adulterous sinner: "He would be at one with others and with God. He would love his neighbour. He would love God Who made and loved him. He would kneel and pray with others and be happy. . . . It was easy to be good. God's yoke was sweet and light. It was better never to have sinned, to have remained always a child, for God loved little children and suffered them to come to Him. It was a terrible and a sad thing to sin" (*P* 143). Echoing the inaugural words of traditional catechetical instruction and droning a litany of childish monosyllables and religious clichés, Stephen determines to repress his adolescent sexual drives by repenting of the one sin that shames him even more than murder. The temptress has reduced his soul to a syphilitic chancre "festering and oozing like a sore, a squalid stream of vice" (*P* 144). Repelled by the lurid imagery of venereal disease, Stephen humbles himself before the "old and weary voice" of his father-priest-confessor. The Church's medicine-man will cure the wound of spiritual invagination, rescue him from the siren, and counsel an innocent "life of grace and virtue and happiness" (*P* 146). The priest invokes the Blessed Virgin Mary as moral guardian of Christian manliness. Chanting simple declarative sentences that echo the Maynooth Catechism, he exhorts his charge to renounce the sins of the flesh, especially masturbation: "It is a terrible sin. It kills the body and it kills the soul. It is the cause of many crimes and misfortunes. Give it up, my child, for God's sake. It is dishonourable and unmanly. . . . Pray to our mother Mary to help you. She will help you, my child. Pray to Our Blessed Lady when that sin comes into your mind" (*P* 144–5).

As penitential prefect of Our Blessed Lady's Sodality, Stephen determines to discipline his senses to the point of masochistic self-abuse and engage in scrupulous works of sacrificial piety. With the help of the Virgin Mary, the young man will sublimate libidinous desire and attempt to recapture, through puritanical self-mortification, the prepubescent calm characteristic of juvenile innocence. He prays: *"O harbinger of day! O light of the pilgrim! Lead us still as thou hast led. In the dark night, across the bleak wilderness guide us on to our Lord Jesus, guide us home"* (*P* 139). What Stephen naïvely fails to realize is that one cannot go home again to the lost womb of sexual latency.

THE BIRD-GIRL: AESTHETIC MUSE

In his return to ritualistic devotion, Stephen becomes involved in an aesthetic love affair with his own soul. The anima, the feminine aspect of the psyche, has won his passion and holds him enthralled. Like Narcissus, Stephen has fallen in love with his projected self-image clothed in female garb. "The attitude of rapture in sacred art, the raised and parted hands, the parted lips and eyes as of one about to swoon, became for him an image of the soul in prayer, humiliated and faint before her Creator" (*P* 150). In the glorified female, "man also perceives his mysterious double; man's soul is Psyche, a woman."[25] The feminine side of Stephen's identity, personified as the soul, swoons in erotic ecstasy before her creator, just as the young man earlier swooned in the welcoming arms of a Dublin prostitute.

The Catholic priesthood offers Stephen a chance to consummate this narcissistic love affair with his psyche. It bequeaths on the soul the magical power of transubstantiation, and it promises a rite of passage into male mysteries that successfully counteract female authority: "No angel or archangel in heaven, no saint, not even the Blessed Virgin herself has the power of a priest of God" (P 158). A Jesuit vocation would guarantee Stephen ascendancy over the Catholic matriarch. By virtue of the "secret knowledge and secret power" of an exclusively masculine fraternity, he would be admitted to the inner sanctum of male religious privilege.

The price, however, of this "awful power of which angels and saints stood in reverence" is an irrevocable act that would "end for ever, in time and in eternity, his freedom" and condemn him to the "grave and ordered and passionless life" of Jesuit conformity (P 160–2). Still painting himself in the images of Lord Byron and the Count of Monte Cristo, Stephen passionately embraces a destiny triumphantly marginal and "elusive of social or religious orders. . . . He was destined to learn his own wisdom apart from others or to learn the wisdom of others himself wandering among the snares of the world" (P 162). He chooses "the misrule and confusion of his father's house" (P 162), the messiness and chaos of sensuous experience, over a "mirthless reflection of the sunken day" (P 160) evinced by the priest's spectral visage. Turning away from this symbolic death's head, Stephen rejects the "eyeless obedience" demanded by Catholic orders and reminiscent of those eagles of authority that originally threatened him with a loss of sight and mastery. He will commit himself, instead, to the pagan priesthood of old Father Daedalus, that "fabulous artificer, . . . a symbol of the artist forging anew in his workshop out of the sluggish matter of the earth a new soaring impalpable imperishable being" (P 169).

Stephen's intellectual choice of an artistic vocation seems to be experientially confirmed by a climactic encounter with a mysterious female who evokes luminous trails of earthly beauty:

A girl stood before him in midstream, alone and still, gazing out to sea. She seemed like one whom magic had changed into the likeness of a strange and beautiful seabird. Her long slender bare legs were delicate as a crane's and pure save where an emerald trail of seaweed had fashioned itself as a sign upon the flesh. Her thighs, fuller and softhued as ivory, were bared almost to the hips where the white fringes of her drawers were like featherings of soft white down. (P 171)

The young woman revealed in Stephen's epiphany amalgamates a plethora of metaphorical features from pagan, Christian, and Celtic iconography. She is at once mortal and angelic, sensuous and serene. Her soft-hued, ivory thighs recall Eileen's ivory hands as well as the Catholic Virgin, Tower of Ivory. Her avian transformation harks back to the Greek myth of Leda and the swan. And because her bosom, like "the breast of some darkplumaged dove," suggests the Holy Ghost of Catholicism, Stephen, as purveyor of the word, imaginatively begets a surrogate Holy Spirit in his ecstatic vision of this semi-mystical muse.[26]

Joyce's irony at this point in the novel is subtle but implicit. If Stephen feels incipient sexual arousal in the presence of exposed female thighs, he quickly sublimates erotic agitation beneath effusions of purple prose. The young man catches sight of an attractive nubile form and immediately detaches himself from emotional participation in the scene. His reaction is self-consciously static, theoretically purged of desire and loathing. Once again, his leap into aesthetic fantasy quenches an initial impulse to approach the girl, to reach out and touch her, or to risk the possibility of social intercourse. Stephen feels he must distance and depersonalize her tantalizing figure through the voyeuristic displacements of oculocentric regard.

As the young woman rises out of the sea, she is reminiscent of Venus, the goddess of love born of the ocean foam. She is pure and virginal, yet "an emerald trail of seaweed" functions as a sign of mortality (and perhaps of Irish nationality) stamped upon her flesh. She belongs to the mundane world of decay and corruption, and the vegetation clinging to her ankle suggests a fetishistic image of emotional entrapment. The woman appears as an "angel of mortal youth and beauty, an envoy from the fair courts of life" (P 172). Tellingly, in his 1904 essay "A Portrait of the Artist," Joyce uses similar phrases in masochistic invocation of a phantasmal prostitute from the red light district of Dublin: "Beneficent one! . . . thou camest timely, as a witch to the agony of self devourer, an envoy from the fair courts of life." (P 263)[27]

Like an Irish Circe, the nymph in *Portrait* has the potential to drag Stephen down into the emerald-green nets of Dublin paralysis. In sociological terms, this attractive young woman, approached and courted, might well threaten Stephen with the kind of domestic entrapment associated with Irish Catholic marriage. The aspiring poet knows that he may look but not touch, admire but not speak. He glorifies the wading girl as an angelic messenger from the "fair courts of life," but he never actually joins her in the teeming ocean waters.[28] His communication is a matter entirely of narcissistic projection. "Her image had passed into his soul for ever and no word had broken the holy silence of his ecstasy" (P 172). Afraid of the "waters circumfluent in space" that symbolize the fluidity of female desire, Stephen is determined to control the world of physiological process by freezing life in the sacrament of art. His "spiritual-heroic refrigerating apparatus" has already begun to implement this psychological flight from woman. His response to this seductive creature is exclusively specular, as he takes refuge in a masculine, visual sexual economy and sublimates tactile and olfactory drives that might move him toward sensuous contact. The mimesis of romantic passion offers Stephen a successfully mediated and comfortably mastered form of sexual satisfaction.[29]

For Joyce's young man, an exercise in scopophilia (love of looking) masquerades as aesthetic delight. If, as Freud suggests, the specular gaze is anal and obsessive – an unconscious expression of a sadistic will to power – then Stephen's cold, pellucid regard penetrates its object through a strategy of phallocentric framing and claims it as a fetishistic trophy to grace the scene of writing. The bird-girl functions as an imaginary symbol of beauty and coherence, of a wholeness and plenitude that mimics the unity of the transcendental signifier. Celebrating the female as a fictive and mystifying center, Stephen seizes the Lacanian *objet petit a* and replicates it as a figure of *différance* – desire playfully, masterfully, and joyously deferred through an endless dissemination of creative *jouissance*. Woman proves to be the blindspot in Stephen's poetic discourse. She is represented as a fantasized paradigm of psychic cohesion, the Other whose realistic fragmentation would threaten the poet's idealized aesthetic project. Because the girl remains a mute, fetishized, and perpetually mediated object of desire, her difference assures psychological stability to the speaking/seeing subject, the authorial I/eye who frames and appropriates her figure.[30]

At nightfall, the exhausted poet feels his soul "swooning into some new world, fantastic, dim, uncertain as under sea, traversed by cloudy shapes and beings. A world, a glimmer, or a flower?" (*P* 172). His spirit seems to embark on an archetypal journey toward the multifoliate rose of Dante's beatific vision. The bird-girl has imaginatively served as Stephen's profane virgin, a Beatrice who ushers him into paradisal happiness. The Dantesque underworld may symbolize the artistic unconscious, but the pre-Raphaelite rose imagery casts satirical light on Stephen's romantic reverie. As the young man attempts to "still the riot of his blood," he swoons in languorous ecstasy. He moodily contemplates an opening flower: "Glimmering and trembling, trembling and unfolding, a breaking light, . . . it spread in endless succession to itself, breaking in full crimson and unfolding and fading to palest rose, leaf by leaf and wave by wave of light, flooding all the heavens with its soft flushes, every flush deeper than other" (*P* 172). Sublimating the sexual component of his experience, Stephen vividly imagines a metaphorical rose engulfing the heavens, and his language of flowers suggests a psychoanalytic exercise in erotic mimesis. The boy's fantasy re-creates a repressed vision of female genitalia spreading in luxuriant rose-pink petals before his aroused phallic consciousness. Stephen's active libido summons veiled images of a woman's body revealing its vulvular mysteries and palpitating with the crimson flush of physical stimulation. Florid prose imitates the orgasmic rhythms of sexual excitement, as tension mounts "leaf by leaf and wave of light by wave of light" until the dream suddenly climaxes in a flood of "soft flushes." Stephen may want to believe that he has purified his sensuous encounter by making it into a mimetic replication of spiritual transcendence, but even his Dantesque beatitude is founded on sexual passion thinly disguised by the language of Freudian displacement.[31]

FLIGHT FROM THE MOTHER

Although the gates of salvation open at the end of Chapter Four, Stephen finds himself, at the beginning of Chapter Five, exiled from the Garden of Eden. Chewing crusts of fried bread, he remembers the turf-colored water in the bath at Clongowes – a spectral image that resonates with associations of death, drowning, and spiritual claustrophobia. As the nascent artist tries to escape the sordid reality of Dublin life by taking shelter in a world of words, he continues to struggle for liberation from the nets of a cloying family life, the demands of Irish nationality, and the stultifying authority of the Catholic religion.

Proclaiming his proud *Non Serviam*, Stephen nevertheless relies on his mother's service for physical nurturance and psychological support. Mary Dedalus washes her son's face and ears, enjoins him to receive the Eucharist, and packs his second-hand clothes in preparation for his exodus to France. Having magically transmuted the power of the female into a static object of aesthetic contemplation, Stephen is once again accosted by ubiquitous reminders of Mother Church and Mother Ireland. He feels compelled simultaneously to reject all three mothers – biological, ecclesiastical, and political. His refusal to take communion at Easter is as much a gesture of rebellion against a pleading Mary Dedalus as it is a rejection of Catholic authority. The image of woman metonymically absorbs all the paralyzing nets that constrain the potential artist. Unlike his companion Cranly, who celebrates mother love, Stephen resolves to detach himself from "the sufferings of women, the weaknesses of their bodies and souls" (*P* 245). He determines to "discover the mode of life or of art" that will allow his spirit to "express itself in unfettered freedom" (*P* 246). In casting off the yoke of matriarchy, Stephen asserts his manhood in fraternal collusion with his classical mentor, old Father Daedalus.

It is not enough, however, to repudiate the female: the artist must successfully usurp her procreative powers. Stephen seems to consider the aesthetic endeavor a kind of couvade – a rite of psychological compensation for the male inability to give birth.[32] He describes the act of aesthetic postcreation in metaphors of parturition, explaining to Lynch: "When we come to the phenomena of artistic conception, artistic gestation and artistic reproduction I require a new terminology and a new personal experience" (*P* 209). When Stephen awakens to "a tremulous morning knowledge, a morning inspiration," his experience is oddly passive: "A spirit filled him, pure as the purest water, sweet as dew, moving as music. But how faintly it was inbreathed, how passionlessly, as if the seraphim themselves were breathing upon him!'' (*P* 217). It soon becomes clear that it is not simply angels who are breathing upon the artist, but the Holy Ghost in a drama that re-enacts the mystery of Christ's Incarnation. The poet welters in a confused haze of light and beauty, but the instant of inspiration is climactic: ''O! In the virgin womb of the imagination the word was made flesh. Gabriel the seraph had come to the virgin's chamber'' (*P* 217).³³

Stephen, possibly awakening from a wet dream, feels inspired to compose a lyrical aubade unwinding in sensuous, liquid verses.³⁴ His soul climaxes in Shelley's ''enchantment of the heart,'' then luxuriates in the rosy afterglow of poetic ecstasy. The moment of inspiration and mental conception simulates a sexual process culminating in erotic *jouissance*. In a strange instance of mental transsexuality, Stephen's imagination is impregnated by the Holy Spirit, and he himself imitates the Virgin Mary giving birth to the Word of God. As the artist falls into a vision of rapturous enchantment, he conflates the ingenuous Emma with Mercedes and the bird-girl, then re-creates this female figure in the awesome, uncanny form of an eternal temptress – a seductive Lilith luring the seraphim from heaven. This courtly villanelle is inspired by a shudder in the loins that engenders not Leda or a burning Troy, but a handful of precious verses: ''he felt the rhythmic movement of a villanelle. . . . The roselike glow sent forth its rays of rhyme'' (*P* 217–18).

The enchantment of the heart that Stephen and Shelley both praised for its radiance now bursts forth into fire and flame – a conflagration strangely ominous in its association with the fires of hell, as well as the more homely hearth-fire lit by the Dean of Studies. The metaphor of smoky praise issuing from a chivalric heart seems puerile at best – part of an ecclesiastical rite complete with swaying censer and ellipsoidal incense-balls. With decadent weariness, Stephen gropes for his tablets and finds, instead, an abandoned cigarette packet. The smoke from the censer of the world is recorded on the cardboard remnant of a package of smokes, all smoked but one. Stephen longs to immerse himself in a Dantesque ambiance of secret roses reminiscent of the multifoliate flower of paradise, but he is forced to fashion a phantasmal rose-strewn path to heaven from the ''great overblown scarlet flowers of tattered wallpaper'' that plaster his dingy room in Dublin. ''He tried to warm his perishing joy in their scarlet glow, imagining a roseway from where he lay upwards to heaven all strewn with scarlet flowers.

Weary! Weary! He too was weary of ardent ways" (P 222).[35]

Unable to win the young and fickle heart of Emma, Stephen re-creates her in baleful aesthetic guise. His composition of the villanelle unfolds as an onanistic, as well as a dialectical exercise. The archaic verse-form has nostalgically been forged from erotic fantasy and the memory of loss. Stephen desires Emma, but he fears the domestic nets associated with a household where young men are "called by their christian names a little too soon" (P 219). In his sacramental verses, Emma is present in the mode of absence as a cloudy, intangible figure. Caught in a blushing moment of "rose and ardent light," her radiant complexion evinces an abstract portrait of a temptress bathed in pink-tinted auras that recall the prostitute at the end of Chapter Two. Stephen remembers Emma the night of the carnival ball – whiteclad, dancing, and flitting like a bird. Her eyes, about to trust him, do not. Her hand seems a soft merchandise that he refuses to purchase. He prefers to define himself as alien to Dublin domesticity, an ascetic monk devoted to secret, hermetic arts. Assuming the role of heretic Franciscan and courting Emma with a web of sophistry whispered in her ear, he plays the devil in clerical garments – a rebellious shaman antagon-istic to the proletarian priest Father Moran.

"Rude brutal anger" over Emma's intimacy with the Catholic prelate momentarily shatters Stephen's idealized fantasy and scatters it in realistic mimesis throughout the Dublin landscape. "He had done well to leave her to flirt with her priest, to toy with a church which was the scullerymaid of christendom" (P 220), he assures himself. Emma's figure is kaleidoscopically reflected in memories of lower-class peasant women – a flowergirl "with damp coarse hair and a hoyden's face," a kitchengirl "with the drawl of a country singer," a girl who mocked him, and a vamp whose "small ripe mouth" made her good enough to eat. "And yet he felt that, however he might revile and mock her image, his anger was also a form of homage" (P 220). Seeing Emma on the steps of the National Library, Stephen wonders if her life might be as "simple and strange as a bird's life" and her heart as "simple and wilful as a bird's" (P 216). But the bird, an emblem of simplicity and trust, quickly melds with the iconography of the inscrutable bat, a creature whose enigmatic flight and dark habitation makes it a symbol of mystery and cunning. "Bat," too, is an Irish slang term for "prostitute" – a suggestion implicitly evoked in the multiple bat-

references that pepper the final pages of *A Portrait*.[36]

Stephen condescends to think of Emma as a younger incarnation of the pregnant woman who tried to seduce Davin in the Ballyhoura hills and who emerges as a symbol of Mother Ireland – a nurturant and guileless female ingenuously bedding the stranger. Emma, too, becomes "a figure of the womanhood of her country, a batlike soul waking to the consciousness of itself in darkness and secrecy and loneliness, tarrying awhile, loveless and sinless" (*P* 221). She prostitutes herself before the priest of Catholicism and, confessing her sins in darkness and secrecy, indulges in a titillating ritual of spiritual self-revelation. Arising slowly from the primordial sludge of Dublin, this Caliban soul, blind and bat-like, will be transformed into an Irish Ariel by Stephen-Prospero, "a priest of eternal imagination, transmuting the daily bread of experience into the radiant body of everliving life" (*P* 221).

Stephen proceeds to compose his own *Pange Lingua*, a "hymn of thanksgiving" on the model of Thomistic verse. The bread of experience assumes artistic immortality, but the wafer that houses Christ's body also suggests an analogous assimiliation of the female body through the sacrament of art. By purging Emma of naturalistic dross, by abstracting her from an Irish domestic scene of horsehair and flirtation and celebrating her *sub specie aeternitatis*, Stephen metaphorically consumes her in aesthetic communion. Erotic union gives way to a spiritual Eucharist, as the poet raises the sacred chalice of devotion before the altar of the muse. Emma, as eternal temptress, surrenders herself to the artist who symbolically – and onanistically – conquers her voluptuous form: "Her nakedness yielded to him, radiant, warm, odorous and lavish-limbed, enfolded him like a shining cloud, enfolded him like water with a liquid life" (*P* 223).[37]

Stephen has paradoxically composed the villanelle out of the same pornographic passion that his Thomistic theory earlier censured. The fires of lust inspire his aubade, a poetic explosion that conceals lascivious motives: "A glow of desire kindled again his soul and fired . . . his body" (*P* 223). Art, once again, promises Stephen logocentric control over the realm of semiotic process. Rejected by Emma, he re-creates her as seductress and muse, uses her as an object of sexual fantasy, then refrigerates her in crystalline spheres of lyrical stasis. Weary of the ardent ways of frustrated passion, he cools his blazing heart through a masturbatory ritual that explodes in both aesthetic and physical *jouissance*. By raising Emma to heights of Circean power that pique her erotic desirability, Stephen magically defuses her flirtatious spell and reduces her to a mystified figure subordinate to and controlled by his priestly imagination.[38]

Does Emma fade out of the novel as the temptress of Stephen's villanelle? Does she "lure the seraphim" and have her will of man through *"languorous look and lavish limb"* (*P* 223)? This is hardly the Emma we recognize from the novel. The formal, highly wrought verses of Stephen's poem reveal his perpetual obsession with the terrifying eroticism of the female. Art enables him temporarily to subdue the archetypal seductress, whose *"eyes have set man's heart ablaze"* from the beginning of time. Against overwhelming enchantment, Stephen arrays the forces of aesthetic transformation. As poet-priest, he transubstantiates the eternal feminine into a disembodied muse that, once out of nature, ceases to threaten. Consigned to the realm of Byzantium, the Circean figure can no longer arouse animal lust or sensuous desire.

Throughout the novel, Stephen has sought the evacuation of affect from language and a re-inscription of his filial self into the symbolic order and law of the Father. By replicating himself in a discursive process of substitutability, he acquires a male aesthetic signature and triumphantly appropriates the female body/text. Inscribing himself into an august company of paternal authority figures (Daedalus, Edmond Dantes, Lord Byron, Dante Alighieri, Father Conmee, Father Arnall, Simon Dedalus, and Cranly), he fabricates an authorial persona purged of unsettling libidinal drives. The eternal temptress he celebrates is a disguised replica of the phallic mother who tantalizes with nurturant pleasure, then obstinately withholds satisfaction. Incestuous attraction to the body of the mother is repressed and displaced onto a radiant icon of female beauty. Emma provides a substitute for the mother (both consubstantial and Catholic Madonna) whose image, in turn, is reproduced in the specular icon of a wading bird-girl, then lyrically transformed into an enchantress idealized out of existence and consigned to the icy realm of Platonic stasis.

The figure of woman as mother/temptress/whore is doubled in the many mirrors of art until she is apotheosized as the virgin goddess of a new artistic religion. The poet simultaneously achieves masturbatory emission and an ejaculatory outburst of *sèmes* lyrically simulating orgasmic *jouissance*. His love is symbolically cryogenic.

Substituting pen for phallus, he penetrates the opaque image of woman as inaccessible Other and, through a series of seminal outpourings, gains onanistic satisfaction from an archetypal figure elevated beyond the unsettling immediacy of sexual difference.

Toward the end of *A Portrait*, Stephen's Platonic reveries give way to flippant remarks and lewd jokes that consign women to the libidinal margins of pornographic amusement. In the company of Lynch, he follows a "sizable hospital nurse" and comments on her cow-like proportions. The predatory young men resemble two "lean hungry greyhounds walking after a heifer" (*P* 248). The "wild spring" turns Stephen's roving eye to voyeuristic gaping at girls "demure and romping. All fair or auburn: no dark ones. They blush better" (*P* 250). The motif of shame and humiliation continues to inform his impressions of female sexuality when he imagines Emma "humbled and saddened by the dark shame of womanhood" (*P* 223) and thinks of menstruation as a fall from childhood innocence. He remarks facetiously that, according to Lynch, statues of women "should always be fully draped, one hand of the woman feeling regretfully her own hinder parts" (*P* 251). In Stephen's mind, woman is still the veiled and mysterious Other, shame-wounded by nature, bovine and buttocks-bound, and ineluctably shackled to the scatological burdens of bodily process.[39]

In his final meeting with Emma, Stephen stabilizes her image in the guise of an idealized Beatrice by opening the "spiritual-heroic refrigerating apparatus, invented and patented in all countries by Dante Alighieri" (*P* 252).[40] He concedes in his diary: "Yes, I liked her today" (*P* 252). But the seeds of friendship or affection will not be allowed to blossom. Rejecting the arms of women, Stephen chooses "the white arms of roads, their promise of close embraces and the black arms of tall ships that stand against the moon, their tale of distant nations" (*P* 252). Nevertheless, he seems to imply that the one hope for salvation residual in the Irish race lies deeply buried in the hearts of women, who serve as repositories for a slumbering national conscience. In order to rouse his countrymen from spiritual torpor, he must learn how to "cast his shadow over the imaginations of their daughters" and insinuate himself into the minds of a responsive female audience.

Throughout *A Portrait*, Stephen has manifested a psychological horror of woman as a figure of immanence, a symbol of unsettling sexual difference, and a perpetual reminder of bodily abjection. At the conclusion of Chapter Five, he prepares to flee from all the women who have served as catalysts in his own adolescent development. His journey into exile will release him from what he perceives as a cloying matriarchal authority. He must blot from his ears "his mother's sobs and reproaches" and strike from his eyes the insistent "image of his mother's face" (*P* 224). Alone and proud, isolated and free, Stephen proclaims joyful allegiance to the masculine fraternity of Daedalus, his priest and patron: "Welcome, O life! I go to encounter for the millionth time the reality of experience and to forge in the smithy of my soul the uncreated conscience of my race. . . . Old father, old artificer, stand me now and ever in good stead" (*P* 252 – 3). The hyperbolic resonance of Stephen's invocation leads us to suspect that his fate will prove Icarian rather than Daedalian. Insofar as women are concerned, he goes to encounter the reality of experience not for the millionth time, but for the first.[41]

Joyce's protagonist has relentlessly attempted to achieve mastery over the outer world by adopting a male model of creation. In the very act of word-shaping, he can impose his will on a resistant environment and reduce the chaotic fluidity of life to the controlled stasis of art. Much of the irony in *A Portrait*, however, results from Joyce's satirical rendering of Stephen's logocentric paradigm. The sociopathic hero, pompous and aloof, passionately gathers phrases for his word-hoard without infusing his "capful of light odes" (*U* 14: 1119) with the generative spark of human sympathy.

Certainly, the reader may feel baffled or uneasy about the degree of irony implicit in Joyce's portrait of the artist as a young narcissist. Stephen/Icarus has flown from one youthful illusion to another – first trusting the rectitude of his Clongowes masters and emulating the Count of Monte Cristo, then sliding into illicit sexual exultation in an initiation ritual immediately undercut by scenes of debased sensuality and emotional self-hatred. As the body, in turn, is disciplined and mortified, a devotion to the priesthood of art displaces the young man's Catholic asceticism. Embracing his new-found mission with all the exuberance of an aesthetic convert, Stephen is left exhausted and swooning before the sanctified icon of a wading girl transformed in his imagination into a mystical muse. Incapable of sustaining this romantic fantasy in the hostile urban environment of Dublin, he takes psychological refuge in vaguely erotic verses generated by the *imago* of an eternal temptress. In the end, nothing is left for the would-be poet but voluntary exile, to be undertaken in a spirit of secrecy, cunning, detachment, and indifference. Toward the conclusion of the novel, Stephen adopts a Wildean pose of triumphant perversity as he proclaims revolutionary freedom and projects a vision of liberating flight "across the kathartic ocean" (FW 185.6) to the haunts of bohemian Paris. Emotionally static and incapable of meaningful connection with other human beings, Stephen is poised in a stance of Icarian impotence. The last diary entries of A Portrait suggest imminent emigration, but they delineate neither flight nor failure.[42]

The text of Joyce's Bildungsroman seems to imply that the developing artist's notorious misogyny will prove to be still another dimension (and limitation) of his youthful priggishness. The pervasive irony that tinges the hero's scrupulous devotions and gives his aesthetic theory that "true scholastic stink" surely informs his relations with women – from his mother and Dante Riordan to Emma and the unnamed bird-girl he transfigures on the beach. In a tone of gentle mockery, Joyce makes clear to his audience that Stephen's fear of women and his contempt for sensuous life are among the many inhibitions that stifle this young man's creativity. Before he can become a true priest of the eternal imagination, Stephen must first divest himself of the spiritual-heroic refrigerating apparatus that characterizes the egocentric aesthete. Narcissism and misogyny are adolescent traits he has to outgrow on the path to artistic maturity. Not until the epic Ulysses will a new model begin to emerge – one that recognizes the need for the intellectual artist to make peace with the mother-lover of his dreams and to incorporate into his masterful work those mysterious breaks, flows, gaps, and ruptures associated with the repressed semiotic flow of male/female desire.

3

INTERPRETING *EXILES*
The Aesthetics of Unconsummated Desire

Where does desire come from? From a mixture of
difference and *inequality*. . . . It is *inequality* that
triggers desire, as a desire – for appropriation.

(Hélène Cixous, "Sorties")

ACT ONE: *PASSIO IRASCIBILIS*

Exiles, Joyce's single dramatic work, served as an important vehicle
for the author's complex, sometimes convoluted investigation of
heterosexual and homoerotic desire. Although *Exiles* may resemble a
turn-of-the-century problem play, it offers, from a psychoanalytic
standpoint, a provocative exploration of sexual and psychic
mobility.[1] Like August Strindberg before him, Joyce is obsessed
with the "name of the Father" as an index of authority and
authorized familial identity. And he knows, instinctively, that the
"merest hint of the mother's infidelity threatens to expose what
Lacan calls the symbolic, . . . which is usually covered over,
sutured, by the representations of . . . the imaginary of chivalry, the
woman's presumed honour."[2] In *Exiles*, Joyce is determined to
inscribe the enigmatic fluctuations of erotic desire into a playful
symbolic context. Sexual urgency is deliberately deferred – both by
Richard Rowan the artist, who sleeps alone in his study and studies
aesthetic parturition; and by Robert Hand, the suitor who courts
Bertha in traditional chivalric guise in order to defer and displace
his own homoerotic admiration for Richard.[3]

Richard has refused to submit to restrictive bourgeois practices
and lives in a common-law marriage with a woman who bears his
child but not his legal name and with a son who is called by the
"nice name they give those children" rather than by the surname
of the father. Denying Bertha and Archie the authorized status of
wife and legitimate heir, he has abdicated patriarchal authority over
the "unauthorized" (illegitimate, dispossessed, un-named) members
of his household. Because he deliberately renounces the role of *pater-
familias*, center of power and law in the family configuration, his

position is ill-defined and decentered by its very refusal to claim wife and child as legal possessions. The two subjects of his domestic hearth, not subject to familial mastery, are liberated and self-determined, theoretically free to author their own identities within the open spaces of paternal absence. Ostensibly disclaiming the rights of a traditional patriarch, Richard eschews stereotypical bourgeois roles and responsibilities. Though a biological progenitor, he rejects phallocratic privilege and abrogates false ideals of sexual fidelity sutured by an imaginary chivalry.[4]

Is Richard challenging Bertha's "presumed honour" by choreographing a titillating scenario of flirtation and sexual indulgence? Is he playing a modern Walter in a self-conscious revision of the tale of patient Griselda? At times his pompous proclamations make him seem an insufferable boor, testing a woman's love for the sheer satisfaction of claiming her spiritual fidelity. Richard's project, however, proves more cunning and metaphorical than earlier renditions of this age-old theme of adultery or the threat thereof. Although his curiosity is piqued, his voyeuristic tendencies are aroused in order to be left unsatisfied – to function as a "spur" to art through the arabesques and traces of abducted desire. Bertha's fidelity is banished to the margins of perpetual doubt, and her marital chastity becomes a matter of undecidability – a gap or aporia at the heart of logocentric control. The satiation of amorous longing is a riddle inscribed in the language of aesthetic desire in order to be reinscribed in the linguistic and symbolic realm of art.[5] *Jouissance* is deferred by a metaphysical quest for a profound, all-consuming love beyond the stirrings of physicality. In Joyce's unusual romantic drama, pleasure is always-already absent in fantasies generated by the libidinal displacements demanded by compensatory creation.

Socially, the public persona of Richard Rowan is acceptable to the Irish in the guise of a bohemian artist affiliated with a woman "not quite his equal." But Bertha, his common-law wife, can be dismissed by the bourgeoisie as a mere "thing" the writer got entangled with. Loveless and friendless, she lives on the margins of Dublin society. "I gave up everything for him," she declares, "religion, family, my own peace. . . . Do you think I am a stone?" (*E* 100). She remains alone and proud – tested by her husband, courted and idealized by Robert, and envied by the chaste (and chastened) Beatrice Justice.[6]

Bertha is the only adult in *Exiles* who is given no surname, though she inherits Richard's family name through their nine-year conjugal association. Her single appellation "Bertha" onomatopoetically suggests the process of birth, as well as the earth in its benevolent and maternal aspects. An early prototype for Molly Bloom as Gea-Tellus, she "is the earth, dark, formless, mother, made beautiful by the moonlit night, darkly conscious of her instincts" (*E* 118). Joyce notes that "Robert likens her to the moon because of her dress. Her age is the completion of a lunar rhythm" (*E* 113). Clothed in lavender and cream, Bertha appears on-stage like an impressionistic vision. If her lunar beauty is reminiscent of the virgin-goddess Diana, her voluptuous physicality evokes the mythic presence of an earth-mother whose consciousness is rooted in instinctual drives. The semiotic dimensions of her fluid, fertile, passionate nature sharply contrast with the logocentric aspirations of both Richard the artist and Robert the sentimental philanderer.[7]

In his notes for *Exiles*, Joyce describes the play as "a rough and tumble between the Marquis de Sade and Freiherr v. Sacher Masoch. . . . Richard's Masochism needs no example" (*E* 124). If Richard is acting out a masochistic need for punishment at the hands of a stalwart competitor, then Robert embodies stereotypical sadistic impulses: "The sadism in Robert's character – his wish to inflict cruelty as a necessary part of sensual pleasure – is apparent only or chiefly in his dealings with women towards whom he is unceasingly attractive because unceasingly aggressive. Towards men, however, he is meek and humble of heart" (*E* 125).[8]

Robert acts the part of a courtly lover, a latter-day Romeo equipped with overblown roses and saccharine compliments. His courtship of Bertha is romantic but evasive, as he tries to confess a secret, inarticulate passion. "There is one word which I have never dared to say to you" (*E* 31), he writes. Upon interrogation, he expresses his feelings in a euphemistic substantive clause: "That I have a deep liking for you" (*E* 31). Adulterous passion, like homosexuality, is evidently a love that dares not speak its name. Just as Leopold Bloom in *Ulysses* will define universal love simply as "the opposite of hatred," Robert Hand tries to diffuse the impact of his avowal by translating "love" into an innocuous proclamation of "deep liking." "Love," a "word known to all men" (*U* 15: 1492–3), appears to be one that few can speak. It can be known but not uttered, thought but not expressed. Bertha tactfully reassures her suitor: "Now you have dared to say it" (*E* 31) – even though Robert has dared nothing and spoken less. The abashed courtier becomes still more elliptical when later interrogated by Richard, who, feigning the role of outraged husband, demands: "Explain to me what is the word you longed and never dared to say to her" (*E* 60). "Yes. I will," Robert replies obediently, only to obfuscate, once again, the referent that seems to defy utterance: "I admire very much the personality of your . . . of . . . your wife. That is the word. I can say it. It is no secret" (*E* 60). Stumbling over still another unutterable word, "mistress," Robert, in a gesture of obeisance meant to acknowledge Richard's conjugal appropriation of Bertha (the kind of appropriation Richard so clearly disdains), has recourse to the social euphemism "wife."

Playing the part of chivalric lover in his conversation with Bertha, Robert complains of sleeplessness and torment and invokes stale romantic metaphors: "Your face is a flower too – but more beautiful. A wild flower blowing in a hedge" (*E* 32). Joyce himself professed in a 1909 love-letter to Nora Barnacle that her eyes were "strange beautiful blue wild-flowers growing in some tangled, rain-drenched hedge" (*SL* 179). And in *Ulysses*, Leopold Bloom, addressing Molly as his "mountain flower," through impassioned wooing wins her heart. But here the sentiment is vacuous and clumsy, a cliché that moves Bertha to amusement rather than passion. She immediately challenges Robert's script: "I am wondering if that is what you say – to the others" (*E* 32). Instinctively, Bertha knows that the rhetoric of idolatry depersonalizes the beloved and denies her free subjectivity.

Swept along by the discourse of courtly love, Robert promises to lavish "long long sweet kisses" of worship over "your eyes. Your lips. All your divine body" (*E* 36). Once he has elevated Bertha to the status of divinity, he can freely proclaim his ardor in tones of humble, swooning adoration accompanied by strains of Wagnerian *Liebestod*. "My life is finished – over," he insists melodramatically. "I want to end it and have done with it. . . . To end it all – death. To fall from a great high cliff, down, right down into the sea. . . . Listening to music and in the arms of the woman I love – the sea, music and death" (*E* 35). The assignation he makes with Bertha is filled with the penumbra of sacramental devotion. With lust cloaked in amorous sentiment, the cavalier can boldly vie for his lady's hand – not to mention her eyes, lips, and the whole of her "divine body" (*E* 36). Bertha, ingenuous but instinctively shrewd, finds Robert's inflated rhetoric as overblown as his roses.

For Robert, the language of courtship is definitely kinetic, and the Janus image of this sticky, romantic effulgence is little more than a pornographic discourse of lascivious compulsion. The moment he is alone with Richard, Robert reverts to homoerotic scripts dictated by male bonding and, in his candid "locker-room" conversation, turns a nostalgic gaze back to those wild nights of drinking and carousing that the bachelors once shared. Their language suggests Nietzschean aspirations: "It was not only a house of revelry; it was to be the hearth of a new life. . . . And in that name all our sins were committed" (*E* 41). As nascent supermen, both men rebelled in their youth against Irish provincialism and, determined to forge a new morality, asserted a "transvaluation of values" through drink, blasphemy, heresy, and womanizing. Robert, however, seems to have confused the existential freedom of Nietzschean liberation with the sybaritic delights of erotic libertinism. A dandy and a roué, he defends hedonistic practices with perverted notions of Aristotelian aesthetics. Recalling St Thomas Aquinas's definition of beauty, *Pulchra sunt quae visa placent*, or "that is beautiful the apprehension of which pleases" (*P* 207), he defines sexual desire as an act of sacerdotal homage. A kiss, he suggests, is an expression of aesthetic devotion: "This stone, for instance . . . is so cool, so polished, so delicate, like a woman's temple. It is silent, it suffers our passion; and it is beautiful. . . . And what is a woman? A work of nature, too, like a stone or a flower or a bird. A kiss is an act of homage" (*E* 41).

Robert longs to idolize woman as a consummate "work of nature" and, aroused by what is common or universal about the female, he articulates an aesthetics of eroticism that seems more representative of the sensibilities of D. H. Lawrence than those of James Joyce. "After all, what is most attractive in even the most beautiful woman," he insists, is her "commonest" qualities: "I mean how her body develops heat when it is pressed, the movement of her blood, how quickly she changes by digestion what she eats into – what shall be nameless" (*E* 41–2). In Lawrentian fashion, Robert celebrates the physical warmth and physiological process of "femaleness" – blood surging, bodily heat, digestion, and excretion. Through adulation of universal sensuous traits, he refuses to personalize feminine beauty. In this biological analogy, Robert reverts to a crude subject/object dichotomy: man is both perceiver and poet, woman the specular object perceived. Later, when Bertha defiantly asks, "Do you think I am a stone?" (*E* 100), she unconsciously challenges such extravagant Platonic homage.

Pledging his troth to Richard as lord and mentor, Robert claims: "I have faith in you, the faith of a disciple in his master" (*E* 44). But Richard, like Christ or Nietzsche, speaks in the metaphorical language of riddle and paradox. He lays claim to a stronger and stranger emotional union, the "faith of a master in the disciple who will betray him" (*E* 44). Richard feels convinced that like Christ and Charles Stewart Parnell, he will be betrayed by friends and disciples and, eventually, by the woman he loves. Like Kierkegaard, he defines ultimate spiritual possession as an act of sacrificial generosity: voluntary renunciation frees the individual from the ponderous burdens of jealousy and desire. Having choreographed the scene of temptation for Bertha and Robert, Richard may then withdraw, like the god of creation, "within or behind or beyond or above his handiwork" and remain indifferent, "paring his finger-nails" (*P* 215).

Despite his earlier renunciation of patriarchal privilege, Richard unwittingly assigns to Bertha the ambiguous status of a conjugal possession to be domestically hoarded or offered to a male competitor. Hence the irony of his parabolic lesson to Archie. "While you have a thing it can be taken from you," he tells his son. "But when you have given it, you have given it. No robber can take it from you. . . . It is yours then for ever when you have given it. It will be yours always" (*E* 46–7). Bertha, evidently, is the thing in question and Robert the potential robber.

Acting according to Richard's directives, Bertha shares the secret of Robert's courtship and describes his wooing in lugubrious detail. Richard, in turn, claims both scientific and aesthetic detachment. As a voyeuristic priest of the eternal imagination, he hears the young woman's penitential confession and carefully draws out every titillating detail. Right down to the last question, "Were you excited?" (*E* 49), he mimics a Catholic prelate scrupulously eliciting sexual information from a penitent in the confessional. How did he kiss you? Was the kiss simple or lingual? "Were you excited? . . . Was he?" (*E* 49). In Catholic theology, the issue of passionate arousal determines the gravity of sexual transgression. Simple dalliance, carried too far, might still entail the commission of merely a venial sin. But if either partner allows him/herself to entertain impure thoughts to the point of physical excitation and consent of the will, the offense becomes mortal – the ethical equivalent of an act of fornication or adultery. It is this same kind of scrupulosity that Richard exercises in his prying interrogation of Bertha. If his wife remained unexcited in response to Robert's temptation, she has not yet "sinned in her heart."[9]

Rowan is setting himself up as godlike artist, playing the manipulative role of writer-director in a drama of potential cuckoldry. Like God the Father, he plans a scenario of temptation that might well precipitate Bertha's sexual fall. The sado-masochistic psychodynamics of his scheme suggest that beneath his brash defiance of bourgeois morality lies a deeply repressed, almost paranoid fear of adultery and conjugal loss. Tormented by the emotional threat of Bertha's infidelity, Richard determines to plunge headlong into the "void of incertitude" and magnanimously offer his spouse to her ardent suitor, since, as he assures Archie, one cannot lose what one refuses to appropriate. At some level of awareness, Richard realizes that, in his role as manipulative voyeur, he can enjoy both the pleasures of vicarious participation and the delights of scopophiliac detachment.

Choreographing Bertha's incipient love affair, Richard maintains an attitude of aesthetic distance that exorcizes kinetic feelings of both desire and loathing. He stages a self-indulgent melodrama for the sake of evincing the "luminosity of doubt." Self-consciously renouncing what he sees as a traditional *male* right to demand assurances of female chastity, he voluntarily embraces a stance of moral incertitude intended to exorcize sexual jealousy. It is significant that Richard protests as his motive for such unconventional behavior Bertha's freedom rather than his own. "I have allowed you complete liberty" (*E* 52), he proclaims. Yet he takes for granted the assumption that Bertha's liberty should be contingent on spousal benevolence. Autonomy of choice is not hers by right, but the implicit gift of an enlightened, somewhat condescending patriarch. Offering Bertha permission to be free, Richard arrogantly presumes that it is he who is responsible for, and has always controlled, her freedom.

Bertha is perhaps correct in her charge that Richard is "unnatural," since he engineers this complex game of conjugal temptation precisely for the purpose of transcending nature. He wants to liberate himself from those troubling emotions of love and hate associated with erotic compulsion; and, as a Nietzschean superman of contemporary art, he desperately tries to fly above and beyond conventional nets of familial commitment. Like that earlier misogynist Stephen Dedalus, he seeks to impose a spiritual-heroic refrigerating apparatus onto the vagaries of an intimate relationship with a woman. Obsessed with a Nietzschean will to power, he attempts to control the semiotic fluidity of feminine desire by invoking logocentric strategies of intellectual mastery. If Stephen fled the adolescent temptress, Richard takes refuge from the vicissitudes of adult sexuality in the luminous incertitude of adulterous betrayal.

When Bertha hurls at Richard the epithet of "mother-killer," she implies that he is somehow guilty of psychological collusion in his own filial alienation. She also suggests that Richard is attempting to kill the mother in herself. Although she approaches her spouse with candor and solicitude, Richard coldly rejects her proffered gift of fidelity. He thrusts both sexual freedom and ethical responsibility onto Bertha, only to revel in her understandable perplexity. He does, in fact, take advantage of her simplicity by using her as a moral and aesthetic pawn to implement his own psychological liberation. Trapped in a confusing labyrinth of inchoate passion, Bertha pleads for some kind of guidance. "Am I to go?" (*E* 55), she asks ingenuously. But Richard has already assimilated his mother's hardness of heart and, with a mask of iron, insists: "Decide yourself. . . . You are free" (*E* 56).[10] Almost maniacally, and with religious determination, he struggles to liberate himself from the *passio irascibilis* that holds him enthralled. "He is jealous, wills and knows his own dishonour and the dishonour of her, to be united with every phase of whose being is love's end" (*E* 114). The transcendence he seeks "must reveal itself as the very immolation of the pleasure of possession on the altar of love" (*E* 114).[11]

At this point in the drama, Joyce assumes an endlessly varied psychic and sexual mobility among his characters. Richard is, for Bertha, Robert, and Beatrice, an elusive object of Lacanian desire who refuses to authorize erotic consummation. The bereft Beatrice displaces her troubled affections onto Robert, who seeks Bertha as a surrogate for homoerotic attachment. All three characters revolve obsessively around Richard, the cunning choreographer of this melodramatic scenario. Frustrated in their passionate attraction to such an idiosyncratic artist, Bertha and Robert are thrust together as unwitting kinsmen to inaugurate a supplementary channel for the expression of repressed libidinal drives.

Richard, in turn, claims aesthetic rather than conjugal rights over the ingenuous Bertha, who proves faithful to him in her fashion. The seed of doubt introduces a note of perpetual desire – a gap or slippage that disseminates itself in the mind of the artist and catalyzes his creative instincts. His beloved, not wholly possessed, must constantly be renewed in his affections through the marriage of true minds that art alone can promise. Doubt, gashing a psychic hole into the seamless web of logocentric self-possession, thrusts the artist onto the edge of emotional incertitude and forces him to lay claim, over and over again, to a dream of love and paradisal communion that always-already eludes him.[12]

ACT TWO: THE CAT-AND-MOUSE GAME

If Richard Rowan assumes the role of "automystic" at the beginning of Act Two, Robert Hand embodies the more debased persona of "automobile" (*E* 113) – a mechanical and pusillanimous stereotype that borders on dramatic farce. Joyce's notes for *Exiles* suggest a vaguely homosexual motivation behind Richard's project: "The bodily possession of Bertha by Robert, repeated often, would certainly bring into almost carnal contact the two men" (*E* 123). Richard longs "to feel the thrill of adultery vicariously and to possess a bound woman Bertha through the organ of his friend" (*E* 125).[13]

When Richard storms Ranelagh Cottage, this "devil for surprises" appears like an avenging angel to catch Robert in the act. The two seem to have changed places in the play's cat-and-mouse game, and Richard takes sadistic pleasure in taunting his victim with proof of adulterous intent. The myopic artist, like Father Dolan in *A Portrait*, sees and knows all. "I was watching you," he declares in a moment of voyeuristic triumph. Robert, the penitent sinner, immediately pleads insanity: "Yes, I was mad. But it was merely lightheadedness" (*E* 59). Like a remorseful child, he protests gratitude for being rescued from temptation and takes a life-long lesson from the master: "I cannot tell you what a relief it is to me that you have spoken – that the danger is passed" (*E* 61).

Arrogant and condescending, Rowan judges his rival fatuous, even lugubrious: "The whole thing made me sad all at once. . . .

Like all men you have a foolish wandering heart" (*E* 61). Richard, of course, sets himself apart and claims exemption from the waywardness that governs "all men's" hearts. Professing the sublime detachment of sexual renunciation, he warns Robert that Bertha cannot be taken either by stealth or by violence: "Steal you could not in my house because the doors were open: nor take by violence if there were no resistance" (*E* 62). By denouncing Robert as a would-be thief, a man guilty of coveting his neighbor's wife, Richard implies that Bertha is a metaphorical possession – a piece of conjugal property which is his by right, but which he voluntarily and magnanimously forsakes. Robert himself reinforces this sense of female objectification when he compares Bertha to Galatea and praises Richard for his labors as a contemporary Pygmalion: "She is yours, your work. . . . And that is why I, too, was drawn to her. You are so strong that you attract me even through her" (*E* 62). Richard, he insists, has artistically sculpted Bertha's character and magically transformed her into a fascinating object of masculine devotion: "You have made her all that she is. A strange and wonderful personality – in my eyes, at least" (*E* 67).[14]

If Robert's description of love was Platonic in Act One, it now degenerates into a vindication of lust as the "law of nature," an obsessive will to power that drives the male to uncontrollable acts of violence: "Those are moments of sheer madness when we feel an intense passion for a woman. We see nothing. We think of nothing. Only to possess her. Call it brutal, bestial, what you will. . . . No man ever yet lived on this earth who did not long to possess – . . . in the flesh – the woman whom he loves. It is nature's law" (*E* 63). It is a law, however, from which Richard claims singular exemption. "What is that to me? Did I vote it?" (*E* 63). "A *lex eterna* stays about him" (*U* 3: 48–9); but, proudly, he rejects it. Richard defiantly embraces the role of Nietzschean superman, the individual who renounces traditional morality and, through a transvaluation of values, becomes a law unto himself. With a note of *hybris*, he contemptuously asserts superiority over nature, identifying himself as "no man" or *Outis*, the epithet Odysseus used in his confrontation with the Cyclops and which, combined with "Zeus," becomes the hero's true name. Like Nietzsche's *Übermensch* in *Joyful Wisdom*, Richard will proclaim "the new, the unique, the incomparable, making laws for ourselves and creating ourselves."[15] Raised above the crowd, he becomes "no man" – a self-generating artist/hero and, in his own mind at least, the superman of a new moral order.

Oblivious of the implications of Richard's avowal, Robert continues to argue not for joyful wisdom, but for the sensual joys of uninhibited passion. Both men and women are polygamous by inclination, he insists, but are prohibited by society from heeding the divine mandate inscribed in their hearts by the finger of God. Robert proposes the "immoral idea" that "a woman, too, has the right to try with many men until she finds love" (*E* 65) and even intends to write a book on the subject – perhaps a novel similar to Joyce's *Ulysses*.

Richard, however, responds to Robert's self-serving plan for sexual revolution with the diversionary tactic of enumerating his own conjugal misdemeanors. After nights of erotic revelry, he habitually courted the practice of rousing Bertha with detailed penitential confessions, then hysterically begging her forgiveness: "I cried beside her bed; and I pierced her heart" (*E* 66). His self-abasing acts of contrition were clearly designed to make Bertha a spiritual accomplice in his sado-masochistic practices. Playing the prodigal son, he demanded that she respond as *Mater Dolorosa* and offer her contrite spouse continual succor. Has Richard "killed . . . the virginity of her soul," he wonders, through such strange and wild expostulations? In repeated trials of her forbearance, was he "feeding the flame of her innocence" with his guilt (*E* 67)? Ironically, Richard never seems to acknowledge that Bertha's heroic renunciation of sexual possessiveness has already preceded his own. Whereas Richard must fight against the *passio irascibilis* in a struggle that lasts nine years and three dramatic acts, he haughtily assumes that Bertha achieved such emotional detachment in the early stages of cohabitation. Richard and Robert, like Joyce their creator, apparently believe that women are "naturally" free of the torments of sexual jealousy.

Richard, moreover, lays claim to a different kind of conjugal prerogative by virtue of his self-defined role as artist-god. During their nine years of exile in Italy, he sought to improve his companion spiritually and intellectually by making her over in the mental image of psychic cohesion dictated by his own narcissistic needs. "I tried to give her a new life" (*E* 67), he boasts, entirely oblivious of the arrogance of such an assertion. Richard fails to realize that this premeditated and supposedly redemptive project was extremely manipulative. Like the sculptor Pygmalion, he set out to fashion Bertha's character as though she were a stone statue or a fictive persona in a nineteenth-century novel. Claiming authorship of her present personality, he redefines her as product (or child) of his fertile imagination and unwittingly exercises artistic authority over the parameters of her emotional life.

Richard's dream of godlike parturition appears all the more evident in an unpublished dramatic fragment documenting powerful fantasies of couvade: "I feel as if I had carried her [Bertha] within my own body, in my womb. . . . Her books, her music, the fire of thought stolen from on high, . . . the grace with which she tends the body we desire – whose work is that? I feel that it is mine. It is my work and the work of others like me. . . . It is we who have conceived her and brought her forth. Our minds flowing together are the womb in which we have borne her."[16] Having "birthed" Bertha from the womb of the intellectual imagination, Richard now complains that his wonderful creation has figuratively emerged stillborn: "She is dead. She lies on my bed. . . . And I know that her body was always my loyal slave" (E 68).

Richard finally reveals the hidden agenda behind his Kierkegaardian act of renunciation when he confesses an obsessive need to liberate himself from the ponderous emotional burden imposed by Bertha's fidelity. "I longed to be betrayed by you and by her – in the dark, in the night – secretly, meanly, craftily. . . . I longed for that passionately and ignobly, to be dishonoured for ever in love and in lust. . . . To be for ever a shameful creature and to build up my soul again out of the ruins of its shame" (E 70). Richard demands the possibility of erotic abjection as a necessary condition for the realization of creative freedom. Using the archetypal image of the phoenix, he intends to sacrifice both himself and Bertha on the altar of adultery, then to reconstruct from the ashes of this metaphorical holocaust a new, impalpable, and imperishable artistic project. Robert, taking up the rhetorical challenge, proposes a "battle of both our souls . . . against all that is false in them and in the world. A battle of your soul against the spectre of fidelity, of mine against the spectre of friendship" (E 70–1). Assuming a *fin de siècle* banner of Nietzschean heroism, Robert plots a moral rebellion against "the misery of what slaves call life" and exults in Dionysiac fantasies of redemption through a single ecstatic moment of *jouissance*, a "blinding instant of passion alone – passion, free, unashamed, irresistible" (E 71).

In his characterization of Richard and Robert, Joyce gives us embryonic versions of Shem and Shaun, the polarized twins of *Finnegans Wake*. Richard, the idealistic poet, manifests "that fierce indignation which lacerated the heart of Swift" (*E* 43). "Fallen from a higher world," he sees himself as an avenging angel filled with "fierce indignation" at human fallibility. He resembles Shakespeare's Ariel – a sprite who, imprisoned in matter, cannot accept life as "cowardly and ignoble" (*E* 43 – 4). Robert, in contrast, protests that he has a nature modeled on Satan or on Shakespeare's Caliban: "I have come up from a lower world and I am filled with astonishment when I find that people have any redeeming virtue at all" (*E* 44). Even Robert's joke about public statuary adds comic resonance to this dramatic portrait of masculine mirror images. Richard, the narcissistic artist, is baffled by the difficulty of "getting down" from the elevated heights of philosophical idealism. Robert, the smiling public man, surveys the scene and declares: "In my time the dunghill was so high" (*E* 43). The scatological analogy suggests that Robert looks out complacently over the dunghill of a desiccated romantic tradition but continues to pile up the dung through his anachronistic, chivalric behavior.

Throughout the second act of *Exiles*, Bertha remains the center and focal point of the play's dramatic action. Like Molly Bloom in *Ulysses*, she is present in the mode of absence, and her figure is all the more powerful for its veiled, mysterious obscurity. When Bertha finally appears on stage, she proves to be a woman who "does things," and her impatience sharply contrasts with the cerebral dialogue of the two men. Having once had the courage to elope with Richard without an explicit invitation, she may well be strong enough to turn the tables on her antagonistic partner and take up his unconventional challenge of adultery. "As I have the name I can have the gains," she threatens. Having earned the name of "whore" through elopement, she might just as well have the gains of sexual freedom in her common-law marriage. When she appeals to Richard for emotional direction, he characteristically refuses counsel. "Your own heart will tell you," he declares. "Who am I that I should call myself master of your heart or of any woman's?" (*E* 75). Richard, who claims to have given birth spiritually to Bertha, stubbornly refuses to exercise conventional prerogatives over his imputed creation. His self-conscious and overdetermined gesture of erotic renunciation proves both patronizing and noble-hearted.

Richard foists the illusion of freedom onto Bertha in order to be free himself – not to court Beatrice, but to liberate his soul from the tormenting anxieties provoked by an uncontrollable (and culturally embedded) desire for exclusive sexual access to the body of the beloved.[17]

Abandoning his wife to the vertigo of existential choice, Richard leaves Bertha and Robert in a state of perplexity and confusion, like dumbfounded actors thrust together without benefit of a script. His strategies of emotional manipulation are particularly complex, since Richard masquerades as what René Girard would call a "model" for both Robert and Bertha, whose mutual attraction has most probably been evinced by Richard's cold-hearted indifference to them both. Robert Hand is shamelessly exploited in his role as the romantic mediator whose ardor provides a spur to resuscitate Richard's repressed desire for Bertha – a yearning revitalized by the ambiguities of Robert's adulterous intent. Nine years earlier, Richard successfully snatched Bertha from Robert's potential grasp by whisking her off to the continent without benefit of clergy. Using the vocabulary of a competitive sexual sweepstakes, he claims, triumphantly: "I played for her against all that you say or can say; and I won" (*E* 40). In order to rekindle the spark of his now-flagging passion, he is obliged to cast Robert in the specious role of sexual rival. Richard apparently demands the deflecting presence of an avid opponent to reinforce his own gratifying illusions of emotional dominance.

Adopting a deceptively liberal stance of amorous indulgence, Richard nonetheless tries to exchange Bertha with Robert for the "use value" of conjugal doubt. In some sense, Bertha proves to be just as much an object of barter as was Freud's Dora. Richard hands over his consort in an act of generosity that reveals the slippage of authoritarian power in an attempt to trade Bertha for a metaphorical wound that will free him psychologically from the bonds of covetousness and from an amorphous conviction of radical lack. Refusing to appropriate the female body in marriage, he makes a dramatic gesture of connubial magnanimity, a grandiloquent "sacrifice."[18] By sublimating lascivious desire to the strictures of aesthetic control, Richard betrays the blind spot in his intellectual project. Because he lusts after the elusive freedom generated by undecidability, conjugal doubt alone can release him from the unsettling constraints of traditional marital commitment.

By doubling the image of his common-law wife, by shattering the stability of her notions of fidelity and affective devotion, Richard can take mental refuge in the role of a detached artist free to re-create, in endless movements of godlike dissemination, a fantasy of his beloved as an imaginary (and unattainable) figure of wholeness and totalizing self-presence.[19]

ACT THREE: THE LUMINOSITY OF DOUBT

The third act of *Exiles* is dominated by a woman. If Richard and Robert articulate a logocentric philosophy based on "ideas and ideas," Bertha cuts through the "pornosophical philotheology" (*U* 15: 109) of both men by persistently and triumphantly expressing the perdurance of female desire. Like Molly Bloom in *Ulysses*, she dwells on amorous reverie and continues to cherish the "great dream" that initially impelled her to elope with Richard, who has ostensibly abandoned his "bride in exile" and is gloriously wedded to his art.

Robert Hand's essay in praise of this "distinguished Irishman" is apparently intended as an allegorical rendering of Richard's domestic drama. In this narrative of exile and return, Bertha becomes analogous to Mother Ireland and Richard to the child who "left her in her hour of need" (*E* 99). Like Kathleen ni Houlihan, Bertha will prove the victorious mother/muse who recalls her wayward son – the man who, through "loneliness and exile," will at last learn to love her (*E* 99). The servant Brigid, like a Greek chorus, prophesies that: "He'll come back to you again. Sure he thinks the sun shines out of your face" (*E* 90). But Bertha somberly demurs: "No, Brigid, that time comes only once in a lifetime. The rest of life is good for nothing except to remember that time" (*E* 91).[20]

The final act of Joyce's drama is filled with riddles, questions, prophecies, and parables. All the characters seem to speak in tongues that hide encoded messages. Bertha instinctively manages to penetrate the convoluted psychodynamics of Richard's manipulation when she accuses: "For your own sake you urged me to it. . . . To be free yourself" (*E* 103). In a conversation with Beatrice, she angrily dismisses the masculine logocentric discourse of "ideas and ideas" (*E* 100). "Do you think I am a stone?" she asks bitterly. "I am very proud of myself, if you want to know. What have they ever done for him? I made him a man. What are they all in his life? No more than dirt under his boots! . . . He can despise me, too, like the rest of them – now. And you can despise me. But you will never humble me, any of you" (*E* 100). Reversing the Pygmalion/Galatea relationship earlier envisaged by Robert, Bertha claims with fierce, maternal pride that it is she who made Richard a man. Through love and passionate devotion, she spiritually gives birth to the mature artist who will, in turn, conceive and bring forth poetic ideas. At this point in the drama, Bertha emerges as a newly born woman, autonomous and free. She asserts, in her own right, a creative liberty that transcends the sexual imbroglio earlier engineered by Richard in his attempt to play choreographer and puppet-master in the drama of both their destinies.[21]

In the final act of the play, Bertha proudly lays claim to the kind of psychological autonomy that Richard has been trying to foist on her in the guise of purported benevolence. "You would like to be free now," he challenges. "You have only to say the word" (*E* 103). When Richard brashly offers Bertha sexual liberty, she seizes the opportunity to assert emotional freedom. She taunts him with a fantasy of nightly trysts with a mysterious lover in acts of unbridled passion: "To meet my lover! Yes! My lover!" (*E* 104). There is an obvious note of mockery in Bertha's declaration of sexual independence, as she wryly comments: "You are a stranger to me. You do not understand anything in me – not one thing in my heart or soul. A stranger! I am living with a stranger!" (*E* 104).

Bertha has spent an unforgettable evening with Robert, but their veiled colloquy remains shrouded in mystery. The spectator, like Richard, is cast into a mire of metaphysical doubt. Robert and Bertha address each other in the figurative language of lovers, a discourse fraught with epistemological uncertainty.

ROBERT: . . . Bertha? What happened last night? What is the truth that I am to tell? . . . Were you mine in that sacred night of love? Or have I dreamed it?

BERTHA [*smiles faintly*]: Remember your dream of me. You dreamed that I was yours last night.

ROBERT: And that is the truth – a dream? That is what I am to tell?

BERTHA: Yes.

ROBERT: . . . Bertha! . . . In all my life only that dream is real. I forget the rest.   (*E* 106)

When Bertha reminds her suitor of his dream of amorous possession during their "sacred night of love," Robert, swept away on a
tide of emotional ecstasy, cannot distinguish reality from dream. If
their conversation is intended to reconstruct the highly coded
language of courtly love, then Robert's assessment should be interpreted literally: the encounter was enacted according to "sacred"
codes of conduct, and whatever intimacy the two lovers shared took
sacramental rather than profane expression. The dialogue has a
Platonic cast, and one might assume from this ambiguous tête-à-tête
that their involvement stopped short of physical consummation.

Joyce, despite his popular reputation as a pornographic author,
rarely gives us explicit representations of sexual coition. After
tantalizing his audience, he invariably transfers erotic climax from
the stage of drama to the scene of writing. Copulation is prepared
for, imagined, fantasized, or recollected. But the moment of physical
climax is always displaced onto a mimetic stage of impassioned
fantasy, a stage of subjective and cultural representation. Erotic
jouissance in the Joycean canon is played out in the register of *écriture*
and endlessly supplemented by inflated reveries in the tumescent
imaginations of his characters.

Robert Hand, like Keats transported by the song of the nightingale, wonders if his experience were a vision or a waking dream.
For a clue to the mystery, we might consult another Keatsian lyric,
"Ode on a Grecian Urn," which suggests that: "Heard melodies
are sweet, but those unheard/Are sweeter." In answer to epistemological queries, the poet would insist: "'Beauty is truth, truth,
beauty,' – that is all/ Ye know on earth, and all ye need to know."
The truth of Robert and Bertha's liaison resides in the lyrical
recollections they privately share. Like the lovers portrayed on the
Grecian urn, they eschew "a heart high-sorrowful and cloyed" by
choosing the "happier love" of unconsummated passion, "forever
warm and still to be enjoyed."[22] The couple can luxuriate in
melodies of erotic expectation inscribed in consciousness by the
suspension of physical release. Robert has dreamt of ecstatic union
with Bertha, but his ineffable dream is all the more powerful for its
lack of sensuous closure. It will take a plethora of forms in his
imagination over a thousand and one nights of delectable fantasy, as
he bears into voluntary exile the sacred chalice of Platonic devotion
to a mistress who will remain "forever panting, and forever young"
in her suitor's romantic memory.

Robert and Bertha mutually construct a dream of love, an imaginary encounter on the stage of aroused desire. Tantalized, they apparently defer physical satisfaction for the sweeter pleasures of erotic dissemination. Their affair seems to have been emotionally and linguistically seminal rather than a transaction involving an "ejaculation of semen within the natural female organ" (U 17: 2283–4). Language inaugurates an irruption of libidinal desire, a diffusion of sensual titillation through the infinitely deferred resonance of a haunting, unsatisfied dream. Bound together in a piquant discourse of amorous longing, the couple has left a gap in experience, creating a phallic wound of ever-living doubt that will, through a reversal (and triangulation) of metaphorical insemination, penetrate and impregnate the womb of Richard's own artistic imagination. Their collusion has freed him, in fantasy if not in fact, from the tedious fears of conjugal possessiveness. Refusing to covet the woman who would be his wife, Richard embraces the restlessness of emotional doubt in lieu of a socially sanctioned bond of law.

By ending the play on a note of paradox, Joyce fails to conclude his drama with the kind of traditional climax anticipated by Aristotelian poetics. He remarks in his notes: "The doubt which clouds the end of the play must be conveyed to the audience not only through Richard's questions to both but also from the dialogue between Robert and Bertha" (E 125). In a drama that deals prominently with the issue of libidinal desire, Joyce titillates his spectator but denies him/her the satisfaction of climactic release. The audience may feel a distinct sense of frustration at this teasing game of authorial manipulation. But, as Joyce would remind us, "doubt is the thing. Life is suspended in doubt like the world in the void. You might find this in some sense treated in Exiles (JJ 557).[23] In his notes for the play, Joyce declares: "All believe that Bertha is Robert's mistress. This belief rubs against his own knowledge of what has been, but he accepts the belief as a bitter food" (E 123). Although Robert chooses to leave Dublin, he evidently does not flee out of guilt or adulterous shame. He acquires the name of Don Giovanni without the gains of physical possession and accepts the salt bread of Dantesque exile as bitter, but inevitable fare. He has, perhaps, tasted the fruits of Eden without consuming the apple whole.[24]

Ultimately, the text of Exiles confounds us with the inevitable confluence of art and life. "You dreamed that I was yours last night," Bertha tells Robert (*E* 106). But what, finally, is the distinction between reality and dream? How much of human experience is real, and how much is a fictional projection of the creative imagination? Love, like art, largely transpires as a waking dream, a fabulation of subjective consciousness. Each individual tends to elevate sexual experience to the status of legend or myth, as the lover invariably weaves the fabric of erotic consummation on the warp and woof of private romantic narrative.

In a play filled with enigmas, Robert's confession of the truth to Richard suggests still further ambiguities. "I failed," Robert avers. "She is yours, as she was nine years ago, when you met her first" (*E* 107). Robert insists that Bertha refused to yield to his entreaties and that he spent an evening of anxious peregrination culminating in a fly-by-night love affair, a "death of the spirit" with an unknown lady in a cab. It is perhaps telling that the stage-directions at this point call for a fishwoman crying "Dublin bay herrings!" (*E* 107). Joyce, in his usual punning manner, may be mocking Robert by implying something fishy about his alibi. The tale Robert narrates could be meant to function as a red herring in this convoluted maze of love and betrayal. Doubt is piled upon doubt, as Richard protests that he will never know the truth about the liaison – "Never in this world" (*E* 102). He hears demonic voices counseling him to despair, despite Robert's assurance that Bertha is still as faithful to Richard as she was nine years earlier. His assertion is deliberately ambiguous. Could Bertha have deceived Richard almost a decade ago, when the three first met? Is Archie, perhaps, Robert's son? "If he were mine," Robert sighs, and identifies himself as Archie's "fairy godfather" (*E* 110).[25]

Despite the accumulation of doubt and ambiguity in *Exiles*, one thing emerges clearly and remains constant throughout the drama – Bertha's powerful and enduring love for Richard. "I have been true to you," she vows. "Last night and always" (*E* 110). "Surely you believe me. I gave you myself – all. I gave up all for you. You took me – and you left me" (*E* 111). Spiritually abandoned during their exile in Rome, Bertha has cherished a living memory of their youthful courtship and its passionate consummation. Like Molly Bloom, she nightly resurrects a life-sustaining vision of her husband in the guise of ardent suitor: "Not a day passes that I do not see ourselves, you and me, as we were when we met first. Every day of my life I see that. Was I not true to you all that time?" (*E* 111).

Bertha, the bride faithful in exile, appeals to her errant spouse in a gesture of profound tenderness and solicitude. By piercing her lover with the phallic weapon of triangulated desire, she inaugurates an ongoing quest for the elusive psychic gratifications of wholeness and self-presence associated with the Lacanian other. Richard, like Stephen's Shakespeare, has suffered "a deep wound of doubt" which can never be healed. "I do not wish to know or to believe," he insists. "I do not care. It is not in the darkness of belief that I desire you. But in restless living wounding doubt. To hold you by no bonds, even of love, to be united with you in body and soul in utter nakedness" (*E* 112). In some sense, Richard is playing Freud's *Fort/Da* game with his common-law wife. By making her disappear as a conjugal possession, he can call her back, inscribed as an object of desire, in the realm of the symbolic order. Through an ostensibly sacrificial gesture, Richard lays claim to the language and mastery of the Father, while Bertha functions as a mystified (M)Other figure whose possible loss engenders an imaginary fissure perpetually sutured through aesthetic fantasy.[26]

The wound itself will nourish the imagination of a writer who takes masochistic pleasure in the luminosity of doubt and proudly internalizes the pain of abjection. "The tusk of the boar has wounded him there where love lies ableeding. . . . There is . . . some goad of the flesh driving him into a new passion, a darker shadow of the first, darkening even his own understanding of himself" (*U* 9: 459–64). The certainty of either love or hate would be disastrous for Rowan the artist, who feels that he must nurture a "living, wounding doubt" as a spur to creativity. The gap in Joyce's aesthetic theory is deducible from the symbolic fissure that insinuates itself like a grain of sand into the oyster-shell of poetic vulnerability, or like the seminal influence that must impregnate the "virgin womb of the [artistic] imagination" (*P* 217). Penetrated by the sudden impact of jealousy, the writer's mind recoils from emotional pain and continually rehearses the traumatic event until trauma has been mastered in the realm of fabulation. Kinesis inaugurates those flights of restless fantasy that impel the insecure artist/lover to conjure alternative fictional worlds.[27]

Richard's infamous wound in *Exiles* metaphorically invaginates his tormented creative consciousness. A perpetual stranger in the home he once knew, he choreographs an uncanny (*unheimlich*) project to detach himself from the umbilical cord of amorous need that links him, like a dependent child or a powerless embryo, to hidden and inaccessible female genital spaces. The cut in his psyche enables him to cut free. Traumatized by the threat of infidelity and conjugal loss, he gives birth in his head to an idealized image of the beloved and continually possesses her anew in the pain of doubt that will undoubtedly hurt him into poetry. Rejecting his *inamorata* as a sexual possession, he embraces her as a mystical figure of coherence and plenitude always-already denied – and thus sought after and pined for until longing erupts in artistic couvade. The emotional scar inaugurated by Richard's sacrificial renunciation of Bertha will be replicated over and over again in his turbulent imagination, as the disruptions of frustrated libidinal desire spur the insecure artist to compensatory acts of parthenogenetic creation.[28]

At the conclusion of *Exiles*, Bertha, the mother/muse of Joyce's drama, has successfully given birth to the artistic hero who will return to her in the role of primordial lover. Asserting the irrepressible dignity of her nature, she draws her spouse into the fluidity of female desire and into the semiotic rhythms of unconsummated passion that burst forth in explosive discharges of creative energy.[29] As in all his later works, Joyce gives the last word in *Exiles* to a woman. Bertha offers Richard a tantalizing invitation to resurrection and emotional renewal so that, together, the couple might strive for, but never fully achieve, a prelapsarian (and wholly imaginary) experience of transcendent *jouissance*.[30] "Forget me, Dick," Bertha pleads. "Forget me and love me again as you did the first time. I want my lover. To meet him, to go to him, to give myself to him. You, Dick. O, my strange wild lover, come back to me again!" (*E* 112).[31]

4

UNCOUPLING *ULYSSES*
Joyce's New Womanly Man

There is only desire and the social, and nothing else.
(Deleuze and Guattari, *Anti-Oedipus*)

The unconscious ceases to be what it is – a factory,
a workshop – to become a theater, a scene and its
staging.   (ibid.)

In *Ulysses*, Joyce depicts an epic hero who is also a pacifist, a Jew,
a *petit bourgeois* businessman, a commercial traveler, a voyeur, an
exhibitionist, and an ostensibly inadequate husband. Because
psychological positions are mobile and transferable in the landscape
of the novel, Leopold Bloom is alternately powerful and obsequious,
feminized and flagellated, politically exalted and socially humiliated.
He emerges as a "new womanly man" and unconventional hero
who seems, paradoxically, to inhabit those marginal spaces on the
edge of social discourse usually reserved for women and for cultural
deviants.

A connoisseur of the sensuous joys of polymorphous perversity,
Bloom proves to be androgynous not only in terms of psychological
temperament but in libidinal orientation, as well. He apparently
retrieves the primordial erotic impulses rejected by Freud in *Civilization and its Discontents* – those primitive olfactory and tactile
responses that the father of psychoanalysis ascribed somewhat
speciously to the female of the species, in contrast to the supposedly
visual and oculocentric sexual economy associated with the male.[1]
Bloom manifests a curious infantile "cloacal obsession" with
excrementa cast off by the body. He smells the pickings of his toe-
nails, relishes the tang of urine in a fried pork kidney, and is
obsessively preoccupied with menstrual excrescences. The Lacanian
phallus is displaced in his symbolic imagination by a fetishistic
concern with breasts and bottoms, feces, menses, urine, and other
physical secretions. Throughout *Ulysses*, "Baby Bloom" finds
himself tantalized by purportedly feminine pulsions that replicate
infantile attachment to the imaginary body of a beneficent and

106

powerful phallic mother: "Be near her ample bedwarmed flesh. Yes, yes" (*U* 4: 238–9). "A warm human plumpness settled down on his brain. . . . Perfume of embraces all him assailed. With hungered flesh obscurely, he mutely craved to adore" (*U* 8: 647–9).

Throughout the novel, most of the female characters take shape as vivid projections of Bloom's richly heterogeneous fantasy life. They are inscribed in his imagination as figures of physical need or sado-masochistic impulse, visceral pity or sensuous attraction. Despite the epicene aspects of his sexual proclivities, Bloom tends to assess women in his environment as amorous objects stoking playful vignettes of the dreaming mind. His farraginous interior monologue offers a penti-mento portrait of Irish society that includes such diverse sources of titillation as the next-door girl with a strong pair of arms and "crooked skirt swinging, whack by whack . . . behind her moving hams" (*U* 4: 164, 172) and a well-dressed lady, gloved and booted, haughtily mounting a carriage in front of the Grosvenor: "Watch! Watch! Silk flash rich stockings white. Watch!" (*U* 5: 130). In a moment of voyeuristic fantasy, Bloom speculates: "Women all for caste till you touch the spot. . . . Possess her once take the starch out of her" (*U* 5: 104–6). He admires Amazonian females like Lady Mountcashel: "Riding astride. Sit her horse like a man. Weightcarry-ing huntress. . . . Strong as a brood mare some of those horsey women" (*U* 8: 343–5); and like Mrs Miriam Dandrade "that sold me her old wraps and black underclothes in the Shelbourne hotel. Divorced Spanish American. . . . Want to be a bull for her. Born courtesan" (*U* 8: 350–7). Women excite or repel him, tease or titillate him; but all of their figurations suggest that in the course of *Ulysses*, Bloom is rewriting the text of turn-of-the-century sex-role enculturation in the discourse of polymorphously perverse desire.

In the persona of Henry Flower, Esquire, Bloom conducts a clandestine epistolary affair with Martha Clifford, a lonely and pathetic working-girl who pines for release from the prison of dreary secretarial duties. Martha complains of boredom and headaches, longs to consummate this illicit liaison with her would-be lover, and takes curious pleasure in his obscene communications. But, like the virtuous Edwardian lady she was raised to be, Martha protests, "I called you naughty boy because I do not like that other world" (*U* 5: 244–5). Too exhausted and bleary-eyed to correct her typographical error, Martha fails to recognize the contradictions implicit in her quest for the "real meaning of that word" she does not like. She assures Henry: "I have never felt myself so much drawn to a man as you. . . . O how I long to meet you. Henry dear, do not deny my request before my patience are exhausted. Then I will tell you all" (*U* 5: 249 – 54). Martha tantalizes her penfriend with promises of forbidden sexual discourse, but her patience and confidence have, indeed, been misplaced in the cautious married man she unwittingly tries to seduce. Bloom, despite a professed interest in social justice, attributes her depression and physical discomfort to menstrual malady rather than situational angst: "Such a bad headache. Has her roses probably" (*U* 5: 285). In "Lotus-Eaters," a chapter of flowers, the exhausted Martha is too busy earning her bread to be greatly concerned about the roses denied her – though she does, apparently, take some kind of masochistic pleasure from the thorns of Bloom's pornographic letters designed to pique erotic curiosity.

In the "Nausicaa" episode, Bloom responds to Gerty MacDowell's sentimental strip-tease with a kind of Zola-esque naturalism. Aroused by her tantalizing display of exhibitionism, he gives the young woman the impression that his strange "dark eyes" are "drinking in her every contour, literally worshipping at her shrine" (*U* 13: 563 – 4). With a little help from Maria Susanna Cummins's *Lamplighter*, Gerty romanticizes this exotic stranger, sanitizes his masturbation, and idealizes his worshipful attentions. As Virgin Mary of Sandymount, she invites the tribute of Bloom's profane ejaculations, reinscribed in adolescent consciousness by that "dream of love, the dictates of her heart that told her he was her all in all, the only man in the world for her for love was the master guide" (*U* 13: 671 – 2).[2]

This "sterling man, a man of inflexible honour to his fingertips" (*U* 13: 694) evaluates the scene with the same phenomenological accuracy one might associate with the comic caricature of Herr Professor Luitpold Blumenduft in "Cyclops": "Near her monthlies, I expect, makes them feel ticklish. . . . How many women in Dublin have it today? Martha, she. . . . Anyhow I got the best of that. . . . Thankful for small mercies. Cheap too. Yours for the asking. Because they want it themselves" (*U* 13: 777 – 90). Bloom's matter-of-fact interpretation of his onanistic encounter with Gerty is fairly mechanical: "My fireworks. Up like a rocket, down like a stick" (*U* 13: 894 – 5). His response may seem self-serving, if not brutal: "Did me good all the same. . . . For this relief much thanks"

(*U* 13: 939–40). But his post-orgasmic thoughts about Gerty are also imbued with feelings of pity and tinged with paternal solicitude. Stunned by his recognition of her lameness, Bloom thinks: "Poor girl! That's why she's left on the shelf and the others did a sprint" (*U* 13: 772–3). He feels grateful to Gerty for reaffirming his sense of manhood and acknowledges that their erotic adventure involved some form of mutuality and communication, "a kind of language between us" (*U* 13: 944).

Bloom sees in this postpubescent girl a figure of his own developing daughter Milly, whom he tenderly recalls in nostalgic reverie now that she has left home for an apprenticeship in photography down in Mullingar and is about to burgeon into a "wild piece of goods": "O, well: she knows how to mind herself. But if not? No, nothing has happened. Of course it might. . . . Ripening now. Vain: very" (*U* 4: 428–31). He remembers Milly's childhood fear of being deserted and the terror she experienced at the first bloody sign of womanly/wombly maturation: "Her growing pains at night, calling, wakening me. Frightened she was when her nature came on her first. Poor child! Strange moment for the mother too" (*U* 13: 1201–3). Just as Molly will later think through Stephen to Bloom, so the husband moves from the incident with Gerty to memories of female fragility and his daughter's growing-pains and finally to that ever-present object of sexual desire dominating his obsessed imagination, the fascinating but elusive figure of Mother-Molly.

The majority of Bloom's reveries about sexual difference seem to circle around reproductive potential, and both mammary endowments and fleshly opulence are high on his list of sex-linked preoccupations. Hence his fascination with Molly's ponderous female bulk as he stares at "her large soft bubs, sloping within her nightdress like a shegoat's udder" (*U* 4: 304–5). Much of Bloom's attention is obliquely focused on imaginary projections of an idealized maternity which he associates with the female body/breast/womb/genitalia. Although he can crassly reduce women to figures of oral, genital, and anal absence ("Three holes, all women" [*U* 11: 1089]), he is the only male in the novel to empathize with "poor Mrs Purefoy" in the throes of a painful *accouchement*: "Three days imagine groaning on a bed with a vinegared handkerchief round her forehead, her belly swollen out. Phew! Dreadful simply! . . . Kill me that would. . . . Life with hard labour" (*U* 8: 373–8). Bloom can imagine the pain of parturition in a vivid evocation of the obstetrical labors of women, and his fantasies later collapse into a dream of masculine couvade. "I so want to be a mother," he declares in "Circe," then metaphorically *"bears eight male yellow and white children . . . handsome, with valuable metallic faces"* (*U* 15: 1817–24). Apparently, Bloom tends to fear what he most desires: woman as mother and fertile creator, the figure of matriarchal power that he tacitly worships in Molly and concretizes in his expressionistic encounter with Bella/Bello the Circean circus-master.

When sex-roles are tested on the stage of language, as they are in "Circe," gender-linked scripts prove absurdly intransigent. Bloom's deepest and most repressed fears erupt in dramatic fantasies of erotic compulsion and sexual loathing in Bella Cohen's ten-shilling whorehouse. Power relations, culturally inscribed in Edwardian consciousness, remain surprisingly stable, as phallocentric authority passes from male to female in a transvestite drama that parodies the psychosexual scripts that dominate 1904 Dublin. Even the "new womanly man" acting out the feminine vulnerability of his epicene nature gives voice to iterations of female helplessness, subservience, and sexual humiliation.[3]

It is only within the heterogeneous representation of Bloom's masculine-feminine, active-passive character that gender identity becomes dynamic and reversible. As Shoshana Felman explains: "Masculinity is not a substance, nor is femininity its empty complement, a *heimlich* womb. . . . Femininity *inhabits* masculinity, inhabits it as otherness, as its own *disruption*. Femininity, in other words, is a pure difference, a signifier, and so is masculinity."[4] In the expressionistic world of "Circe," Joyce explores that specular icon of feminine gender that inhabits the male cultural imagination. Bella/Bello Cohen, as fetishistic embodiment of the phallic mother, serves as a screen image for Bloom's projected fantasy of his own somewhat willful and tyrannical spouse. He himself is transformed into a woman and then into a pig through a "substitutive signifying chain which subverts . . . the clear-cut polarity, the symmetrical dual opposition, of male and female, masculine and feminine."[5] As Daniel Ferrer observes, "Bloom's masochistic phantasy paradoxically takes the form of a kind of breaking-in of Bella/Bello: the masculinization of the dominating woman is quite as important as the pseudo-feminization of the victim. The game is double-edged."[6]

What is in question in the "Circe" episode is Leopold Bloom's culturally constructed manhood and the phallic signifier that affirms or denies his status as male/father/husband in a twentieth-century Oedipal configuration – the "Daddy-Mommy-Me" triangle defined by Deleuze and Guattari in *Anti-Oedipus* and replicated in religious trinitarian models. In the course of the chapter, Bloom temporarily adopts a schizoid position characterized, in Deleuzian terms, by libidinal viscosity: "flows ooze, they traverse the triangle, breaking apart its vertices."[7] Exploring repressed bisexual drives that challenge traditional domestic arrangements, Bloom moves in and out of the restrictive frame of reproductive triangulation dictated by culturally inscribed paradigms of masculine sexuality. The chapter offers a plurality of signs confirming Bloom's psychological androgyny. He is first male, then female; and, finally, at the "Bip" of a trouser button, he regains his precarious sense of Oedipal identity.

The primordial sign of Bloom's maleness, his phallus, is first symbolically present, then absent in a game of sexual metamorphosis and phallic veiling that entails both cross-dressing and imaginary genital transformation. Bloom is symbolically castrated by Bello, the imperious semitic circus-master who, as priestess of a Levitican sacrifice mimicking exaggerated circumcision, "debags" her timid victim.[8] In Circean fashion, she porcines the obsequious male who admits to being a secret "adorer of the adulterous rump" (*U* 15: 2839). A pagan devotee and worshipper of the voluptuous female body, Bloom admires precisely those aspects of physical form that Molly scorns as impersonal features of animal passivity, the "same two lumps of lard" that fail to confirm personal attractiveness.

The phallic icon of Bloom's socially sanctioned manhood is present in the mode of absence as he acts out a bizarre trans-sexual metempsychosis. Paradoxically, when the prominent signifiers of Bloom's epicene personality – his sympathy, gentleness, vulnerability, and solicitude – are reinscribed in an ostensibly female register, they are radically transformed in the context of cultural interpretation. With Bloom's metamorphosis into a woman, his compassion and gentleness give way to masochistic subservience. Although this modern-day Odysseus is recognizably androgynous, his most sympathetic and endearing qualities take on absurd dramatic resonance when the ground of gender changes from male to female. What is admirable in the emotionally bisexual male becomes a sign of debilitating weakness on the part of a defenseless, quaking "womanly woman" exploited by the "manly man" of Victorian pornography. Bella/Bello has leapt from the pages of Frank Harris, of Huysmans's *A Rebours*, and of titillating texts like Sacher-Masoch's *Venus in Furs* to perpetrate lascivious acts of brutality on Poldy's feminized body.[9] Hence Bloom's ignominious fall from manhood when Bello orders:

> Down! (*he taps her on the shoulder with his fan*) Incline feet forward! Slide left foot one pace back! You will fall. . . . On the hands down!

BLOOM

(*her eyes upturned in the sign of admiration, closing, yaps*) Truffles!
(*With a piercing epileptic cry she sinks on all fours, grunting, snuffling, rooting at his feet: then lies, shamming dead, with eyes shut tight, trembling eyelids, bowed upon the ground in the attitude of most excellent master.*)

BELLO

(*with bobbed hair, purple gills, fat moustache rings round his shaven mouth, in mountaineer's puttees, green silverbuttoned coat, sport skirt and alpine hat with moorcock's feather, his hands stuck deep in his breeches pockets, places his heel on her neck and grinds it in*) Footstool! Feel my entire weight. Bow, bondslave, before the throne of your despot's glorious heels so glistening in their proud erectness.

BLOOM

(*enthralled, bleats*) I promise never to disobey. (*U* 15: 2847–64)

Joyce seems to be suggesting, like Deleuze and Guattari, that cultural laws of gender are constant insofar as they are manifest in contemporary social representation. The whoremistress acquires all the accoutrements of imperialistic power as soon as she dons male trousers and sprouts a moustache. As ringmaster and tyrannous phallic mother, Bella/Bello demeans, humiliates, and tortures her obsequious victim. A battered Bloom succumbs to ritual degradation and becomes the ham-holocaust to be slaughtered and skewered, then served up as "fat hamrashers" (*U* 15: 2896) in a sumptuous, non-kosher cannibalistic feast. Both Amazonian woman and effeminate male, enacting transvestite and trans-sexual roles of Edwardian pantomime, are inscribed in a melodrama of sado-masochistic catharsis.[10]

Bloom has given birth to the figure of Bello in his own tortured imagination, projecting his psychic need for punishment into the powerful *imago* of a manly woman, a carnivalesque embellishment of his generally supine spouse. Bella/Bello plays on Bloom's guilt and conjugal inadequacy – irrational responses evoked by his paternal failure to engender a viable male heir. "If it's healthy it's from the mother," he thinks. "If not from the man" (*U* 6: 329). Cross-dressing offers a mode of phallic veiling, a cover for his repressed sense of genital mutilation. If the child Rudy is metaphorically represented as a surrogate penis in Bloom's sexual imagination, then the grieving father must continually be punished for his son's death through psychological enactments of symbolic castration. Freud emphasizes in *The Interpretation of Dreams* the interchangeability of paternal and filial positions in the language of the unconscious. Having sired a son who was unable to survive, Bloom mentally changes places with the neonate and expresses his horror of filial loss through emotional rejection of phallic power. He internalizes both the guilt elicited by poor papa's suicide and the pain of little Rudy's death. Father, child, and phallus occupy the same psychological position in Bloom's unconscious, and all have become pathological symptoms of loss and bereavement.

The impotent Bloom, sonless and fatherless, is defined in terms of phallic lack: having nothing (but a daughter) to show for a lifetime of heterosexual engagement, he reverts to passive, homosexual, or feminized subject-positions that demand a posture of phallic subjugation. Unmanned by a socially defined pathology of male shame and sexual inadequacy, he adopts an ostensibly feminine persona. If "all is lost" in terms of traditional Oedipal triangulation, then the only hope of escape from psychic breakdown resides in the schizoid position of mental flow, process, viscosity, and disruption – a chaotic metamorphosis of shifting sexual identities enacted on the discursive stage of Circean pantomime.[11]

At this point in the carnivalesque fantasy, tropes are reified, and signifiers of sex and gender prove absurdly interchangeable. The swinish behavior of lascivious males is mythically hypostasized, first by allusion to the Homeric narrative of Circe the evil temptress, then in a Joycean expressionistic drama that allows Bloom to realize his most shameful, anarchic, and deeply repressed libidinal drives. The text of Joyce's pantomime reinforces those fetishistic signs attributed by the unconscious to the omnipotent phallic mother –

an imperious female who sporadically offers nurturance but enjoys, at the same time, invidious power to demean, de-sex, and castrate the defenseless male. The phallic sign of masculine identity, once subverted or repressed, releases a flood of male fantasies depicted by the psyche in female guise. Traditional signs of gender-related authority seem indelibly inscribed on twentieth-century cultural consciousness, albeit in atavistic form.

In her male incarnation, Bella/Bello becomes authoritarian and violently sadistic, torturing Bloom to the point of absolute alterity. He is other, *"l'autre"* – first trembling in shame before his masterful captor, then enslaved to her dictates, and finally derided as a "maid of all work" trained to "fetch and carry" (*U* 15: 3086–8) in the chaotic bordello of Joyce's fictive imagination. As soon as Bloom's gender changes from male to female, his androgynous attributes are deracinated from their masculine context and conflated with cultural stereotypes of feminine fragility. The new womanly man is reduced to the archaic subject-position of powerless womanly woman, as the female aspects of bisexual desire erupt in comic mockery. Compassion degenerates into impotence, androgyny into transvestite humiliation. The dramatic text is uprooted from realistic mimesis, and expressionistic drama gives rise to jubilant *écriture*. The narrative explodes in a riot of cathartic comedy, as "Circe" enunciates the polyphonic novel's "underlying unconscious: sexuality and death. Out of the dialogue . . . the structural dyads of carnival appear: high and low, birth and agony, food and excrement, praise and curses, laughter and tears."[12] The poles of Joyce's dialogic imagination prove to be those of Bakhtin's carnival, as desire, unrestrained, flows through the schizoid gap between binary oppositional constructs: subject/object, male/female, death/birth, excrement/nurture, blood/milk.

In his/her female incarnation, Poldy/Paula manifests all the signs of feminine gender dictated by the ritual inscriptions of sex-role stereotypes. S/he colludes in his/her own victimization by meeting the erotic demands of the prostitutes and consenting to sado-masochistic practices. "O, it's hell itself!" (*U* 15: 2908) screams L. Paula Bloom, who nevertheless allows gestures of physical defilement to be perpetrated on his/her effeminate flesh by Bello, Zoe, Florry, and the bordello cook, Mrs Keogh. Bowing at the feet of Bello, Bloom acknowledges his/her authority as "Master! Mistress! Mantamer!" (*U* 15: 3062). Auctioned off to the highest bidder, s/he undergoes various animal metamorphoses as horse, cow, and chicken: "Four-teen hands high. Touch and examine shis points. Handle hrim. This downy skin, these soft muscles, this tender flesh. If I had only my gold piercer here! And quite easy to milk. Three newlaid gallons a day" (*U* 15: 3103 – 5). The defenseless Bloom is forced to give milk and lay eggs in agricultural postures that parody his/her mammary obsession and henpecked connubial role.[13]

It is clear from role-reversals in "Circe" that, in terms of cultural representation, female gender confers parodic marginality. Woman seems destined to play the part of *l'autre*, alienated other in the specular projections of the male libidinal imagination. When Bloom is auctioned by Bello in a satirical rendition of the bourgeois marriage market, his feminized genitalia become literal objects of commercial exchange. Feminine sexuality, represented as a hole or Freudian absence, absorbs a plethora of masculine fantasies that fill the castrated signature envisaged at the heart of female identity. Bello "*bares his arm and plunges it elbowdeep in Bloom's vulva*," exclaiming "There's fine depth for you!" (*U* 15: 3089 – 90) in mock imitation of heterosexual penetration and homosexual fisting. The victim's genitals are visibly mutilated as indelible signs of woman's enslavement to male phallocentric desire. "That give you a hardon?" (*U* 15: 3090) Bello inquires. Then s/he orders: "Let them all come. . . . Bring all your powers of fascination to bear on them. Pander to their Gomorrahan vices" (*U* 15: 3114 – 22). Bello savagely violates the vaginal hole denied the wholeness of sexual integrity. Every female orifice, it would appear, is for sale and on display; every hole can be purchased, raped, or penetrated for the purpose of phallic satisfaction.[14] And a good woman, raped, knows, like the disgraced cuckold, what to do: "Die and be damned to you if you have any sense of decency or grace about you" (*U* 15: 3204 – 5). In this expressionistic battle of the sexes, the power of an imaginary phallic mother manifests itself as monstrous and obscene. As textual icon of matriarchal authority, Bello assumes the right to debase and colonize Bloom's vulnerable, objectified, mock-female body.

As woman/Jew/victim, the hapless Poldy is reduced to little more than a cipher of racial and sexual oppression. The male/female drama of courtship and conquest unfolds as an age-old atavistic tale:

Woman, undoing with sweet pudor her belt of rushrope, offers
her allmoist yoni to man's lingam. Short time after man presents
woman with pieces of jungle meat. Woman shows joy and covers
herself with featherskins. Man loves her yoni fiercely with big
lingam, the stiff one. (*he cries*) *Coactus volui*. Then giddy woman
will run about. Strong man grapses woman's wrist. Woman
squeals, bites, spucks. Man, now fierce angry, strikes woman's
fat yadgana. (*U* 15: 2549 – 55)

This primitive tableau of meat and mating, of giddy flirtation and
animal friction, pornographically climaxes in sexual violence.
Brutality inhabits the underside of romantic courtship, and if the
playmate of this behemoth lover dares to arouse his lust, she must
suffer the consequences of bestial cupidity.

When Bloom is transformed into a woman by Bella/Bello, he loses
his dignity along with the accoutrements of masculine pride. The
repressed feminine tendencies of this heroic androgyne erupt in a
ludic play of erotic madness. The bellicose matriarchal figure, usur-
ping the male role that Poldy is hesitant to enact, becomes a
nightmare fantasy of the stereotypical virago – a phallic mother
invested with all the privileges of uninhibited patriarchal authority.
The semiology of gender remains unchanged, as various *dramatis
personae* appear in transvestite or trans-sexual guises. Even the
comedy of language cannot alter the binary codes of gender or the
deeply embedded sex-roles inscribed in societal consciousness. The
text seems to evoke the pervasive cultural fear that woman, granted
phallic authority, would persecute her mate with unbridled ferocity;
and that man, bereft of the kind of patriarchal power that buttresses
an illusory sense of dominance and mastery, would sink helplessly
into sexual degradation.

BELLO

What else are you good for, an impotent thing like you? . . .
Up! Up! Manx cat! What have we here? Where's your curly
teapot gone to or who docked it on you, cockyolly? Sing, birdy,
sing. It's as limp as a boy of six's doing his pooly behind a cart.
Buy a bucket or sell your pump. . . . Can you do a man's job?
(*U* 15: 3127 – 32)

When sex-roles are again comically reversed, a feminized Bella
plays the saccharine part of an ethereal nymph who incarnates the

Edwardian womanly ideal – an icon of grace and reverence, unsullied by either food or feces. "We immortals," proclaims the nymph, "have not such a place and no hair there either. We are stonecold and pure. We eat electric light" (*U* 15: 3392–3). This self-glorified, asexual image of the female is no more attractive than her opposite narrative number, Bello the sadistic ringmaster. "You have broken the spell," Bloom insists. "The last straw. If there were only ethereal where would you all be, postulants and novices? Shy but willing like an ass pissing" (*U* 15: 3449–51). Because sexual violence contaminates both ethereal and aggressive icons, the mirror image of Bloom's virginal seductress is a demonic succubus intent on castration. The saintly sprite, offended by Bloom's erotic indictment, grabs a poniard and strikes at his loins, then "*flees from him unveiled, her plaster cast cracking, a cloud of stench escaping from the cracks*" (*U* 15: 3469–70). Recognizing the antagonistic Bello emerging from angelic disguise, Bloom mimics abusive phallic authority and insults the transvestite (or hermaphroditic) impersonator: "Fool someone else, not me. . . . Rut. Onions. Stale. Sulphur. Grease. . . . Mutton dressed as lamb. . . . I'm not a triple screw propeller. . . . Clean your nailless middle finger first, your bully's cold spunk is dripping from your cockscomb" (*U* 15: 3477–93).

Joyce's polytropic man soon relinquishes this ill-fitting role of brutal *machismo* when he witnesses a dramatic enactment of his wife's seduction by that Dublin Don Giovanni, Blazes Boylan. Here the "coronado" [*cornuto*] husband wears a visible signature of cuckoldry, the antlered hat-rack of conjugal infamy.[15] He serves as eager flunkey to Molly's suitor, whose penile equipment is ostentatiously on show:

BOYLAN
(*to Bloom, over his shoulder*) You can apply your eye to the keyhole and play with yourself while I just go through her a few times.

BLOOM
Thank you, sir. I will, sir. May I bring two men chums to witness the deed and take a snapshot? (*he holds out an ointment jar*) Vaseline, sir? Orangeflower . . .? Lukewarm water. . .?

KITTY
(*from the sofa*) Tell us, Florry. Tell us. What . . .
(*Florry whispers to her. Whispering lovewords murmur, liplapping loudly, poppysmic plopslop.*)

MINA KENNEDY

(*her eyes upturned*) O, it must be like the scent of geraniums and lovely peaches! O, he simply idolises every bit of her! Stuck together! Covered with kisses!

LYDIA DOUCE

(*her mouth opening*) Yumyum, O, he's carrying her round the room doing it! Ride a cockhorse. You could hear them in Paris and New York. Like mouthfuls of strawberries and cream.

KITTY

(*laughing*) Hee hee hee.

BOYLAN'S VOICE

(*sweetly, hoarsely, in the pit of his stomach*) Ah! Godblazegruk-brukarchkhrasht!

MARION'S VOICE

(*hoarsely, sweetly, rising to her throat*) O! Weeshwashtkissinapooisthnapoohuck? (*U* 15: 3788–813)

Bloom's gaze is transfixed before the scene of ritual conquest, as he yells locker-room cheers through the keyhole and urges his sexual surrogate to prodigious heights of erotic performance: "(*his eyes wildly dilated, clasps himself*) Show! Hide! Show! Plough her! More! Shoot!" (*U* 15: 3815–16).

The presence-absence of Boylan's ithyphallic member signifies for the excited onlooker both masochistic humiliation and scopophiliac *jouissance*. In this outrageous enactment of caricatured cuckoldry, the timorous Bloom relives the pain of conjugal loss in the mode of voyeuristic farce. He mentally panders to the lascivious Boylan, whose virility signifies the kind of erotic potency glaringly absent from Bloom's own sexual relations with his wife. Participating as flunkey at the scene of Molly's infidelity, Bloom self-consciously reinterprets the signs of connubial disruption from the privileged perspective of dramatic choreographer. Acting as technical director of the comedy, he symbolically sutures the wound of cuckoldry by dramatizing marital transgression in the stylized frame of a turn-of-the-century peepshow. The seriously embattled scenario of *Exiles* is here replayed as *Commedia del'Arte*.

Like a clownish rendition of Richard Rowan, Bloom revises the text of his wife's adultery in a grotesque fantasy that resembles

French farce, not to mention the titillating fabulations of Victorian pornography embodied in *Sweets of Sin*. By imaginatively colluding in the subversion of marital stability, by up-ending traditional expectations and putting his own phallic powers deliberately under erasure, Bloom participates in the carnivalesque comedy not as unwitting victim, but as the author/actor/director of this play of infidelity. Through the dual role of playwright and spectator, he is able, like Sacher-Masoch's fictive Severin, to reduce his ignominious situation to an absurdly masochistic drama. In the course of "Circe," Bloom becomes author and reader of his own domestic narrative, gaining artistic control over emotional trauma by re-creating the dread event in exaggerated detail on the stage of a highly charged erotic (and perverse) imagination.[16]

A projection of deeply embedded guilt, this preposterous dramatic fantasy offers Bloom the gratifications of both aesthetic mastery and psychological catharsis. In the dreamscape of "Circe," Bloom doffs the culturally inscribed role of irate cuckold to wear the costume of flunkey; but, like a dramatist who plays the Fool in a script of his own making, he asserts authorial primacy as godlike director of the scene. As playwright and participant, Bloom witnesses his wife's afternoon tryst from the standpoint of God, Shakespeare, and scopophiliac voyeur. He imitates that picaresque "playwright who wrote the folio of this world and wrote it badly, . . . the lord of things as they are," the hangman-god who "is doubtless all in all in all of us, ostler and butcher, and would be bawd and cuckold too but that in the economy of heaven, foretold by Hamlet, there are no more marriages, glorified man, an androgynous angel, being a wife unto himself" (*U* 9: 1047–52). Playing bawd and cuckold onstage, Bloom strives to become in his own imagination a self-sufficient and self-delighting "wife unto himself" by framing his spouse and her lover, gazing at them through a keyhole, and satisfying his own libidinous urges in masturbatory acts of playful postcreation.[17]

In "Circe," Bloom's polymorphous perversity and his masochistic longing for protection/punishment at the hands of a powerful woman have imploded in rich, hallucinatory, and schizoid images. The expressionistic drama depicts Bloom's repressed terror and obsessive fascination with the *imago* of a manly female, a fascistic figure of sensual domination. Libidinal desire gives rise to a polymorphous dissemination of sexual signifiers that destroy the univocal, phallocentric drives of masculinity and articulate deepseated trans-sexual fantasies embedded in the psyche of Joyce's womanly man. "Circe" evokes what Hélène Cixous delineates as "a proliferating, maternal femininity. A phantasmic meld of men, males, gentlemen, monarchs, princes, orphans, flowers, mothers, breasts gravitates about a wonderful 'sun of energy' . . . that bombards and disintegrates these ephemeral amorous anomalies so that they can be recomposed in other bodies for new passions."[18]

By the end of the "Circe" episode, Bloom has apparently been purged of both guilt and sexual humiliation in an odyssey that resembles Deleuzian schizoanalysis more than Freudian psycho-analysis.[19] Ready to reassert the feminine dimensions of his androgynous personality, he pursues the inebriate Stephen and rescues the nascent poet from the grasp of the Dublin watch, those ubiquitous policemen who signify the abuse of patriarchal power and the illegitimate authority of the threatening Father. At the conclu-sion of the chapter, Stephen lies semi-conscious and battered at the feet of his ersatz spiritual guardian. But the nature of the relation-ship between the two men is highly ambiguous. Is Bloom symbolic-ally assuming the Homeric role of adoptive paternity, as critics have traditionally suggested? Or is he subverting the name and law of the Father in an act that replicates the movements of maternal nurturance and care? It might be argued that Bloom and Stephen come together not in Homeric filiation, but through a shared masculine bond that hinges on their mutual dread of maternal abjec-tion.[20]

Bloom's ostensible reward at the end of "Circe" is a somewhat sentimentalized evocation of the lamb-like and erudite Etonian scholar little Rudy might have become:

BLOOM

(*Communes with the night*) Face reminds me of his poor mother . . .
(*he murmurs*) . . . swear that I will always hail, ever conceal,
never reveal, any part or parts, art or arts . . .
  (*Silent, thoughtful, alert he stands on guard, his fingers at his lips in the attitude of secret master. Against the dark wall a figure appears slowly, a fairy boy of eleven, a changeling, kidnapped, dressed in an Eton suit with glass shoes and a little bronze helmet, holding a book in his hand. He reads from right to left inaudibly, smiling, kissing the page.*)

BLOOM

(*wonderstruck, calls inaudibly*) Rudy!

RUDY

(*gazes, unseeing, into Bloom's eyes and goes on reading, kissing, smiling. He has a delicate mauve face. On his suit he has diamond and ruby buttons. In his free left hand he holds a slim ivory cane with a violet bowknot. A white lambkin peeps out of his waistcoat pocket.*) (*U* 15: 4949–67)

As Cheryl Herr observes, the "highly artificial and bizarrely cross-coded Rudy needs to be understood by reference to the several discourses constituting him," since "the primary frame of reference is the pantomime: Rudy is both silent harlequin and the hero of the twentieth-century panto."[21] Although the text embodies that phallic sign of Bloom's procreative powers, the male child he once engendered, the ghost of his dead son can be resuscitated only in the magical, inchoate fairy-world evoked by the pantomime's Grand Transformation scene. Because of the interchangeability of relational positions in the language of the unconscious, the specter evokes an aching reminiscence of paternal desire and filial loss – a final, enigmatic figure of the disappointed father gazing out through the unseeing eyes of a phantasmal, ever-living son.

In the concluding tableau of "Circe," Bloom the bereft father is coupled with the memory of a lost son in the presence of an adoptive surrogate whom he guards and protects with tender solicitude. But in some sense, Bloom has become more of a *mother* to Stephen than a substitute father. He symbolically supplants the terrifying specter of Mary Dedalus, whose withered hand points a finger of guilt as the ghost-mother counsels repentance and refuses to utter the word of love "known to all men."[22] Turning the Oedipal paradigm inside-out in a gesture of psychic couvade, Bloom enacts his longing for male motherhood through a fantasy that places the (surrogate) father at the origin and center of filial resurrection. Like the poet Mallarmé mourning at the "Tomb of Anatole," he plays out the parthenogenetic roles of both father and mother in a posture of male maternity that Hélène Cixous identifies with the legendary stance of Pygmalion: the "old dream: to be god the mother. The best mother, the second mother, the one who gives the second birth." The "death of the cherished son" gives rise in such cases to a "dream of marriage between father and son. – And there's no mother then."[23]

The conclusion of "Circe" stands the Freudian family romance on its head by amalgamating and shifting subject-positions in the domestic triangle "Daddy-Mommy-Me." Bloom adopts a maternal position *vis-à-vis* Stephen, who slips into an inebriate pose of infantile helplessness and resembles a narcissistic child. Substituting Stephen for Rudy, Bloom establishes a temporary homoerotic alliance with the younger man. Oedipal categories are further confused when, at the end of "Eumaeus," the two go off *"to be married by Father Maher"* *(U* 16: 1887) in a scene that parodies the kind of resolution dictated by conventional fiction.[24]

In a multi-layered, revolutionary narrative, Joyce deliberately subverts the expected codes of Aristotelian denouement. He tantalizes his reader to interpret Bloom's meeting with Stephen through the epic grid of Homer's *Odyssey* as the triumphant reunion of Odysseus and Telemachus. Such a reading, however, ascribes to momentary affiliation the kind of metaphysical meaning undermined by Joyce's richly experimental text. Although Stephen may relate to Bloom with openness and affection, any attempt to identify the older man as transubstantial, consubstantial, or even sub-substantial father founders on the rock of undecidability, since the father/son opposition is itself an Oedipal construct whose essentialist premisses refuse mimetic replication.[25]

The final chapters of Joyce's novel mock what Deleuze and Guattari identify as Oedipal imperialism by proposing an infinite regress of substitutability in the family's sex-stereotyped scripts. If Bloom assumes a maternal subject-position in his friendship with Stephen, he adopts a similar stance in relation to Molly, while simultaneously exacting nurture from his spouse in the role of benevolent phallic mother. The voyage of Bloom/Odysseus leads to Nostos, a nostalgic return to the bed of Mother-Molly and the womb/tomb of both conjugal and filial affection. Bloom goes home in the company of a young man whom he offers as gift to a Penelopean figure who remains for him the symbolic center around which his dreams perpetually circulate. Molly inhabits Bloom's emotional world in the guise of maternal *imago* and Circean seductress – an archetypal projection of male need and erotic demand elevated to the wholeness and plenitude of imaginary (M)Other. "Ithaca" concludes the man's epic (his)story. Leopold Bloom is last seen in mythic motion, *en route* to a "square round Sinbad the Sailor roc's auk's egg in the night of the bed of all the auks of the rocs of Darkinbad the Brightdayler" (*U* 17: 2328 – 30) – in progress toward that enigmatic point of female/maternal origin associated with the mysteries of "bridebed, childbed, bed of death" (*U* 3: 396).

Bloom's polymorphously perverse delight in the comforting, voluptuous presence of Mother-Molly is nostalgic in the root-sense of the Greek word for "return." As Jane Gallop remarks, nostalgia refers to "a regret for a lost past that occurs as a result of a present view of that past moment." The word may connote either the languor of homesickness or the remorse evoked by unsatisfied desire. "Both the principal definitions relate to a return, the first in the wish to return to a place, . . . the second in the wish to return to a time."[26] Bloom obsessively tries to go back to that far-off time of his inaugural love-making with Molly on Howth to reclaim a world and a place of amorous satisfaction, of erotic origins dissociated from the subsequent trauma of filial loss and paternal failure. Warm female flesh signifies a protective matrix of maternal and spousal love that once valorized Baby-Bloom in the position of an integrated subject and sheltered him from the confusions of psychic fragmentation.

The magic of Howth becomes for both Leopold and Molly a central axis for erotic nostalgia and impassioned fantasy. Each psychologically portrays the experience to him/herself in terms of emotional valorization by the other, an ecstatic self-mirroring that replicates the delights of pre-Oedipal bonding. The scene re-presents an imaginary fulfillment of the spiral of identity – a prelapsarian moment of Edenic happiness joyously recollected in Bloomian tableau and later embellished on the myth-making looms of Molly's Penelopean tapestries.

In a reverie framed by two copulating flies, Bloom celebrates those wondrous moments of tactile pleasure and infantile delight:

> Glowing wine on his palate lingered swallowed. Crushing in the winepress grapes of Burgundy. Sun's heat it is. Seems to a secret touch telling me memory. Touched his sense moistened remembered. Hidden under wild ferns on Howth below us bay sleeping: sky. No sound. The sky. The bay purple by the Lion's head. Green by Drumleck. Yellowgreen towards Sutton. Fields of undersea, the lines faint brown in grass, buried cities. Pillowed on my coat she had her hair, earwigs in the heather scrub my hand under her nape, you'll toss me all. O wonder! Coolsoft with ointments her hand touched me, caressed: her eyes upon me

did not turn away. Ravished over her I lay, full lips full open, kissed her mouth. Yum. Softly she gave me in my mouth the seedcake warm and chewed. Mawkish pulp her mouth had mumbled sweetsour of her spittle. Joy: I ate it: joy. Young life, her lips that gave me pouting. Soft warm sticky gumjelly lips. Flowers her eyes were, take me, willing eyes. Pebbles fell. She lay still. A goat. No-one. High on Ben Howth rhododendrons a nannygoat walking surefooted, dropping currants. Screened under ferns she laughed warmfolded. Wildly I lay on her, kissed her: eyes, lips, her stretched neck beating, woman's breasts full in her blouse of nun's veiling, fat nipples upright. Hot I tongued her. She kissed me. I was kissed. All yielding she tossed my hair. Kissed, she kissed me.

  Me. And me now.

  Stuck, the flies buzzed. (*U* 8:897–918)

A glass of burgundy releases a physical memory of the pent-up "secret touch" associated in Bloom's mind with animal heat and bodily moisture, with flowers and defloration, and with an impressionistic riot of sensuous colors swirling around a sundrenched purple bay. In this joyous game of "laugh and lie down," it is Bloom who feels like a vulnerable Adonis ravished by the seductive Venus who lies throbbing and receptive beneath his trembling body. "Flowers her eyes were, take me, willing eyes" (*U* 8: 910). A younger Bloom-self regresses to a mode of infantile pleasure as he tongues "woman's breasts full in her blouse of nun's veiling, fat nipples upright" (*U* 8: 914–15). The perfume of flowers and the taste of food are mingled in the seedcake Molly shares with Bloom, like a mother feeding a child with predigested pablum or a bird nourishing its young: "Softly she gave me in my mouth the seedcake warm and chewed" (*U* 8: 907). The "sweetsour" spittle suggests vaginal secretions, and Molly's "soft warm sticky gumjelly lips" offer a foretaste of the vulval "lips full open" that welcome her excited lover. This ritual exchange of eucharistic seedcake anticipates sexual communion with the mother/lover/wife of Bloom's amorous fantasies.[27] "Wildly I lay on her, kissed her: eyes, lips, her stretched neck beating," Bloom thinks, with a sense of wonder at the emotional pulsations that bring man and woman together in a timeless, rhapsodic embrace. The rhetoric of love proves metaphoric and oxymoronic: "lay" implies a passivity contradicted by the urgency of masculine libidinal drives, which are tempered, in turn, by sentimental feelings of tenderness and care.

In this lyrical reminiscence, Bloom is both ravisher and ravished, Molly both lover and beloved. The repressed romantic sensibilities of the novel erupt in a representation of male/female bonding that imitates, for both partners, the pleasures of pre-Oedipal, oceanic union and captures the reciprocity of ecstatic *jouissance*. The author titillates us with the thrill of sexual arousal, of highly charged emotion and about-to-be-satisfied desire. The actual moment of physical climax, however, is withheld from the scene of writing. Bloom's vivid recollection focuses on the tantalizing joys of foreplay, on anticipatory arousal rather than heterosexual release. In the textual frame before us, two buzzing flies copulate. Molly and Leopold do not (yet) come together – though they are always-already locked in a passionate embrace phantasmatically inscribed in the textual unconscious of Joyce's swirling, circular discursive matrix.

As Christine van Boheemen remarks, "the ideas of *coniunctio*, of communion, of the return to paradise . . . do not just disappear from the consciousness of the text. They are incorporated into the consciousness of the characters as the presence of their absence," so that "the blissful happiness of resolution informs the text as permanent and unattainable desire."[28] Molly embodies, for Bloom, that figure of totalizing self-presence for which he perpetually pines – an unattainable object of romantic fulfillment sealed in the inaccessible world of the imaginary. From the point of view of Joyce's modern epic, Molly occupies the nostalgic place of mythic (M)Other, the "eternal feminine" that psychically centers male libidinal fantasy. By the time narrative focalization shifts to the female subject-position of "Penelope," Molly, portrayed from the standpoint of speaking/desiring subject rather than specular/desirable object, relates an entirely different (her)story of memory and desire.

5

MOLLY BLOOM
The Woman's Story

She *inscribes* what she is saying because she does not
deny unconscious drives the unmanageable part they
play in speech.

(Hélène Cixous, "Sorties")

what else were we given all those desires for

(*U* 18: 1397–8)

Man's desire and woman's are strangers to each
other.

(Luce Irigaray, *This Sex Which Is Not One*)

SPECULUM OF THE OTHER MOLLY

Molly Bloom emerges in the "Penelope" episode of *Ulysses* like a
fragmented image in a cubist painting seen from a number of simul-
taneous but conflicting perspectives. She has been portrayed in a
wide range of paradigmatic feminine roles, from latter-day Emma
Bovary to mythic earth-goddess – as a sensuous Irish matron whose
emotional resources are rapidly dwindling, and in the metaphorical
guise of a serene Gea-Tellus who replicates the maternal and seductive aspects of the archetypal female. If one were to judge from
current critical debate, Molly would seem to be either a fictional
embodiment of the "eternal feminine" or a middle-aged, cranky,
and erotically-minded housewife frightened of losing her tenuous
powers of sexual allure.[1]

Joyce encouraged an epic interpretation of her figure when he
confessed in a letter to Harriet Weaver that he had "tried to depict
the earth which is prehuman and presumably posthuman" (*Letters* I,
180). But to Frank Budgen he sketched Molly's more fleshly aspects,
describing her as "perfectly sane full amoral fertilisable untrustworthy engaging shrewd limited prudent indifferent *Weib*. *Ich bin der
Fleish der stets bejaht*" (*Letters* I, 170). By labeling Molly the "flesh
that always affirms," Joyce invites his readers to approach the
"Penelope" episode voyeuristically, as a textual exhibition of

126

feminine sexuality revealed through uncensored and unsublimated stream-of-consciousness monologue.

In mapping the enigmatic territory of feminine desire, Joyce tried to simulate the mysterious and polymorphous iterations of a woman's psyche, constructing a female subject that has much in common with the Lacanian "woman-creature" of contemporary psychoanalytic theory. Molly has traditionally been excluded from male discursivity because she "speaks fluid," and her subvocal iterations imitate the amorphous and irrational utterances of hysterical speech. Her unpunctuated soliloquy flows out of Joyce's fictional representation of a rich and capacious stream-of-consciousness that draws freely on those preverbal, prediscursive dimensions of language described by Julia Kristeva as semiotic – a threatening and subversive discourse associated with pre-Oedipal attachment to the body, voice, and pulsions of an imaginary maternal figure. Although Molly's sinuous prose-poetry flows from a phallic pen, it nonetheless offers a linguistic paradigm of *écriture féminine*, as *jouissance* is deferred by the free play of a woman character's imagination over the elusive terrain of sexual difference.[2]

Molly Bloom's "feminine writing" has always seemed both perplexing and paradoxical, rooted as it is in the heteroglossia of male and female polyphonic voices inherited from nineteenth-century sexual/textual metadiscursive conventions. In a tantalizing confession of marital infidelity, Molly depicts herself to herself through the language of pornographic fantasy. Her monologue unfolds as psychic masquerade, a curious rehearsal of erotic desire encoded in a frame of sentimental Victorian fiction. Playing the dialogic roles of both analyst and analysand, Molly reads the text of her own adulterous tale with all the style and panache of a proud, unrepentant Emma Bovary. What overflows the margins of her graphic narrative is unsettling sexual desire masked in ostensible libidinous pleasure. As the Penelopean web of Molly's discourse transgresses the boundaries of Edwardian sex-role stereotypes, the voice of a lusty vamp gives way to the complaints of a destabilized ego – fluid and fragile, insecure and vulnerable. Desirous, like Bloom, of the lost satisfactions of pre-Oedipal nurturance, Molly unconsciously displaces infantile need onto an obsessive search for emotional presence. In Joyce's implicit paradigm of psychological development, the female self, detached from the male-biased rhetoric of cultural inscription, is mentally split and schizophrenically fragmented. It reads its sexual identity marginally, through a masculine Logos needed to valorize the feminine ego. Because Molly sees and judges herself through a fantasmatic grid of male surveillance, she reads her own sexual experiences "against herself" in a monologue that gives startling evidence of emotional alienation from the matrifocal ground of feminine desire. As in much of Joyce's work, the maternal figure is present in the mode of absence, an unattainable and imaginary theological center that focuses the subject's fantasies of self-representation.

In the context of more traditional psychoanalytic space, Molly would seem to manifest a concentric narcissistic sexual economy, formulated according to the classical Freudian view of female sexuality in terms of a continual preoccupation with self and body. Most readers have tended to agree that Molly is selfish and egotistical, "a woman whose love for herself seems an intrinsic part of her character."[3] Darcy O'Brien, for instance, dismisses her as a "comic example of a self-loving woman" and complains that her "narcissism is of such proportions that one is hard pressed to discover amid her effusions any kind of love . . . except self-love."[4] Those dimensions of her personality that have long been analyzed in terms of a narcissistic aetiology may, however, be symptoms of a reaction formation – an attempt, on Molly's part, to compensate psychologically for the original trauma of maternal desertion.

Joyce, in his notes for the "Penelope" episode, declared that Molly is "jealous of men" and "hates women."[5] But if she is portrayed as a woman who "hates women," then she *also* hates herself – or, at least, struggles to handle the repercussions of diminished self-esteem. It is precisely what has been erased from the text – the figure of the absent mother – that forms in Molly's narrative a psychological gap crucial to her understanding of sexual difference. Although barely cognizant of Lunita Laredo, Molly acknowledges "being jewess looking after my mother" (*U* 18: 1184 – 5) and exhibits many of the debilitating consequences of long-term mother absence. Deprived of oral gratification, physical warmth, and solicitous presence shortly after birth, Molly was forced at an early age to relinquish her mother as primary love object. Without direct experience of mother-daughter symbiosis, she identified in childhood with a mythic evocation of the beautiful, seductive, and powerful woman who won Daddy's affections only to go

128

away. If Molly seems to exhibit narcissistic tendencies, it is largely because the trauma of maternal abjection has enunciated the ground of problematic ego-development.[6]

Cut off from attachment to her "moon-mother" Lunita, Molly constructs a myth of origins that imagines the plenitude of feminine nurture as an always-already absent object of desire. "My mother, whoever she was," muses Molly, "might have given me a nicer name" (*U* 19: 846 – 7). She cannot mimetically represent the archetypal female as milk-giver and breast-giver, a beneficent source of female identification through mother-daughter symbiosis. Traumatized by primordial loss, the girl-child compulsively re-creates an idealized image of her mother as an unattainable icon, an imaginary figure constructed around the exotic traces of a glamorous, Spanish-sounding name. Molly's own emotional needs tend to reproduce, in turn, Lunita's shadowy history.[7] Unable to reclaim the mother of childhood longing, Molly tries to *become* the woman who abandoned her by attempting continually to reinscribe in consciousness the wound of parental desertion. "Ive my mothers eyes and figure anyhow" (*U* 18: 890 – 1), she reassures herself. Transferring the womanly/wombly affections of Lunita to the register of Oedipal approval, she seeks to appropriate the veiled phallus of the father in compensation for those sensuous satisfactions attributed in fantasy to an all-powerful phallic mother.[8]

Though an earth-mother in Joyce's imagination and the Gea-Tellus of Bloom's own psychological projections, Molly more closely resembles the legendary Persephone in search of a long-lost Demeter. Some sin there must have been – an apple tasted (like Eve's), a pomegranate half-devoured (like Persephone's), to deprive the girl-child of her female origin, that *heimlich* womb that once nurtured and protected. Cast into an *unheimlich* world of male authority, judgment, and tacit supervision, Molly grew to adolescence under the panoptical eye of an inept and bumbling patriarch who casually prohibited his daughter's emotional needs for pre-Oedipal nurture. Exploring the forbidden mystery of male desire by re-enacting the history of maternal seduction, Molly is trapped in the "discourse-desire-law of man's desire" and loses the ability to imagine a maternal figure of mythic and psychosexual satisfaction. Molly has experienced, in the words of Luce Irigaray, "an exile, an extradition, an exmatriation, from this/her economy of desire."[9] Her fabulated origins have been reduced to primeval simplicity –

to the archetypal dream of an austere, impenetrable moon-mother, an always-already absent and unattainable love-object. The moon turns its face away from a daughter who is left isolated and psychologically castrated. Without the imaginary presence of a nurturant female parent, the infant cries alone in the Plutonian night, calls for Ceres/Demeter until the cries of longing are transferred to the father/lover who prohibits an incestuous expression of daughterly desire.

Molly Bloom's discourse is fluid and feminine, deracinated and polymorphic, uncontained by the limits of logocentric authority. But the contours of her monologue are fearfully phallomorphic, determined by the pervasive presence of a male register of desire. Woman, for Molly, is represented mimetically as an absence that threatens masculine power and phallic domination. By her own defiant rejection of male logic and restraint, Molly replicates the register of female castration, "a *hole* in men's signifying economy. A nothing that might cause the ultimate destruction, the splintering, the break in their systems of 'presence,' or 're-presentation' and 'representation.'"[10]

Spewing forth words in uncontrolled, fluid, voluminous volubility, Molly exudes verbiage in a semi-hysterical outburst of exuberance and anxiety. Post-coital depression reflects and re-presents a deeper, more embedded melancholia, the maternal object-loss that must have been interpreted, both consciously and unconsciously, as an ego-loss inaugurating infantile abjection. Bereft of the mother that everywhere fills the landscape of her unconscious, Molly continues to enact a scenario of perpetual bereavement. The maternal figure, appearing in fantasy as a little moon, beloved but "lunatic" and unstable, represents that bisexual presence hidden, veiled, and ultimately prohibited by the authoritarian law of the Father against incestuous appropriation.

Starved of feminine nurture, Molly identifies narcissistically with the bisexual mother of infant yearning who "becomes a substitute for the erotic cathexis."[11] Her narcissism spins around an axis of oral deprivation, a symptom psychologically displaced onto the orally fixated male: "like some kind of a big infant . . . they want everything in their mouth" (*U* 18: 582–3). Longing to suck the breasts of a mother who denies her bodily contact, Molly makes a fetish of her own milk-giving and pleasure-giving breasts. "*Amor matris*, . . . the only true thing in life" (*U* 9: 842–3) has engendered a futile object cathexis. Yearning for the metaphysical presence of (M)Other love, Molly transfers intra-psychic desire to the male penis/phallus/progenitor and seeks a "substitutable signifier" for mammary/umbilical connection. Locked in oral fixation, she wants to ingest and assimilate the phallic presence that substitutes for a maternal breast. But the aetiology of such hysterical, all-consuming desire is melancholic – a regression from object-cathexis to the narcissistic oral phase of the libido. Melancholia, Freud tells us, "behaves like an open wound, drawing to itself cathectic energy from all sides . . . and draining the ego until it is utterly depleted."[12]

Molly has clearly internalized the bisexual/phallic mother, the mythic lunar presence whose inconstancy forever forms an emotional scar sutured by the abandoned daughter's brash pose of vanity and insouciance. She is caught in a Freudian dilemma, since she must "inscribe herself in the masculine, phallic way of relating to origin, that involves repetition, representation, reproduction." In giving birth to her daughter Milly, Molly "will be her mother and yet not her mother, nor her daughter as mother, with no closure of the circle or the spiral of identity."[13]

The idealized maternal figure has been internalized as a harsh super ego, a female *imago* whose gaze, unseen, will always judge the girl-child unworthy of affection. The fantasized genital insufficiency of the mother, held responsible in a Freudian schema for the "fact of castration," is shamefully reproduced in the narcissistic wound of maternal absence. The girl-child feels herself deprived of both penis and idealized phallic parent and, in a gesture of irrational atonement for this double castration, seeks to play the role of genital proxy for the veiled sex of a transcendent, mythic mother. "The girl's only way to redeem her personal value, and value in general, would be to seduce the father, and persuade him to express, if not admit, some interest in her."[14] To valorize her fragile identity as female/child/woman/beloved, Molly must seduce not only Major Brian Cooper Tweedy, but a signifying chain of Tweedy clones who function psychologically as paternal surrogates.

Bound to her father in a complex web of Oedipal emotions, Molly aspired to replace the lascivious Lunita in Daddy's adoring eyes. She unconsciously internalized a masculine stereotype of feminine desirability and began to emulate the imaginary (male-constructed) temptress who seduced the ingenuous Tweedy, then left him alone with the fruit of their illicit union. Molly, perceiving herself through her father's eyes, came of age in an environment of psychic alienation and, as an Oedipal strategy for mental survival, fashioned a seductive self-image wholly dependent on masculine approval. As Jane Gallop observes, the "father, possessor of the phallus, must desire the daughter in order to give her value"; but the father's veiled emotional seduction of his child takes place through the aegis of patriarchal authority. Paradoxically, the "daughter submits to the father's rule, which prohibits the father's desire, the father's penis, out of the desire to seduce the father by doing his bidding and thus pleasing him."[15]

Having initially courted the attentions of a detached and distant patriarch, Molly now feels neurotically compelled to repeat her childhood conquest in the numerous flirtations of adult life. As a young girl in Gibraltar, she managed to attract the interest of Lieutenant Harry Mulvey, a naval officer enthralled by her charms, but willing to substitute manual titillation for the more dangerous pleasures of adult sexuality. Similarly, the British officer Gardner flattered and fawned over Molly after her marriage to Bloom, but the two probably shared the delights of heavy petting rather than consummating an adulterous liaison.

If Molly seeks a virile lover to confirm her female identity, why does she choose to marry Leopold Bloom? Her psychological project is decidedly ambivalent. Just as Bloom obsessively searches for a surrogate to replace, through phallic presence, both his dead father Rudolph and his infant son Rudy, so Molly directs her unconscious energies toward a repressed and futile quest for the imaginary figure of an absent mother. As Freud would remind us, the neurotic personality, unable successfully to analyze traumatic experience, is invariably destined to repeat it.[16] Searching for the patriarchal signifier that will heal the gap of maternal absence, Molly reverts to a pre-Oedipal model of emotional satisfaction in her conjugal relationship with Leopold Bloom.[17]

Molly's attraction to her husband is clearly a mode of psychological compromise. Forever seeking the lost female parent, Molly finds in Bloom the "new womanly man" who can compensate, in some sense, for earlier maternal desertion. Leopold courts the precocious Molly, the "Oriental prize of Dublin," by exercising the androgynous charms of a "masculine feminine passive active" mate (*U* 17: 289–90). Ethnically semitic, he reminds her of her Jewess-looking mother and exhibits a foreign demeanor that proves to be slightly epicene. Molly remarks that "he was very handsome at that time trying to look like lord Byron," whom she judges, in turn, "too beautiful for a man" (U 18: 208 – 10). Demanding a filial relationship with Mother-Molly, Bloom pledges a symbiotic troth of unshakable, non-judgmental devotion, and, in turn, symbolically acts the part of surrogate mother in his relationship to an insecure and vulnerable spouse. In her marriage to Leopold, Molly attempts to reinstate a fantasized emotional paradigm of maternal-infant symbiosis. She seeks sensuous and psychological gratifications that will allow her a "return to the experience of primary love – the possibility of regressing to the infantile stage of a sense of oneness, no reality testing, and a tranquil sense of well-being in which all needs are satisfied."[18]

From a psychoanalytic perspective, the Molly-Leopold-Boylan triangle figuratively reinstates, with a difference, the Oedipal relationship at the heart of familial association. Molly unconsciously choreographs a bizarre configuration in which Leopold plays nurturant mother and affective emotional partner; Boylan is cast in the role of distant, idealized, authoritarian father; and Molly herself tries to re-enact both the pre-Oedipal script of infant-mother attachment and the Oedipal drama of paternal seduction. On the morning of 16 June 1904, she reads the cards to predict a fortune that is already predestined: the cards have been stacked by Molly's childhood isolation and infantile psychic needs.[19]

In the course of cohabitation with Leopold Bloom, Molly has grown more and more daughterly vis-à-vis her husband. Although she thinks of men in general, and of Bloom in particular, as infants yearning for the amniotic peace of a mother's womb, she herself is deliberately infantilized in relation to an uxorious spouse. While complaining about male helplessness, Molly depends on Bloom to serve her breakfast in bed, purchase salacious reading-material (like Sweets of Sin), and nourish her with precious and expensive cream. Bloom once suggested milking her postpartum "bubs" into the tea, but it is he who now provides mother's milk (or cream) to a bed-ridden spouse. Like a child making outrageous demands on its parents, Molly orders Poldy to serve her breakfast in bed, buy her gifts of garters and face lotion, and, finally, to leave her alone to play at afternoon games with a virile lover. Although Bloom may be replaced in his partner's erotic affections, he knows he will never be ousted from his filial/parental roles of caretaker and nurturer. In Bloom's romantic eyes, the sun shines for Molly and will continue to illumine her features, despite the "blazing and boiling" ardor of Blazes Boylan's sexual attentions. Unlike Molly's more *macho* suitors, Bloom unconsciously craves a fetishistic, polymorphous sexuality. He provides Molly with tender, maternal care and seeks, in turn, the psychological reinforcement of non-aggressive, childish erotic rites.[20] Having regressed, in some sense, to the anal stage of infantile sexuality, Bloom worships at the "altar of the adulterous rump" and takes sensuous pleasure in the osculation of the "melonsmellonous hemispheres" of his wife's voluptuous bottom.[21]

Instinctively, Molly knows that Bloom will offer her the kind of unstinted devotion usually associated with mother-love. "The sun shines for you he said the day we were lying among the rhododendrons on Howth head . . . I was a flower of the mountain yes so we are flowers all a womans body" (*U* 18: 1571 – 7). "I liked the way he made love then he knew the way to take a woman when he sent me the 8 big poppies because mine was the 8th" (*U* 18: 328 – 30). Sharing the birthday of the Blessed Virgin Mary, 8 September, Molly remains ever virginal in her husband's enamored imagination. When Bloom proclaims that the "sun shines" for the woman he loves, he poetically attests to what Freud would call "overvaluation of the love object." Whereas Boylan flatters Molly with a pragmatic gift of food and wine (peaches and port), Bloom sends her eight full-blown poppies, lyrical symbols of flaming affection and impressionistic tokens of the female genitalia. If there's "a touch of the artist about old Bloom" (*U* 10: 582 – 3), courtship brought both aesthetic and pornographic impulses to the fore. We know that Molly considered his titillating epistles "only natural" and took masturbatory pleasure in such explicit *écriture*. On Valentine's Day, 1888, Bloom sent Molly the following acrostic:

> *Poets oft have sung in rhyme*
> *Of music sweet their praise divine.*
> *Let them hymn it nine times nine.*
> *Dearer far than song or wine.*
> *You are mine. The world is mine.* (*U* 17: 412 – 16)

Two days after Molly's eighteenth birthday and the gift of "8 big poppies," the world, metaphorically, became Bloom's. Molly and Leopold "anticipatorily consummated" their marriage and, nine months later, Molly gave birth to their daughter Milly.

Although Molly thinks that Bloom "looked more like a man with his beard a bit grown" in the hospital (*U* 18: 30) and that he ought to "smoke a pipe like father to get the smell of a man" (*U* 18: 508–9), she would clearly feel uncomfortable, even threatened, were she married to a surrogate Tweedy. Molly is fascinated by father-figures like Mulvey, Gardner, and Boylan; but she also feels insecure and diminished in their presence, for she knows that these "manly men" will constantly judge her harshly and that she must play the stereotypical role of seductress in order to please such demanding suitors. "I hate that pretending of all things" (*U* 18: 491), Molly thinks to herself. And yet her flirtation with aggressive males requires the perpetual adoption of a false self-system – a set of roles defined by the cliché-ridden rhetoric of Edwardian courtship and pulp yellow novels of the day.

Molly's psychosexual quest is obviously problematic: while searching for the lost mother of childhood fantasy, she is simultaneously compelled to re-enact the family romance of Oedipal attraction. She suffers from a proverbial Freudian separation of emotional and erotic satisfactions and wants both maternal solicitude from a womanly spouse and the thrill of aggressively heterosexual coition. Reared without a positive model of conjugal co-operation, she goes outside her home, as did Lunita before her, to verify a volatile and insecure self-image. Thus Boylan, her "organizer," becomes an authority figure she wants to please and placate – not only by song and professional competence, but through erotic expertise as well.

Initially, Molly interprets her own sexuality as naïve readers have usually interpreted *Ulysses* – tacitly (and pornographically) assuming a relentless female fascination with phallic potency. She self-consciously adopts the melodramatic role of seductress, and her tone is smug and self-satisfied until the gradual detumescence of erotic intensity leaves her disenchanted with the few moments of genital friction provided by the self-serving Boylan. Deserted by this careless and uncaring Don Juan, Molly retreats from libidinal engorgement to a sense of disappointment and melancholia. The four, five, or six climaxes she purportedly enjoyed with Boylan have left her feeling bereft and unsatisfied. Female desire flows around the impassioned recollection of sexual contact, but memory is imbued with the vacuous residue of copulation without sentiment, coupling without *jouissance*.

Certainly, Molly's explicit language, exuberance, and celebration of sensuous delight have all contributed to an impression of sexual freedom and erotic enjoyment. Celebrating Boylan's virility with Rabelaisian enthusiasm, she observes: "he must have come 3 or 4 times with that tremendous big red brute of a thing he has . . . I never in all my life felt anyone had one the size of that to make you feel full up he must have eaten a whole sheep" (U 18: 143 – 51). But her praise for Boylan's agility quickly wanes, as she acknowledges the impersonality and sadism of his sexual attentions: "whats the idea making us like that with a big hole in the middle of us or like a Stallion driving it up into you because thats all they want out of you with that determined vicious look in his eye" (U 18: 151 – 3). Molly resents "all the pleasure those men get out of a woman" (U 18: 583) and suspects her lover of savage satisfaction in the infliction of physical pain. Remembering his rough foreplay, she notices "the mark of his teeth still where he tried to bite the nipple . . . arent they fearful trying to hurt you" (U 18: 569 – 70). The brawny Boylan apparently ignores Molly's own sexual needs and proffers few signs of tenderness or affection.

On the afternoon of 16 June 1904, Molly is enacting a psychological drama patterned on unresolved Oedipal fixations. She admires Boylan's potency and yields to his love-making with a kind of masochistic self-abandon, thrilled by his stallion-like frenzy and by "that tremendous big red brute of a thing" which she metaphorically compares to a blunt weapon, "like iron" or a "thick crowbar" (U 18: 147 – 8).[22] After all, she must be punished – over and over again – for erotically desiring Tweedy and depriving her father of Lunita's conjugal affections. But her sexual script, dictated by the classical conventions of nineteenth-century pornography, proves to be demeaning rather than cathartic.[23] It leaves her feeling victimized and abandoned, contemptuous of Boylan's phallic mastery and angry at his physical crudeness. "One thing I didn't like," she complains, was "his slapping me behind . . . though I laughed Im not a horse or an ass" (U 18: 122 – 3). Boylan has played the stereotypical role of lascivious patriarch, spanking his erotic object and dismissing her as an afternoon amusement. His love-making involves little more than phallic-narcissistic sexploitation, urged on by anal-sadistic tendencies. He treats Molly like a giant breast/body to be voraciously devoured, to be physically enjoyed and casually eliminated. In search of a phallic substitute for

Lunita's nurturant love, Molly finds in this emotional scenario little more than a psychological replication of the earlier wound of maternal desertion.

Is Molly, at least, sexually satisfied by Boylan? She attests to the pleasures of vaginal orgasm and brags of protracted climax. But is the "untrustworthy . . . *Weib*" a reliable narrator? Or does she exhibit a kind of pornotopic inflation when she recalls how "he made me spend the 2nd time tickling me behind with his finger I was coming for about 5 minutes with my legs round him. . . . O Lord I wanted to shout out all sorts of things fuck or shit or anything at all" (*U* 18: 586–9)? The invocation of long-censored four-letter words would seem to testify to erotic liberation. But immediately after Molly's exuberant declaration of sexual freedom, her joy is deflated by fears of feminine inferiority. Even at the height of sensuous excitement, she worries about orgasmic strain, wrinkles, and male disapproval. Only in perverse fantasy can she challenge the limits of Victorian discourse or defy traditional sex-roles. It is somewhat shocking that at the moment of supposed climax, Molly sees herself as specular object rather than experiencing subject. Unselfconscious pleasure is tainted by a pervasive fear of patriarchal judgment, and her primary concern remains the pursuit of Boylan's tenuous favor. She imagines herself free to "shout . . . anything" (*U* 18: 588–9) were she liberated from the constraints of male censure. But in actual fact, Molly feels sexually insecure and perpetually on trial before the father-figure she so urgently aims to please. She *wants* to shout that four-letter word known to all men, but does not. Inhibited by the need "not to look ugly," she is tormented by anxiety about "those lines from the strain" (*U* 18: 589) and, conforming to a sexual script that could have been dictated by *Sweets of Sin*, congratulates herself on remaining seductive and tantalizing, despite the rigors of love-making: "I gave my eyes that look with my hair a bit loose from the tumbling and my tongue between my lips up to him the savage brute" (*U* 18: 592–4).

It seems telling that every celebration of Boylan's penile prowess immediately gives way to expressions of anger and resentment over a conviction of female inferiority. Like the goddess Juno in Ovid's *Metamorphoses*, Molly is convinced that men get more pleasure from sex than do women: "nice invention they made for women for him to get all the pleasure" (*U* 18: 157). And despite her claims concerning vaginal orgasm, she pre-empts *The Hite Report* by confessing to occasions of self-induced climax: "no satisfaction in it pretending to like it till he comes and then finish it off myself anyway" (*U* 18: 98–9). If Bloom believes that his wife has been satisfied by their sexual practices, then Molly has apparently been "faking it" with her husband. Only the most suspicious of readers would entertain the possibility that she engages in a similar deception with Blazes Boylan – or even with herself.[24]

MOLLY BLOOM AND EDWARDIAN SEXUAL SCRIPTS

It is clear from Molly's childhood and education that her sole experience of power in a male-dominated society is contingent on her ability to attract, manipulate, and influence powerful men. Sheldon Brivic complains that Molly's "version of neurotic compromise is to give up, as a woman, the real world of power for the dream world of love."[25] But in turn-of-the-century Ireland, Molly has few genuine choices. Living in a neurotic social environment and confined to Edwardian sexual scripts, she has become addicted to masculine validation of feminine self-worth. Like Gerty MacDowell in "Nausicaa," Molly is male-identified and chooses to play the role of seductive vamp, a persona that reinforces patterns of earlier childhood experience. Trapped in a debilitating prison of gender-stereotypes, she unconsciously tries to imitate the alluring temptress portrayed in popular pornography. Molly may read a genre of novels different from the romances that Gerty so voraciously devours; but like her younger counterpart in *Ulysses*, she is doomed to construct a media-controlled self-image.

If, as Joyce tells us, Molly is "jealous of men," her sentiments go far beyond the kind of anatomical penis-envy hypothesized by Freud. Like many contemporary feminists, Molly feels dissatisfied with woman's condition of social and cultural powerlessness and, though lacking rhetorical skills to articulate her discontent, decries the violent consequences of male political aggression.[26] The generals of the Boer War, she believes, should have resolved territorial issues in hand-to-hand combat or in a limited military arena: "they could have made their peace in the beginning or old oom Paul and the rest of the other old Krugers go and fight it out between them instead of dragging on for years killing any finelooking men there were" (*U* 18: 394–6). She disdains war as a waste of beautiful young bodies mutilated as cannon-fodder by power-mad politicians but resents the fact that Gardner, who died of enteric fever in the Boer War, was not "even decently shot" (*U* 18: 397). Like Bloom, Molly takes a non-violent, pacifist stance when she proposes the novel idea that universal matriarchy would make the earth a more utopian community: "itd be much better for the world to be governed by the women in it you wouldnt see women going and killing one another and slaughtering when do you ever see women rolling around drunk like they do or gambling every penny they have and losing it on horses yes because a woman whatever she does she knows where to stop" (*U* 18: 1434–9). If Joyce planned in his notes to portray Molly as a misanthrope arbitrarily hurling invective at members of both sexes, his authorial intentions were clearly modified as "Penelope" evolved into an epic articulation of the repressed female story embedded in a male master-narrative. Molly's monologue exhibits such endearing human qualities of psychological ambivalence and emotional vulnerability that the reader is subtly seduced by the "magnolious expansiveness" (*Letters* I, 173) of her mellifluous discourse.

Whereas critics delight in citing Molly's misogynist indictment of women as "a dreadful lot of bitches," they often ignore its proto-feminist conclusion: "I suppose its all the troubles we have makes us so snappy" (*U* 18: 1459–60).[27] Like Joyce, Molly diagnoses shrewishness as a symptom of female frustration, and, by acknowledging the debilitating consequences of gender-based tribulations, whether physiological or culturally induced, she expresses a good deal of commiseration for woman's inequitable lot. At a number of points in her soliloquy, narcissistic sentiments of impatience or self-pity expand into broader feelings of communion with her long-suffering sisters, whom she sees as the more enduring, altruistic, and sensitive sex.[28]

Molly, we learn, has troubles enough of her own, especially those attendant on her recent foray into adultery. Even when she feels perturbed at Boylan's boorish insensitivity, she continues to worry about the impression she makes on her egotistical lover. "I wonder was he satisfied with me," she muses. "I wonder is he awake thinking of me or dreaming" (*U* 18: 121–5). Not only is there little question of love in the liaison, but Molly appears to be in some doubt as to whether Boylan cares for her at all. She would feel far more secure in her plan to soak this wealthy bachelor for money and gifts if only she "could find out whether he likes me" (*U* 18: 412 – 13). Invariably, her thoughts return to an ever-present fear of ageing and ugliness: "I looked a bit washy of course when I looked close in the handglass powdering" (*U* 18: 413 – 14). Despite a powerful need to placate this insensitive suitor, Molly strongly resents cultural inscriptions of female submission to weighty and imperious males: "always having to lie down for them . . . can you ever be up to men the way it takes them" (*U* 18: 416 – 20).

Molly takes it for granted that "the woman is beauty of course thats admitted" (*U* 18: 559 – 60), especially when "compared with what a man looks like with his two bags full and his other thing hanging down out of him or sticking up at you like a hatrack" (*U* 18: 542 – 4). She scorns male exhibitionist tendencies and disdains men who regard the phallus "as if it was 1 of the 7 wonders of the world" (*U* 18: 551 – 2). But Molly cannot herself identify with the aesthetic ideal embodied in "those statues in the museum" or with the *Photobits* nymph immured in the bedroom of 7 Eccles Street. Her self-image is more perverse and pornographic: "Im a little like that dirty bitch in that Spanish photo he has" (*U* 18: 563 – 4). Again, an unconscious denigration of feminine behavior extends even to herself. If Molly believes that women can act like "a dreadful lot of bitches," she can also be harsher on herself than any of the lot. Her casual identification with the "nude señorita" (*U* 17: 1810) depicted in a pornographic postcard reveals a startling residue of contempt for the female body, as well as feelings of sexual abasement unconsciously associated with her exotic Spanish mother.

One could, of course, make a similarly strong case for an earlier attitude of adolescent narcissism on Molly's part. As a child, she seems to have been as self-absorbed as Issy Earwicker, the primping daughter and purported temptress of *Finnegans Wake*. Molly loved, at the age of ten, cavorting before the fire in a "little bit of a short shift" and felt flattered by the attentions of the "fellow opposite" voyeuristically "watching with the lights out" (*U* 18: 919 – 22). "I used to love myself then stripped at the washstand dabbing and creaming" (*U* 18: 922 – 3), she confesses, and recalls being fascinated with her budding breasts, "shaking and dancing about in my blouse . . . I loved looking down at them" (*U* 18: 850 – 1). She still seems to admire the "peachy" thighs that allure Boylan: "I bet he never saw a better pair of thighs than that look how white they are the smoothest place is right there between this bit here how soft like a peach" (U 18: 1144–6). It is not clear, however, that the mature Molly retains the kind of delight in her body that she felt as a nubile girl.[29]

As a middle-aged matron, Molly is filled with anxiety about the loss of physical attractiveness. She worries that her "belly is a bit too big," considers giving up stout at dinner, and wonders about the efficacy of *antifat*. Molly has been conditioned to fear unsightly flab and feels panicky at the thought of her body running to fat. Like Gerty MacDowell, she is duped by advertised panaceas and feels confident that if only she could purchase "one of those kidfitting corsets . . . obviating that unsightly broad appearance across the lower back to reduce flesh" (U 18: 446–50), she could hide a protruding abdomen and please the most critical of suitors.

When Molly observes that she used to love herself as a girl, she unwittingly implies that the prepubescent self-confidence she once enjoyed has waned with middle age. In a brief narcissistic reverie, she thinks: "God I wouldnt mind being a man and get up on a lovely woman" (U 18: 1146–7). Later, she admits that her breasts "excite myself sometimes its well for men all the amount of pleasure they get off a womans body were so round and white for them always I wished I was one myself for a change just to try with that thing they have swelling up on you so hard and at the same time so soft when you touch it" (U 18: 1379–81). Despite her earlier contempt for male anatomy, Molly indulges in a number of transsexual fantasies that exhibit what seems to be a fairly natural curiosity about sexual difference. Men, she speculates, are "all mad to get in there where they come out of" because the womb/vagina must provide an embryonic haven: "yes because theres a wonderful feeling there so tender all the time" (U 18: 806–9). Longing for the maternal flesh/sanctuary/nurturance prematurely denied her, Molly understandably envies a univocal phallic presence that can penetrate the body of the mother and engender feelings of security and tenderness associated with pre-Oedipal bonding.

Socially conditioned to regard other women as enemies and sexual competitors, Molly tends to dismiss every female of her acquaintance as too old, thin, harsh, idiosyncratic, or demented to pose a threat to her own attractiveness and erotic supremacy. That miserly "old faggot" Mrs Riordan was driven to religious devotion and puritanical prudishness when she lost her husband, because "no man would look at her twice." "I hope Ill never be like her"

(*U* 18: 4 – 12), Molly comments acerbically. She expresses similar contempt for the aged Mrs Rubio, who wore a "switch of false hair" and remained "vain about her appearance . . . with all her religion domineering" (*U* 18: 752 – 4). It is the terrible fear of being ignored and isolated, like the niggardly Mrs Riordan, or superstitiously pious, like the fatuous Mrs Rubio, that threatens Molly with the specter of an ominously bleak senility.

Although she recognizes the inequities of Edwardian sexual scripts, Molly never seriously contemplates the possibility of altering those cultural and political structures responsible for gender discrimination. Her socialized premisses about sexual privilege, along with a repressed horror of ageing and debilitation, lead her pessimistically to conclude: "as for being a woman as soon as youre old they might as well throw you out in the bottom of the ashpit" (*U* 18: 746 – 7). Knowing that a metaphorical rubbish heap awaits her long before the grave, she has already begun to enunciate mental panic. If society banishes females who are old, ill, or unattractive, then a woman's only recourse is to cling desperately to whatever scraps of youth and beauty she possesses for as long as she is able. Life for a middle-aged woman in turn-of-the-century Ireland degenerates into a losing battle against the imminent loss of physical attributes. In an open market geared to the demands of a male libidinal economy, women must patiently wait for the Prince Charming of their dreams, then continually labor to retain his favor through assiduous devotion to all the cosmetic strategies suggested in the *Gentlewoman* and other ladies' magazines of the day.

The suitor whose interest Molly most avidly courts is, finally, neither Blazes Boylan nor Stephen Dedalus, but Leopold Paula Bloom. Despite the fact that she has just inaugurated her role as adulteress on the afternoon of 16 June 1904 ("anyhow its done now once and for all with all the talk of the world about it people make its only the first time after that its just the ordinary do it and think no more about it" [*U* 18: 101 – 2]), and that she has thereby enjoyed her first complete sexual experience in almost eleven years, Molly is still compulsively preoccupied with the issue of Bloom's continuing affection. Having so recently taken an extramarital lover, she projects her own feelings of guilt onto her spouse by courting suspicions that he might be having a secret love affair: "he came somewhere Im sure by his appetite anyway love its not or hed be off his feed thinking of her so either it was one of those night women

142

. . . or else if its not that its some little bitch or other he got in with somewhere or picked up on the sly . . . 1 woman is not enough for them" (*U* 18: 34 – 60). Molly's jealousy becomes a leitmotif of the chapter and continues almost to the end of her soliloquy: "I wonder was it her Josie off her head with my castoffs hes such a born liar too no hed never have the courage with a married woman" (*U* 18: 1252 – 4). Unaware of Bloom's sexual dysfunction, Molly concludes that "he couldnt possibly do without it that long" (*U* 18: 76), then tries to piece together shreds of evidence to expose the name and nature of his hypothetical infidelity.

Vigorously protesting that she doesn't "care two straws now who he does it with" (*U* 18: 53 – 4), Molly, as usual, protests too much. She cares so passionately, in fact, that her attention is always focused a little above or beyond her husband's image. If Bloom-Ulysses slaughters Molly's suitors, real or imaginary, in his head, Joyce's modern-day Penelope is engaged in an analogous project to disarm her ostensible competitors. She mentally demolishes, one by one, those women she believes have caught Bloom's attention or have expressed the least sign of interest in his masculine regard. Molly indicts the pathetic Miss Stack, an "old maid" (and emaciated version of Beatrice Justice) who retrieves flowers from the wastebasket and offers them to the bedridden Bloom; that "slut" Mary Driscoll, a domestic servant guilty of "padding out her false bottom to excite him" (*U* 18: 56 – 7); and Josie Powell Breen, a nondescript woman whom Bloom briefly courted before his marriage. Molly marshals her most powerful rhetoric against this rather insipid catalogue of putative enemies. Having dismissed the brazen Mary Driscoll from her employment on a charge of stealing oysters (though the girl's real crime was the possession of garters that might have been fetishistic favors from Bloom), she justifies her jealousy by proclaiming: "I couldnt even touch him if I thought he was with a dirty barefaced liar and sloven like that one" (*U* 18: 73 – 4).

Molly bitterly resents what she perceives to be an inequitable double standard governing male-female relationships: "they [men] can go and get whatever they like from anything at all with a skirt on it and were not to ask any questions but they want to know where were you where are you going" (*U* 18: 297 – 300). She accuses Bloom of voyeuristically "skulking" after her during their courtship and resents his invasion of her sexual privacy. Proverbially contradictory, Molly ascribes to her husband the same kind of envy and suspiciousness that she herself exhibits throughout "Penelope."

If Molly had few female friends before her marriage, she seems to have abandoned even those when she assumed her proper status as a respectable married lady. In the early days of her courtship, she took pleasure in snatching Bloom away from the hapless Josie Powell, then tantalizing the rejected wallflower: "because I used to tell her a good bit of what went on between us not all but just enough to make her mouth water" (*U* 18: 214–16). Although Molly abdicates responsibility for alienating this female friend, it is clear that she considers her conquest of Bloom a rather smug and enviable victory. Josie "didnt darken the door much after we were married" and eventually wound up with a "dotty husband" who wears his muddy boots to bed "when the maggot takes him" (*U* 18: 216–23). Molly's own insecurities compel her to drive away competitive female acquaintances, then to complain that women lack the kind of intimate camaraderie and social support apparently enjoyed by males: men "have friends they can talk to weve none" (*U* 18: 1456–7).

Convinced that she could intimidate a matron like Josie and that a younger woman would get wise to Bloom's idiosyncrasies ("if they only knew him as well as I do" [*U* 18: 45–6]), Molly summons to her aid the amusing rationalization of male menopause. Bloom's wandering eye is surely just a passing phase, not to be taken seriously, "because all men get a bit like that at his age especially getting on to forty" (*U* 18: 50–1). Thinking about "Mrs Maybrick that poisoned her husband," Molly argues that it would be "only natural" for a woman to get rid of an intolerable partner: "of course some men can be dreadfully aggravating drive you mad . . . she must have been madly in love with the other fellow to run the chance of being hanged O she didnt care if that was her nature what could she do" [*U* 18: 237–44]). Molly protests: "Id rather die 20 times over than marry another of their sex" (*U* 18: 231–2). She, of course, does not *want* to "marry another" because she intends to retain (and resuscitate the interest of) her present mate. The knowledge of Bloom's strange habits gives her a kind of security: "hed never find another woman like me to put up with him the way I do . . . hes not natural like the rest of the world" (*U* 18: 232–3, 268); "nobody understands his cracked ideas but me" (*U* 18: 1407).

Molly secretly takes pride in her perplexed but extraordinary relationship with Bloom, characterized by an intriguing mixture of tolerance, affection, jealousy, and exasperation. Her spouse, she complains, is annoyingly "pigheaded" (*U* 18: 363), but "hes not proud out of nothing" (*U* 18: 17), is "not such a fool" (*U* 18: 81), and has "a few brains" (*U* 18: 321–2) in his head. He knows, in fact, a lot about a mixed-up number of things, even though, if asked a question, he might pretentiously "say its from the Greek" and "leave us as wise as we were before" (*U* 18: 241–2). Molly's acquisition of a responsible husband, the possession of a "finelooking daughter," and her recent attraction of a wealthy lover offer proof of success in a world where female status is other-directed and contingent on rewards for the satisfaction of male libidinal desire. Women, Molly observes, "try to walk on you" if they "know youve no man" (*U* 18: 473–4). She then proceeds to judge her spinster competitors accordingly. Brashly asserting her superiority over the unmarried "Kathleen Kearney and her lot of squealers Miss This Miss That Miss Theother lot of sparrowfarts skitting around talking about politics . . . Irish homemade beauties" (*U* 18: 878–81), she challenges: "let them get a husband first thats fit to be looked at and a daughter like mine or see if they can excite a swell with money that can pick and choose whoever he wants like Boylan . . . or the voice either" (*U* 18: 892–6). Molly is perhaps overly defensive in her expression of feminine vanity. The implicit braggadocio of her erotic and (only secondarily) professional accomplishments betrays, once again, a faltering and unstable self-image.

Harking back to her youth in Gibraltar, Molly tells a poignant tale of childhood isolation. Hester Stanhope, her one female friend, was "awfully fond" of Molly, her "dearest Doggerina," whom she fawned over and comforted during a terrifying thunderstorm: "the night of the storm I slept in her bed she had her arms round me then we were fighting in the morning with the pillow what fun" (*U* 18: 641–3). Mrs Stanhope is the closest thing to a mother-surrogate, elder sister, or "kissing cousin" that Molly has ever known. Molly notes that "we were like cousins" (*U* 18: 641), though she cannot initially recall Hester's first name. There is a subtle suggestion of lesbian attraction in their physical intimacy in bed, as well as in the pillow-fight that follows the next morning. But if Hester is a maternal substitute, the friendship shared by the two women degenerates in classic Oedipal fashion.

145

"Wogger," Mrs Stanhope's husband, apparently made eyes at the nubile Molly, and Hester quickly removed him to Paris, safe from the scene of incipient temptation. One suspects that Mrs Stanhope may have deliberately obscured her address on the envelope she sent, as well. Molly remembers: "he was watching me whenever he got an opportunity" (*U* 18: 643). Dearest Doggerina, for her part, is also keeping a steady eye on Wogger. And the older man's perceived or imagined desire sparks in her the first stirrings of erotic excitement. Echoing Gerty MacDowell, Molly recalls how "our eyes met I felt something go through me like all needles my eyes were dancing . . . after when I looked at myself in the glass hardly recognised myself the change. . . . I had a splendid skin from the sun and the excitement like a rose . . . it wouldnt have been nice on account of her but I could have stopped it in time" (*U* 18: 645 – 52). In the first blush of sexual awakening, Molly proves as vain as Issy Earwicker. Enthralled by her mirror image, she imagines her body blossoming "like a rose" into the newly discovered thrill of sensuous desire, apparently inaugurated by the physiological change attributable to menstrual roses and female fecundity.

After the Stanhopes' departure for Paris, Molly mourns a lost female friendship and, for the second time, feels deserted by a matriarchal figure.[30] Desperate for companionship, she sends herself letters "with bits of paper in them so bored sometimes I could fight" (*U* 18: 699). Life "got as dull as the devil after they went I was almost planning to run away mad out of it somewhere were never easy where we are . . . waiting always waiting" (*U* 18: 676 – 8). On the desolate Rock of Gibraltar, the beleaguered adolescent dreams of a handsome prince who will rescue her from emotional imprisonment in a remote and inaccessible peninsular ("penisolate" *FW* 3. 6) fortress.

Longing for the love and emotional presence symbolized by a fairy-tale figure able to storm the Rock for her sake, Molly finds her Irish Prince Charming in Lieutenant Harry Mulvey, the "secret admirer" who woos her with a love letter and wins her girlish heart. "Mulveys was the first . . . an admirer he signed it I near jumped out of my skin" (*U* 18: 748, 762). *In medias res*, Molly – in the middle of her monologue and at the chronological center of her life – looks back fondly on the early days of virginal flirtation. Mulvey's initial kiss seemed magical and transcendent: "I remember shall I wear a white rose . . . he was the first man kissed me under the Moorish wall . . . it never entered my head what kissing meant till he put his tongue in my mouth'' (*U* 18: 768 – 71). The thrill of lingual penetration awakened this "sleeping beauty" from an adolescent sexual slumber. As a teenager in Gibraltar, the precocious nymphette could wear the white rose of virginity or the red rose of passion. Poised precariously between innocence and experience, she could choose the role of *ingénue* or seductress, virgin or vamp. Mulvey, like Odysseus and Sinbad (and like Eveline's Frank), is a sailor "off the sea" whose life suggests exotic travels. The young naval officer has seen a bit of the world, and he would like to see more of Molly Tweedy than Victorian propriety and virginal reticence allow. The fifteen-year-old Molly is curious but sexually ignorant – and perhaps more naïve about love-making than her nautical suitor acknowledges.

Bereft of a maternal role model, the young girl must rely for sex education on her prurient advisor Mrs Rubio and on the witch-like warnings of the ancient Ines. It is difficult for Molly to heed the pious remonstrations of the former, whom she remembers "near 80 or 100 her face a mass of wrinkles" (*U* 18: 753). The more practical admonitions of Ines make a stronger impression. With her knowledge of sexuality confined to wives' tales and folklore, Molly refuses to "go all the way" with Mulvey "for fear you never know consumption or leave me with a child embarazada that old servant Ines told me that one drop even if it got into you at all after I tried with the Banana" (*U* 18: 801 – 3). The curious adolescent, confusing syphilis with consumption, and engaging in masturbatory experiments with a banana, is a source of both comedy and pathos. Fear of pregnancy, a genuine and justifiable concern, is a dominant theme in Molly's youthful flirtation. She feels horrified at the thought that even one drop of semen could make her pregnant and, cognizant of her mother's sexual history, is doubtless aware of the heavy consequences of being left *embarazada* in the port of Gibraltar. With a pang of regret, Molly recalls her promise to Mulvey that they could consummate their sexual liaison if only she were married and had a legal cover: "he said hed come back . . . and if I was married hed do it to me and I promised him yes faithfully" (*U* 18: 820 – 2). Haunted by the memory of this frustrated love affair, Molly confesses: "Id let him block me now" (*U* 18: 822).

The adolescent Molly tantalizes Mulvey and exercises all the allurements she has learned from life as a daughter of the garrison. She has her thin blouse "open for his last day" but refuses direct tactile contact: "he caressed them outside they love doing that its the roundness . . . he wanted to touch mine with his for a moment but I wouldn't let him" (*U* 18: 796 – 800). In her first Circean scenario, Molly self-consciously plays the role of sexual temptress and gets a certain thrill from arousing, then refusing immediate gratification to her excited suitor: "I tormented the life out of him first tickling him I loved rousing that dog in the hotel . . . he was shy all the same I liked him like that moaning" (*U* 18: 812 – 14). Syntactically conflating Mulvey with a stray cur, Molly treats him like an animal – to be teased, petted, and finally rewarded. And she takes exultant pride in her mature ability to gain the upper hand in the game of "catch as catch can." Although Mulvey is a lusty sailor who would presumably be "hot on for it" (*U* 18: 1412), Molly "pulls him off into [her] handkerchief" (*U* 18: 809 – 10) and manages to satisfy him with digital stimulation. Mulvey gratefully responds like an animal being trained by little Doggerina, a beast obedient to its mistress's piquant commands.[31]

Given the facts of Molly's sex education (or lack thereof) and social inhibitions, her amorous response to Mulvey seems surprisingly uninhibited. She murmurs "yum" in sensuous wonder, allows him to caress her breasts, and curiously inspects his phallic anatomy. Aware of her own virginal limits and confident of her ability to curb male libidinous urges, Molly delights in a first-hand experience that proves more instructive than earlier researches with a banana. "I made him blush a little when I got over him that way when I unbuttoned him and took his out and drew back the skin it had a kind of eye in it theyre all Buttons men down the middle on the wrong side of them Molly darling he called me" (*U* 18: 814 – 17). She thinks of the penis as a tube or pole, indented with an eye like a needle, and "button-like" at the end. And though she refuses to expose breast or belly, Molly examines her lover's genitals, opens her thighs suggestively beneath a protective petticoat, and feels no compunctions about petting her excited partner to orgasm. She even treasures her semen-stained handkerchief for weeks after Mulvey's departure, preferring its smell to the cheap Spanish perfume available in Gibraltar.

Molly's adolescent encounter with Mulvey sets the stage for the mythic resonances that will be retrieved in her imagination at the end of the "Penelope" episode. The comic elements of this inaugural experience are absorbed by the larger, more exotic scene of romantic reverie. As Molly and Mulvey lie together on the Rock of Gibraltar, the "highest rock in existence" and the ancient pillar of mediterranean civilization, the setting is vaguely reminiscent of Byron's *Don Juan* and suggestive of a primordial Garden of Eden: "we lay over the firtree cove a wild place . . . the galleries and the casemates and those frightful rocks and Saint Michaels cave with the icicles . . . hanging down . . . yes the sea and the sky you could do what you liked lie there for ever" (*U* 18: 789–92). Poised on a giant phallic promontory, the lovers enact infertile rites allied with the splendors of a beautiful but barren landscape. The wild sea crashes beneath, and an "awful deepdown torrent" holds them suspended in a rhapsodic moment of insatiable desire. By the time Molly celebrates her rapturous ecstasy with Bloom on Howth Head, she gives to this lyrical scene the cumulative weight of mythic memory. Together, Molly and Leopold will consummate an act left unconsummated in Gibraltar and, through the passion of their love-making, experience a romantic epiphany sufficiently powerful to revive, sixteen years later, the smouldering embers of a moribund marriage.

MOLLY AND LEOPOLD: CONJUGAL ESTRANGEMENT

Throughout the text of *Ulysses*, Joyce teases and titillates our voyeuristic sensibilities and invites us to construct a male-centered vision of Molly as eternal temptress – the insatiable female, the perpetually receptive vagina/mouth/womb of pornographic fantasy. It is not until the "Penelope" episode that he attempts to disclose the woman's story embedded in a predominantly male epic narrative. Homer left Penelope mute and weaving, a symbolic figure of spousal fidelity. Joyce gives voice to her contemporary counter-part's exuberant iterations, cast in the discourse of sexual volubility. Hence the half-century of critical confusion as to the exact nature of Molly's pre- and post-marital erotic liaisons. It is surely one of the great curiosities of modern literature that readers for almost forty years persisted in a literal interpretation of the list of lovers dictated at the end of "Ithaca."[32]

Assuming Mulvey to be the first term of his [Bloom's] series,

Penrose, Bartell d'Arcy, professor Goodwin, Julius Mastiansky, John Henry Menton, Father Bernard Corrigan, a farmer at the Royal Dublin Society's Horse Show, Maggot O'Reilly, Matthew Dillon, Valentine Blake Dillon (Lord Mayor of Dublin), Christopher Callinan, Lenehan, an Italian organgrinder, an unknown gentleman in the Gaiety Theatre, Benjamin Dollard, Simon Dedalus, Andrew (Pisser) Burke, Joseph Cuffe, Wisdom Hely, Alderman John Hooper, Dr Francis Brady, Father Sebastian of Mount Argus, a bootblack at the General Post Office, Hugh E. (Blazes) Boylan and so each and so on to no last term. (*U* 17: 2133–42)

In the course of her monologue, Molly expresses scorn or derision for the majority of the twenty-five males on the list; and she seems to have had only a passing social glance from, or professional acquaintance with, almost all the rest. Molly dismisses Menton as "that big babbyface" who "had the impudence to make up to me one time" (*U* 18: 39–42). And her contact with a farmer at the Dublin Society's Horse Show or with a bootblack at the General Post Office must have been limited to a cursory moment of lascivious interest. She thinks Simon Dedalus a fool and remembers with disgust Lenehan's impudent fondling. As Hugh Kenner observes, the "Penelope" episode exposes the Ithacan catalogue as nothing more than "a list of past occasions for twinges of Bloomian jealousy."[33] Molly has evidently remained faithful to Bloom in her fashion. And with the possible exception of the enigmatic Gardner, a suitor unknown to the Ithacan consciousness, Molly's "lovers" before Boylan were apparently restricted to the realm of flirtation or fantasy. The suitors named in "Ithaca" are males perceived through Bloom's jealous but boastful imagination. He seems to believe, like many husbands, that his wife's voluptuous figure must be a constant source of sexual temptation for other men, who cannot refrain from ogling her with lust in their hearts.

Molly's own perception of these alleged suitors is more realistic and critical. She once exchanged passionate embraces with Bartell D'Arcy "on the choir steps" and plans to use the incident to tantalize Bloom at some later date. Her liaison with Gardner was most probably limited to heavy petting, since Molly spends so little time thinking about this more recent British admirer. But the kind of excitement, guilt, agitation, and confusion that she associates with her present affair with Boylan seems to indicate that adultery is a novel experience for her. Were this not the first time Molly had consummated the act with a gentleman-suitor, one doubts that either she or her husband would manifest such an obsessive pre-occupation with the event throughout the day of 16 June and the early morning hours of 17 June 1904.

Molly's love affair with Boylan appears to be her first experience of "complete carnal intercourse, with ejaculation of semen within the natural female organ" (U 17: 2278-9) in ten and a half years. There is little wonder, then, that she feels aroused by his ardor and exaggerates the magnitude of his prowess. Even as Molly celebrates Boylan's stud performance, however, her seduction of such a "swell" is filled with ulterior motives. Molly's thoughts about Boylan, like her memories of Mulvey, Gardner, Wogger, and the rest, are all suffused with an awareness of Bloom. When Molly expresses the desire for a romantic "kiss long and hot down to your soul," she thinks: "I wish some man or other would take me sometime when hes there and kiss me in his arms" (U 18: 104-6). The focus of this fantasy is not sensuous pleasure but the excitation of conjugal jealousy: it is important that Bloom be present as voyeuristic witness to the deed. Similarly, Molly feels convinced that Bloom left her alone earlier in the afternoon "because he has an idea about him and me hes not such a fool" (U 18: 81). Rationalizing her afternoon tryst, Molly implies that the encounter was "plotted and planned" by her husband rather than herself: "its all his own fault if I am an adulteress" (U 18: 1516).

"I suppose he thinks Im finished out and laid on the shelf" (U 18: 1021-2), she speculates. And this pervasive fear – that her husband's sexual indifference is a sign of emotional rejection – dominates her monologue. Worried that Bloom might rekindle his earlier interest in Josie Breen, Molly reassures herself: "I could quite easily get him to make it up any time" by titillating his fetishistic curiosity. "I know plenty of ways ask him to tuck down the collar of my blouse or touch him with my veil and gloves" (U 18: 186-90). The "plentiful ways" in Molly's treasure-trove of erotic tactics range from subtle seductive gestures to obscene titillations. As she sinks further into post-coital depression, layers of social civility are peeled back to expose torrents of psychological recrimination.

Angered by her husband's inept performance of oral sex, Molly makes Bello-like plans to punish him: "he does it all wrong too thinking only of his own pleasure his tongue is too flat or I dont know what he forgets that wethen I dont Ill make him do it again if he doesnt mind himself and lock him down to sleep in the coalcellar with the blackbeetles" (*U* 18: 1249 – 52). Left physically frustrated, she temporarily plays the role of punitive phallic mother and, in this particular Freudian revenge fantasy, imagines incarcerating her spouse in the cellar – a cold and *unheimlich* womb-tomb indeed. Molly is evidently too inexperienced to instruct Bloom in the art of cunnilingus. Somewhat confused about the nature of her own physical responses ("I dont know what he forgets"), she cannot articulate her desire for clitoral stimulation even to herself, much less to Bloom; and she soon loses patience with the "perverse" experiment which contributes, she believes, to her husband's pleasure rather than her own.[34]

Molly strongly resents Bloom's neglect of what she considers proper intercourse and his pursuit of polymorphously perverse satisfactions. He kisses his wife's bottom and is willing to try cunnilingus, with little fear of lips, labia, or vulva; but he apparently refuses contact with the mysterious and threatening vaginal interior and either practices *coitus interruptus* or brings himself off through frictional contact with his wife's melonsmellonous hemispheres. One would assume the latter, since Molly is used to practicing a primitive form of birth-control and, heeding nineteenth-century popular folklore, allows Boylan to ejaculate "within the natural female organ" only the last of the three, four, or five times they make love. She seems satisfied with external ejaculation and resents Bloom for his refusal even to broach the forbidden cave of Calypso. Oblivious of Bloom's sexual dysfunction, Molly feels confused and angry at his apparent rejection of her genital spaces and still-fertile womb. And though she contemplates the possibility of having another child ("not off him [Boylan] though" [*U* 18: 166 – 7]), progeny is not the issue. She is worried about being "all washed up" in Bloom's affections and determines to resuscitate his flagging erotic interest.[35]

As the soliloquy progresses, Molly gets more in touch with the source of her repressed hostility. Furious at her husband, she entertains sadistic fantasies of sexual confrontation the following morning:

Ill start dressing myself to go out . . . Ill put on my best shift
and drawers let him have a good eyeful out of that to make his
micky stand for him Ill let him know if thats what he wanted
that his wife is fucked yes and damn well fucked too up to my
neck nearly not by him 5 or 6 times handrunning theres the
mark of his spunk on the clean sheet I wouldnt bother to even
iron it out that ought to satisfy him if you dont believe me feel
my belly unless I made him stand there and put him into me Ive
a mind to tell him every scrap and make him do it in front of
me serve him right (*U* 18: 1508 – 16)

There is a manic quality about this colorful erotic scenario that
implies a harsh challenge to her reluctant spouse for a decade of
conjugal neglect. Defending her adultery as an act of sexual
exasperation, Molly exonerates herself of responsibility and lays the
guilt entirely on Bloom. She argues that cuckoldry is precisely
"what he wanted" – a masochistic penance expiating marital
"omissions." If the nature of Molly's pornographic project is not
entirely clear, its import is unmistakable. She seems to envisage a
scene tantamout to Bloom's earlier fantasies of humiliation in
"Circe" when, cast in the role of Boylan's flunkey, he voyeuristically peered through a keyhole in a perverse act of titillation and
self-punishment. Similarly, Molly contemplates arousing her
husband by flaunting her afternoon adultery, then coercively
demanding sexual satisfaction in a scene modeled on Leopold von
Sacher-Masoch's *Venus in Furs*. The one salient point that emerges
from the diatribe is Molly's frustration with Bloom and her
desperate desire to win him back. "Ill just give him one more
chance" (*U* 18: 1497 – 8), she resolves – articulating, simultaneously, the resolution to give *herself* another chance to solicit the
sexual attentions of a wandering husband.

MATERNAL RELATIONSHIP: MOLLY AND MILLY

If Molly finally reverts to memories of youth and joy at the end of
"Penelope," it is largely because she is so dissatisfied with the
present that her one sanctuary would seem to be a nostalgic invocation of past experience or future possibility. The satisfactions of
family life have been somewhat ambivalent for Molly, who never
knew her own mother and who now regards maternity as an

uncomfortable reminder of physical deterioration. As Milly grows in age and grace, she becomes a sexual rival to a mother who needs constant reassurance of continuing attractiveness. Thus Molly complains of her daughter's stubbornness, "long tongue," brash behavior and sassy conduct. She regrets having slapped Milly for talking back, but her recollection of the incident suggests that it stands out as a rare instance of physical punishment. Although Molly roundly criticizes her daughter, she recognizes in the girl a younger version of herself and tries to comprehend the motives for Milly's obstreperous behavior. "I was just like that myself," she confesses: "they darent order me about the place" (*U* 18: 1077–8). As Bloom observes, Milly is a little Molly – the "same thing watered down." Milly has proved to be "in great demand" with young Dublin males, and her seductive skills have apparently been learned from Mom. In a burst of comically ingenuous rhetoric, Molly laments the fact that her daughter is not yet sufficiently sensitive to understand or fully enjoy the pleasures of female sexuality: "of course she cant feel anything deep yet I never came properly till I was what 22 or so it went into the wrong place always only the usual girls nonsense and giggling" (*U* 18: 1050–2).

This middle-aged mother and adolescent daughter experience the kind of conflict that would seem inevitable in a twentieth-century nuclear family. But Molly's cavalier attitude toward Milly may well reflect her own repressed anger at Lunita Laredo's earlier desertion. As Nancy Chodorow observes, a woman's experience of mothering will be highly colored by pre-Oedipal maternal attachment. Especially in the mothering of girl-children, "her identification with her mother and her reexperience of self as child may lead to conflict over those particular issues from a mother's own childhood which remain unresolved." Motherhood "may be a (fantasized) attempt to make reparation to a mother's own mother for the injuries she did (also in fantasy). . . . Alternatively, it may be a way to get back at her mother for (fantasized) injuries."[36] Molly, in fact, has few available role models for nurturant maternity. Abandoned in infancy by her moon-mother Lunita, she longs to re-create that "ideal home" denied her in childhood, but has limited resources for implementing such dreams of domestic bliss. Because Molly's notion of female parenting was defined negatively, by detachment and insouciance, she has a great deal of difficulty relating successfully to her own adolescent daughter.

It is somewhat amusing that the infinitely contradictory Molly nevertheless chastises Milly for contradicting: "answering me like a fishwoman when I asked to go for a half a stone of potatoes . . . till I gave her 2 damn fine cracks across the ear . . . she had me that exasperated of course contradicting" (*U* 18: 1067 – 73). Unwittingly punning, Molly complains that Milly's "tongue is a bit too long for my taste" (*U* 18: 1033), in contrast to Bloom's tongue, which she judges literally "too flat" to suit her pleasure during oral sex. Understandably, Molly feels chagrined when her blooming daughter criticizes her for immodest behavior or suggestive attire: "your blouse is open too low she says to me the pan calling the kettle blackbottom" (*U* 18: 1033 – 4). If one recalls Molly's opening her blouse to tantalize Mulvey and the role played by her low cleavage the afternoon of Bloom's marriage proposal, it seems a bit comical that Milly should complain about the very tactics that issued in her birth – sexual strategies that the young girl will undoubtedly employ in her budding romance with Bannon.

But Molly, like any middle-class mother, is not anxious to see her daughter blossom into a tantalizing sexual morsel or to watch her inaugurate those seductive rites that will lead to the perilous game of "laugh and lie down." And so she corrects Milly's behavior at every opportunity. Although Molly "loved herself" when she was a girl in Gibraltar and delighted in a striptease that nightly amused a voyeuristic neighbor, she reprimands Milly for a similar tendency toward exhibitionism: "I had to tell her not to cock her legs up like that on show on the windowsill before all the people passing they all look at her like me when I was her age" (*U* 18: 1034 – 6). Molly has clearly begun to see her daughter as a competitor for male attention and is loath to relinquish her own sexual priority.

Molly, of course, criticizes Milly for precisely those faults she acknowledges in herself. By imitating her mother, Milly plays the role of disconcerting emotional looking-glass: she offers a living reflection of the younger Molly in the full flower of adolescence. The mother, feeling the blossom of youth daily withering and aware of the inevitable disappointments of middle age, is understandably hesitant to recognize her daughter's womanly independence. But Milly has reached her menarche and is biologically a mature female, capable of bearing a child. The girl experienced her first menstrual period or "catamenic hemorrhage" on 15 September 1903, "9 months and 1 day" before the evening of Molly's soliloquy (*U* 17:

2287 – 9). Since that time, mother and daughter have shared an intuitive bond of womanly understanding, "a preestablished natural comprehension in incomprehension" (*U* 17: 2289 – 90) that makes Bloom feel conspicuously marginal. In Bloom's eyes, Molly and Milly appear to be conspiring in an act of surveillance designed to circumscribe his "complete corporal liberty of action" (*U* 17: 2291 – 2). Whether or not the two women are actually plotting together is questionable, since their ostensible collusion may be nothing more than a paranoid projection of Bloom's guilty conscience. What is salient in this disclosure, however, is that Milly's menarche has produced a strange, inarticulate, and unprecedented link with her mother. As "consummated females," the two sense a physical liaison that precipitates a new-found emotional communion. Despite prolific parental complaints, Mother-Molly is willing to sympathize with her daughter's growing pains and, in so doing, begins to retrieve the maternal sentiments that tie her emotionally both to the estranged adolescent and to a wayward Odyssean spouse.

MOLLY AND LEOPOLD:
RECONCILIATION AND COMMUNION

By presenting Stephen Dedalus in the "Ithaca" episode as a surrogate for Blazes Boylan, Bloom invokes a psychological strategy worthy of Homer's Odysseus. Having spiritually adopted Stephen to replace his lost son Rudy, Bloom finds it "only natural" to attempt to share his beloved wife with the poet/professor who might successfully distract her from the brawny suitor who has recently claimed her attentions. Molly sarcastically comments: "what is he driving at now showing him my photo . . . I wonder he didn't make him a present of it altogether and me too" (*U* 18: 1302 – 5). If Molly accuses her husband of laying an emotional trap for her with Stephen as bait, she nevertheless springs eagerly into the net. It is Stephen, in fact, whose amorphous image begins to dominate her fantasies and to supersede Boylan as an object of romantic reverie.

Molly tells herself that "itll be grand if I can only get in with a handsome young poet at my age" (*U* 18: 1358 – 9). She immediately proceeds to convince herself that such a May/July liaison would be feasible, since Stephen must be a mature young man in his twenties: "I wonder is he too young hes about wait . . .

I suppose hes 20 or more Im not too old for him if hes 23 or 24"
(*U* 18: 1326 – 8). At Bloom's implicit suggestion, Molly imagines
herself in the role of matriarchal muse: "they all write about some
woman in their poetry well I suppose he wont find many like me"
(*U* 18: 1333 – 4). Characteristically, she thinks of poetry in terms of
the "fine young" body of the poet, whose firm flesh might provide
"some consolation for a woman like that lovely little statue he
bought . . . theres real beauty and poetry for you" (*U* 18:
1348 – 51). Molly's aesthetic model is, appropriately, a figurine of
Narcissus, a sculpture so tantalizing that it makes her want to
perform fellatio – on the statue, the body of Stephen Dedalus, or
any of "those fine young men . . . down in Margate strand
bathingplace" (*U* 18: 1345 – 6).

Imagining such euphoria, Molly is suddenly alarmed at the
thought of Boylan: "O but then what am I going to do about him
though" (*U* 18: 1366 – 7). Compared to these fantasies of erotic
delight, Molly's egotistical lover becomes an annoying encum-
brance. He cannot compete with inflated dreams of an author who
would immortalize her charms: "Ill read and study all I can find or
learn a bit off by heart if I knew who he likes so he wont think me
stupid if he thinks all women are the same and I can teach him the
other part Ill make him feel all over him till he half faints under me
then hell write about me lover and mistress publicly too with our 2
photographs in all the papers when he becomes famous" (*U* 18:
1361 – 6). The promise of both fame and scandalous publicity
provides a fairly compelling lure for the romantic Molly, who envisions a release from conjugal boredom through illicit union with
a bohemian writer.

By the time she has fabulated a deliciously provocative liaison
with Stephen, Molly is ready to judge Boylan a self-centered fool,
an "ignoramus that doesnt know poetry from a cabbage" (*U* 18:
1370 – 1). Although this potent suitor seems to have a gargantuan
sexual appetite and a surprisingly short refractory period, Molly
expresses growing disenchantment with his rudeness and playful acts
of sexual aggression: "one thing I didnt like his slapping me
behind" (*U* 18: 122). Boylan apparently considers their love-making
a trivial amusement. "Of course," Molly thinks, "hes right enough
in his way to pass the time as a joke" (*U* 18: 1375 – 6). She knows
that such an egotistical male will never provide her with the kind of
emotional satisfaction she so deeply craves ("sure you might as well

be in bed with what with a lion" [*U* 18: 1376 – 7]) and chooses the lionous Leopold over the lionized, bestial Boylan.

It is, finally, Stephen Dedalus who functions as catalyst in the "disintegration of [Molly's amorous] obsession" (*U* 17: 939). Despite fantasies of the young poet serving an erotic apprenticeship under her tutelage, Molly is also able to think of him as a surrogate son and to feel pity for this "stray dog" of an author. Her earliest memories of Stephen remind her of Rudy: "I saw him driving down to the Kingsbridge station with his father and mother I was in mourning thats 11 years ago now yes hed be 11" (*U* 18: 1305 – 7). Stephen was eleven when Molly last saw him, and she connects the incident with her loss of a son who, she thinks, would now be eleven had he lived. Although Molly may seem callous in her remark about the pointlessness of ritual grief, she is obviously trying to cope with earlier emotional trauma when she wonders: "what was the good in going into mourning for what was neither one thing nor the other . . . of course he insisted hed go into mourning for the cat" (*U* 18: 1307 – 10). A few moments later, she lets down her guard and recalls the handmade jacket used as a funeral shroud for her innocent lamb/child: "I suppose I oughtnt to have buried him in that little woolly jacket I knitted crying as I was . . . but I knew well Id never have another our 1st death too it was we were never the same since" (*U* 18: 1448 – 50). She has evidently been forced to develop various psychological strategies to sublimate the bereavement over her son's death – surely a life-shattering event for a young woman in the full bloom of procreative potential. Molly is invoking one of the many rationalizations that have allowed her to handle the loss of her baby. By imagining Stephen as "a darling little fellow in his lord Fauntleroy suit" (*U* 18: 1311 – 12), she unconsciously entertains the prospect óf spiritually adopting this roving Irish bard and placing him in an appropriately filial role.

When Molly identifies Stephen as the "young stranger neither dark nor fair" (*U* 18: 1316) who appeared on the cards earlier in the day, she assures herself that the poet must be in his mid-twenties. But when she feels solicitous and maternal, she describes him as "hardly 20" (*U* 18: 1462), a boy not much older than her daughter Milly. In a rare moment of explicit resentment at Lunita Laredo's desertion, Molly sees herself as substitute caretaker to the renegade Stephen: "where would they all of them be if they hadnt all a mother to look after them what I never had thats why I suppose hes running wild now out at night away from his books and studies . . . well its a poor case that those that have a fine son like that theyre not satisfied and I none" (*U* 18: 1441 – 5). Like Bloom, Molly desperately longs for a surrogate son to replace little Rudy; and, like her husband, she mentally adopts Stephen and imagines him as a full-fledged member of the household – a pampered guest who could study in the room upstairs, sleep in Milly's bed, instruct his hostess in Italian, and enjoy the sumptuous breakfast that she (or Bloom) would prepare.

In Molly's mind, Stephen has already been transformed into a figure of the absent child; and, like Telemachus, he is accompanied in her imagination by the father so long absent from Penelope's still-fertile bed. As surrogate son, Stephen binds Molly to the wandering husband who has recently found in her warm female presence an Edenic land of "milk and honey." The association with Stephen proves crucial to the episode, for it distracts Molly from her earlier obsession with Boylan and re-focuses her imaginative energies on Bloom as the cherished Byronic lover of her youth.

When Molly considers confessing her adultery to her husband, one begins to suspect that the encounter with Boylan has been part of an unconscious ploy to attract an errant spouse. At the conclusion of her soliloquy, Molly is plotting to rekindle Bloom's interest: "Ill tighten my bottom well and let out a few smutty words . . . now make him want me thats the only way" (*U* 18: 1530 – 40). If the only way to win him back is to appeal to his coprophiliac obsession, Molly will pull out all the stops and make use of whatever tricks or fetishes required. She is determined to wake Bloom from his sexual slumbers and re-ignite the flames of their mutual passion. Molly dismisses, one by one, the competing suitors who have wooed and temporarily won her favor: she rejects Boylan as a fool, Gardner as a ghost, and Stephen as an innocent child. In the end, she comes back to her husband Leopold as the "strange wild lover" of youthful reverie.

Molly returns in fantasy to memories of Gibraltar at a time when the *ingénue* could still wear the white rose of virginity and when the red rose of womanhood was just about to flower. As she sinks into sleep, the sun of her imagination rises and illumines the dreams of this mountain-flower blossoming on the hill of Howth. The Bloom of her youth has given her burgeoning images of poetry. In the conclusion of her monlogue, Molly re-enacts the thrill of unconsummated passion that holds the two lovers suspended in a prelapsarian world of pulsating desire: "God of heaven theres nothing like nature the wild mountains then the sea and the waves rushing then the beautiful country with fields of oats and wheat and all kinds of things and all the fine cattle going about that would do your heart good to see rivers and lakes and flowers all sorts of shapes and smells and colours springing up even out of the ditches" (*U* 18: 1558–63). Like Adam and Eve in the Edenic garden, Leopold and Molly are united in a Rousseau-esque dream of romantic innocence. As flower of the mountain, Molly fashions from sublimated sexual drives a resounding lyrical crescendo celebrating the raptures of erotic *jouissance*:

> yes he said I was a flower of the mountain yes so we are flowers all a womans body yes that was one true thing he said in his life and the sun shines for you today yes that was why I liked him because I saw he understood or felt what a woman is and . . . I gave him all the pleasure I could leading him on till he asked me to say yes and I wouldnt answer first only looked out over the sea and the sky I was thinking of so many things he didnt know of . . . and O that awful deepdown torrent O and the sea the sea crimson sometimes like fire and the glorious sunsets and the figtrees in the Alameda gardens . . . yes when I put the rose in my hair like the Andalusian girls used . . . and I thought well as well him as another and then I asked him with my eyes . . . and drew him down to me so he could feel my breasts all perfume yes and his heart was going like mad and yes I said yes I will Yes. (*U* 18: 1576–609)

A flower of Gibraltar and Howth, Molly says "yes" to Leopold and herself becomes a Bloom.[37] She knows that sexual and marital consent are in this case identical, and her feelings about both suggest a strong attraction to Bloom's epicene personality – a fascination that will not only endure but prevail through sixteen storm-tossed years of bourgeois marriage.

In the androgynous Leopold Bloom/Henry Flower, Molly finds a sympathetic love-object whose nurturant qualities provide a psychological surrogate for the absent mother of childhood abjection. On an unconscious, latent and symbolic level, the man-womanly Bloom satisfies Molly's repressed longing for pre-Oedipal (comm)union. His penis metaphorically "flowers" as phallic signifier in a substitution and reversal of the lost maternal breast, in accordance with Freud's formulation that "when sucking has come to an end, the penis also becomes heir of the mother's nipple."[38] In the mythic guise of Eve/Persephone, Molly, tasting the seed of forbidden fruit, returns it seasoned with spittle to the mouth of a maternal surrogate, to inseminate the fertile and receptive male with her own mimetically nurturant seed(cake). Molly feeds Bloom with the spittle/seedcake/Ceres-cake that she herself desires, offers nurture as he sucks her breasts, and symbolically re-enacts the mother/child drama of reciprocal love and psychic valorization denied her in infancy. At the end of "Penelope," she tantalizes her lover with a poetic pablum that resuscitates his manhood and wins, in turn, the seminal gift of sexual/phallic/fetishistic completion.

As Joyce's idealized paradigm of the Jewish "family man," Bloom embodies those Oriental qualities associated in Molly's imagination with the lost Lunita. Molly displays a keen perception of and appreciation for her husband's "difference" from the others: he is warm, considerate, caring, sensitive, and "polite to old women." Her real concern, of course, is that he be polite and loving to her, no matter what her age or physical appearance. She desperately longs for that *heimlich* womb and nurturant presence obliterated from childhood memory by Lunita's untimely desertion. It is Bloom who offers his blossoming mountain flower not only eight full-blown (opiate) poppies, but the unqualified gift of non-judgmental affection associated with mother-love. Enamored of this dark semitic stranger, a virginal Molly says "yes" to her solicitous suitor and to the "awful deepdown torrent" of heterosexual passion that both replicates and redefines the frustrated pulsions of infantile desire.

The emotional gaps in Molly's past engender, throughout "Penelope," a subversive feminine discourse that defies logocentric boundaries, borders on the margins of hysteria, and, in its melancholic quest for the absent (M)Other, longs to suture the wound of pre-Oedipal separation. In being "not all," Molly evinces a "supplementary *jouissance*," a *jouissance* "of the body . . . *beyond the phallus*."[39] She perpetually seeks to heal the trauma of maternal abjection by re-creating the polyphonous rhythms and lyrical echolalias of semiotic communication.[40] Leopold Bloom serves as a channel, a surrogate, an instrument for the articulation of primordial feminine desire – ruptured in its futile search for an original, oceanic union with the imaginary mother, but temporarily healed in fantasized recollections of erotic joy and orgasmic transcendence shared, at the height of youthful exuberance, with an androgynous son/husband/lover.

Throughout *Ulysses*, sexual identities are indeterminate and polymorphous, psychologically mobile and perpetually transferable. Joyce's novel mockingly reproduces the Oedipal triangle of "Daddy-Mommy-Me" only to shatter and disrupt the dictates of its culturally embedded scenario. Molly and Leopold reciprocally occupy complementary subject-positions of beneficent phallic mother and blissfully dependent *infans*. Each oscillates, by turn, between a subjective articulation of polymorphously perverse desire and the valorizing role of Lacanian *objet a*. Although Stephen temporarily plays a surrogate son binding Molly and Leopold together as Oedipal parents, this Freudian family romance quickly gives way to a nostalgic mother-child coupling, with the new womanly man and psychologically bisexual woman at its enigmatic nexus. Poldy plays "Mommy" to a bedsteadfast spouse who takes shape as mythic (M)Other in his own heterogeneous imagination. And Molly, historically in love with an absent female figure, learns to reconstruct the maternal subject-position through, and in relation to, an uxorious spouse.

In the Blooms' unusual conjugal configuration, the patriarchal subject-position of authoritarian Daddy remains conspicuously vacant. It is temporarily occupied by such caricatured males as Major Brian Cooper Tweedy and the indomitable Blazes Boylan. But the voice of authority is radically diffused in the carnivalesque atmosphere of 7 Eccles Street and disrupted by the "thousand break-flows" of pre-Oedipal (and anti-Oedipal) desire that revels in libidinal viscosity: "Flows ooze, they traverse the triangle, breaking apart its vertices."[41] This anarchic ménage brings us, in Deleuzian terms, "yet another message and another code: everyone is bi-sexual, everyone has two sexes" in a schizoid world of polymor-phously perverse "desiring machines."[42] Lunita Laredo and Major Tweedy, Rudolph, Ellen Higgins, Millicent and Rudy Bloom all lie together in the great conjugal bed of psychological filiation.

Both Molly and Leopold handle the Lacanian experience of radical "lack" by nostalgically endowing one another with theological wholeness and plenitude. Their reveries of salutary presence belong to an always-already absent world of prelapsarian bliss. As Bertha declares in *Exiles*, romantic epiphany "comes only once in a lifetime. The rest of life is good for nothing except to remember that time" (*E* 91). And it is precisely this act of poetic remembering, of re-collecting transitory moments of love and (imaginary) communion and recasting them in aesthetic form, that gives joy, delight, and ecstatic *jouissance* to the psychic horizons of an "all too human," and all too mortal, physicality.

6

READING *FINNEGANS WAKE*
The Feminiairity which Breathes Content

Voice! . . . the frantic descent deeper deeper to where
a voice that doesn't know itself is lost in the sea's
churning. . . . Agony – the spoken "word"
exploded, blown to bits.

(Hélène Cixous, "Sorties")

ALP AND HCE

In *Finnegans Wake*, as in *Ulysses*, Joyce again sets up a repressive
Oedipal triangle in order to mock, destroy, and obliterate it. In this
most revolutionary and avant-garde of texts, the obsessive, logocentric reality of the male, along with the *idée fixe* of patriarchal
authority ("awethorrorty" [*FW* 516. 19]), has been ossified into
stony impotence. The compulsive desire for mastery has hardened
into the rocky sensibility of Finn MacCool, an ancient Irish giant
helplessly shaking a "meandering male fist" (*FW* 123. 10). The
masculine persona of Humphrey Chimpden Earwicker, a
"patrified" hero or *Immensipater* (*FW* 87. 11, 342. 26), is paralyzed
in phallocentric rigidity.[1] In contrast, Anna Livia Plurabelle
embodies the "woman creature" who speaks fluid and remains free.
The traditional hero, dead and outmoded from the beginning of the
book, has to be dreamt into waking, into "Array! Surrection," by
Anna's life-giving riverrun.

Anna Livia Plurabelle emerges in *Finnegans Wake* as Joyce's all-
including, most farraginous archetype. She is open, fluid, and
forever "yea-saying" to the rushing torrent of temporal phenomena
associated with the given moment of cosmic experience. Even more
than Molly Bloom, Anna captures the semiotic rhythms of the
capacious unconscious and the free flow of fertile libidinal desire. As
mother and lover of men and women, she leaps into the lap of old
Father Ocean, the watery grave of death and resurrection, until, in
the persona of ALP, womb merges with tomb to continue the
endless process of evaporation and vaporous redistribution that
characterizes cosmic regeneration.

It is with *Finnegans Wake* that Joyceans tend to divide into two separate camps – those who, like Joseph Campbell and Henry Robinson, attempt to extract from the text a recognizable narrative and those who celebrate the *Wake* as a post-structuralist *oeuvre*, free of character, story, or identifiable subjects.[2] Although I recognize the need to suspend traditional notions of "go-ahead plot" in the *Wake*, it nonetheless seems fruitful to extrapolate tessellated, fragmented *personae* from the *Wake*'s labyrinthine prose and to interpret these fabulated subjects in terms of mythic, sexual, psychoanalytic, and cultural productions. I tend to speak of ALP as though this "alphybettyformed" female were rounded and identifiable in the Joycean text while, at the same time, bracketing an ever-present awareness of the impossibility of discussing figures from the *Wake* apart from their textual/contextual discursive matrix. One appeals to tropes and rhetorical figures, acknowledging the extended metaphorical dimensions of a polysemic linguistic construct that arises from and perpetually reflects the intractable, polymorphously perverse dimensions of an ineffable textual unconscious.

The persona of Anna Livia Plurabelle in the *Wake* is both riverwoman and gadfly, a flowing stream and a "kindly fowl." Scratching and burrowing, searching the litter of all the dungheaps on the planet, she busily roots out the "literature" (French *littérature*, both litter and letter) that will produce a missive to vindicate her husband. An unquenchable source of movement and curiosity, she is also the busy, pecking hen about to give birth to the primordial egg from which the world of art can be generated. The egg becomes Humpty Dumpty, or HCE in his ovular persona, precipitously balanced on the wall of a male-constructed civilization and dependent on ALP for continuing vitality. *Finnegans Wake* might, in some sense, be interpreted as a magnificent couvade, a hymn by the male artist to those feminine creative powers that man can only imitate through art or war – through a poetic reshaping of the material world or by aggressive conflict that asserts a phallocentric will to power in grandiose acts of conquest and destruction.

"Allalivial, allalluvial!" (*FW* 213. 32). All alive are part of that divine being Allah, here "done" by Joyce in a feminine mode. Unlike the Judeo-Christian God, omnipotent and omniscient, the female mother/goddess is immanent in the world of nature. Her "omni" qualities are less than plenipotentiary and manifest an all-encompassing alliance with life and love, rather than with the knowledge and power traditionally ascribed to a patriarchal deity. If old Father Ocean reveals himself as a wrathful Poseidon, Mother Anna flows through the land nourishing and rejuvenating her children without the bitter, acerbic sting of her salt-sea father.

Wishing us "teems of times and happy returns" (*FW* 215. 22–3), Joyce celebrates "Annah the Allmaziful" (*FW* 104. 1): "Anna was, Livia is, Plurabelle's to be" (*FW* 215. 24). Playing the "trinity scholard," the artist feminizes and Latinizes the eternal Trinity of Catholicism – the three-personed god resurrected in female form. Blending east and west, "sanscreed" with "eryan" (*FW* 215. 26–7), he offers Anna Livia, in all her plurabilities, as a multifarious, tripartite mother goddess who embraces the Viconian cycles of history ("Ordovico or viricordo" [*FW* 215. 23]), as well as the muck-laden reality of "Dear Dirty Dumpling" (*FW* 215. 13–14), both city and husband, "foostherfather of fingalls and dotthergills" (*FW* 215. 14).

Joyce's mythic invocation appeals to a trinitarian deity whose emanation is both Catholic and Freudian. In her ancient identity as Annah, ALP embodies the archetypal female – Heva, Eve, and Lilith, mother of the race and progenitrix of all the daughter-sons that presently people the earth. As legendary matriarch, she manifests the inarticulate, atavistic powers worshipped by prehistoric pagan races. She is the Great Mother that preceded Hera and Zeus in the Greek pantheon and later functioned as the Ceres-figure of the Eleusinian cults. But she also plays the role of Cybele, exotic and destructive goddess worshipped and feared as proverbial temptress. In more contemporary terms, Anna bears in her wake the mysterious forces of the id and the buried libido erupting from the subterranean world of a farraginous textual unconscious.

HEN VERSUS HUN: THE FIRST BOOK OF GUINNESSES

In the introductory chapter of *Finnegans Wake*, the archetypal Anna appears in different, contradictory guises. On the one hand, she is the "gnarlybird," a diminutive damsel who caricatures the busy, chattering, gadabout female. Her gossip serves as a repository of cultural fragmentation and offers a contemporary analogue to the religious gospel of an earlier age. In another incarnation, ALP becomes the strong-willed Grace O'Malley, the Prankquean-pirate who challenges Jarl van Hoother, steals his sons, and is ultimately reconciled to a life of bourgeois domesticity.

In a 1905 letter, Joyce wrote to his brother Stanislaus: "I am sure
. . . that the whole structure of heroism is, and always was, a
damned lie" (*Letters* II, 81); and, in the course of the *Wake*, he
boldly reveals the deception behind heroic pretensions to patriarchal
authority and military grandeur.³ In a polymorphous impersonation
of the British war hero Willingdone/Wellington that shapeshifts into
the French/Corsican Napoleon, HCE embodies the kind of masculine aggression that Joyce perpetually satirizes. Willingdone is a self-
styled imperialist who *thinks* himself great in all things, in guilt and
in glory; but in actual fact, he is simply a pretentious, vulnerable
human being subject to irritation and arousal by the taunting,
seductive "jinnies": "This is the jinnies with their legahorns feint-
ing to read in their handmade's book of stralegy while making their
war undisides the Willingdone. The jinnies is a cooin her hand and
the jinnies is a ravin her hair and the Willingdone git the band up"
(*FW* 8. 31–4; French *bander*, "to have an erection"). Infuriated, the
general sends a scatological message to these female temptresses and
their military entourage: "Cherry jinnies. Figtreeyou! Damn fairy
ann, Voutre" (*FW* 9. 13–14).⁴
    Like God the Father or a petulant child, HCE demands that his
"will be done" even when military maneuvers prove irrational or
the field of battle degenerates into a sordid erotic "skirtmish."
Throughout *Finnegans Wake*, man disposes and disperses; he erects,
then destroys the political foundations of a civilization jerrybuilt to
resemble the chaosmos of Babel. The male is "Bygmester Finnegan,
of the Stuttering Hand" (*FW* 4. 18), a putative master of both
language and law, and an Ibsenian Master Builder constantly
subject to tragic hubris and a fatal fall precipitated by a "collupsus
of his back promises" (*FW* 5. 27–8). Significantly, the Wellington
Monument in Phoenix Park stands as the slumbering giant's ithyphallic member in the mythic topography of the *Wake*.⁵
    It is the female, in contrast, who burrows in the dungheap of
dissonant experience and rescues the orts, scraps, and fragments of
a more tentative and polyvalent bricolage constitutive of "femaline"
culture. Anna Livia, as Biddy the Hen and chambermaid of history,
serves as guardian of humankind's sacred word-hoard – those
"litters from aloft" that dazzle the primitive Mutt and Jute. "What
a mnice old mness it all mnakes! A middenhide hoard of objects"
(*FW* 19. 7–8). In this runic claybook lie "miscegenations on
miscegenations" that "lived und laughed ant loved end left" (*FW*

18. 20 – 1). Their fantastic tale will prove intelligible to the "abced-minded" scholar willing to excavate the muck and detritus of this mysterious "allaphbed" (*FW* 18. 17 – 18). Entombed in the cemetery-dungheap are the primordial parents, lying face to face or "fux to fux" (*FW* 177. 36) in a surrealistic archeological grave. Earwicker, that "gyant Forficules," will some day rise like a phoenix from the garbage dump of history. Fallen in battle, he will nonetheless be resurrected by "Amni the fay," who presently collects a litter of letters to vindicate her spouse.

If ALP as gnarlybird seems obsequious and diminished, she projects, in the role of Grace O'Malley, the sixteenth-century Irish pirate, an archetypal image of folkloric witch – a fiercely independent and willful woman who poses a genuine threat to male domination. As Prankquean, Grace challenges the smug Jarl van Hoother, an indigenous aristocrat ensconced in Howth Castle. The earl presides over an all-male fortress whose only female resident is treated as a dummy or doll – an inert sexual plaything bound in incestuous alliance with the prepubescent "jiminis." Into this masculine stronghold bursts Grace O'Malley, brash and sphinx-like, to pose a riddle of sexual/conjugal/creative import: "why do I am alook alike a poss of porterpease?" (*FW* 21. 18 – 19). When the earl, stony and marmoreal, not only refuses to answer but "shuts" (shits and shuts the door) in her face, the Prankquean retaliates by kidnapping the two jiminies in turn. Magically transforming their twin personalities, she bequeaths on each the balanced, androgynous aspect missing from van Hoother's company. Grace changes the melancholic Tristopher into a "luderman" and teaches the playful Hilary the tragic seriousness of life. Her rain/reign offers the boon of female fertility to the otherwise parched, constipated, and anal-obsessive Jarl.

On the Prankquean's third visit, van Hoother dons his seven-layered martial costume and emerges to fight the witch-like warrior. Like Willingdone before him, he engages in a scatological battle with his uppity opponent. "And he clopped his rude hand to his eacy hitch and he ordurd and his thick spch spck for her to shut up shop, dappy. And the duppy shot the shutter clup. . . . And they all drank free. For one man in his armour was a fat match always for any girls under shurts" (*FW* 23. 3 – 9). In the thundering attack that conflates defecation with military "skirtmish," either van Hoother defeats and sexually conquers the Prankquean, who is

168

tamed by conjugal affiliation; or, alternatively, he is bested by the mother/daughter team that colludes to outwit him. (In the latter case, the dummy, finally roused to life and allied with the Prankquean in a new "duppy" incarnation, secretly opens the door of the castle for Mummy while Daddy goes forth in proud display.) Is the boastful Jarl defeated by his Amazonian opponent? Or are we to take the Swiftian paraphrase literally and assume that the male figure emerges victorious over the mother/daughter team allied in their "shurts" against him? In either case, male and female are reconciled in a felicitous scene of family peace: "And that was the first peace of illiterative porthery in all the flamend floody flatuous world. . . . The prankquean was to hold her dummyship and the jimminies was to keep the peacewave and van Hoother was to git the wind up. Thus the hearsomeness of the burger felicitates the whole of the polis" (*FW* 23. 9–15).[6]

ALP, as peacefugle or pirate, "a parody's bird, a peri potmother" (*FW* 11. 9), emerges as the dominant force of emotional conjunction in the narrative. Taming the military ardor of a patriarchal male, she integrates hostile family members in peaceful communion and serves as catalyst for a larger reign of bourgeois felicity through the "whole of the polis." The family, Joyce implies, reflects the political macrocosm in Viconian microcosm. From the dialectic of warring male/female desires, domestic synthesis is, at least temporarily, possible.

"CONTINUARRATION": THE TALE OF ANNA LIVIA

O tell me all about Anna Livia! I want to hear all about Anna Livia. Well, you know Anna Livia? Yes, of course, we all know Anna Livia. Tell me all. Tell me now. You'll die when you hear. (*FW* 196. 1–6)

The tale told of Anna Livia by the ancient Irish washerwomen at the ford is a narrative "Minxing marrage and making loof" (*FW* 196. 24). And it is, inevitably, the story of Humphrey Chimpden Earwicker, that "duddurty devil" her husband, who fell from grace when he "thried to two in the Fiendish park" and has to vindicate his "awful old reppe" (or reputation) of lascivious male desire (*FW* 196. 10–15). The tale/tail of their marriage is a bifurcated narrative, spliced together from gossip and hearsay by the crones who make the Adam and Eve story a part of the river's oral history (herstory).[7] Marriage, they imply, is a social mirage demanded by man-made civilization, an institution which captures woman in the double persona of wife and minx, seductress and nurturer.

The first question that concerns the washerwomen is one of legitimacy. Were ALP and HCE legally married? Were the banns of matrimony loosened or celebrated? Or were the two merely spliced together in a union of nature? "Was her banns never loosened in Adam and Eve's or were him and her but captain spliced? For mine ether duck I thee drake. And by my wildgaze I thee gander" (*FW* 197. 11–14). The conjectures suggest that HCE and ALP assumed from the beginning that "what's sauce for the goose is sauce for the gander." Anna "can show all her lines, with love, license to play. And if they don't remarry that hook and eye may!" (*FW* 197. 15–17). It is not clear whether the washerwomen accuse ALP of libertine behaviour with a number of men after her marriage or with HCE and his personae illegitimately before the wedding. In any case, their speculations about the union become increasingly violent, until they assume that Humphrey used force to win his bride: "he raped her home, Sabrine asthore, in a parakeet's cage" (*FW* 197. 21–2). The union takes on mythic resonances recalling the rape of the Sabine women, as well as Milton's Sabrina fair, gleaming goddess of the river.

Of Daneviking extraction, that "gran Phenician rover" (*FW* 197. 31) HCE combines Viking arrogance with Phoenician wiliness and an economic heritage as a wandering "marchantman," sailor, seacaptain and whaler (like Mulvey, Odysseus, and Sinbad). As a trader, he "erned his lille [Danish, 'little'] Bunbath hard, our staly bred" by the "wet of his prow" (*FW* 198. 5–7). Humphrey won Anna by the sweat of his brow and by the semen of his prow – thus combining Adam's curse with the *machismo* characteristics that adhere to his Viking heritage. (In another incarnation, he becomes the *Wake*'s Norwegian sea captain wooing a tailor's daughter.) Anna serves Humphrey a quotidian diet of daily bread that proves both nurturant and stale, life-sustaining and diminishing. The bold Phoenician sailor searches for his mummy in the hindmoist waters of Anna's riverrun: "Don't you know he was kaldt a bairn of the brine, Wasserbourne the waterbaby? Havemmarea, so he was! H.C.E. has a codfisck ee" (*FW* 198. 7–9). Humphrey evidently exhibits "cod's eyes" as he greedily glares at Anna, his bride-prize of war, who embodies both the Blessed Virgin Mary (*Ave Maria*) and a military trophy of successful conquest. Like Shem and Shaun at their geometry lesson, he seeks a primordial return to the embryonic waters of an "eternal geomater" (*FW* 296. 31–297. 1) through sexual congress (*Gè mèter* = Greek, "Mother Earth").

Anna, claim the crones, is "nearly as badher as him herself" (*FW* 198. 9). A brash temptress, she tantalizes her drooling seducer in much the same way that Molly titillated Mulvey. The ingenuous Anna does not hesitate "to go in till him, her erring cheef, and tickle the pontiff aisy-oisy . . . Letting on she didn't care, sina feza, me absantee, him man in passession, the proxenete!" (*FW* 198. 12–17). Serving as her own procuress, she challenges male authority with the tickling fluency of female river-speech, then feigns indifference and lets the proud Humphrey play the male/*macho* role of "man in passession."

The narrative of Anna Livia is, of course, shaped by the voyeuristic voices of the washerwomen. Both narrator and auditor function as comic *dramatis personae*, and both display a powerful emotional investment in the tale. "O, tell me all I want to hear," the auditor begs. "Tell us in franca langua. And call a spate a spate" (*FW* 198. 14–19). As one old woman spits up a spate of accusations and lascivious details, the other excitedly demands frank language and chides the narrator for using exotic jargon. Both women delve into the dirty laundry of Anna's past and spin a tale of female sexuality that affords them the salacious delights of pornography. Part of the fun is casting aspersions on Anna's character: "For coxyt sake and is that what she is? Botlettle I thought she'd act that loa. . . . Sure she can't fiddan a dee, with bow or abandon! . . . Well, I never now heard the like of that! Tell me moher. Tell me moatst" (*FW* 198. 22–8).

Unconsciously invoking Freudian strategies, the women go back to Anna's childhood to search for a clue to her sexual behavior. Anna's grandfather, the River Humber, was apparently an authoritarian patriarch, somber and atavistic: "Well, old Humber was as glommen as grampus, with the tares at his thor and the buboes for ages, . . . with his dander up, and his fringe combed over his eygs" (*FW* 198. 28–30; 199. 5–6). This fierce, primitive authority figure demands obsequious responses from all of his charges, plies them with questions, and examines their estuarial depths with a harsh, judgmental hand/eye.

The virginal Anna, vulnerable and ingenuous, might have felt herself threatened by grandpa's incestuous gaze. "And there she was, Anna Livia, she darent catch a winkle of sleep, purling around like a chit of a child" (FW 199. 11–12). The demure damsel is pliable and obedient: "she'd cook him up blooms of fisk and lay to his heartsfoot her meddery eygs, yayis, and staynish beacons on toasc and a cupenhave so weeshywashy of Greenland's tay" (FW 199. 15–18). These Danish delicacies from Copenhagen and Greenland suggest a Nordic feast worthy of the great Finn himself. No question here about female duties in the preparation of a sumptuous breakfast, all washed down with the tea that suggests female sexuality in the novel's hermeneutic code. Woman is nurturer to man's alimentary and sexual needs. As in *Ulysses*, food and love are conflated, and the word "yes" serves as an exuberant affirmation of life's fertile possibilities.

Like Molly Bloom, the matronly Anna is definitely male-identified.[8] Grandfather and husband meld together into a single masculine paradigm in the midst of a morning meal. In an effort to please her irascible spouse, ALP works her fingers (and knees) to the bone. For the pleasure/*plaisir* of her greedy partner, she labors "for to plaise that man hog . . . till her pyrraknees shrunk to nutmeg graters while her togglejoints shuck with goyt" (FW 199. 20–2). Such feminine altruism is ill rewarded by a husband who goes on a hunger strike and refuses to be satisfied by any of her life-giving favors: "my hardey Hek he'd kast them frome him, with a stour of scorn" (FW 199. 24–5).

Like Maria in "Clay," Anna takes comfort in songs that celebrate "*The Heart Bowed Down*" to her lord and master and humms a "balfy bit" to elevate her spirits. She tries to please her partner sexually by the titillations of fellatio, but her efforts meet with mixed success: "What harm if she knew how to cockle her mouth! And not a mag out of Hum no more than out of the mangle weight. Is that a faith? That's the fact" (FW 199. 31–3). As the boundaries of fact and fiction are eradicated, the two washerwomen express faith in the historical truth of their topping tale of tupping and tepping. With her "frostivying tresses dasht with virevlies" (FW 199. 36) and robed in "a period gown of changeable jade" (FW 200. 2), Anna tries to arouse her husband's flagging sexual interest. Piquing his appetite, she serves as procuress for HCE, "throwing all the neiss little whores in the world at him" (FW 200.

29 – 30). Anna challenges her spouse's manhood by casting the spoils of war – both male and female – into "Humpy's apron" (*FW* 200. 32) to satisfy his languishing homo- and heterosexual desires.

Like Molly Bloom planning the seduction of an errant husband, Anna complains of her partner's impotence in a letter she writes to lighten her heart and expresses the desire to recapture his waning attentions. As the washerwomen listen to the epistolary voice of Anna Livia, they recognize in its message of vanity and lamentation some of the typical concerns of any Dublin matron. *"By earth and the cloudy but I badly want a brandnew bankside, bedamp and I do, and a plumper at that!" (FW* 201. 5 – 6). ALP's first request from her earthbound hubby and from the "old woman in the sky" is for a corset or girdle to contain her overflowing riverrun – a female undergarment similar to the boned corset that caught Molly's eye in the *Gentlewoman*. Characteristically, Anna has internalized the grief she feels over conjugal estrangement by projecting HCE's lack of interest onto her own fading charms. She complains of being *"wore out"* from *"waiting for my old Dane hodder dodderer, my life in death companion, my frugal key of our larder, my much-altered camel's hump . . . to wake himself out of his winter's doze and bore me down like he used to"* (*FW* 201. 7 – 12). With the blood of Danevikings in his veins, HCE the hod-carrier has degenerated into a disappointing sexual partner – a dotty old gentleman who resembles a "doddered" tree, shattered and infirm. Anna's letter, vindicating Humphrey of sexual criminality by protesting his age and erotic infirmity, suggests the senility, illness, and impotence of this "life in death companion." Anna grieves for the loss of her "maymoon's honey," now reduced to a "Decemberer" fool whose "camel's hump" is "much altered" in this May/December marriage. Yet she expresses the hope that he is merely hibernating and that, like the dead Osiris/Adonis/Attis of ancient fertility rites, he will be resurrected "out of his winter's doze" and resume a manly posture with the full force of sexual renewal.[9]

Meanwhile, Anna waits – lovingly, patiently, and devotedly – for her sleeping, slumbering giant to wake himself and assumes responsibility for a shrinking domestic economy. As industrious as Molly during the lean years of her marriage to Bloom (Molly sold second-hand clothes and played the piano in a coffee-palace), Anna offers to hire herself out as a washerwoman or seamstress to keep the family in *"horsebrose and milk"* (*FW* 201. 15–16). Bound to onerous maternal and spousal duties, she nevertheless dreams, like Molly before her, of liberating herself from her snug domestic nest and leaping away to the careless freedom she once knew as a seaside girl. She clings to fantasies of recapturing her promiscuous adolescence, of escaping *"to the slobs della Tolka or the plage au Clontarf to feale the gay aire of my salt troublin bay"* (*FW* 201. 18–19).

The washerwomen, meanwhile, are transfixed in voyeuristic expectation of the "hazelhatchery part" of Anna's salacious biography. Like the narrator of "Ithaca" cataloguing Molly's lovers, and like Molly exaggerating the number of times she and Boylan had sex, the crones excitedly forage for every titilating detail. "How many times did she do it?" they wonder, as they try to verify questions of when, how, where, and with whom. As self-proclaimed guardians of female virtue, they are simultaneously fascinated and scandalized by the story of ALP's profligacy. The spinsters delineate her adventures with a kind of Rabelaisian relish – though their voyeuristic investment makes them less than reliable narrators. How many children had she, and who were their fathers, they wonder. "How many aleveens had she in tool?" (*FW* 201. 27). Popular opinion suggests "a hundred eleven, wan bywan bywan." Having bred this gargantuan brood, Anna "can't remember half of the cradlenames she smacked on them" (*FW* 201. 29–32). In the face of such prodigious fecundity, the women remark smugly, "They did well to rechristien her Pluhurabelle" (*FW* 201. 35), the whore of multiple beauties. The one hundred and eleven progeny she has borne imply a long line of fertile progenitors, embraced with wild abandon by Anna in her sensuous, alluring youth.

As the prurient crones comment and crow over Anna's erotic experiments, they accuse her of adolescent frivolity: "She must have been a gadabout in her day, so she must, more than most. Shoal she was, gidgad. . . . Tell me, tell me, how cam she camlin through all her fellows" (*FW* 202. 4–8). Rumor has it that she was a veritable childish devil or "diveline." The virginal Anna threw away her chastity, that pearl of great price, and squandered her virtue with bucks of the town: "Casting her perils before our swains . . . Linking one and knocking the next, tapting a flank and tipting a jutty" (*FW* 202. 8–11). Bursting with curiosity, the washerwomen follow the chronology of Anna's lovers and try to trace her fluid meanderings back to an ınitial act of virginal violation, the original sin that forfeited her chastity. They are ironically oblivious of the fact "that each one who enters imagines himself to be the first to enter whereas he is always the last term of a preceding series even if the first term of a succeeding one, each imagining himself to be first, last, only and alone, whereas he is neither first nor last nor only nor alone in a series originating in and repeated to infinity" (*U* 17: 2127–31). "Waiwhou was the first thurever burst?" they ask excitedly, trying to determine the mysterious identity of the male who initially burst the hymen of Anna's seed-bed (*FW* 202. 12–13). The first of Anna's multiple lovers is an amorphous deity, not "who" but "Waiwhou," a superhuman power that reigns as Thor/Thur, the omnipotent father/lover/patriarch. Thor, the thunder-bearer and hammer-hurler of ancient Nordic myth, provides a divine model for Daddy, the god in the sky that bursts his raincloud in a shower that fills the river and fertilizes her soil.

According to the washerwomen, the paradigm of that primordial defloration was war-like and violent. Either Anna was conquered by planned seduction "in a tactic attack" (*FW* 202. 13) or she was wooed and won "in single combat" (*FW* 202. 14). Metaphors of love and war mingle in the narrative, as the female becomes prey to a Daneviking's prowess and yields her virginity, in a moment of weakness, to the enemy who attacks the fortress of her chastity. This allegory of military conquest goes back to the *Roman de la Rose*, Spenser's *Fairie Queene*, and numerous medieval and Renaissance texts that envision the soul as virginal victim, stormed and conquered by an alien seducer. To the prurient spinsters, it is inconceivable that the prodigal Anna could have given herself freely in an act of erotic delight, since their model of sexuality is both aggressive and puritanical. They assume that woman is innocent prey to the libidinous desires of the male and that the victimized virgin must be raped or seduced by a phallic predator: "Tinker, tilar, souldrer, salor, Pieman Peace or Polistaman" (*FW* 202. 14–15).

The washerwomen long to discover the name of this mysterious suitor: "That's the thing I'm elwys on edge to esk" (*FW* 202. 15). But Anna admits to some confusion about her first love affair: "She sid herself she hardly knows whuon the annals her graveller was, a dynast of Leinster, a wolf of the sea, or what he did or how blyth she played or how, when, why, where and who offon he jumpnad her and how it was gave her away" (*FW* 202. 23–6). That first "graveller" proved a grave-dealer, a "deathsman of the soul" who left her gravid with potential life. Topographically, her despoiler contaminated her river-water by gravelling her soil-bed and polluting the purity of her virginal stream. Was that first seducer a king or a sea-wolf, a dynast or a pirate? Anna does not know. She cannot recall "how it was gave her away" because the reason (both causal and rational) is irrelevant. All those logocentric questions of "how, when, why, where and who offon" adhere to the fabric of an artificial social structure irrelevant to sexual union. In the traditional wedding ceremony, Anna would have been given away by her father; but in the trans-social world of *Finnegans Wake*, the syntactical construction "gave her away" is notably bereft of an identifiable subject. The pronoun "who" has been replaced by "how," and the inviolate daughter/bride implicitly gives *herself* to the father/lover who claims her virginity.

Liberated from traditional family attachments, the ingenuous girl yields to her lover in a moment of consummate ecstasy. Her innocence and fluidity, her lilting form and shimmering movements, sharply contrast with the ponderous gait of her stony, patriarchal suitor. "She was just a young thin pale soft shy slim slip of a thing then, sauntering, by silvamoonlake and he was a heavy trudging lurching lieabroad of a Curraghman, making his hay for whose sun to shine on, as tough as the oaktrees" (*FW* 202. 26–30). In the persona of an earth-bound, lumbering farmer, HCE hardly seems worthy of Anna's nubile charms, though she apparently capitulates "with nymphant shame" when he gives her "the tigris eye! O happy fault! Me wish it was he!" (*FW* 202. 33–4). As Tigris and Euphrates meet, Joyce recalls the cradle of civilization and the Garden of Eden, where sin and culture were born simultaneously. The story is Joyce's version of the fall of Adam and Eve, the "happy fault" of original sin that gave birth to the shame of mortality and the glories of Christianity. Here the fault evokes sheer sensuous delight, rather than the Christ-centered promise of future redemption. Man and woman fall together into erotic pleasure to rise again and be redeemed in their offspring. This is the primordial lesson of the Garden of Eden/Erin, Ireland's little "split pea" of a biblical story of Genesis (Guinnesses).

But, one of the washerwomen protests, the tale at this point is "anacheronistic." Anna's first liaison was not with HCE, but with an earlier lover "when nullahs were nowhere, in county Wickenlow,

garden of Erin, before she ever dreamt she'd lave Kilbride and go
foaming under Horsepass bridge, . . . to wend her ways byandby,
. . . for all her golden lifey in the barleyfields and pennylotts of
Humphrey's fordofhurdlestown and lie with a landleaper, well-
ingtonorseher" (*FW* 202. 36 – 203. 1 – 7). Before she lay with the
composite hero Wellington/Norseman/Horsa/Finn, Anna Liffey, in
an earlier incarnation, made love in a Wicklow "garden of Erin,"
a utopian landscape where "the hand of man has never set foot"
(*FW* 203. 15 – 16). Somewhere between the Alaskan tundra (Yokan)
and the ovular vale of Avoca (Ovoca), the innocent Anna had her
first sexual experience. The place is a fantasy fairyland rather than
a geographical locale: "Dell me where, the fairy ferse time!"
(*FW* 203. 16). Anna's very first lover was apparently a "holy
man," the "local heremite, Michael Arklow" – an Irish archangel
and hermit/priest dwelling in a Celtic dell somewhere in the heart
of the Hibernian hinterlands. Arklow is a spiritualized HCE persona
portrayed in a sanctified, mock-heroic incarnation. The time of the
"natural nuptials" between Anna and Michael is equally equivocal:
the union takes place "one venersderg in junojuly" (*FW* 203.
19 – 20), a winter's Venus-day ripe for venereal perambulations,
when ALP could play Juno and goddess, the ox-eyed woman in
search of her man.

Anna emerges as a teasing *ingénue* with "kindling curves you
simply can't stop feeling" and "singimari saffron strumans of hair"
that weave a web of feminine charm around her shy but willing
lover. The traditional Irish analogue to the tale is the hagiography
of St Kevin of Glendalough, the hermit tempted by a threatening
female. In Joyce's mock-heroic version of the narrative, the monk
does *not* cast the temptress Cathleen into the lake; instead, he
embraces the lake/river as a holy water/lover. Arklow parts the
"reignbeau's heavenarches" of Anna's saffron tresses, "deepdark
and ample like this red bog at sundown," and immerses himself in
her silt-laden streams. Goaded by her "enamelled eyes," indigo and
enticing, the monk is seduced into "vierge violetian" – a virginal
violation that baptizes Michael in the amorous waters of the violet
Liffey (*FW* 203. 22 – 9).

Characteristically, the pious hermit protests his innocence and
projects his desire onto the woman he lusts after. The lapsed celibate
claims he was seduced by the lascivious Anna: "He cuddle not help
himself, thurso that hot on him, he had to forget the monk in the

man" (*FW* 203. 32–4). As he showers the beautiful maiden with kisses, Arklow warns her "never to" succumb to his erotic titillations. With "niver to, niver to, nevar" (*FW* 203. 36) on his lips, the monk fondles his lover, "rubbing her up and smoothing her down," plying her with "kiss akiss after kisokushk" (*FW* 203. 35), until the "vierge" to be violated is vertiginously aroused. The preamble to this "holy communion" is described in tantalizing, lubricious prose. But the parting and mingling of Anna's hindmoist waters is an act that occurs almost entirely off-stage. The reader can only imagine the mad monk Michael plunging with salacious delight into the "majik wavus" of Anna's "elfun . . . meshes." We are told, opaquely, that "Simba the Slayer of his Oga is slewd" (*FW* 203. 32), as the monk relinquishes his prurient vows of celibacy.[10] Losing male reason and logocentric control, Michael kisses Anna's "freckled forehead" and immerses himself in the life-giving waters of her mortal stream. (The figure of Shaun/Kevin later portrayed in Book IV is far more restrained.)

Anna, for her part, "hielt her souff" (held her breath, panted in ecstasy).[11] Yielding her virginity to this bold priest's entreaties, she revels in the sexual initiation that inaugurates her river/womanhood: "she ruz two feet hire in her aisne aestumation. And steppes on stilts ever since" (*FW* 204. 2–3). The ecstasy of love-making elevates Anna's ingenuous self-image; she emerges from the erotic moment whole, hearty, and transcendent. The virginal "sacrifice" proved an act of psychic healing that gave her a sense of personal integration. If the rent (or hole) caused by coition was experienced as a physical wound, her monk/priest/lover provided verbal balm and healing kisses: "That was kissuahealing with bantur for balm! O, wasn't he the bold priest? And wasn't she the naughty Livvy?" (*FW* 204. 3–5). No longer a maid, Anna delights in her newly acquired status of womanhood and is filled with the pride of feminine consummation. Her estuaries have risen, and her sense of self is bright and untarnished. She has emerged from the stream of her youth into the full flower of maturity as woman and river, Anna Livia/Anna Liffey.

The sobriety of this sacramental rite of passage is immediately undercut by the voyeuristic gossip of the washerwomen, who continue to excoriate the "naughty Livvy" for the imputed sins of her youth. The hermit Arklow, violating a vestal virgin with all the guilt and excitement of sacred sin, believed that he took the flower of Anna's womanhood. Rumor has it, however, that "two lads in scoutsch breeches went through her before that, Barefoot Burn and

Wallowme Wade, . . . before she had a hint of a hair at her fanny to hide or a bossom to tempt a birch canoedler" (*FW* 204. 5–9). These lascivious scouts defiled her long before she had pubic hair or the nub of a bosom and snatched the unripe fruit of her budding sexuality. Even before that, in an incident that mimics the rape of Leda by Zeus in the form of a swan, the innocent Anna "all unraidy, too faint to buoy the fairiest rider, too frail to flirt with a cygnet's plume, . . . was licked by a hound, Chirripa-Chirruta, while poing her pee, pure and simple" (*FW* 204. 10–13). The young girl was vulnerable even while urinating. Naïve and helpless, she was violated by a dog that caught her with her knickers down during "shearingtime." Thus was the *ingénue* taken against her will by a rapacious hound in a scene that suggests a conflation of rape and oral sex. (Female micturition is apparently a source of polymorphously perverse arousal for HCE, whose voyeuristic interest in his daughter Issy's urination and in the titillating tinklings of two girls in Phoenix Park may well be constitutive of his mysterious sin.)

Further back in her infantile past, at the dawn of protohistory, "first of all, worst of all, the wiggly livvly, she sideslipped out by a gap in the Devil's glen while Sally her nurse was sound asleep in a sloot and, feefee fiefie, fell over a spillway before she found her stride" (*FW* 204. 14–17). In her early sexual researches, the wiggly, elusive child experienced a primordial fall: the rivulet lost her innocence to "stagnant black pools" and lay and laughed amid blushing hawthorns.[12]

Ultimately, of course, Anna's sexual fall into womanhood is shrouded in ambiguity and mystery. Joyce acknowledges, like Freud before him, the erotic delights of polymorphous perversity that characterize infantile sexual experiments. Anna, it seems, lost her virginity when she escaped the surveillance of her nurse and fell over a spillway, but the exact nature of the event remains obscure. Is the child innocent and free ("innocefree") as her laughter, and Joyce's Yeatsian pun, would suggest? Or is she guilty of a mysterious autoerotic transgression? We do not know, and neither Joyce nor the washerwomen will tell us, since their story appeals to the inarticulate guilt of childhood eroticism. Anna's "virginal violation" at the hands of a godly monk, two boy scouts, a hound, and viscous black pools of rainwater comprises a sexual aporia woven into the tapestry of the *Wake*. It becomes part of the unfathomable "eternal geomater" that Shem and Shaun will try, unsuccessfully, to penetrate and unravel.

The washerwomen who tell us the tale of Anna Livia perceive themselves moral guardians of Dear Dirty Dublin. In charge of the town's dirty linen, they simultaneously clean the undergarments and scour the secrets of a sinful populace, interpreting the history of ALP through a palimpsest of gossip and popular cliché. They see the world through Gerty MacDowell eyes and impose a soap-opera vision of experience onto their sudsy, soporific story. But like the river itself, the narrative of ALP must "never stop" and demands "continuarration." "You're not there yet. I amstel waiting. Garonne, garonne!" (*FW* 205. 14–15). In this makeshift, "Wakeschrift" tale of HCE's resurrection, the old women cite ample proof of Humphrey's impotence. "Her Chuff Exsquire," with white mane and hoary (whory) locks, has suffered the extinction of both chivalric heroism and courtly love. Without the "role of a royss in his turgos the turrible" (*FW* 205. 29), he must forgo regal stature and, like Turko the Terrible, become invisible – a deposed king reduced to vapid pantomime.

The resourceful Anna, however, determines to "frame a plan" to resuscitate her spouse. She borrows a mailsack from her "swapson" Shaun the Post, then makes herself "tidal to join in the mascarete" (*FW* 206. 13–14). Transforming herself into a magical shape-changer, Anna moves from stream to river to tidal estuary and, at each turn, assumes a new cosmetic persona in the masquerade of life. In ritual fashion, she arrays herself for a seductive bridal union with HCE. She mingles nature with civilized beauty, the decorative landscape of Ireland with trivial social charms. "Then, mother-naked, she sampood herself with galawater and fraguant pistania mud, wupper and lauar, from crown to sole" (*FW* 206. 30–2). She washes in a sacred bath of holy water and mud and lets her hair fall in winding coils to the seashore. She bathes in the flowers and mud of existence, cleansing her body with the silt of society and making soap from the effluvia of daily life. "Dirty cleans" (*U* 4: 481), Bloom notes in *Ulysses*. And here the muck of Anna's silty soil mingles with her river-water as she washes "allover her little mary" with leafmould, "turfentide and serpenthyme" (*FW* 206. 34–6). Joyce's prose imitates the rhapsodies of the biblical Song of Songs in evoking a shimmering fantasy of feminine splendor: "Peeld gold of waxwork her jellybelly and her grains of incense anguille bronze" (*FW* 206. 36–207. 1).

Like any mediterranean bride in spring, Anna weaves garlands for her hair "of meadowgrass and riverflags," "bulrush and waterweed," and the surrealistic "fallen griefs of weeping willow" (*FW* 207. 2 – 4). Covering herself in "shellmarble bangles," she resembles an eastern bride ornamented with bracelets, anklets, armlets, amulets, and necklaces of every description. Sending for her "boudeloire maids," this Baudelaire of the cosmetic paint-box creates herself anew in feminine finery to impress "His Affluence" HCE. Begging only for a "minnikin" of his precious time, she escapes from her distracted mate and flees "with her mealiebag slang over her shulder" (*FW* 207. 18 – 19). HCE's "cock striking mine" makes a "bridely sign" of conjugal possession. But the clever bride/matron beautifies herself to attract, then distract, her partner and escape his cloying protectorate. Once a "pearl of great price," ALP has now become an "oysterface" matron equipped with a peasant mealiebag that evokes resonances of both womb and word-sack – a catch-all, carry-all that protects the word of female gossip and the sacred Logos of future incarnations. This embryonic sac(k) recalls the "virgin womb of the imagination" essential to the delivery of mail/art/word/life.

In another guise, Anna Livia is "no electress at all" – no regal or electrifying seductress – but "old Moppa Necessity" (*FW* 207. 29), the reality principle that manifests itself as mother to ingenuity and invention. More atavistic than electrifying, ALP resembles a "bushman woman, the dearest little moma ever you saw" (*FW* 207. 34 – 5). Not a beautyqueen, she is, instead, a "judyqueen," caught between youth and senility and bound to maternal duties that make her a "punch and judy" puppet of domestic frustration. The fluid river-woman is a female Proteus, and we are warned to "saise her quirk for the bicker she lives the slicker she grows. Save us and tagus!" (*FW* 208. 1 – 2). As she matures, Anna becomes all the more elusive and incomprehensible. Losing the narcissistic focus of adolescent self-centeredness, she slips into and out of the thousand protean shapes demanded by nurturance and sympathetic projection. As the boundaries of her ego gradually dissolve, this mother/woman begins to assume the multiple personalities of those in the realm of her care.

ALP's environmental garb, described in gargantuan proportions, evokes the Rabelaisian atmosphere of the earlier comic catalogues in the "Cyclops" episode of *Ulysses*. Her clogs are "a pair of ploughfields"; Anna wears "owlglassy bicycles" for eyeglasses and protects her pudenda ("hydeaspects") with a "fishnetzeveil" (*FW* 208. 4–11). She takes Sugarloaf Mountain as a hat, "with a gaudy-quiviry peak and a band of gorse for an arnoment and a hundred streamers dancing off it" (*FW* 208. 7–9). Her "blackstripe tan joseph was sequansewn and teddybearlined, with wavy rushgreen epaulettes" (*FW* 208. 16–18). In fact, "everyone that saw her said the dowce little delia looked a bit queer" (*FW* 208. 29–30). Anna takes such pride in her appearance that they say "the darling murrayed her mirror" (*FW* 208. 35) in a narcissistic nuptial that both consummates and murders the adolescent ego.

As fertile mother and womb of the world, Anna hides in her "nabsack" (womb, wordsack, female genitalia) all the "plurabilities" that she bestows on her progeny.[13] "Anna high life" impartially distributes a hoard of presents, both good and evil, to "her furzeborn sons and dribblederry daughters, a thousand and one of them, and wickerpotluck for each of them" (*FW* 210. 4–6). In the riotous catalogue that follows, Joyce introduces his own authorial signature in the person of Sunny Twimjim, the boy from Clongowes Wood College – an institution now demoted to a kind of savage outpost of Christianity. Through Anna's beneficence, the author receives "a Congoswood cross on the back" (*FW* 211. 5) to be borne on the new *Via Dolorosa* of aesthetic martyrdom. Shem/Seumas, Sunny's shade or fictional alter ego, sports the traditional poetic crown of laurel that gives the illusion of feeling big – though, in fact, the poetic crown of momentary glory is interchangeable with the artistic crown of thorns decorating the exiled Twimjim.

After a catalogue of Anna's maternal gifts to her children, the Dublin washerwomen reassert the central paradigm of *Finnegans Wake*: "every telling has a taling and that's the he and the she of it" (*FW* 213. 12). Every tale is both history and herstory, reflecting the binomial bifurcation of male/female conflict polarized around kinetic patterns of amorous desire. Man and woman clash, fall, and sexually collide to give birth to a new breed/brood of daughter/sons that will re-enact age-old sagas of marital/martial conquest. The male rises to phallic grandeur only to fall into the womb of his hind-moist mother/wife, and his seed is cast on the waters of humanity to be brought to fruition in endless cycles of racial renewal.

Every story has a "taling" – a tell-tale narrative base rooted in irrational forces of conflict and creativity. More often than not, public · myth and legend are constructed around a private hermeneutic code obscuring a seminal story of unresolved sexual conflict. Impelled by erotic desire, man and woman love, clash, fight, and do "the coupler's will" (*U* 3: 47). The thrill of Eros drives them to pursue, resist, and eventually capitulate to the consummation of natural law. From sexual congress come children who must learn both the laws of nature and the secrets of the universe, from grandaddy's martial arts to the more anarchic elements of grandma's grammar.

All taling has a tail or end in an eschatology that climaxes in the dissolution of that final distinction between self and other, between subjective personality and objective impotence. The subject loses its will and reason and is re-absorbed into larger, impersonal cycles that "begin again" the endless drama of human existence. "It saon is late. 'Tis endless now. . . . Wharnow are alle her childer, say? In kingdome gone or power to come or gloria be to them farther? Allalivial, allalluvial!" (*FW* 213. 15–32).

Out of universal suffering, we turn as a tribe to that patriarchal potentate, "the great Finnleader himself in his joakimono on his statue riding the high horse there forehengist" (*FW* 214. 11–12). The author Giacomo Joyce writes himself into this Möbius strip of a narrative when he puts the Finnleader "in his joakimono" and makes a lexical joke of authority and patriarchal pretension. The "*Immensipater*" (*FW* 342. 26) is little more than an anachronistic clown sprung, fully blown, from the head of a facetious Giacomo. Though riding a high horse, this stupefied "awethorrorty" (*FW* 516. 19) figure is paralyzed and frozen, confined to a stone pedestal that immobilizes him in haughty but impotent pride.

The Dublin washerwomen, inadvertently skeptical, implicitly reject an omnipotent Lord and patriarchal divinity by directing their prayers to a more earthly and compassionate goddess, the holy "Maria, full of grease" (*FW* 214. 18). This new proletarian protector is both divine intercessor and female drudge, bearing the "load" of earthly toil in her spiritual dealings with the deity. The crones call on female saints to mitigate the wrath of an angry god and, in a more atavistic invocation, importune "Icis," the Egyptian Isis who resurrected Osiris by restoring his castrated manhood. In a burst of Catholic devotion, the women pray to "marthared mary allacook" (Margaret Mary Alacoque from "Eveline"), the self-martyred saint who now appears as both cook and "kook" in a new proletarian dispensation.[14]

Uttering semi-religious orisons, the washerwomen remind us that the promise of paradise comes each evening with sunset and urge us to: "Wait till the honeying of the lune, love! Die eve, little eve, die!" (*FW* 215. 3–4). As the "little eve" reminiscent of our first mother fades into sunset, a new life of moonlight, dream, romance, and fantasy will be born again. "Anna Livia, trinkettoes" emerges as boon companion and twinkling star, drinking and twinkling at eventide, "the queer old skeowsha anyhow." She embraces and revitalizes her "quare old" mate, "Dear Dirty Dumpling, foosther-father of fingalls and dotthergills" (*FW* 215. 12–14). In the incarnation of Finn MacCool, HCE is father to an atavistic race of preternatural progeny – son/daughters with fins and gills who comprise an androgynous species. The hermaphroditic Humphrey inaugurates a primordial polis of social organization: "*Hircus Civis Eblanensis!*" Celebrated as the legendary "goat" founder of Dublin, he functions as mythic progenitor of the Irish race: "He had buckgoat paps on him, soft ones for orphans. Ho, Lord! Twins of his bosom. Lord save us!" (*FW* 215. 27–9). Nurturing twin antagonists in his bosom, he fosters the sons who will eventually defy, castrate, and supersede their impotent father.

Like Beckettian *dramatis personae*, the washerwomen feel convinced that talk can "save us" (*FW* 215. 34). So long as they continue to narrate a story, to articulate the stirrings of consciousness in fabulated oral history and myth, they remain part of a "tale told of Shaun or Shem" (*FW* 215. 35) – a tale of waking and resurrection, of "teems of times and happy returns. The seim anew" (*FW* 215. 22–3). And so the women celebrate all "Livia's daughter-sons" in a song of life and renewal that transcends their earlier social concerns of legitimacy and sexual sin, of gossip and puritanical judgment. Out of Anna's fall comes a proliferation of progeny, each with a different personal cry that makes it unique in time and space.

The moral and ethical questions raised with salacious interest at the beginning of the chapter now dissolve into universal, cosmic cycles of racial continuity as the women themselves, with the coming of evening, fade into a dark, atavistic landscape to become part of the rocks and trees and stones that unite them with great Mother Earth. Enveloped by night, the crones sink into the heaviness of slumber: "My foos won't moos. I feel as old as yonder elm" (*FW* 215. 34–5). They fall into the quotidian death of sleep and darkness, that obscure region of dream and dissolution that absorbs the waking mind and makes consciousness part of an alien, inanimate world. As the two women fuse with the cosmos surrounding them, the distinction between self and other, between conscious identity and inanimate matter, is gradually effaced. The chattering voices of the crones are lost in the distance, and the episode ends with a murmuring music echoing Anna's evensong: "Beside the rivering waters of, hitherandthithering waters of. Night!" (*FW* 216. 4 – 5). As the women fade into a darkening landscape, the voice of the river arises from the book's textual unconscious and floods the night world of *Finnegans Wake*.

MAMAFESTA

A "commodius vicus of recirculation" (*FW* 3. 2) brings us back to ALP's letter in Book I, Chapter 5, and forward to its fuller, more embellished form in Book IV. Joyce originally wrote the latter version for the "mamafesta" chapter but put it aside and incorporated it into Book IV fourteen years later.[15] Each of the multiple versions of the letter serves as a textual paradigm for the *Wake* itself, acting as a semiotic microcosm of the linguistic macrocosm in which it has, like a puzzle or rebus, been playfully embedded.[16] The letter is one of the central aporias of the book, an enigmatic document whose gaps and fragmented utterances reflect, in miniature, the polysemic discourse of its fabulative matrix. Dictated by Anna to Shem her scribe, the epistle "writ by one and rede by two and trouved by a poule in the parco" (*FW* 201. 1 – 2) was reportedly "rede" (both read and understood) by the twin sons Shem and Shaun. Posted and lost, it was finally "trouved" (French, *trouver*, "found, verified, and proved true") by a "poule" or French hen in the Phoenix Park, the alleged site of HCE's sin. The hen is, in turn, an androgynous ALP-ish fowl who serves the function of a twentieth-century Paul, a purveyor of the Joycean gospel through scatterings of gossipy good news to the modern world.

Beginning with a tripartite invocation to "Annah the Allmaziful [rather than Allah the Allmerciful], the Everliving, the Bringer of Plurabilities," Joyce offers a feminized version of the Lord's Prayer: "haloed be her eve, her singtime sung, her rill be run, unhemmed as it is uneven!" (*FW* 104. 1 – 3). We are told that her "untitled mamafesta memorialising the Mosthighest has gone by many names" (*FW* 104. 4 – 5) collected in a riotous Rabelaisian catalogue of over one hundred titles (*FW* 104. 5–107. 7). The missive, identified as a "proteiform graph" and a "polyhedron of scripture" (*FW* 107. 8), definitely signifies a writing whose weird, cuneiform (or cunniform) letters prove indecipherable to those "naif alphabetters" who would interpret the text as the scribbling of "a purely deliquescent recidivist [an unreformed criminal], possibly ambidextrous, snubnosed probably and presenting a strangely profound rainbowl in his (or her) occiput" (*FW* 107. 9–12). To both the "eternal chimerahunter" and the lust-loving scholar, the text "has shown a very sexmosaic of nymphosis" (*FW* 107. 13–14). Or, to put it another way, "*Honi soit qui mal y pense.*" The letter is a perplexing text whose polysemic utterances are shot through with the kind of gaps, slippages, holes, and protuberances that allow its reader to project his/her unconscious preoccupations (rooted metaphorically in the "occiput," or back part of the skull) onto the amorphous content of this *tabula* semi-*rasa*, "tabularasing his [HCE's] obliteration" (*FW* 50. 12). Curiosity has invaginated the folds or *plis* in a document once buried, then picked (or pecked) up – sent, lost, found, and finally resurrected from the dungheap of history by Biddy the hen.

The letter has been reduced to a puzzle of graphemes that implicitly graph a sexual history buried in the tissue of the epistle's integument. We are promised the pornographic titillations of "nymphosis" (Greek *nympheusis*, "wedding") and a collage of dirty pictures. Joyce uses the word "ambidextrous" here, as in "Circe," to suggest the elusive, bisexual identity of its author, "snubnosed" like a woman or a castrated male and exhibiting a "profound rainbowl" of fertile indentation. The rainbow promise of biblical history (male to male, Yahweh to Noah) is transmuted into a vaginal hole/bowl to catch the fecundating rain/ejaculate/tea squidsquirted onto the receptive (female) page/tissue. The text calls our attention to its margins or "*bordereau*" (French, "inventory") to reveal "a multiplicity of personalities inflicted on the documents or document and some prevision of virtual crime or crimes" (*FW* 107. 24–6). So fragmented is the letter that we do not know if it constitutes a single text or many, whether it "previews" one crime or multiple transgressions. We "must grope on till Zerogh hour" (*FW* 107. 21–2), in search of that female "zeroine" who complements *Ain Soph*, the ineffable One of Kabbalistic mystery.

The text of this holy epistle (sacred and shot full of holes) is about marriage and copulation, a titillating "sexmosaic" of bodily parts melded together in the institutional union of one flesh promised in a wedding ceremony that gives the impression ("under the closed eyes of the inspectors" [*FW* 107. 28–9], at least), that two are made one and "coalesce, their contrarieties eliminated, in one stable somebody similarly as by the providential warring of heartshaker with housebreaker and of dramdrinker against freethinker" (*FW* 107. 29–32). The female temptress (heartshaker) rouses masculine desire and violent need until the semi-inebriate (dramdrinking) male is moved to acts of possessivenes and destruction. But the promises of institutional marriage prove little more than a tantalizing illusion perpetrated for the sake of birthing "more generations and still more generations," despite the "jolting series of prearranged disappointments" (*FW* 107. 33–5) that characterizes conjugal life. This bull of a male begins to resemble a castrated ox, perpetually humping to fend off the disillusionments of bourgeois life: "it's as semper as oxhousehumper!" (*FW* 107. 34).[17]

The letter from "Boston (Mass.)" (*FW* 111. 9–10) is described as a "radiooscillating epiepistle" (*FW* 108. 24), and the Shaun-like professor who explicates the text urges us, first, to examine its envelope: "to concentrate solely on the literal sense or even the psychological content of any document to the sore neglect of the enveloping facts themselves circumstantiating it is . . . hurtful to sound sense" (*FW* 109. 12–15).[18] Here, as so often happens in the *Wake*, the literal text is (en)gendered as an eroticized sexual/textual object open to the specular gaze of a lascivious-minded male. The letter's scriptural polyhedron takes the form of Anna's sexual delta, as letter and writer are fused in fantasy, and ALP's hindmoist hemispheres, suggestively draped in "evolutionary clothing . . . full of local colour and personal perfume," are lovingly fondled "by the deft hand of an [impotent] expert" (*FW* 109. 23–30). Beneath the "feminine clothiering" of Anna's embroidered female writing is inscribed the imprint of that "feminine fiction, stranger than the facts" (*FW* 109. 31–2), the deltoid site of copulation and conception, whose life-giving potential transforms egg and ejaculate into a unique human being, and whose genitalia "a little to the rere" (*FW* 109. 33) are the bodily source of that life-writing indigenous to every "femaline" author. A tale potentially resides in ALP's tail, an evolutionary "hystry" (*FW* 535. 18) or womb-story that "parently" looks backward to "the ginnandgo gap between antediluvious and annadominant" (*FW* 14. 16–17) and a "lost histereve" (*FW* 214. 1) of biblical origins; and forward to the fruitful "Wooming" (*FW* 603. 1) of "one fledge, one brood" (*FW* 378. 4), the "child we all love to place our hope in for ever" (*FW* 621. 31–7). Just as the chaotic "allaphbed" of literal letters gestates in a mysterious "proteiform" writing to inscribe meaning into signifiers that bear arbitrary, socially imposed significance; so, too, Anna's "cunniform" scripture generates those embryonic forms which, as mature subjects, will produce "the grandest gynecollege histories" (*FW* 389. 9).[19]

It is clear from the body of this epistolary teaser that sex and text are one: ALP has inscribed a feminine fiction into the fragmented rhetoric of her letter, and it is only by examining the text's deltoid holes that one begins to penetrate the mystery of female sexual/ textual desire. As Shari Benstock notes, the "letter/dream of desire starts and ends in the woman's body – in the River Liffey – the keys to which are given by Anna Livia through her 'Lps.' located at the mouth of the river, in the labia of the vaginal canal. Riding the river's wave, the letter rests in the 'Gyre O' of the vagina." According to Benstock,

> Anna Livia insures that Earwicker's secret is safe by hiding the letter in the one place he would not think to look, a place he knows *too* well, and one he assumes can only be filled by him. . . . In order to read the letter's message, the reader must first strip the woman and next penetrate her body; the envelope must be torn and the letter removed. . . . Such a process violates the hymeneal covering of the vagina where the letter is lodged, ruptures its protective layers, an infringement that . . . opens the letter to ambiguity, destroying the inviolate nature of its authority.[20]

The text warns that "we are in for a sequentiality of improbable possibles" (*FW* 110. 15). One might as well forget Aristotle's *Poetics* ("Harrystotalies" [*FW* 110. 17]) with its "patrilinear plop" (*FW* 279. 4), along with those logocentric categories bound to be violated by the hen-woman's semiotic discourse. Aristotle's seminal theories about logic, poetics, and epistemology are blatantly challenged by the ovular *écriture* of ALP as "original hen," "an illegible downfumbed by an unelgible" (*FW* 482. 21).[21] "That's the point of eschatology our book of kills reaches for now in soandso many

counterpoint words. What can't be coded can be decorded if an ear
aye sieze what no eye ere grieved for" (*FW* 482. 33–6). As in the
"Nestor" episode of *Ulysses*, the investigative scholar hypothesizes
about the Aristotelian concept of "the possible as possible" and
links it to those "souls impossibilised" through acts of onanism or
contraception. The events recounted in ALP's narrative "are
probably as like those which may have taken place as any others
which never took person" (*FW* 110. 19–21). In the voice of Shaun,
Joyce obliquely contemplates the central mystery of ontology: why
should anything *be* rather than not? Is birth merely an accident of
nature or can one conceive of (and by virtue of) a *lex eterna*
originating in divine providence, a "coupler's will" choreographing
human generation? (In *Ulysses*, Stephen chooses the latter theory,
Bloom the former.) In more colloquial terms, "Which came first,
the chicken or the egg?" Joyce opts for the "coerogenal" hen/hun
(*FW* 616. 20),[22] Biddy Doran, scratching up a fragmented epistle
from the dungheap of human history:

> The bird in the case was Belinda of the Dorans, a more than
> quinquegintarian (Terziis prize with Serni medal, Cheepalizzy's
> Hane Exposition) and what she was scratching at the hour of
> klokking twelve looked for all this zogzag world like a
> goodishsized sheet of letterpaper originating by transhipt from
> Boston (Mass.) of the last of the first to Dear whom it proceded
> to mention Maggy well & allathome's health well only the hate
> turned the mild on *the van* Houtens and the general's elections
> with a *lovely* face of some born gentleman with a beautiful present
> of wedding cakes for dear thankyou Chriesty and with grand
> funferall of poor Father Michael don't forget unto life's &
> Muggy well how are you Maggy & hopes soon to hear well &
> must now close it with fondest to the twoinns with four
> crosskisses for holy paul holey corner holipoli whollyisland pee ess
> from (locust may eat all but this sign shall they never)
> affectionate largelooking tache of tch. (*FW* 111. 5–20)

The mamafesta purportedly contains everything from "A" to
"O" (*FW* 94. 21–2), Alpha to Omega, first to Greek-alphabetic
last. It is written "scotographically" (*FW* 412. 3), in a
night/nought/not-writing, so that a photographic "negative" inversion of Aristotelian logic evinces a feminine semiotic discourse.[23] It
replicates the sacramental hole of Anna's sexual delta, the zero of a

yonic aperture whose darkness masks the life-giving faculty that proves both mysterious and holy. In terms of Joyce's post-Freudian pornosophical philotheology, the "hole" of the female conjoins with the penile "whole" of the male to create a "holipoli" (or holy city/family) based on the Viconian emergence of a *gens* or (hoi-poloi) gentile class. The whole island of Ireland is washed by the Gulfstream and by the seminal tea-stain that transmits vitality to future descendants of the Porter couple.

The letter directs the love-play of feminine desire toward solicitude for "allathome's health" and toward the magical wedding-cake that signifies a sacramental or Eucharistic communion between male and female, "dear thankyou Chriesty."[24] Here Anna Livia defends her husband largely by way of diversionary tactics: he is portrayed as a "Real Absence," the text's embedded theological subject and "Reverend . . . majesty" (*FW* 615. 13), reflected in the diminutive form of an Irish "Maggy" (the dark persona of his daughter Issy, but also a pedestrian Muggy/mugger/muggee, victimized by relentless verbal mugging on the part of his accusers).

The letter's night/not-writing gives a laundered account of ALP's angry retort to the Dubliners who calumniate her spouse and get their "comeuppance" in the epistle of Book IV. Ostensibly talking about the weather and complaining of the summer heat, Anna offers a blessing of domestic health intended to palliate differences and reduce this hostile band to milky-mild placidity. She defuses gossip by appealing to HCE's domestic rights (assured by the "general's elections" of Ireland's republic), his military success in the guise of Willingdone/Wellington, his beneficent reign as Jarl van Hoother, and his aristocratic lineage as "some born gentleman" bearing the bounty of a troth and wedding-cakes. HCE, she implies, is an honorable man true to his matrimonial vows. He has recently laid to rest his competitor Father Michael (an amalgamation of Anna's first lover, Michael Arklow, with the adulterous Father Michael [of the Honuphrius and Anita scandal] with whom Anita/ALP "has formerly committed double sacrilege" [*FW* 573. 3]) in a great "funferall" that celebrates the *Immensipater*'s own victory and resurrection.

Anna "hopes soon to hear well," as opposed to ill, about her persecuted husband, and she closes her mamafesta with fond maternal greetings to the twins, who have doubled their parents' hopes by replicating the images of their forebears. Children and parents

190

double-cross one another "with four crosskisses," as they exchange an affectionate embrace that prophesies future cross-purposes when the Oedipal youngsters mature into potentially parricidal progeny. The cross of parenthood bears its own particular brand of martyrdom, and the gospel of this universal domestic drama will, in turn, be spread by "holy paul" to the gentiles of a modern Dublin/ Heliotropolis. The "masterbilker's" ejaculatory tea-stain inscribes the text with a male cross-signature that proves invulnerable to the gnawings of rapacious insec(s)ts and the jawings of loquacious gossipers.[25]

In this incarnation, the mamafesta is a "culious" example of pleasant/peasant Irish poetry, an epistolary exercise in restraint and diplomacy that recalls the original Greek association between the word for "poet" and that for "maker." Using subtle feminine wiles, ALP adopts a "stralegy"/strategy of effusive solicitude, killing her husband's enemies with kindness. The letter reincarnated in Book IV will be less conciliatory, as Anna's dammed-up riverrun finally explodes in torrents of logorrhea against HCE's accusers, "Mucksrats" (*FW* 615. 16) and "Wriggling reptiles" (*FW* 616. 16). This version of the missive is as ladylike as the journalistic outpourings of a languishing Lydia sipping tea; the final epistle, in contrast, will take fire and bristle with the spousal fury of a veritable virago. "Sneakers in the grass, keep off!" (*FW* 615. 28–9). "Stringstly is it forbidden by the honorary tenth commendmant to shall not bare full sweetness against a nighboor's wiles. What those slimes up the cavern door around you, keenin, (the lies is coming out on them frecklefully) had the shames to suggest can we ever? Never! So may the low forget him their trespasses" (*FW* 615. 32–6).

In her fowlish incarnation as Biddy Doran, the kindly ALP proves a model of love and renewal: "she just feels she was kind of born to lay and love eggs (trust her to propagate the species)" (*FW* 112. 13–14). A "good lay" and a devoted wife, ALP is passionately committed to the public exposure of the truth about her somewhat schizophrenic spouse (or triphrenic, in keeping with his "trilithon sign" [*FW* 119. 17]), who dallies and dances with "apple harlots" and projects himself into the role of the three soldiers who suspiciously survey his actions in the park. As Patrick McCarthy notes, "Anna Livia apparently wants to vindicate her husband but somehow makes matters worse by saying that he had three personalities and his weakness was dancing with young girls."[26] "All shwants (schwrites) ischt tell the cock's trootabout him . . . Yet is it but an old story, the tale of a Treestone [Tristan] with one Ysold [Iseult]'' (*FW* 113. 11 – 19).

The world, apparently, is filled with stories of older men (like King Mark in the Tristan tale) lusting ''erogenously'' (*FW* 115. 14) after young female flesh, ''grisly old Sykos'' who do their ''unsmiling bit on 'alices, . . . yung and easily freudened'' (*FW* 115. 21 – 3). Here the letter's narrative seems to fuse with still another pornographic tale of ''*prostituta in herba*,'' a young woman who ''deliberatively'' somersaults off her ''bisexcycle, at the main entrance of curate's perpetual soutane suit with her one to see and awoh!'' (*FW* 115. 15 – 17) – a digression proposed by the exegete to satisfy his own lascivious obsessions and to transfer sexual culpability onto the female/temptress/victim. ''*Est modest in verbos*. Let a prostitute be whoso stands before a door and winks or parks herself in the fornix near a makeussin wall (sinsin! sinsin!)'' (*FW* 116. 16 – 18). Recalling Earwicker's crime by the Magazine Wall, the narrator excitedly peers (with a ''pudendascope'') at the fantasized figure of a ''neurasthene nympholept . . . under her lubricitous meiosis'' (*FW* 115. 30 – 4), the eternal temptress as nymphomanic adolescent.

Psychoanalytic interpretation quickly gives way to socialist rhetoric on the part of this arrogant lecturer whose ''steady monologuy of the interiors'' (*FW* 119. 32 – 3) usurps the signifying space of ''this oldworld epistola of their weatherings and their marryings and their buryings and their natural selections'' (*FW* 117. 27 – 8). Protesting to the contrary, he has nevertheless allowed masculine egotism and pedantic scholarship to deform ALP's feminine writing, now reduced to ''a miseffectual whyacinthinous riot of blots and blurs and bars and balls and hoops and wriggles and juxtaposed jottings linked by spurts of speed'' (*FW* 118. 28 – 30). Or is the text's obscurity due, in part, to the ''quadrifoil jab'' of another professorial fork/pen/penis (that of Brotfressor Prenderguest [*FW* 124. 15]) expressing hostility toward female ''wholeness'' by recurrently poking the feminine body/text with a penetrating instrument that fragments the narrative tissue of Anna's epistle and blindly reduces it to an artifact in Braille?

Shari Benstock, assessing the psychoanalytic subject-positions of Anna and her daughter in the *Wake*'s night-writing, concludes:

The writing of *Finnegans Wake* both inhabits and is inhabited by

woman, by ALP and Issy, who are present in the transparent
space of the hymeneal folds, in the silences of the historically
interweaved, overlapped, and spiralling story, who constitute the
absent center of the *Wake* universe, who are to be found inside
the mirror, in the bar between the conscious and the
unconscious, between dreaming and waking, between signifier
and signified – both inside and outside the fabric they weave.
These two – who are one in desire – are capable of providing
the origin of the text that exists outside the text, the frame for
the dreamstory that is both outside and within itself: they are the
letter (of desire) that violates and is violated.[27]

ALP AND HCE: THEIR BED OF TRIAL

When Joyce finally portrays HCE and ALP attempting to satisfy
connubial desire, the parodic scene travesties traditional notions of
romantic love. In their incarnation as the pub-keeping Porters, the
couple lie upon their bed of trial and awkwardly attempt to make
love – despite the interruptions of crying children, the threat of
impotence, and the inconvenience of mechanical contraception.
Joyce's graphic stage-directions would send chills down the spine of
a Lawrentian sentimentalist.[28] "Man with nightcap, in bed, fore.
Woman, with curlpins, hind. Discovered. Side point of view. First
position of harmony. . . . Man looking round, beastly expression,
fishy eyes, paralleliped homoplatts, ghazometron pondus, exhibits
rage. . . . Woman, sitting, looks at ceiling, haggish expression,
peaky nose, trekant mouth, fithery wight, exhibits fear. . . .
Closeup. Play!" (*FW* 559. 20–9).

Such "culious" cinematography of an "allnights newseryreel"
(*FW* 489. 35) attempts to capture a fairly typical moment in the life
of a middle-aged couple. Gone are the days of uninhibited passion
and unselfconscious love-making. Sexual congress is dominated by
Anna's frazzled "hesitency" skeptically manifest in a "haggish
expression." Her husband is hardly a passionate Don Juan, as he
screws up his fishy eyes and, with a bestial expression, exhibits rage
at libidinal frustration. Just as he dons "man's gummy article,
pink" in preparation for the amorous event, a child's cry off-stage
interrupts Humphrey's work in progress.

"Airwaked" by Jerry's howl, Anna leaps out of bed and rushes to the child's side. She comforts her restive son by exorcising the phantom father from the boy's childish imagination. Rehearsing the "hystorical leavesdroppings" of Humphrey's sin in the Phoenix park, she insists that the threatening father/god/patriarch is nothing but a Freudian nightmare:

> You were dreamend, dear. The pawdrag? The fawthrig? Shoe! Hear are no phanthares in the room at all, avikkeen. No bad bold faathern, dear one. . . . Gothgorod father godown followay tomollow the lucky load to Lublin for make his thoroughbass grossman's bigness. . . .
> Sonly all in your imagination, dim. Poor little brittle magic nation, dim of mind! (*FW* 565. 18–32)

Porter, a bourgeois pub-keeper and urban grocer, "our hugest commercial emporialist" (*FW* 589. 9–10), is lost in the Babbitt-like ritual of mercantile labor. Enslaved to the materialistic demands of running a business and earning a living for his family, he is sapped of both energy and power. All his phallic potency is channeled into the business of selling Bass ale and keeping afloat on the river of twentieth-century commerce.

In a moment of lustful exhibitionism, HCE deigns to "present wappon, blade drawn to the full" before the "infant Isabella" (*FW* 566. 21–3). But this incestuous indiscretion (or dream thereof) is sharply reprimanded by Anna, who chides her husband in good bog latin:

> – *Vidu, porkego! Ili vi rigardas. Returnu, porkego! Maldelikato!* [Look, pig! They're watching us! Return, pig. Indelicate!] (*FW* 566. 26–7)

As HCE's erect phallus is transformed in his masculine imagination into a gigantic monument, "a stark pointing pole" and "dunleary obelisk" of amazing "lungitube" comparable to the Wellington Monument in Phoenix Park, Anna warns him to shield his weapon with a condom: "I must see a buntingcap of so a pinky on the point" (*FW* 567. 7). Here feminine prudence induces Humphrey to control the fertility of his regal monolith. A Humpty Dumpty fallen from his wall, the deposed patriarch must bequeath his paternal authority to the twin sons who, even now, are "trowelling a gravetrench for their fourinhand forebears" (*FW* 572. 5–6), "two very blizky little portereens after their bredscrums, Jerkoff and

Eatsup" (*FW* 563. 23 – 4).[29]

Humphrey, clearly threatened by the fractious children who usurp Anna's scattered emotional energies, explodes in lascivious fury. Abandoning all trappings of romance, he asserts a legal right to his wife's body, the "access to one's partner" guaranteed by Church law. "Legalentitled," he screams. "Accesstopartnuzz. Notwildebeestsch. Byrightofoaptz. Twainbeonerflsh. Haveandholdpp" (*FW* 571. 28 – 9). The sacred vows of wedlock are mangled by HCE's urgent libidinal need, apparently exacerbated by Issy's lubricious tinklings: "Listen, listen! . . . Annshee lispes privily" (*FW* 571. 24 – 6). Claiming conjugal privilege, he warns his wife to yield to his desires, as both "provideforsacrifice" (*FW* 571. 32 – 3).[30]

In the Roman guise of Honophrius and Anita, HCE and ALP proceed to enact a salacious parody of ecclesiastical rulings on Roman Catholic marriage – a Joycean satire of Church interference in the bedroom, "perhaps the commonest of all cases arising out of umbrella history" (*FW* 573. 35 – 6). Along with various consorts, man and wife engage in a comic catalogue of lascivious, perverse, and incestuous practices. The question is one of conjugal right: "Has he hegemony and shall she submit?" (*FW* 573. 32). Is payment of the "marriage debt" valid if "tendered to creditor under cover of a crossed cheque" (*FW* 574. 14)? Surprisingly, this murky litigation ends in a court judgment favoring the couple's right (and the woman's endorsement) to limit fertility by means of a "good washable pink" (*FW* 574. 25) rubber cheque that checks conception.[31] The never-born soul "impossibilised" by contraceptive practice has no legal rights, since "no property in law can exist in a corpse" (*FW* 576. 5).

HCE and ALP are free to "keep to their rights and be ware of duty frees" (*FW* 576. 35 – 6). Courtship, Joyce suggests, is a "mirror-minded curiositease" (*FW* 576. 24), a titillating "collideorscape" (*FW* 143. 28) of narcissistic gratification. But it ends abruptly when male and female agree to mortgage sexual pleasure for the onerous responsibilities of parenthood: "prick this man and tittup this woman, our forced payrents" (*FW* 576. 26 – 7). In institutional coupling, man and woman seek another self, a comforting alter ego to stave off isolation: "guide them through the labyrinth of their samilikes and the alteregoases of their pseudoselves, . . . from loss of bearings deliver them" (*FW* 576. 32 – 5). "Commit no miracles. . . . Let earwigger's wivable teach you the dance!" (*FW* 579. 13 – 25).

Anna and Humphrey, "basilisk glorious with his weeniequeenie" (*FW* 577. 2), impelled by resurgent faith in erotic pleasure, take up, once again, the dance of wedded love, though "woman's the prey" (582. 31–2). "At half past quick in the morning" (*FW* 583. 30), the couple "photoflash" their love-making in a windowshade silhouette observed by "patrolman Seekersenn" (*FW* 586. 28) and forthwith reported to a Dublin crowd. The coupling is described as a metaphorical horse-race ("old pairamere goes it a gallop, a gallop" [*FW* 583. 12]) and in terms of a spirited cricket match ("she had to kicker, too thick of the wick of her pixy's loomph" [*FW* 583. 32–3]). After Anna warns her husband not to break the condom, "for fear he'd tyre and burst his dunlops and waken her bornybarnies making his boobybabies" (*FW* 584. 13–14), HCE manages triumphantly to shoot his bolt into this "auricular of Malthus." He deliberately refrains from "wetting the tea." Both have paid the marriage-debt and become one: "O I you O you me!" (*FW* 584. 34). "Humperfeldt and Anunska" are "wedded now evermore in annastomoses" (*FW* 585. 22–3) and settle down in the "fourth position of solution" to await the coming of dawn (*FW* 590. 22–3).[32]

CYCLICAL RETURN

In the "wholemole millwheeling vicociclometer" of Joyce's *Wake*, we witness a "tetradomational gazebocroticon . . . autokinatonetically" rehearsing the cycles of Viconian history, those "homely codes, known as eggburst, eggblend, eggburial and hatch-as-hatch can" (*FW* 614. 27–33). Male and female are united in that bisexual, "coerogenal hun" (*FW* 616. 20) that celebrates the coming of the dawn and calls us to resurrection. The voice that proffers benediction is strangely polymorphous and disembodied: "Sandhyas! Sandhyas! Sandhyas!" it proclaims (*FW* 593. 1), fusing the Catholic *Sanctus* with the Sanskrit word for peace, *Samdhi*. Joyce parodies the Indian borrowings of Eliot's *Waste Land* and chants a blessing as ambiguous as that of his poet-predecessor. Convinced that Eliot had plagiarized parts of *Ulysses*, he wreaks vengeance by peppering the *Wake* with Eliotic parodies. HCE's love-making on his bed of trial climaxes with the rooster-cry *Cocorico!*, even though Humphrey is "long past conquering cock of the morgans" (*FW* 584. 24–5) and his procreative potential has been deliberately

circumscribed. Lightning flashes and the rain comes; but the act is
self-consciously sterile, and no seed will fertilize Anna's ageing
delta.

It is Anna Livia, however, who rouses Humphrey from the
reveries of his night-long slumber and calls him to "Array! Surrection!" (*FW* 593. 2 – 3) in the new Egyptian city of Heliotropolis.
Like the immortal Phoenix, he will rise from the ashes of sleep and
death, from the "hundering blundering dunderfunder of plundersundered manhood" to return triumphant, "renascenent; fincarnate
. . . awike in wave risurging into chrest" (*FW* 596. 2 – 6). The
"supernoctural" event climaxes on a note of "joyance" – of
Joycean joy and sexual *jouissance*. Resurrection transpires in a single,
eternal moment, as the sun rises and the Hindu great year,
"madamanvantora" (*FW* 598. 33) renews its cycles. "Father Times
and Mother Spacies," the "old man of the sea and the old woman
in the sky," oversee this cosmic pantomime (*FW* 599. 34 – 5; 600.
2 – 3).

The lyrical voice of Anna, rejuvenating her husband and
celebrating the dawn, gradually begins to emerge from the chaosmos
of Joyce's *ricorso*. ALP remembers the "polycarp pool" where she
was spawned of "Deltas Piscium and Sagittariastrion" and
concludes that "once we lave 'tis alve and vale" (*FW* 600. 5 – 7).
Although she prepares to say "hail and farewell" to spouse and
family, she nonetheless proclaims, triumphantly, "let it be!"
(*FW* 600. 12): "Be! Verb umprincipiant through the trancitive
spaces" (*FW* 594. 2 – 3). The injunction inaugurates a jubilant
hymn to the "given" world of quotidian experience, the keys to
which are bequeathed to the race by the dying river-goddess.

The holy Saint Kevin "Hydrophilos" may come to terms with
"the feminiairity which breathes content" (*FW* 606. 22 – 3) by
taking refuge in a human chalice, "a priest's postcreated portable
altare cum balneo" (*FW* 605. 7 – 8) or "tubbathaltar" (*FW* 606. 2).[33]
But in so doing, he exorcizes the feminine principle and chooses
baptismal celibacy, the spiritual "regeneration of all man by affu-
sion of," rather than immersion in, the holy sister/water of female
creation (*FW* 606. 11). He will never understand "the first and last
rittlerattle of the anniverse; when is a nam nought a nam"
(*FW* 607. 10 – 12), that is, when he is dead or impotent (deprived
of manhood), or when man (generic) is female (specific). According
to this paradoxical tautology, a man is not a man when he is a god,

a corpse, or a woman. In the last case, the feminine genital center is symbolized as a "nought" or hollow space. Then "pubably it resymbles a pelvic or some kvind [Danish, 'woman'] . . . a wenchyoumaycuddler" (*FW* 608. 23–5).

Gradually, the polymorphous, bisexual discourse of Book IV gives way to the lyrical voice of Anna Livia, murmuring her final monologue as she flows out to sea. "Soft morning, city! Lsp! I am leafy speafing" (*FW* 619. 20). Her lisping narrative is filled with fluid "l" and "f" sounds and with open vowels that suggest the yonic spaces of female interiority: "I am leafy, your goolden, so you called me, may me life, yea your goolden" (*FW* 619. 29–30). But her dying message, recalling the golden days of courtship, is one of resurrection, as she exhorts her spouse to arise with the dawn and attempts, simultaneously, to arouse his flagging sexual interest. "Rise up, man of the hooths, you have slept so long! . . . Rise up now and aruse!" (*FW* 619. 25–9). She offers him a clean shirt, double brogues, and a "brandnew big green belt" (*FW* 620. 2) symbolic of Erin/Eireen/Eire. Always, she assures him, "your wish was mewill" (*FW* 620. 27). And it continues to be so, as Anna proffers the girl/child Isabel to take her place in Humphrey's bed. "It's Phoenix, dear. And the flame is, hear!" (*FW* 621. 1–2). The couple's joy in passionate communion may be finished, but the flame of youthful attraction can still be sparked, phoenix-like, by memories of amorous delight.

HCE is apparently old and impotent.[34] Anna, however, has only to close her eyes to remember her husband, along with each of the male progeny he has engendered, as "a youth in his florizel, a boy in innocence, peeling a twig, a child beside a weenywhite steed" (*FW* 621. 30–1). She likes to envisage Humphrey in terms of "the child we all love to place our hope in for ever" – the offspring who reflects the virile energies of its father before he assumed the martial role of a blustering Willingdone on his "big white harse." Casting off "the weight of old fletch," and "laving" (loving, leaving, washing) her husband's flaccid penis, ALP tries to arouse this aged consort with strategies of prepubescent titillation. "Reach down. A lil mo. So. Draw back your glave. Hot and hairy, hugon, is your hand! Here's where the falskin begins. Smoos as an infams. One time you told you'd been burnt in ice. And one time it was chemicalled after you taking a lifeness" (*FW* 621. 24–33). Anna suggests that Humphrey's "hot and hairy" member has been metaphorically scarred by love-wounds – by the "icy fire" of passion and by numerous erotic deaths. The uncircumcised phallus reminds her of a child's, and she tries to arouse the polymorphous potential associated with infantile (and senile) stimulation.

As man and wife stroll together through the waking metropolis of Dublin, their perambulations suggest matitudinal love-play. Anna complains of Humphrey's "big strides" and demands "a gentle motion all around." "You'll crush me antilopes I saved so long for. They're Penisole's. And the two goodiest shoeshoes" (*FW* 622. 8–12). Sex in the morning, she implies, should be salubrious for the health. And "it seems so long since, ages since," she and "possumbotts" have shared this kind of innocent pleasure. Their early-morning promenade becomes a mimetic journey through *Finnegans Wake*.[35] ALP recalls her husband in his incarnation as Jarl van Hoother, the chastened lord who is now "a fine sport . . . and a proper old promnentory. His door always open" (*FW* 623. 5–7). She cites her own role as Biddy the Hen, burrowing in the litter of culture to unearth the "traumscrapt from Maston, Boss" (*FW* 623. 36). "Scratching it and patching at with a prompt from a primer. And what scrips of nutsnolleges I pecked up me meself. Every letter is a hard but yours sure is the hardest crux ever" (*FW* 623. 31–3).

"Sometime then, somewhere there, I wrote me hopes and buried the page when I heard Thy voice, ruddery dunner, so loud that none but, and left it to lie till a kissmiss coming. So content me now" (*FW* 624. 3–6). The romantic hopes of girlhood were apparently repressed when Anna felt herself responding to the thundering voice of HCE, the paternal surrogate who wooed and won her affections. But respectable cohabitation with Bygmister Humphrey has meant perpetual accommodation to a shrinking economy and diminishing expectations. Like Leopold Bloom, and like Ibsen's Solness, Earwicker is notorious for ingenious building schemes that meet with little success: "All your graundplotting and the little it brought! Humps, when you hised us and dumps, when you doused us! . . . On limpidy marge I've made me hoom. Park and a pub for me. . . . One of these fine days, lewdy culler, you must redoform again" (*FW* 624. 12–20). Anna, benevolently assures this "grand owld marauder" (*FW* 624. 27) that, despite his failures and his fading potency, "you done me fine!" (*FW* 624. 35). "How glad you'll be I waked you!" she proclaims. "How well you'll feel! For ever after" (*FW* 625. 33–4). Though faltering and breathless, Anna tries to resuscitate her husband with tender recollections of adolescent courtship. "Remember! Why there that moment and us two only? I was but a teen, a tiler's dot" (*FW* 626. 8–9). Diminutive and ingenuous, the impressionable teen lost her heart to the "swaggering swell" who boasted a resemblance to her father: "The swankysuits was boosting always, sure him, he was like to me fad" (*FW* 626. 9–10).

Frail and haggard, the dying Anna still remembers the gentle moments of courtship when, light-hearted and laughing, her oak of a lover would stand against her "in your bark and tan billows of branches for to fan me coolly" (*FW* 626. 22–3). Despite the military echoes of Irish political strife in HCE's black-and-tan garb, the scene is filled with tenderness and solicitude. Anna, gently yielding her bank-side's parting, would "lie as quiet as a moss" (*FW* 626. 23) and freely submit to love-making.

> One time you'd stand fornenst me, fairly laughing. . . . And one
> time you'd rush upon me, darkly roaring, like a great black
> shadow with a sheeny stare to perce me rawly. And I'd frozen
> up and pray for thawe. . . . My lips went livid for from the joy
> of fear. . . . How you said how you'd give me the keys of me
> heart. And we'd be married till delth to uspart. . . . And can it
> be it's nnow fforvell? Illas! (*FW* 626. 21–34)

With fearful joy, Anna experienced wild extremes in HCE's passion – from a gentle, solicitous coupling to fierce, aggressive penetration. Like Thor "darkly roaring," or like Zeus raping Leda, HCE would rush upon his beloved as "a great black shadow" in a storm of libidinous desire. With a "sheeny" (shiny and semitic) visage, this semi-divine lover took his partner so violently that her heart was frozen by the wintry gusts of impersonal frenzy. Like a wind whipping the cheeks of Anna's face and buttocks, the powerful father/lover came upon her with a tempestuous force that seemed both epiphanic and apocalyptic: "Wrhps, that wind as if out of norewere! As on the night of the Apophanypes. Jumpst shootst throbbst into me mouth like a bogue and arrohs! Ludegude of the Lashlanns, how he whips me cheeks! Sea, sea! . . . Remember!" (*FW* 626. 4–8).[36]

Viking and Visigoth ("Vulking Corsergoth"), playing Vulcan to Anna's Venus, the staunch HCE stormed this "princeable girl," the "pet of everyone," with little regard for aristocratic lineage. His conquest of Anna was tantamout to the invasion of Ireland by the Vikings or to the colonization of India by imperial powers: "the invision of Indelond. And, by Thorror, you looked it!" (*FW* 626. 26–9). Penetrated and colonized by the "horrible" Thor/Zeus/ Humphrey, Anna was raped, occupied, and conquered by promises of lawful wedlock: "And we'd be married till delth to uspart. And though dev do espart. O mine!" (*FW* 626. 31–2).

Suddenly roused from reveries of youthful submission, Anna proclaims: "Only, no, now it's me who's got to give. . . . And can it be it's nnow fforvell?" (*FW* 626. 32–3). As the light and her eyesight fail simultaneously, all that she loves begins to fade. With some confusion, she wonders if her family is receding, or if it is she who is being transformed by the shadow of death. "But you're changing, acoolsha, you're changing from me, I can feel. Or is it me is? I'm getting mixed. Brightening up and tightening down. Yes, you're changing, sonhusband, and you're turning, I can feel you, for a daughterwife from the hills again. Imlamaya" (*FW* 626. 35–6; 627. 1–3).

The resurrected Humphrey has rejected Anna in favor of his daughter/wife Isabel, a nubile stream flowing from the Himalayas in mimetic imitation of ALP. A rivulet following the course of her mother, Issy is "coming. Swimming in my hindmoist. Diveltaking on me tail" (*FW* 627. 3–4). Like a fish or a duckling pursuing its parent, the playful sprite is born of the moist foam of Anna's riverrun. "Just a whisk brisk sly spry spink spank sprint of a thing theresomere, saultering. Saltarella come to her own" (*FW* 627. 4–6). Anna blesses the couple that will conjugate in her absence – the son/husband of her waking, aroused to seek a younger woman to satisfy his rejuvenated manhood. "I pity your oldself I was used to. Now a younger's there" (*FW* 627. 6). Although Anna predicts the sundering of this incestuous union, she bequeaths on the couple a sacramental benediction: "Try not to part! Be happy, dear ones! May I be wrong! For she'll be sweet for you as I was sweet when I came down out of me mother" (*FW* 627. 7–9).

The sweetness and innocence of her daughter Issy reminds Anna of her own traumatic separation from the *magna mater* that once protected her in the "great blue bedroom" of the sky. Why did she ever abandon the peace and silence of that ethereal sanctuary, "the air so quiet, scarce a cloud"? "I could have stayed up there for

always only. It's something fails us. First we feel. Then we fall"
(*FW* 627. 9–11). In true Plotinian fashion, Joyce describes the
initial stirrings of sexual desire that lead the individual toward
change and maturation – the need, absence, or gap in experience
that draws us forward into sexual union. Feeling the impetus of both
desire and sympathy, the self abandons the splendid isolation of
prepubescent wholeness and falls into the painful perturbations of
Eros. The calm torpor of sexual latency gives way to a turbulent
dialectic of emotional conflict and amorous gratification.

Knowing that "something fails us," we fall into sin and into
language. We yield to a restless desire for personal communication
that leaves us forever unsatisfied by the lack – the astonishing gap
and failure of articulation – that always separates signifier from
signified, and each individual from an/Other's subjectivity.[37] The
self is isolated in a hostile universe, where communication is faulty
and understanding rare. "A hundred cares, a tithe of troubles and
is there one who understands me? One in a thousand of years of the
nights?" (*FW* 627. 14–16).

As Anna flows into the sea of death, she confesses to years of
"soffran" from the loss of children and lovers. And though she will
be replaced by a younger beauty, falling from the hills in the fertile
spring rains, she expresses stoic indifference to the cycles that will
go on after her death: "And let her rain now if she likes. Gently
or strongly as she likes. Anyway let her rain for my time is come"
(*FW* 627. 11–13). Anna has, at least, the solace of knowing that she
cared for those who needed her: "I done me best when I was let"
(*FW* 627. 13). She takes comfort, too, from "Tobecontinued's
tale," a story of perpetual cosmic reincarnation, and from the
knowledge that "there'll still be sealskers" (Danish, *elske*, "to love")
– both self-lovers and romantic lovers, long after her departure
(*FW* 626. 18–19). But as she realizes that Father Time, in the guise
of an angry Poseidon, has come to claim her, Anna casts off the
altruistic roles of wife and mother that have so long defined her
position in the universe. She divests herself of spousal and maternal
duties and regards her domestic affiliations from the selfish perspective of pre-marital freedom. Sacrosanct family ties appear utterly
diminished: "All me life I have been lived among them but now
they are becoming lothed to me. And I am lothing their little warm
tricks. And lothing their mean cosy turns. And all the greedy gushes
out through their small souls. And all the lazy leaks down over their

brash bodies. How small it's all!'' (*FW* 627. 16–20).

Anna acknowledges that as a young child/bride, lilting in her loyalty and oblivious of faults, she romantically exaggerated her husband's mythic stature: ''I thought you were all glittering with the noblest of carriage. You're only a bumpkin. I thought you the great in all things, in guilt and in glory. You're but a puny'' (*FW* 627. 21–4). And so she turns home to her wild, primitive ancestors, a Celtic race of lesbian sea-hags that celebrate life through wild dances and ecstatic din.

> I can seen meself among them, allaniuvia pulchrabelled. How she was handsome, the wild Amazia, when she would seize to my other breast! And what is she weird, haughty Niluna, that she will snatch from my ownest hair! For 'tis they are the stormies. Ho hang! Hang ho! And the clash of our cries till we spring to be free. (*FW* 627. 27–32)

Already, she envisions herself transformed, singing hymns of freedom with her sister-waters the ''stormies.'' Although Anna has served as an archetypal figure of the altruistic, nurturant mother, her thoughts before death cast off the emotional ties, as well as the stereotypical female roles, that have shackled her for so long. She retains a female identity that is ever elusive and that dares, in the end, to question a lifetime of dedication and self-sacrifice. At the close of her life, love and loathing are fused, and both are lost in the ''bitter ending'' of mortality.

Wearied now, and ''moananoaning'' with anguish, Anna rushes to embrace her ''cold mad feary father'' in the ultimate bond of an Oedipal union that proves both terrible and annihilating. This ''therrble'' sea-god ''bearing down on me now under whitespread wings'' is a composite of Thor, Poseidon, Zeus, the Holy Spirit, and Anna's first seducer, Michael ''from Arkangels'' (*FW* 628. 2–5, 9–10). At the climactic moment of personal extinction, Anna heroically leaps into the waiting arms of her immortal father/lover. Engulfed by old Father Ocean, the river Anna Liffey will nonetheless rise as cloud-vapor and begin again the endless cycles of biological renewal. At the conclusion of *Finnegans Wake*, womb flows into tomb, bearing on her tumultuous river-waters a solitary leaf ''a way a lone a last a loved a long the'' (*FW* 628. 15–16) riverrun of cosmic life.[38]

Joyce gives the last (and the first) word in *Finnegans Wake*, ''the''

(French, "tea"), to a woman. At the final sounding (or scripting) of this single syllable, the book turns back upon itself and, like a resurrected Finnegan, refuses closure and begins again – but with a difference. It is with the fading utterance of ALP's definite article that we realize the endless, indefinite semiosis of *Finnegans Wake*. In a moment of epiphany that brings us back to the book's beginning, tracing, as it were, the infinite structure of a Möbius strip, we are implicitly commissioned to re-read the entire text as an explosive extension of Anna's lyrical riverrun. Having taken for granted the socially sanctioned assurance of a male narrative voice, we must climb aboard the "bisexcycle" of reader-response and circle through the book once more, with a paradoxically belated foreknowledge of a work ubiquitously inscribed with the provocative iterations of feminine writing.

RICORSO
Anna Livia Plurabelle and Écriture Féminine

How does one decode the complex structures of Eros and sexuality within Joyce's farraginous textual production? What, precisely, is the nature of the verbal coup that Joyce perpetrates in *Finnegans Wake*, and what is its relationship to *écriture féminine?* The elusive concept of "feminine writing" has been recently instantiated in literary theory by such diverse critics as Julia Kristeva, Hélène Cixous, Luce Irigaray, Alice Jardine, and Toril Moi. The common denominator among these various, if sometimes contradictory thinkers, is the shared assumption that *écriture féminine* is an attempt to "write the body" and to incorporate into discourse those subversive, semiotic rhythms that Kristeva has allied with the body, voice, and pulsions of pre-Oedipal contact between infant and mother – those polysemic and polyglottic iterations that challenge the name and the law of the Father by poetically subverting the univocal discourse associated with phallocentric master narratives.

At the 1975 James Joyce Symposium in Paris, Philippe Sollers, waving a bright red copy of *Finnegans Wake*, exclaimed triumphantly: "Je vous montre une révolution!"[1] He explained in "Joyce and Co.": "Joyce represents the same ambition as Freud: to analyze two thousand years of manwomankind. . . . He writes not in langwidge (language as the edge of the wedge with which id is wed – Joyce's translation for Lacan's *lalangue*) but in bursting flows of language (Joyce's *l'élangues*): jumps, cuts – singular plural."[2] Like Sollers, Margot Norris in *The Decentered Universe of "Finnegans Wake"* finds encoded in the obvious linguistic subversiveness of the *Wake* an implicit challenge to the patriarchal culture which it parodically replicates and defies. Colin MacCabe takes a similar stance in *James Joyce and the Revolution of the Word* by marshaling forceful evidence from psycholinguistics to suggest the *Wake*'s radical development of a non-phallocentric feminine discourse: "If the 'masculine monosyllables' (190. 35) serve as the fixed point around which the rhythm flows, it is the feminine stream which provides the movement. Language is a constant struggle between a 'feminine libido' which threatens to break all boundaries and a 'male fist' which threatens to fix everything in place."[3]

In opposition to Sollers and Co., a number of contemporary feminist critics argue that Joyce's "masterwork" ultimately glorifies the "sameold gamebold adomic structure" (*FW* 615. 6) of androcentric language and history – an atomic/Adamic game of linguistic punning that reduces to mockery Anna Livia's continuous, run-on language and makes women little more than marginal figures in a male-dominated society. Sandra Gilbert and Susan Gubar argue in *No Man's Land* that "Joyce is taking upon himself the Holy Office of pronouncing that woman, both linguistically and biologically, is wholly orifice."[4] Joyce's puns, they contend,

> offer more consistently assertive instances of the ways in which male writers can transform the *materna lingua* into a *patrius sermo*. For, containing the powerful charm of etymological commentary within themselves, such multiple usages suggest not a linguistic *jouissance* rebelliously disrupting the decorum of the text, but a linguistic *puissance* fortifying the writer's sentences with "densest condensation hard." As we do in the presence of all puns, we (laughingly) groan at the author's authoritative neologisms because he has defeated us, even charmed us, by demonstrating his mastery of the mystery of multiple etymologies.[5]

A deconstructive reader, on the one hand, would be tempted to join Sollers, Norris, MacCabe, and the *Tel Quel* school in celebrating the *Wake* as a linguistic subversion of the name and the law of the Father, a revolution of the word that disrupts the traditional symbolic order and challenges bourgeois practices allied with the repressed desires of a male libidinal economy. Thus Kristeva can cite Joyce's final opus as exemplary of those bisexual, polyphonic rhythms associated with the poetic resonance of maternal utterance; whereas a more resistant reader might identify the lexical disseminations of *Wake*an language in the context described by the French collective *Psych et Po* as "the discourse of the narcissistic son (the female son)" which "only acts as writing in order to deny, repress, censure – but in order to exploit it, the mortgaged place, henceforth an unavoidable obstacle, of the mother's body."[6]

In the latter case, the archetypal womb of Anna Livia Plurabelle, the eternal geomater whose sexual delta both centers the son and exiles him from embryonic bliss, becomes *unheimlich*, a maternal haven that expels its inhabitants and inaugurates the perplexing aporia of male sexuality. In Joyce's writing, the name of the Father proves to be a primary patriarchal signifier continually rendered impotent by the act of verbal castration performed by a rebellious son who defies the authoritarian progenitor. Wielding pen over penis, word over the ineptly stuttered iterations of his castrated predecessor, the impudent son forges the name and authority of the Father in letters that litter a world of his own androgynous making.

Julia Kristeva has revealed in the poetic language of *Finnegans Wake* a carnivalesque discourse contingent on the notion of heterogeneity. The semiotic disposition of Joyce's experimental text is "anterior to naming, to the One, to the father, and consequently, maternally connoted." Like all poetic language, Joyce's *Wake*speak is "from a synchronic point of view, a mark of the workings of drives (appropriation/rejection, orality/anality, love/hate, life/death) and, from a diachronic point of view, [it] stems from the archaisms of the semiotic body." Through poetic discourse, the "subject-in-process appropriates to itself this archaic, instinctual, and maternal territory."[7] The *Wake* would seem to posit the lyrical "pleasure of merging with a rediscovered, hypostasized maternal body," identified by Kristeva as the lost "phallic Mother who gathers us all into orality and anality, into the pleasure of fusion and rejection."[8]

In Anna Livia Plurabelle's lilting, lyrical utterances, Joyce taps what Kristeva delineates as the "pre-thetic" semiotic *chora* of "articulations heterogeneous to signification and to the sign." "As the addressee of every demand, the mother occupies the place of alterity. Her replete body, the receptacle and guarantor of demands, takes the place of all narcissistic, hence imaginary, effects and gratifications."[9] In psychoanalytic terms, the fantasized phallic mother melds with a de-identifying oceanic whole that assimilates both male and female authority and offers a mirror of that illusory plenitude ascribed by the subject to the inscrutable Other. In this "drury" world of anxiety and narcissism, the maternal figure provides a symbol of fetishistic displacement for the individual searching for embryonic bliss and seeking a return to infant omnipotence. But the trauma of *ananke*, the introduction of a reality principle that bursts the illusion of infantile grace, haunts the under-side of prelapsarian happiness. In pre-Oedipal bonding, the child is wholly dependent on a beneficent mother who both valorizes its existence and satisfies its physical needs. This amorphous maternal figure can titillate but refuse sensory satisfaction: arousing desire, she may, at will, either grant or withhold the vital pleasures of mammary nurturance. The phallic matriarch offers stimulation and exoneration, a promise of pain and pleasure that fills in the gaps of disrupted patriarchal authority and suggests a fetishistic supplement to the lost potency of the castrated Father.

In *Finnegans Wake*, Anna Livia Plurabelle adopts a "femaline" river-speech that writes itself against the stony language of male symbolic discourse. Naming herself in the language of maternal connotation, she challenges the authority of the male as Logos and law-giver through utterances that combine symbolic and semiotic linguistic practices in a letter whose literal meaning can never fully be decoded. Anna flows through the *Wake* into an inundating phallic motherhood. As the River Liffey, she ingests and assimilates the male ground of existence – the paternal mountain (HCE/Finnegan) gradually eroded by the sinuous course of a female *fleuve* embracing its banks. Her phallic potential is metaphorically manifested in the one hundred and eleven (or thousand and one) children who project the creative power of the mother into the male-dominated world of patriarchal privilege: "her furzeborn sons and dribblederry daughters" (*FW* 210. 4–5) In opposition to the phallocentric discourse of the Father, Anna "speaks fluid" and, through the subversive *parole* of "gramma's grammar," restructures the Lacan-ian letter of the unconscious in a revolutionary "femaline mamafesta." She reinscribes a rhythmic, maternal, semiotic voice into the primordial hill of creative chaos, the litter of letters that suggests the scriptural elements of the Logos, the compositional units of the Kabbalah whose mystic import was initially formulated through sacred books that articulate the androgynous voice of Adam Kaedmon.

At the beginning of the *Wake*, Joyce depicts a metaphorical mound of preconscious signifiers, a lexical word-heap in which both HCE and ALP are buried "fux to fux" (*FW* 177. 36). The light-ning explosion of a Viconian Father-God, a transcendental signifier of authority and mastery, erupts in a thunderburst of seminal poten-tial – obscure, incomprehensible, and definitely threatening to awestruck inhabitants of the planet. It is the task of Anna Livia to reinvent the symbol-system of Thor the hammer-hurler, old Father Ocean into whose stormy waters she ultimately flows. ALP is mistress of a fluid, feminine discourse that assimilates patriarchal language and reiterates its ominous warnings in sympathetic, creative form. If the paternal voice is imperious and sonorous, the "mother tongue" of ALP is reduced, finally, to a whisper of polyphonic labial "Lps" in the last lyrical passages of the *Wake*. Anna's provocative river-speech constantly subverts phallocentric discourse and chants lisping libidinal iterations that arise out of the unconscious and appeal to a collective, Jungian racial memory.

In *Finnegans Wake*, Anna Livia is the source of an explosive, hysterical bisexual discourse. She spews forth words in flagrant violation of the symbolic law of the Father, re-playing the scenes of psychological life in the world of the imaginary. Her fluidity is fluvial, and the effluvia of quotidian experience – of desire and guilt, fear and sexual fascination – are carried off into the oceanic tides of a Father/God/transcendental signifier. Her origins are mythically associated with the vaporous ether that produces rainclouds and thunderstorms, fertility and flood. Just as in hysterical discourse vagina and mouth are one, so Anna's womb/delta is rife with words and with children, menstural itera-tions and periodic rhapsodies. The two poles of the body are conflated, and hysteria prevails. Through perpetual verbal gymnastics, Anna Livia is outmaneuvering the symbolic order in linguistic utterances that flood the text with a semiotic flow that proves unconstrained and untranscribable.

According to Hélène Cixous, woman "doesn't create a monarchy of her body or her desire. . . . Her libido is cosmic, just as her unconscious is worldwide. . . . She alone . . . has never ceased to hear what-comes-before-language reverberating. . . . Her rising: is not erection. But diffusion. Not the shaft. The vessel."[10]

Unleashed and raging, she belongs to the race of waves. She arises, she approaches, she lifts up, she reaches, covers over, washes a shore, flows embracing the cliff's least undulation, already she is another, arising again, throwing the fringed vastness of her body up high, follows herself, and covers over, uncovers, polishes, makes the stone body shine with the gentle undeserting ebbs, which return to the shoreless nonorigin, as if she recalled herself in order to come again as never before.[11]

The name of the Father in *Finnegans Wake*, like the unutterable Tetragrammaton of Yahweh, cannot be spoken. It floats, detached from its paternal signifier, in the shadow of the text, constantly present in the mode of absence. Inaccessible to human articulation, the progenitor's presence erupts in those explosions of patriarchal authority that signify a transcendent law, a power of judgment so ominous as to inaugurate the Viconian fear-words of human speech. The discourse of the Father suggests paternal power projected through imaginary tropes onto a world of nature that invites appropriation but eludes human mastery. The archetypal patriarch, "the great Finnleader himself in his joakimono on his statue riding the high horse there forehengist" (*FW* 214. 11–12), longs to inscribe his phallocratic signature onto the resistant body of a resilient Mother Earth. Obsessed with a will to power and domination, he seeks to subjugate Gea-Tellus, the goddess of nature and world, who always escapes his aggressive attempts at conquest. "The pawdrag? The fawthrig? Shoe! Hear are no phanthares in the room at all, avikkeen. No bad bold faathern" (*FW* 565. 18–20). HCE's "dunleary obelisk," of amazing "lungitube," has "phoenishly" fallen, along with Finnegan from his ladder and Humpty Dumpty from his wall. "First we feel. Then we fall" (*FW* 627. 11).

The powerful figure of Gea-Tellus gives way in *Finnegans Wake* to an archetypal image of female fluidity evinced through an endless riverrun of maternal/pre-Oedipal pulsions. If the world is a text that inscribes the symbol-system of phallocratic law onto the consciousness of every individual, then the object of the creative artist is to subvert the law and language of the Father by adopting the feminine *langue* of maternal desire. Exuding excrescences of hysterical speech, female discourse revels in a fluid, metamorphic mode. Its polysemic dissemination of verbal meaning suggests a scattering of male seed (or *sèmes*) in fields of maternal mud, the *boue* that gives birth to those brain-children created by artist and imaginary muse in an act of radical, subversive copulation.

Finnegans Wake writes itself in the wake of Anna's riverrun by scattering seeds of male logic in babbling, carnivalesque play. The meaning of the text resides in slippage – in those symbolic gaps that deracinate language from logical formulations and create a world of words that indefinitely defers both meaning and closure. Anna's letter is not merely part of the larger text, but a microcosmic mamafesta that forms a nexus in the *Wake*'s linguistic unconscious. The whole of the *Wake* flows from the eggburst of ALP's henmissive, a litter of letters that subverts the gospel of grandpa's repressive Oedipal codes.

In the text of the *Wake*, speech has given way to polyphonic discourse, and the voice that dominates Joyce's metaphorical muttering is the voice of a female creator reintegrating the fragments of a murdered godhead, breathing life into the limbs of a sexually moribund spouse, and calling the male husband/father/divinity to arise from the ashes of sleep and death, from the "hundering blundering dunderfunder of plundersundered manhood," to awake "renascenent; fincarnate" (*FW* 596. 4) in a "supernoctural" moment of "Array! Surrection!" (*FW* 593. 2–3). Anna, the *mater* (*Die Mutter*) that mutters her river-speech throughout the text, reinscribes a maternal message into a world potentially embryonic in the middenheap of history. The mud of creation blends earth and feces, silt and sludge, to give birth to a universe of meaning. The significance of grandma's grammar finally resists logocentric interpretation and remains insistently fluid, fragmented, enigmatic, and incomprehensible. It subverts and eludes the male symbolic register that forever attempts to master the *jouissance* of female (and bisexual) desire.

How, finally, should a feminist reader approach Joyce? If this were an Ithacan catechetical question, the response would be obvious, though polymorphous: with care, certainly; with a sense of delight and appreciation; with skepticism and circumspection; and with a carnivalesque spirit of fun, play, amusement, and curiosity. From certain parallactic perspectives, Joyce's postmodern *oeuvre* can be envisaged as contiguous with the projects of feminist fabulation. Like *écriture féminine*, his writing annuls classical notions of identity and origin, of metaphysical authority and textual closure. Exploring those schizoid gaps between socially constructed binary oppositions, it plays with an endless dissemination of sexual difference that eludes the Oedipal configurations of patriarchal power.

Although Joyce depicts, in the world of *Dubliners*, a misogynist society dominated by archaic sexual stereotypes, he mocks and challenges at every point the stultifying sex-role attributions that prove ubiquitous in turn-of-the-century Ireland. His canon evolves from a seeringly realistic portrait of Edwardian sexual politics, Irish puritanism, and Celtic sentimentality to the subversive textual exposition of Molly Bloom's climactic utterances and Anna Livia Plurabelle's river-speech – a polyglottic discourse arising from the linguistic unconscious of the text itself. Joyce's writing flows sinuously, like ALP's riverrun, from the dramatization of repression in *Dubliners* and *A Portrait of the Artist* to the exuberant affirmation of an unrepressed language of desire in *Ulysses* and *Finnegans Wake*. A female story dialogically emerges from Joyce's master narrative, appropriates its textual authority, and gradually deconstructs the linguistic codes essential to the logocentric and phallocentric discourse not only of "dear dirty Dublin" but of western patriarchal culture.

Joyce, imagining himself in the role of "femaline" creator, adopts a female subject-position and incorporates into the symbolic register of his writing the semiotic pulsions of a pre-referential (M)Other tongue that continually subverts the *patrius sermo* of his literary forebears. Unlike a modernist such as D. H. Lawrence, he never attempts to speak for all women or to compose literary guidebooks to successful heterosexuality. By playing a multiplicity of parts in the Circean drama of fictional fabulation and imaginatively oscillating between gender polarities, he releases from the textual unconscious of *Finnegans Wake* revolutionary iterations of a culturally repressed language of bisexual desire.

> So. Avelaval. My leaves have drifted from me. All. But one
> clings still. I'll bear it on me. To remind me of. Lff! . . . End
> here. Us then. Finn, again! Take. Bussoftlhee, mememormee!
> Till thousendsthee. Lps. The keys to. Given! A way a lone a last
> a loved a long the (*FW* 628. 6 – 7, 13 – 16)

The last word of *Finnegans Wake* is uttered by Anna Livia Plurabelle, but it is the weakest word in the language – the definite article which, by definition, seeks a substantive as its complement. The *Wake* ends on a note of insatiable desire: the word "the" reaches out, futilely, for a compatible term to introduce. The Logos, sought, eludes the desiring speaker eager to sustain the salutary metaphysical presence of verbal affirmation. Linguistic longing remains unsatisfied, and the text refuses closure in a way that a scholarly study, or an individual life, cannot.

NOTES

INTRODUCTION: DEFUSING THE PATRIARCHAL CAN(N)ON

1 Jacques Lacan, *Feminine Sexuality*, p. 87. Lacan notes that "Freud revealed this imaginary function of the phallus . . . to be the pivot of the symbolic process that completes *in both sexes* the questioning of the sex by the castration complex" (*Ecrits: A Selection*, p. 198).

2 Arthur Power, *Conversations*, p. 35. See Carolyn Heilbrun's "Afterword" to *Women in Joyce* for a description of Joyce as a "man who hated women" (pp. 215–16). Bonnie Scott's *Joyce and Feminism* and Richard Brown's *James Joyce and Sexuality* offer excellent accounts of Joyce's feminist backgrounds.

3 Julia Kristeva, *Desire in Language*, pp. 50, 116. Jacques Lacan also describes "how everything gets ascribed to the woman in so far as she represents, in the phallocentric dialectic, the absolute Other" (*Feminine Sexuality*, p. 95).

4 Simone de Beauvoir, *The Second Sex*, pp. 239–40.

5 Karen Horney, *Feminine Psychology*, pp. 134–5.

6 Cheri Register, "American Feminist Literary Criticism."

7 An Oedipal theme pervades Joyce's writing, and many of his heroes find themselves in psychic conflict with a maternal figure. Stephen Dedalus is haunted by Mother Ireland and Mother Church, institutions sustained by the matronage of Mary Dedalus, who returns in *Ulysses* as an engulfing specter, a ghost that threatens to devour her son and destroy his artistic potential. Sheldon Brivic offers an extensive discussion of the Oedipal complexities of *A Portrait* in the first section of *Joyce Between Freud and Jung*, "Stephen Oedipus" (pp. 15–83). In "The Song of the Wandering Aengus," Mark Shechner argues that the whole of Joyce's work rests on a "psychic base of oral need and oral insufficiency" and that *Portrait*, *Ulysses*, and *Finnegans Wake* all embody an unconscious quest for the lost and nurturant mother. According to Shechner, Joyce's central fantasy, prefigured in his narrative essay "A Portrait of the Artist," "is one of ecstatic oral merger with an omnibus whore/Virgin/saint/muse/temptress whose very ambiguity is emblematic

of the missing mother" (pp. 84, 78).

8 See Ruth Bauerle, "Bertha's Role in *Exiles*."

9 Jacqueline Rose explains that for Lacan, "men and women are only ever in language. . . . . All speaking beings must line themselves up on one side or the other of this division, but anyone can cross over and inscribe themselves on the opposite side from that to which they are anatomically destined" (*Sexuality*, p. 73). Rose notes that Lacanian psychoanalysis "shifts the concept of bisexuality – not an undifferentiated sexual nature prior to symbolic difference (Freud's earlier sense), but the availability to all subjects of both positions in relation to that difference itself" (ibid., p. 73n).

10 Philip Toynbee, "A Study of James Joyce's *Ulysses*," p. 282; Marilyn French, *The Book as World*, p. 259.

11 For realistic exposures of Molly, see David Hayman, "The Empirical Molly," and Elaine Unkeless, "The Conventional Molly Bloom."

12 See Margot Norris, *The Decentered Universe of "Finnegans Wake"*; Colin MacCabe, *James Joyce and the Revolution of the Word*; and Stephen Heath, "Joyce in Language," "Ambiviolences," and "Trames de lecture."

13 Julia Kristeva, *Polylogue*, p. 16. Translation mine.

14 ibid.

15 Jacques Lacan's *Séminaire XX: Encore* celebrates woman as "not-all," the anti-universal *par excellence*, the "pure space" of supplementary *jouissance* that partakes of the infinite. Lacan writes: "There is no such thing as *The* woman, where the definite article stands for the universal. There is no such thing as *The* woman since of her essence, . . . she is not all. . . . It none the less remains that if she is excluded by the nature of things, it is precisely that in being not all, she has, in relation to what the phallic function designates of *jouissance*, a supplementary *jouissance*" (*Feminine Sexuality*, p. 144). The French term *"jouissance"* cannot, in effect, be translated into English, since it conflates notions of sexual orgasm, intellectual enjoyment, sensuous pleasure, and emotional ecstasy. See Jacques Lacan, *Ecrits: A Selection*, p. x. As Betsy Wing explains in the glossary accompanying her translation of Hélène Cixous and Catherine Clément, *The Newly Born Woman*, "total sexual ecstasy" is the most common connotation of *jouissance*, "but in contemporary French philosophical, psychoanalytic, and political usage, it does not stop there, and to equate it with orgasm would be an oversimplication." *Jouissance* is "a word with *simultaneously* sexual, political, and economic overtones. Total access, total participation, as well as total ecstasy are implied. At the simplest level of meaning – metaphorical – woman's capacity for multiple orgasm indicates that she has the potential to attain something more than Total, something extra – abundance and waste, . . . Real and unrepresentable" (Cixous and Clément, *The Newly Born Woman*, p. 165).

16 In *Nora: The Real Life of Molly Bloom*, Brenda Maddox offers a fascinating biographical portrait of Nora Barnacle Joyce, the Galway

girl who fled to the continent with an egotistical genius who demanded a lifetime of nurturance and support.

17 Although Joyce makes covert reference to Freudian theory as "the new Viennese school Mr. Magee spoke of" (*U* 9: 780) in the "Scylla and Charybdis" chapter of *Ulysses*, he always claimed to distrust the notions of Freudian psychoanalysis. Freud, he felt, was far too reductive and mechanical in his interpretation of symbols, "a house being a womb, a fire a phallus" (*JJ* 382). Nevertheless, critics like Frank Budgen, Richard Ellmann, and Elliott Gose all suspect Joyce of fairly heavy, if unacknowledged, reliance on the popular theories of Freudian psychology "in the air" among the intelligentsia of Europe in the first two decades of this century. In *The Consciousness of Joyce*, Richard Ellmann includes among the holdings of Joyce's 1920 library Freud's *Psychopathology of Everyday Life* (1917 German edition); *A Childhood Memory of Leonardo da Vinci* (1910 German edition); and Ernest Jones's study *The Problem of Hamlet and the Oedipus Conflict* (1911 German edition). Ellmann hypothesizes, furthermore, that Joyce made conscious use of Freudian theory in his composition of *Ulysses* while scrupulously avoiding "Freud's classical model of family relations as Joyce had sampled it." The relevance of Joyce's early acquaintaince with Freud's writing "can hardly be overstressed. The three essays 'burst in upon his porcelain revery' with their transformations, combinations, and divisions of self, their picture of its abasements and suppressed appetites and ambivalences, which were as yet largely untapped for conscious literature" (pp. 54–6 and Appendix). For further discussion of Joyce's use of Freudian sources, see Elliott B. Gose, Jr, *Transformation*, pp. 95–101; and John Bishop, *Joyce's Book of the Dark*, pp. 15–18 and *passim*.

18 For an excellent glossary of Lacanian terminology, see Alan Sheridan's "Translator's Note," in Jacques Lacan, *Ecrits: A Selection*, pp. vii–xii. In describing Lacanian desire, Sheridan explains that the "human individual sets out with a particular organism, with certain biological needs, which are satisfied by certain objects. . . . All speech is demand; it presupposes the Other to whom it is addressed, whose very signifiers it takes over in its formulation . . . there is no adequation between the need and the demand that conveys it; indeed, it is the gap between them that constitutes desire. . . . Desire . . . is not an appetite: it is essentially excentric and insatiable" (p. viii). Noting the function of radical lack (*manque*) in the construction of the Lacanian subject, Jacqueline Rose observes: "The mirror image is central to Lacan's account of subjectivity, because its apparent smoothness and totality is a myth. The image in which we first recognise ourselves is a *misrecognition*. . . . For Lacan the subject is constituted through language – the mirror image represents the moment when the subject is located in an order outside itself to which it will henceforth refer. . . . Language can only operate by designating an object in its absence. . . . Symbolisation starts, therefore, when the child gets its first sense that

something could be missing; words stand for objects. . . . . For Lacan, the subject can only operate within language by constantly repeating that moment of fundamental and irreducible division. The subject is therefore constituted in language *as* this division or splitting" (*Sexuality*, pp. 53–4). Lacan writes that "desire is neither the appetite for satisfaction, nor the demand for love, but the difference resulting from the subtraction of the first from the second, the very phenomenon of their splitting" (*Feminine Sexuality*, p. 81).

19 Toril Moi, *Sexual/Textual Politics*, p. 8.

20 Hélène Cixous, "The Laugh of the Medusa"; Julia Kristeva, *Revolution*, p. 17. (I refer to the name of the Lacanian Father in the upper case, and to the biological or Freudian father in the lower case.) For Kristeva, as for Deleuze and Guattari, the pre-thetic "schizophrenic flow" exists "only through language, appropriating and displacing the signifier to practice *within it* the heterogeneous generating of the 'desiring machine' " (ibid.). Kristeva insists that just as "the feminine is defined as marginal under patriarchy, so the semiotic is marginal to language," and that one must "view this repression of the feminine in terms of *positionality* rather than of essences" (Toril Moi, *Sexual/Textual Politics*, p. 166). She takes the controversial stance that "men can also be constructed as marginal by the symbolic order, as her analyses of male avant-garde artists (Joyce, Céline, Artaud, Mallarmé, Lautréamont) have shown" (ibid.). Throughout the following study, I have assumed, like Kristeva, that a male author can successfully adopt and speak from a feminine subject-position in a work of fiction.

21 In *Sexual Politics*, Kate Millett alludes to Joyce as a modernist anomaly, but objects to his ostensibly derogatory portraits of woman as "nature," "unspoiled primeval understanding," and the "eternal feminine" (p. 285). More recently, Sandra M. Gilbert and Susan Gubar, in *No Man's Land*, have launched a frontal attack on Joyce for his inauguration of "a new patrilinguistic epoch." They indict both *Ulysses* and *Finnegans Wake* as male-biased projects of linguistic mastery perpetrating a "feat of legerdemain in which the *materna lingua* dissolved and resolved itself into a newly empowered *patrius sermo*" (p. 260).

22 See Judith Fetterley, *The Resisting Reader*.

1: THROUGH A CRACKED LOOKING-GLASS

1 Engaged in controversy with Grant Richards over the publication of *Dubliners*, Joyce declared: "My intention was to write a chapter of the moral history of my country and I chose Dublin for the scene because that city seemed to me the centre of paralysis. I have tried to present it to the indifferent public under four of its aspects: childhood, adolescence, maturity and public life. The stories are arranged in this order. I have written it for the most part in a style of scrupulous

meanness'' (*Letters* II, 134). ''It is not my fault that the odour of ashpits and old weeds and offal hangs round my stories. I seriously believe that you will retard the course of civilisation in Ireland by preventing the Irish people from having one good look at themselves in my nicely polished looking-glass'' (*Letters* I, 63–4).

2 Jacqueline Rose observes: ''Sexuality belongs in this area of instability played out in the register of demand and desire, each sex coming to stand, mythically and exclusively, for that which could satisfy and complete the other'' (*Sexuality*, p. 56). In *''Dubliners*: Women in Irish Society,'' Florence Walzl examines Joyce's female characters within the context of Dublin culture and analyzes gender attributions operative in late nineteenth-century Ireland. She concludes that ''when Joyce pits men against women in his tales, it can be proved that drastic economic and social pressures actually forced Dubliners into such situations of frustration, deprivation, and hostility. He spares neither sex'' (p. 53).

3 Jane Gallop, *Feminism and Psychoanalysis*, pp. 173–4. ''The demand for love,'' writes Lacan, ''can only suffer from a desire whose signifier is alien to it. If the desire of the mother *is* the phallus, then the child wishes to be the phallus so as to satisfy this desire'' (*Feminine Sexuality*, p. 83).

4 Phillip Herring, in *Joyce's Uncertainty Principle*, successfully anatomizes the ''gnomonic nature'' of language in ''The Sisters'' – a language filled with ellipses, hiatuses, silences, malapropisms, and empty, ritualistic dialogue (pp. 11–18). According to Jean-Michel Rabaté in ''Silence in *Dubliners*,'' the incomplete figure of the dead or absent father is inscribed in the text of *Dubliners* ''until finally everything will appear hinged on the silent name of the capitalised Father'' (p. 48).

5 See Waisbren and Walzl, ''Paresis and the Priest''; J. B. Lyons, *James Joyce and Medicine*, pp. 84–91; and Zack Bowen, ''Joyce's Prophylactic Paralysis: Exposure in *Dubliners*.'' Hugh Kenner, in ''Signs on a White Field,'' comments on the ironic contrast between Joyce's tale of two sisters mourning a deceased sibling and the biblical narrative detailing Christ's resurrection of Lazarus at the behest of Mary and Martha in St John's gospel. ''This brother lies in his coffin unresurrected. . . . We may guess at what went wrong with Father Flynn. He grasped that God did not choose him – perhaps out of nonexistence? And, prompted by the enigma of the title, we may even divine the story's scriptural model'' (p. 210).

6 In tracing ''Joyce's Revision of 'The Sisters': From Epicleti to Modern Fiction,'' L. J. Morrissey focuses on the progressive inconclusiveness of Joyce's text and its metamorphosis from a ''readerly'' narrative in the first-published *Homestead* version to a ''writerly'' offering in *Dubliners*. ''As our desire to create an enclosed, single, readerly text is increasingly frustrated, our sensitivity to the 'word' of the writerly text is sharply increased'' (p. 48).

7 Juliet Mitchell notes: ''The identity that seems to be that of the subject is in fact a mirage arising when the subject forms an image of itself by

identifying with others' perception of it. . . . . Lacan's human subject is
. . . a being that can only conceptualise itself when it is mirrored back
to itself from the position of another's desire'' (in Mitchell and Rose,
Feminine Sexuality, p. 5). In ''Joyce: The (R)use of Writing,'' Hélène
Cixous offers a paradigmatic Freudian reading of ''The Sisters'' that
concludes: ''Desire (a homosexuality which is only admitted in the dark
folds of a confessional) is eclipsed here, so swiftly, almost unnoticed, by
the desire to kill'' (p. 24).

8 Ellie Ragland-Sullivan, in *Jacques Lacan and the Philosophy of
Psychoanalysis*, sees as the fundamental premiss of Lacanian theory the
''contention that the human psyche is composed of two different
'subjects': an objectlike narcissistic subject of *being*, and a *speaking*
subject.'' The ''first of the Lacanian subjects (the *moi*) gives rise to and
remains perpetually entwined with the second (the *je*) for the duration
of all conscious life. . . . The Lacanian ego (*moi*) . . . is an ideal ego
whose elemental form is irretrievable in conscious life, but it is reflected
in its chosen identificatory objects (alter egos or ego ideals). The subject
of speech (S or *je*) is distinct from the subject of identifications (ego or
moi), but they interact all the same. The conscious subject, thus
viewed, is made up of 'inmixed' symbolic chains'' (pp. 1–4).

9 Gallop, *Feminism and Psychoanalysis*, p. 64. In *A Scrupulous Meanness*,
Edward Brandabur interprets the charge of ''pederasty'' literally and
concludes that the boy in ''An Encounter,'' like his predecessor in
''The Sisters,'' ''is lured by the mystery of initiation into a
sadomasochistic system with a degenerate old man'' (p. 49). Donald
Torchiana, in *Backgrounds for Joyce's ''Dubliners,''* provides a more
historical interpretation of the encouter, suggesting that ''Joyce presents
us with a recrudescence of the sinister puritanism recalling Cromwell
and his sadistic cruelties in Ireland'' (p. 45).

10 A number of readers have questioned Frank's sincerity and wondered if
his intentions toward Eveline are, in fact, honorable. David Wright
reminds us in *Characters of Joyce* that ''the word 'frank' appears elsewhere
in *Dubliners*'' in a ''generally ironical'' context and that '''going to
Buenos Aires' was once a common euphemism for 'becoming a
prostitute''' (pp. 24–5). In *The Pound Era*, Hugh Kenner emphasizes
the implausibility of Frank's marriage proposal and suggests that this
randy sailor ''may have been less than Frank.'' Eveline simply ''has a
fiction in her head which arranges for her the very little she knows of
a man named Frank.'' Her ''daydream of escape'' is founded on a
fictional construct tinged with the rhetoric of ''shopgirls' romances
printed in magazines.'' Reflecting the illusions of popular culture at the
turn of the century, Eveline feeds on sentimental fantasies, imagining ''a
home waiting for her'' in a foreign land and a beautiful future with her
handsome lover. In this ironic evocation of a ''real Dublin . . . and a
fictitious Buenos Aires,'' Joyce deliberately maximizes Eveline's
''ignorance and her pathos, and emphasizes his earliest and most constant insight, that people live in stories that structure their worlds''

(pp. 34–9). See also Bonnie Scott's biographical discussion of Margaret/Eveline in *Joyce and Feminism*, pp. 60–1.

11 Gallop, *Feminism and Psychoanalysis*, p. 113. On "Derevaun Seraun," William Tindall cites Patrick Henchy of Dublin's National Library to suggest that the words are "corrupt Gaelic for 'the end of pleasure is pain' " (*A Reader's Guide to James Joyce*, p. 22). On the basis of information given him by John Garvin, Donald Torchiana translates the phrase as "Worms are the only end" (*Backgrounds for Joyce's "Dubliners,"* p. 75). In "Some Notes on Language and Atmosphere in *Dubliners*," Johannes Hedberg offers a similar reading of this demotic Galwegian Irish to mean "only end: maggots" (p. 117). Joyce's own assessment of the Irish domestic worship of hearth and home was recorded in a letter to Nora during their courtship – a communication which details a maternal death similar to that described in "Eveline": "My home was simply a middle-class affair ruined by spendthrift habits which I have inherited. My mother was slowly killed, I think, by my father's ill-treatment, by years of trouble, and by my cynical frankness of conduct. When I looked on her face as she lay in her coffin – a face gray and wasted with cancer – I understood that I was looking on the face of a victim and I cursed the system which had made her a victim" (*Letters* II, 48).

12 In response to the printer's objection to "Two Gallants," Joyce asked in a letter to Grant Richards: "Is it the small gold coin . . . or the code of honour which the two gallants live by which shocks him? . . . I would strongly recommend to him the chapters wherein Ferrero examines the moral code of the soldier and (incidentally) of the gallant" (*Letters* II, 132–3). In *Joyce's Politics*, Dominic Manganiello explains that in Guglielmo Ferrero's book *L'Europa giovane* "the moral code of the soldier consists in arousing men's 'inert brutality.' Ferrero associates this militaristic activity, which he considered typical of the Germanic races, with the art of gallantry" (p. 50). See also Robert Spoo, " 'Una Piccola Nuvoletta': Ferrero's *Young Europe* and Joyce's Mature *Dubliners* Stories." There is some disagreement as to whether the young woman filched the coin from her employer or saved what would have been a considerable amount of money from her hard-earned slavey's wages.

13 As Florence Walzl observes, "the frustration of Dublin's women – a consequence of their dull, empty rounds of existence – results in a circular plot in which the evils of the first generation are visited upon the second." In both "Eveline" and "The Boarding House," "each girl makes a life choice that insures her a repetition of her mother's life." Walzl concludes: "As mothers, so daughters. It is clear in these stories that the situation of the first generation becomes the condition of the second and that mothers tend to transform their daughters into replicas of themselves" ("*Dubliners*: Women in Irish Society," pp. 47–9). For a summary of the Dorans' future domestic troubles, see Fritz Senn, " 'The Boarding House' Seen as a Tale of Misdirection," p. 412.

14 Hélène Cixous remarks that "Chandler is one of those men who lived curled up in a foetal position, not daring to move lest they be flung out into the outside world. He secretes his own protective cocoon, with childlike, womanlike care. He is still gently nestling within his illusions, preparing his secret self to be born to the glorious destiny of a poet" (*The Exile of James Joyce*, p. 91). According to Bonnie Scott, the "Chandlers have different fantasies of a happy life – Chandler's centering upon modest artistic acclaim; Annie's, upon the popular media's concept of house beautiful. Both are delusions in which one spouse fails to participate" (*Joyce and Feminism*, p. 63). Scott also culls from Joyce's letters evidence that he, like Chandler, felt "typical paternal jealousy" at the birth of his son Giorgio and was troubled by a "sense of rivalry" for Nora's divided attentions (p. 69). On 4 December 1905, Joyce wrote to his Aunt Josephine: "I imagine the present relations between Nora and myself are about to suffer some alteration. . . . It is possible that I am partly to blame. . . . I daresay I am a difficult person for any woman to put up with but on the other hand I have no intention of changing. Nora does not seem to make much difference between me and the rest of the men she has known. . . . I am not a very domestic animal – after all, I suppose I am an artist – and sometimes when I think of the free and happy life which I have (or had) every talent to live I am in a fit of despair" (*Letters* II, 128–9).

15 Sigmund Freud, "Femininity," in *New Introductory Lectures*, pp. 133–4.

16 Chandler, says Donald Torchiana, "is the prisoner of love, and his prison is what has passed for love in his altogether loveless life" (*Backgrounds for Joyce's "Dubliners,"* p. 133). It is ironic that "Little Chandler admires Byron, though for the wrong poem" (p. 131). Torchiana believes that Joyce chose as the prototype for Chandler's character one of the lesser lights of the Irish Renaissance, George Roberts, whose sentimental, "snivelling" poetry Joyce complained about in a January 1905 letter to Stanislaus.

17 As Philip Slater points out in *The Glory of Hera*, in a household that is mother-dominant and father-avoidant, the woman tends to treat her son as a substitute husband. At times, she may relate to him as an idealized spouse; but such maternal devotion is often characterized by a "deeply narcissistic ambivalence." The mother "does not respond to the child as a separate person, but as both an expression of and cure for her narcissistic wounds. Her need for self-expansion and vindication requires her both to exalt and to belittle her son, to feed on and to destroy him" (p. 33). Such a pattern of socialization results in a vicious cycle: "A society which derogates women produces envious mothers who produce narcissistic males who are prone to derogate women" (p. 45). Reacting against a formidable matriarchal figure, boys develop an unstable self-image that demands continual validation in the outer world. (Consider Jimmy Doyle, Ignatius Gallaher, Little Chandler, and Farrington.) In *Dubliners*, men tend to flee the prison of

a matrifocal household for the sanctuary of the Irish pub, Guinness ale, and a bantering relationship of easy good-fellowship with male cronies who are also in flight from domestic entrapment.

18 Florence Walzl, analyzing Maria as a typal paradigm, remarks that "the narrative modulates between Maria as a Virgin Mary figure . . . and the figure of a Celtic witch in her physical appearance and troublemaking" ("A Book of Signs and Symbols," p. 120). Mary Reynolds believes that "the witchlike appearance of Maria . . . clearly owes something to the presence of another virgin in *Inferno* 20, the prophetess Manto" ("The Dantean Design," p. 125). Richard Brown sees George Moore's story "Mildred Lawson" as an influence on Joyce's portrait of Maria (*James Joyce and Sexuality*, pp. 127–8).

19 Maria omits the following verse from Balfe's *Bohemian Girl*:

> I dream'd that suitors besought my hand,
> That knights upon bended knee,
> And with vows no maiden heart could withstand
> That they pledged their faith to me.
> And I dream'd that one of this noble host
> Came forth my hand to claim;
> Yet I also dream'd, which charmed me most,
> That you loved me still the same.

For an excellent discussion of Joyce's use of *The Bohemian Girl*, see R.B. Kershner, *Joyce, Bakhtin, and Popular Literature*, pp. 63–8.

20 In " 'A Painful Case': The Movement of a Story through a Shift in Voice," Suzanne Katz Hyman offers a revealing analysis of the way in which Duffy uses language as a mode of logocentric control. A "walking embodiment of the Cartesian split," Duffy has recourse to aphorism, cliché, and self-irony for purposes of intellectual detachment. He manipulates language "to color and control experience so as to make it manageable." At the end of the story, when "language gives way to silence," the tale culminates in two non-verbal images: one of venal lovers, and the other a sinister, worm-like train (pp. 111, 115, 117–18). Donald Torchiana reminds us that Duffy is a failed and ironic Tristan, whose "residence in Chapelizod suggests the relevance of the Tristan and Isolde legend" from Richard Wagner's opera (*Backgrounds for Joyce's "Dubliners,"* p. 165).

21 Unlike Richard Ellmann and Bjorn Tysdael, Bonnie Scott is convinced that Joyce's essays "Drama and Life" and "Ibsen's New Drama" manifest a "distinct interest in women's experience" and illustrate a keen "admiration for Ibsen's feminism" (*Joyce and Feminism*, p. 47). In "What is a Woman . . . a Symbol of?: A Lacanian Reading of Joyce's 'The Dead'," Garry Leonard observes: "Gabriel desires to be the desire of woman – of Gretta – because she can then provide what he lacks, or rather protect him from realizing that he lacks anything. Gretta is Gabriel's symptom; something which, if he could only have it, would complete him. The symptom emits something of infinite

value, yet indecipherable – like distant music." See also Jacques Lacan, "Joyce le symptôme."

22 In *Notes for Joyce*, Don Gifford summarizes the poignant narrative of the western Irish ballad, "The Lass of Aughrim": "The lass, relatively low born, is seduced and abandoned by a Lord. With her child in her arms she seeks the Lord in his castle or tower and is deceived and turned away by the Lord's mother, who apparently imitates her son's voice through the closed door. The quoted lines are a variant of the Lass's complaint as she stands in the rain at that point. Rejected, as she thinks, the Lass puts to sea, and she and her child are drowned. . . . The ballad closes with the Lord's lament and with the curse he calls down on his mother" (p. 83). According to Richard Ellmann, Joyce was quite fond of the ballad, which he urged Nora Barnacle's mother to sing for him on a visit to Galway. He found the song's final verses especially moving:

> If you'll be the lass of Aughrim
> As I am taking you mean to be
> Tell me the first token
> That passed between you and me.
>
> O don't you remember
> That night on yon lean hill
> When we both met together
> Which I am sorry now to tell.
>
> The rain falls on my yellow locks
> And the dew it wets my skin;
> My babe lies cold within my arms
> Lord Gregory let me in. (*JJ* 286)

23 Without question, Furey has been elevated in Gretta's fantasy life to the status of romantic hero and mystified courtly lover. Lacan asks: "Indeed, why not acknowledge that if there is no virility which castration does not consecrate, then for the woman it is a castrated lover or a dead man (or even both at the same time) who hides behind the veil where he calls on her adoration" (*Feminine Sexuality*, p. 95). See also Ruth Bauerle, "Date Rape, Mate Rape."

24 Mark Osteen, in "Gabriel's Sarcasm: A Lost Line in 'The Dead,'" argues for the textual restoration of "a sentence, present in those late-stage Maunsel proofs but absent from all published versions" of "The Dead" and here inserted in brackets from the *James Joyce Archive*. Vincent Pecora makes a convincing case in "'The Dead' and the Generosity of the Word" for Gabriel's unconscious duplicity in his sentimental self-laceration and construction of a "myth of generous self-sacrifice" geared to appropriate Gretta's melodramatic narrative.

25 In the passion-vanity dialectic described by René Girard in *Deceit, Desire and the Novel*, Michael Furey exemplifies the "passionate person . . . distinguished by his emotional autonomy, by the spontaneity of his

desires, by his absolute indifference to the opinion of Others" (p. 19). Gabriel, in contrast, acts as a *vaniteux* whose desire is contingent on both external and internal mediation. Such mediated passion, Girard tells us, "defines desire *according to Another*" (p. 4), and it is only the other's desire, "real or presumed, which makes this object infinitely desirable in the eyes of the subject" (p. 7). Michael Furey proves, for Gabriel, to be "both the instigator of desire and a relentless guardian forbidding its fulfillment" (p. 35). According to Brenda Maddox, the fictional Michael Furey is a composite character based on the object of Nora Barnacle's "first serious crush," Michael Feeney, who died at the age of sixteen of typhoid and pneumonia in February, 1897; and on her "later admirer, Michael Bodkin," who died at twenty of tuberculosis in February, 1900 (*Nora*, pp. 15–17).

26 According to Lacan, "woman is a symptom" for masculine desire (*Feminine Sexuality*, p. 168). "For the soul to come into being, she, the woman, is differentiated from it, and this has always been the case" (p. 156). At the "level of fiction which is commonly labelled sexual commerce," the speaking subject has "recourse to the imaginary register" and "sexual difference gets transposed into the question with which the Other, from the place of its lack, interrogates the subject on *jouissance*" (pp. 120–1). Jacqueline Rose explains: "As negative to the man, woman becomes a total object of fantasy (or an object of total fantasy), elevated into the place of the Other and made to stand for its truth. Since the place of the Other is also the place of God, this is the ultimate form of mystification" (*Sexuality*, p. 74). See also Jacques Derrida, "Fors."

27 Joseph Buttigieg interprets the scene as the sudden eruption of "involuntary memory" into Gabriel's firmly defended consciousness: "What Gabriel experiences in this scene is a loss of control. The paralyzed world of habit to which he is accustomed collapses as realities he has long been blind to arise like Lazarus from the dead. Gabriel suffers a defeat or a fall, but he also obtains, for a brief moment, a new vision. . . . His egocentrism surrenders to generosity and sympathy" (*A Portrait of the Artist*, p. 38).

28 Jacques Lacan, *Feminine Sexuality*, p. 141. Vincent Pecora charges that in "the name of Michael Furey, his legendary hero and personal saint, Gabriel sacrifices himself to the past, and to the dead, more profoundly than any of his compatriots does. Moreover, he appears completely assured of the sincerity of his gesture. . . . Gabriel has reproduced in himself . . . the story of Christ." In Pecora's view, "Gabriel in no way overcomes or transcends the conditions of his existence. Rather, he merely recapitulates them unconsciously" "'The Dead' and the Generosity of the Word," (p. 243).

29 Like Richard Ellmann, Florence Walzl sees the story as a journey of development "from insularity and egotism to humanitarianism and love" ("Gabriel and Michael: The Conclusion of 'The Dead'"). Donald Torchiana interprets the ending as a symbolic evocation of the

resurrection of the Irish imagination: "The grace of snow . . . has indeed about it something of the harbinger of the Easter Lily. Moreover, a wise man from the East of Ireland has experienced an epiphany, just as the feast, service, and ending of the book demand. . . . 'The Dead' in the long run is a story of growth and life and spring" (*Backgrounds for Joyce's "Dubliners,"* p. 253). Edward Brandabur, in contrast, diagnoses Gabriel as a neurotic victim of "compulsive sadomasochism" whose hostility towards his wife finds "an effective mythic and psychological structure in the story of Michael Furey" (*A Scrupulous Meanness*, p. 122). Charles Peake, in less vehement terms, interprets the book's culminating paragraph as a "critical evocation of resignation to spiritual death" (*James Joyce: The Citizen and the Artist*, p. 53). Mary Reynolds shares this assessment when she compares the "vision of a frozen Ireland" at the end of "The Dead" to Dante's description of a frozen world in the final canto of the *Inferno*. "The closing sentence of 'The Dead' recalls frozen Cocytus, Dante's last image of despair" ("The Dantean Design," p. 124). And finally, Vincent Pecora offers a powerful post-structuralist argument for the story's seering criticism of "institutionalized codes" and "the ideologically supported transformation of one set of illusions into another" ("'The Dead' and the Generosity of the Word," p. 237). Gabriel, says Pecora, "mythologizes his existence in a literary emancipation that can in fact only repeat the contradictions and anxieties he longs to overcome" (p. 234).

2: STEPHEN DEDALUS AND WOMEN

1 Stephen is clearly being inaugurated into the Lacanian symbolic register of male phallogocentrism. "As the first signifier of the social or Symbolic order," writes Ellie Ragland-Sullivan, "the Phallus commands exchange and communication. But it also symbolizes the nonclosure and disunity that it introduces permanently into the human subject by replacing the simultaneity of perception with the deferred nature of language and consciousness" (*Jacques Lacan*, p. 281). See also Christine van Boheemen, *The Novel as Family Romance*, pp. 14–16.

2 As Anika Lemaire explains, according to Lacanian theory, the childish "*infans* does not yet have language at his disposal. In the circuit of exchange between the parents, permutations of the 'I' and 'thou,' the subject is designated by a 'he' " (*Jacques Lacan*, p. 69). At the moment of *Spaltung*, the child "recuperates himself as a distinct entity as opposed to the primary merging of himself with his mother" (p. 57). Parallel to the Oedipus, he "acquires full use of language through the appropriation of the grammatical category of the 'I'. The young child, who at first designates himself by his forename followed by the third person singular of the verb, realizes in a second stage the full assumption of his personality" (p. 8). The iteration of the *infans* as subject of

utterance hinges on a pre-Oedipal movement from lack to desire, then from desire to demand, a process whereby the subject "alienates himself in language, creates himself and fashions himself at will" (p. 161). In order to construct the ego, the individual "constitutes himself in discourse by splitting into two parts: subject of utterance and unconscious subject" (p. 161).

3 Quoting Jung on "The Significance of the Father" (an essay found in Joyce's library), Jean Kimball observes that enuresis or bed-wetting may be seen, in Freudian terms, as "an infantile sexual substitute" ("Freud, Leonardo, and Joyce," p. 170). Hence the importance of maternal ministrations after Stephen has wet the bed. If the horn is interpreted as a "phallic synonym," then the sailor's hornpipe suggests repressed erotic interest in the mother. Stephen unconsciously identifies his female parent as a phallic mother whom he sexually desires but simultaneously fears. Kimball points out that "as early as 1911 or 1912 Joyce owned Freud's essay on Leonardo, which highlights the artist's relationship with his mother," and that he probably read Freud's 1905 publication of *Three Essays on the Theory of Sexuality*, "which focused on the crucial effect of infant sexuality on the psychological destiny of the adult" (p. 165). For a list of the psychology books in Joyce's library and a discussion of their possible influence, see Richard Ellmann, *The Consciousness of Joyce*, pp. 53–9, and Appendix, pp. 109 and 114–115.

4 Chester Anderson argues in "Baby Tuckoo: Joyce's 'Features of Infancy'" that in this scene Stephen "is threatened with 'castration' in the most classic way: by having his eyes pulled out, as Oedipus himself pulled out his with Jocasta's brooch." Anderson identifies Dante as the "terrible mother" or castrator and feels "it is important that the threat comes from Dante, the 'bad' mother split from the 'nice'" (p. 149). Anderson's distinction, however, obscures the revelation of Mary Dedalus as a female authority-figure. According to Freud, as the reality principle supersedes the pleasure principle, the ego must "achieve a progressive conquest of the id." The ego "seeks to bring the influence of the external world to bear upon the id and its tendencies, and endeavors to substitute the reality principle for the pleasure principle which reigns unrestrictedly in the id" (*Complete Psychological Works*, Vol. 19, pp. 56, 25).

5 Dorothy Dinnerstein, *The Mermaid and the Minotaur*, p. 28.

6 Nancy Chodorow, *The Reproduction of Mothering*, p. 122. In *Powers of Horror*, Julia Kristeva suggests the hypothesis that "maternal authority is experienced first and above all, after the first essentially oral frustration, as sphincteral training. It is as if, while having been forever immersed in the symbolics of language, the human being experienced, in addition, an *authority* that was a . . . repetition of the *laws* of language. Through frustrations and prohibitions, this authority shapes the body into a *territory* having areas, orifices, points and lines, surfaces and hollows, where the archaic power of mastery and neglect, of the differentiation of proper-clean and improper-dirty, possible and impossible, is

impressed and exerted. It is a 'binary logic,' a primal mapping of the body. . . . Maternal authority is the trustee of that mapping of the self's clean and proper body; it is distinguished from paternal laws within which, with the phallic phase and acquisition of language, the destiny of man will take shape" (pp. 71–2).

7 In her essay on "The Dread of Woman," Karen Horney postulates that at the juncture between pre-Oedipal attachment and Oedipal separation, the young boy "feels or instinctively judges that his penis is much too small for his mother's genital and reacts with the dread of his own inadequacy, of being rejected and derided." The male child's frustration arouses a "twofold fury in him: first through the thrusting back of his libido upon itself, and secondly, through the wounding of his masculine self-regard." The boy's "reaction to that wound and to the dread of his mother that follows from it is obviously to withdraw his libido from her and to concentrate it on himself and his genital. . . . The female genital no longer exists for him" (*Feminine Psychology*, pp. 142–4).

8 Simone de Beauvoir, *The Second Sex*, p. 136.

9 ibid., p. 129.

10 ibid., p. 135.

11 Nancy Chodorow tells us that a child's dread of the mother is necessarily ambivalent: "Although a boy fears her, he also finds her seductive and attractive. He cannot dismiss and ignore her. Boys and men develop psychological and cultural/ideological mechanisms to cope with their fears without giving up women altogether. They create folk legends, beliefs, and poems that ward off the dread by externalizing and objectifying women. . . . On the one hand, they glorify and adore. . . . On the other, they disparage" (*The Reproduction of Mothering*, p. 183).

12 Chodorow explains: "Denial of sense of connectedness and isolation of affect may be more characteristic of masculine development and may produce a more rigid and punitive superego. . . . Boys come to define themselves as more separate and distinct, with a greater sense of more rigid ego boundaries and differentiation. . . . Men's endopsychic object-world tends to be more fixed and simpler, and the masculine heritage of the Oedipus complex is that relational issues tend to be more repressed. Masculine personality, then, comes to be defined more in terms of denial of relation and connection" (ibid., p. 169).

13 See Michel Foucault's discussion of the similarities among educational, penal, and military institutions in *Discipline and Punish*.

14 Philip Slater, *The Glory of Hera*, pp. 416, 439.

15 In Charles Rossman's view, Stephen perceives Emma "in a blend of falsifying images: first, as a vaguely religious figure, a nunlike innocent with a 'cowled head'; then, on the tram step below him, as a temptress trying to coax him out of his protective isolation, down from his height." The poem that he writes in her honor "substitutes for lived experience, refining the human actors out of existence. Here art, like

religious grace in chapter three, signifies experiential death" ("Stephen Dedalus," pp. 118–20). Hélène Cixous offers an incisive critique of Stephen's narcissistic exercise: "The motto of the Jesuits, nailed down by its four full-stops, is opposed to the vague, floating, mysterious evocation of the woman's name. In the act of writing, both the real woman and the dream woman fade away; only the trace of a kiss remains. The poet embraces himself. . . . He longs to be metamorphosed; . . . the artist gives himself poetry and writing in the place of the beloved" (*The Exile of James Joyce*, pp. 404–6). For a comprehensive discussion of Stephen's imitation of Dumas's Count of Monte Cristo, see R. B. Kershner, *Joyce, Bakhtin, and Popular Literature*, pp. 195–212. For an excellent analysis of Joyce's development of the character of Emma Clery from its inception in *Stephen Hero*, see Bonnie Scott, *Joyce and Feminism*, pp. 133–55.

16 Jacques Derrida, via Mallarmé, insists that the noun *spur* is related "to the verb to *spurn*, that is, to disdain, to rebuff, to reject scornfully." The artistic spur (*éperon*) of creativity must be spurned as a physical presence in order to be re-created aesthetically as an object of desire (*Spurs/Eperons*, p. 41). Stephen's behavior, at this point, conforms to Jacques Lacan's analysis of courtly love: "It is an altogether refined way of making up for the absence of sexual relation by pretending that it is we who put up an obstacle to it. . . . For the man, whose lady was entirely, in the most servile sense of the term, his female subject, courtly love is the only way of coming off elegantly from the absence of sexual relation" (*Feminine Sexuality*, p. 141).

17 Jane Gallop comments: "Written language is a further mediation over oral, and it is in the written, mediated, more symbolic dimension that we find the mark of the father" (*Feminism and Psychoanalysis*, p. 130). Jacques Derrida declares in *Spurs/Eperons* that aesthetic style "also uses its spur (*éperon*) as a means of protection against the terrifying, blinding, mortal threat (of that) which *presents* itself, which obstinately thrusts itself into view. And style thereby protects the presence, the content, the thing itself . . . on the condition that it should not *already* . . . be that gaping chasm which has been deflowered in the unveiling of the difference" (p. 39). See also Maud Ellmann, "Disremembering Dedalus."

18 As Julia Kristeva explains in *Powers of Horror*, abjection is a "precondition of narcissism" evoked by a "prohibition placed on the maternal body" (pp. 13–14). "We are no longer within the sphere of the unconscious but at the limit of primal repression that, nevertheless, has discovered an intrinsically corporeal and already signifying brand, symptom, and sign: repugnance, disgust, abjection. There is an effervescence of object and sign – not of desire but of intolerable significance" (p. 11). "The body's inside, in that case, shows up in order to compensate for the collapse of the border between inside and outside. . . . The abjection of those flows from within suddenly become the sole 'object' of sexual desire – a true 'ab-ject' where man,

frightened, crosses over the horror of maternal bowels and, in an immersion that enables him to avoid coming face to face with an other, spares himself the risk of castration" (p. 53).

19 Julia Kristeva asks in *Powers of Horror*: "Why does *corporeal waste*, menstrual blood and excrement, or everything that is assimilated to them, from nail-parings to decay, represent – like a metaphor that would have become incarnate – the objective frailty of symbolic order? . . . Excrement and its equivalents (decay, infection, disease, corpse, etc.) stand for the danger to identity that comes from without: the ego threatened by the non-ego, society threatened by its outside, life by death" (p. 71).

20 The language of this description is based on the murkier prose of a Nietzschean reverie that Joyce recorded as an "Epiphany" in 1903: "What moves upon me from the darkness subtle and murmurous as a flood, passionate and fierce with an indecent movement of the loins? What leaps, crying in answer, out of me, as eagle to eagle in mid air, crying to overcome, crying for an iniquitous abandonment?" (Scholes and Kain, *Workshop*, p. 41).

21 Jeanne McKnight tells us that "Joyce's manuscript notes for *Stephen Hero* suggest that he had once intended Stephen's sexual initiation to have been oral. The plan was for Stephen to participate in *Soixanteneuf*" ("Unlocking the Word-Hoard," p. 427). See also Scholes and Kain, *Workshop*, p. 71.

22 Hélène Cixous believes that until Anna Livia, Joyce's "portraits of women are far from appealing or charming: he sees woman as a mixture of two simplified aspects, the one attracting and the other repelling, her arms held out in welcome but also to grasp and hold, her flesh welcoming in order to bury and absorb. She is the contradiction to the artist's decision to fly away. . . . By her animal or mineral nature, woman can stand for pure beauty, and by her *difference*, by vagueness and aloofness, she may become partially divine, so that her distant image becomes the icon before which Joyce likes to prostrate himself" (*The Exile of James Joyce*, pp. 485–6).

23 Cixous notes that the hell of Father Arnall's sermon "is a model of organisation for physical and mental torture, a model of order and elegance in sadism, and thus could not fail to captivate Stephen's still rebellious mind. . . . Stephen indeed denies his sins, but cannot avoid hearing their language, which is a travesty of his own. . . . It is the artist in him that has been put to the torture. . . . Nietzsche used to say that 'I fear that we cannot rid ourselves of the notion of God, because we still believe in grammar'; it is this belief in grammar that is slowly dying in these convulsions of language and of Stephen's mind" (ibid., pp. 327–30).

24 Beauvoir, *The Second Sex*, pp. 150–1. Sheldon Brivic feels that "sexual desire is linked in Stephen's mind to dread of being reduced to a woman" ("Joyce in Progress," p. 315).

25 Beauvoir, *The Second Sex*, pp. 166–7.

26 Anthony Roche, in an article on "Stephen's Vision," suggests an analogy between this passage and the Gaelic *aisling* or vision-poem, with its "open declaration of sensual delight." "Magic and metamorphosis are invoked at the very outset of the description of the girl; they work with the bird similes (the images of a seabird, a crane, swan's down, and dove) to suggest the world of Celtic legend where the children of Lir were magically transformed into swans, the souls of those who died young took flight for the Otherworld in the shape of birds" (p. 328). See also F. L. Radford, "Daedalus and the Bird-Girl."

27 In *The Ordeal of Stephen Dedalus*, Edmund Epstein identifies this woman as a prostitute; the text, however, seems to counterpoint her image with the Nighttown setting. For Epstein, the bird-girl "is the earth itself, the 'vegetable chaos' of earthly life" (p. 99). Charles Rossman feels that the wading girl "is the mirror of Stephen's emotional state, the self-serving projection of a doomed yearning. She is the natural descendant of the imagined 'harlots with gleaming jewel eyes,' who had previously stimulated Stephen's orgies of auto-eroticism" ("Stephen Dedalus," p. 121).

28 Florence Howe, in a feminist critique of the scene's realistic context, sees the delicate, crane-like figure as "land-bound." She feels that Stephen's "ambivalence towards the young girl is at once a combination of his earlier idealistic view of women and his experience with a prostitute as well as his way of moving past that to declaim himself a man and an artist. . . . The artist can fly and create, even in motion. We women are of the earth. . . . The male artist, whether he is Stephen or Joyce or someone else, must conceive his power, or his difference from women, must take his measure against them, must finally define the two sexes as different species" ("Feminism and Literature," pp. 263–4). In *A Portrait of the Artist*, Joseph Buttigieg offers a scathing indictment of Stephen's aesthetic posture in response to the vision of the bird-girl. In order to sustain his "angelic flight," Stephen "must become hardened in his haughtiness, confirmed in his cold remoteness, and ossified in his dehumanized aesthetics" (p. 75). "Through the imagination he expects to shed his temporality. . . . Stephen is as human as those around him; what makes him different is the illusory feeling of disembodiment" (p. 72).

29 Stephen's epiphany is "sacramental" insofar as it proves to be the "outward sign of an inward grace." Compare the fervid invocation in the narrative essay "A Portrait of the Artist": "Thou wert sacramental imprinting thine indelible mark, of very visible grace. A litany must honour thee: Lady of Apple Trees, Kind Wisdom, Sweet Flower of Dusk" (*P* 264). The protagonist of Joyce's 1904 essay turns away from "waders, into whose childish or girlish hair, girlish or childish dresses, the very wilfulness of the sea had entered" (*P* 262). The woman he praises seems to combine characteristics later ascribed to Emma, the bird-girl, and the eternal temptress. His prayer climaxes in a flood of romantic ecstasy: "A kiss: and they leap together, indivisible, upwards,

radiant lips and eyes, their bodies sounding with the triumph of harps!'' (*P* 264).

30 Toril Moi, in *Sexual/Textual Politics*, observes that ''Freud's own texts, particularly 'The Uncanny,' theorize the *gaze* as a phallic activity linked to the anal desire for sadistic mastery of the object. The specularizing philosopher is the potent master of his insight. . . . As long as the master's scopophilia (i.e. 'love of looking') remains satisfied, his domination is secure'' (p. 134). Alan Sheridan explains in Jacques Lacan's *Ecrits: A Selection* that the Lacanian ''*objet petit a*'' connotes '' '*autre*' (other), the concept having been developed out of the Freudian 'object' and Lacan's own exploitation of 'otherness'. The '*petit a*' (small 'a') differentiates the object from (while relating it to) the '*Autre*' or '*grand Autre*' (the capitalized 'Other'). . . . Lacan insists that '*objet petit a*' should remain untranslated, thus acquiring, as it were, the status of an algebraic sign'' (p. xi). According to Lacan, ''What was seen, but only from the side of the man, was that what he relates to is the *objet a*, and that the whole of his realisation in the sexual relation comes down to fantasy'' (*Feminine Sexuality*, p. 157). In *Sexuality in the Field of Vision*, Jacqueline Rose describes the *objet a* as ''Lacan's formula for the lost object which underpins symbolisation, cause of and 'stand in' for desire. What the man relates to is this object. . . . As the place onto which lack is projected, and through which it is simultaneously disavowed, woman is a 'symptom,' for the man'' (p. 72).

31 As Bonnie Scott points out, Stephen's romantic swooning mimics the euphoria of post-orgasmic release. He ''reclines on a nurturing mother earth, then falls into a sleep that is also a fall into a flushed womb through rose-like labia'' (*James Joyce*, p. 88). For an illumination of Joyce's use of ''symbolism strongly reminiscent of the *Paradiso*,'' see Barbara Seward, ''The Artist and the Rose,'' p. 58.

32 For further discussion of Joyce's art as couvade, see R. Barrie Walkley, ''The Bloom of Motherhood,'' and Jeanne Perreault, ''Male Maternity in *Ulysses*.''

33 Mary Reynolds convincingly argues that Gabriele d'Annunzio's first novel, *The Child of Pleasure*, ''furnished the model for the villanelle section of Chapter Five'' (*Joyce and Dante*, p. 181). Hence the intrusion of an angelic Gabriel into Stephen's bedchamber. Reynolds also believes that the villanelle episode is intended to reflect the design of Dante's *Vita Nuova* through ''the relation of the writing of love poetry to the artistic development of the poet,'' and that this particular example of intertextuality was inspired by still another Dante/Gabriel: ''The copy of the *Vita Nuova* that Joyce bought in Trieste was a deluxe illustrated version of the first pre-Raphaelite edition of 1902,'' with illustrations by Dante Gabriel Rosetti (ibid., p. 178). Reynolds's textual parallels between *Vita Nuova* and *Portrait* are striking (ibid., Appendix, pp. 256–64). For further discussion of Joyce's belated addition of the villanelle section to Chapter Five of *Portrait*, see Hans Walter Gabler, ''The Seven Lost Years of *A Portrait*.''

34 Whether or not Stephen has experienced nocturnal emission has long
been a matter of debate among Joyceans. Hugh Kenner seems to have
inaugurated the "wet dream school" in *Dublin's Joyce* (p. 123). According to Bernard Benstock, an "examination of Joyce's technique reveals
that the origins of the poem are not in spiritual dream surfacing near
dawn to quasi-consciousness, but in the slow awakening to the realisation of a nocturnal emission. It is not just Stephen's soul that is 'all
dewy wet' " (*The Undiscover'd Country*, p. 153). But Benstock also
suggests that Stephen's "involuntary ejaculation" is followed, towards
the end of his poetic composition, by "voluntary masturbation," as
"sexual fantasy envelops the naked body of a compliant Emma"
(p. 154). In a recent article on "The Villanelle Perplex," Robert Day
insists that Stephen has not had a wet dream, but that he does masturbate in this "scene of onanistic composition," or "remote-control sex"
(p. 79).

35 Hélène Cixous observes that in Stephen's romantic rhetoric, the word
"heart" is usually "equated with 'flesh,' and the 'heart's cry' with the
cry of desire. 'Soul' is associated with 'nakedness,' meaning the real
body of woman." In this instance, "his heart's cry is but the sublimation of a more elementary appeal which uses poetry as dissimulation,
rhythm as replacement, and music to disguise its frustration" (*The Exile
of James Joyce*, p. 498). These purplish passages, says Bernard Benstock,
"should be enough indication that the final poem is not intended to be
read as evidence of poetic maturity: the mood is pre-Raphaelite with
a vengeance" (*The Undiscover'd Country*, p. 150).

36 See Elaine Unkeless, "Bats and Sanguivorous Bugaboos."

37 In "The Villanelle Perplex," Robert Day reminds us that "the letters
to Nora of 1909, which seem to have been involved in the imagery of
the prose sections of this passage, abound in references to masturbation
while writing or reading the words of love . . . (*SL* 184–86, 190–91)."
Day believes that Joyce gives us "as clear a description of self-induced
orgasm and liquids pouring forth as Stephen's fancy language and the
1914 obscenity laws will permit; he is now violating his own precious
thing with profane hands" (p. 79).

38 In Joseph Buttigieg's judgment, Stephen simply "transforms his lust
into a villanelle. He escapes and avoids the potential embarrassment of
human sexual encounter by wallowing self-indulgently in the unreal
beauty of words. He totally abandons the tangible universe in order to
derive his pleasure safely from the solitary savoring of his own verbal
contrivances" (*A Portrait of the Artist*, p. 67). In contrast, Robert Scholes
defends the villanelle as a "muse-poem," the celebration of a "great
poetical archetype." He argues that "Joyce intended the poem to be
the product of genuine inspiration. . . . It is at this point that Stephen
ceases to be an esthete and becomes a poet" ("Stephen Dedalus, Poet
or Esthete?" pp. 478–80). Robert Day, assessing the poem "from the
point of view of a seeker after wholeness, harmony and radiance,"
finds it "a hodgepodge of cliché and a farrago of nonsense" ("The

Villanelle Perplex," p. 82). "Talent is there, but Cupid gets in the way" (p. 83).

39 Compare the young Joyce's own misogynist remarks, recorded on 2 February 1904 by his brother Stanislaus: "Woman is an animal that micturates once a day, defecates once a week, menstruates once a month, and parturates once a year" (*Dublin Diary*, p. 11 n). In *Powers of Horror*, Julia Kristeva argues that menstrual blood connotes physiological abjection and threatens the symbolic order because it "stands for the danger issuing from within the identity (social or sexual); it threatens the relationship between the sexes within a social aggregate and, through internalization, the identity of each sex in the face of sexual difference" (p. 71). The notion of *defilement* that menstrual excrescences evince "is the translinguistic spoor of the most archaic boundaries of the self's clean and proper body" (p. 73).

40 As Bernard Benstock explains, the "surface implication of this magniloquent phrase is that Dante is somehow responsible for a platonically antiseptic attitude for men to hide behind when dealing with unresponsive women." Stephen's "infatuation with Emma is a matter of bestowing upon her Beatrice qualities . . . and then, heroically adjusting to his vast disappointment, citing Dante as his predecessor" (*The Undiscover'd Country*, p. 97).

41 In her study of morals and gender, *In a Different Voice*, Carol Gilligan postulates that Stephen Dedalus provides an excellent example of a young man acting out a masculine "adolescent ideal" embodied in a narcissistic "concept of the separate self and of moral principles uncompromised by the constraints of reality" (p. 98). "In Stephen's simpler construction, separation seemed the empowering condition of free and full self-expression, while attachment appeared a paralyzing entrapment and caring an inevitable prelude to compromise. . . . For Stephen, leaving childhood means renouncing relationships in order to protect his freedom of self-expression" (p. 157).

42 For Joseph Buttigieg, Stephen's narcissism and intellectual isolation invoke a spiritual simony that sacrifices the values of love and care for the dubious prize of aesthetic detachment. "One cannot help noticing the total absence of love in Stephen, and the close connection between his coldness and his unswervingly ironic stance" (*A Portrait of the Artist*, p. 90). Stephen's "flight from suffering amounts to a flight from love. . . . Stephen's existence becomes a work of art and ceases to be a 'life,' that is, a history" (p. 93).

3: INTERPRETING *EXILES*

1 One of the reasons that *Exiles* is such a perplexing dramatic experiment is the very indeterminacy of its genre. Searching for an appropriate form, Joyce vertiginously mixes conventions and swerves from one dramatic genre to another. What begins as a comedy of manners quickly

moves in the direction of romantic parody, melodrama, moral parable, and farce. Some of the play's idiosyncrasies might be attributable to what Robert Adams identifies as the "buried piling on which Joyce's play seems to have been constructed, . . . Scribe's libretto for Meyerbeer's opera, *Robert le Diable*. As a piece of stagecraft, Scribe's piece is a juvenile shocker in the lowest traditions of Victorian melodrama" ("Light on Joyce's *Exiles*," p. 98). In the opinion of Mary Reynolds, the origins of *Exiles* are decidedly Dantesque. The play, she tells us, "reproduces in part the closing episode of Dante's *Purgatorio*," when "Dante is reunited with Beatrice and receives from her the assurance that his poetic mission has divine validation. . . . Richard Rowan, the artist-hero of *Exiles*, defines a conception of love in a dialectic of moral freedom, and Joyce here deliberately constructs a modern and relativist interpretation of Dante's sequence" (*Joyce and Dante*, p. 165). According to Reynolds, Richard Rowan "is clearly a Joycean interpretation of the artist-pilgrim of the *Divine Comedy*. But whereas "Dante's exploration of the 'struggle of the soul' is theologically-directed, Joyce's comes near to being psychoanalytically directed" (ibid., p. 172).

2 Jane Gallop, *Feminism and Psychoanalysis*, p. 48. In his essay on "The Meaning of the Phallus," Jacques Lacan explains the critical distinction between sexual need and erotic desire: "What is thus alienated in needs . . . reappears in a residue which then presents itself in man as desire. . . . The phenomenology which emerges from analytic experience is certainly such as to demonstrate the paradoxical, deviant, erratic, eccentric and even scandalous character by which desire is distinguished from need. . . . Demand in itself bears on something other than the satisfactions which it calls for" (*Feminine Sexuality*, p. 80).

3 Joyce's emulation of Ben Jonson probably influenced the fact that he gave his *dramatis personae* in *Exiles* a set of comic, almost parodic verbal handles. Richard Rowan is associated with the "rowan tree," a Eurasian tree of the apple family with red, berry-like pomes. His surname recalls Hamilton Rowan, although he denies lineal descent from the Irish patriot. The word "Rowan" further suggests a sense of firmness and mastery subliminally associated with a "rower" or captain. Robert Hand, in turn, is identified as an aspiring "manipulator" (from the Latin *manus*). He wants a hand in everything and tries to intrude in Richard's domestic situation by forcefully laying hands on Bertha. Robert proves to be a phallic imposter whose hands are everywhere, grasping for Bertha as lover, then reaching for Richard as leader and master. Rowan comes to the cottage to demand that Robert unhand Bertha; but instead, like Pilate, he washes his hands of the situation and goes off to pare his fingernails as the would-be lovers sort out their moral dilemma. A surprising number of references to hands are scattered in stage-directions throughout the play.

4 Rowan has refused to "mark the product of copulation with his own name" or reduce his partner to an "anonymous worker, the machine in

the service of a master proprietor who will put his trademark upon the finished product" (Luce Irigaray, *Speculum of the Other Woman*, p. 23). Calling himself a "socialist artist," Joyce wrote to Stanislaus in May 1905: "I cannot tell you how strange I feel sometimes in my attempt to live a more civilised life than my contemporaries. But why should I have brought Nora to a priest or a lawyer to make her swear away her life to me? And why should I superimpose on my child the very troublesome burden of belief which my father and mother superimposed on me?" (*Letters* II, 89).

5 This riddle, in turn, raises still another question. Has Richard indeed relinquished the phallus as "emblem of man's appropriative relation to the virgin" (Luce Irigaray, *Speculum of the Other Woman*, p. 42)? Or has he, instead, appropriated the womb, the original signifier of absence and mystery, by making himself the origin of aesthetic and imaginary creations that erase woman's sexual/reproductive authority?

6 It is interesting that Joyce intended to give Bertha a youthful history of love and loss, of amorous grief similar to that of Nora Barnacle and Michael "Sonny" Bodkin in actual life and of Gretta Conroy and Michael Furey in the *Dubliners* story "The Dead." In his notes for the play, Joyce imagines Bertha weeping over Rahoon, over "him whom her love has killed, the dark boy whom, as the earth, she embraces in death and disintegration. He is her buried life, her past. . . . His symbols are music and the sea, liquid formless earth. . . . She is the Magdalen who weeps remembering the loves she could not return" (*E* 118). Bertha remains friendless and alone, protesting in an unpublished fragment of dialogue: "I was too simple and uneducated" (Robert Adams, "Light on Joyce's *Exiles*?", p. 91). Although Beatrice Justice could be a potential friend to Bertha, she is cast by Joyce in the role of antagonist and foil. Beatrice is described as "a slender dark woman of 27 years" (*E* 16), dressed like a spinster and appearing like a shade. Joyce notes that "her mind is an abandoned cold temple in which hymns have risen heavenward in a distant past but where now a doddering priest offers alone and hopelessly prayers to the Most High" (*E* 119). Beatrice has served as Richard's editor and ostensible inspiration, a virgin offered a novena of letters over the nine years of Rowan's exile. Richard implies, moreover, that his flight from Ireland was meant as a judgment against this unfaithful Mercedes who, in a moment of weakness, sinned in a garden by pledging her troth to Robert with a kiss and a garter.

7 Until recently, few critics have acknowledged the centrality of Bertha's role in *Exiles*. Hugh Kenner claims that Bertha is a "neurotic woman" and a "parody of the exiled Eve" (*Dublin's Joyce*, p. 89). His view is shared by Carole Brown and Leo Knuth, who see the play's female protagonist as "little more than a psychological satellite," "annoyingly imperceptive," and "neither empathic nor discerning" ("Joyce's Exiles," p. 16). William Tindall indicts Bertha as Richard's "stooge," a woman who gullibly colludes in her own sado-masochistic victimization

(*A Reader's Guide to James Joyce*, p. 111). And Theo Dombrowski, romanticizing Richard's ideal love, concludes that Bertha "does not want freedom" but "desires love as a kind of bondage" ("The Problem of Love," p. 123). One of Bertha's few critical defenders is Darcy O'Brien, who celebrates Joyce's heroine as a symbol of innocence and a "secular Madonna . . . who bestows her soul's virginity in love, that unnatural phenomenon which occurs but once" (*Conscience*, pp. 64–5). Ruth Bauerle, in her essay on "Bertha's Role in *Exiles*," offers convincing evidence that Bertha might be considered the "dominating figure of the drama." See also Celeste Loughman's essay "Bertha, Victress, in Joyce's *Exiles*" and Bernard Benstock's discussion of *Exiles* in *A Companion to Joyce Studies*.

8 According to Richard Ellmann, Joyce fashioned the character of Robert Hand through a conflation of Oliver St John Gogarty, Vincent Cosgrave, Thomas Kettle, and Roberto Prezioso. "From his experiences with them Joyce drew the picture of friendship which appears in the play: a friend is someone who wants to possess your mind . . . and your wife's body, and longs to prove himself your disciple by betraying you" (*JJ* 356). Joyce evidently took much of his inspiration for *Exiles* from Prezioso's dalliance with Nora – an interest which Joyce himself at first encouraged. Prezioso was a Venetian journalist who befriended Joyce in Trieste and "had a reputation of success with women." He began making regular calls on Nora, and Joyce followed the flirtation as though it were a scientific experiment. When Prezioso, however, "endeavored to become Nora's lover rather than her admirer" in 1911 or 1912, Joyce sought him out and "expostulated with him in the name of friendship and broken confidence." In a semi-public spectacle, Prezioso was left weeping and humiliated in the Piazza Dante. Ellmann notes that "Joyce was half-responsible for Prezioso's conduct, in an experiment at being author of his own life as well as of his work. No doubt he was taking too much upon himself, but he did not do so for pleasure, except perhaps the pleasure of self-laceration" (*JJ* 316–17). See also Hélène Cixous, *The Exile of James Joyce*, p. 534. Cixous claims that Joyce slapped Prezioso, but I can find no biographical evidence of such uncharacteristic physical violence on Joyce's part.

9 In *James Joyce and Sexuality*, Richard Brown notes Joyce's satire of the sexual undercurrents of the Catholic confession and identifies this scene as a parody of the sacrament of penance. "Much of the tension of the play," he tells us, "arises from the sexual inquisition to which Richard subjects Bertha" (p. 128). According to Michel Foucault, it was the Catholic pastoral of the seventeenth century which gave rise to the construction of a sexual discourse modeled on a rigorous and detailed confessional investigation, "an entire painstaking review of the sexual act in its very unfolding." The priest was to examine a penitent in confession with the understanding that "everything had to be told. A twofold evolution tended to make the flesh into the root of all evil, shifting the most important moment of transgression from the act itself to

the stirrings – so difficult to perceive and formulate – of desire. . . . Discourse, therefore, had to trace the meeting line of the body and the soul, following all its meanderings. . . . The Christian pastoral prescribed as a fundamental duty the task of passing everything having to do with sex through the endless mill of speech" (*History of Sexuality*, pp. 19–21).

10 A maternal ghost overshadows Rowan's consciousness, spurred to rebellion against Mother Ireland by a matriarchal judge that "turned aside from me and from mine" (*E* 23). Still fighting the haunting specter, Richard protests that it was, finally, his mother who drove him away. "On account of her I lived years in exile and poverty too" (*E* 23). She rejected her grandson as "a child of sin and shame," nameless and godless. On behalf of himself and his son, Richard raises an angry cry of rebellion against the parent who bore him, then thrust him from her heart and affections. Yet it is her aspect – hard, cold, detached, and pitiless – that he purportedly seeks to emulate, proclaiming: "It is her spirit I need" (*E* 25).

11 Joyce remarks that "Bertha's state when abandoned spiritually by Richard . . . is like that of Jesus in the garden of olives. It is the soul of woman left naked and alone that it may come to an understanding of its own nature. . . . Through these experiences she will suffuse her own reborn temperament with the wonder of her soul at its own solitude and at her beauty, formed and dissolving itself eternally amid the clouds of mortality" (*E* 115). If Bertha, as Joyce suggests, is to be perceived as a Christ-figure, Richard becomes God the Father, an all-seeing patriarch testing Bertha's faith through abandonment and suffering. Bertha resembles the scapegoat about to be sacrificed for the sins of humankind – in this case, male sins of jealousy and emotional avarice. In a symbolic drama that borders on allegory, Joyce has given us *two* Christ-figures – Bertha the victim and Richard the narcissistic man/god. Joyce admits in his notes for *Exiles* that Richard initiates this existential trial largely out of self-interest: "He is in fact fighting for his own hand, for his own emotional dignity and liberation in which Bertha, no less and no more than Beatrice or any other woman is co-involved. He does not use the language of adoration and his character must seem a little unloving. But it is a fact that for nearly two thousand years the women of Christendom have prayed to and kissed the naked image of one who had neither wife nor mistress nor sister" (*E* 120).

12 It is not surprising that readers have, for the most part, found Joyce's "semi-autobiographical" protagonist arrogant and annoying, if not insufferable. Darcy O'Brien sees Rowan as "a man driven by an unpleasant alliance of principle, perversity, and lust," not to mention voyeurism, masochism, and homosexual urges (*Conscience*, pp. 60–1). Hugh Kenner describes him as a "lonely deity" obsessed with a need for mastery over all the characters in the drama ("Joyce's *Exiles*," p. 395). And Clive Hart judges Richard "consistently pompous, overmeticulous, and masochistic," especially in his interaction with

Bertha, "the only person in the play who is at all sympathetic" (*James Joyce's "Ulysses,"* pp. 26–7). Perhaps the strongest indictment comes from Edward Brandabur, who believes that Rowan suffers from a sado-masochistic pathology in which "the neurotic both directs and plays conflicting roles" of torturer and victim. Controlled, in actuality, by a "spiritual allegiance to his dead mother," Richard proves a moral and aesthetic failure in the enactment of his narcissistic project (*A Scrupulous Meanness*, pp. 138, 131). John MacNicholas, in an excellent survey of "The Stage History of *Exiles*," points out that literary critics have often had difficulty liking the play because Richard is himself so unlikeable. "Apparently, only Harold Pinter has staged *Exiles* with unqualified success," perhaps because "Joyce was struggling toward a new kind of theater. Ambiguity and stylized silences are at the center of this theatrical technique" (pp. 11, 23). Bernard Benstock believes that in Joyce's drama of "three cat and mouse acts" (*E* 123), Rowan "is the major cat, a role that he tries to monopolize throughout but may have to relinquish before the end" (*"Exiles,"* p. 368). Benstock disagrees with those critics who see "Rowan as the dominant force in *Exiles*, the introspective and philosophical hero modeled by his creator on himself and therefore sacrosanct" (p. 377). Richard Brown, however, defends Rowan as a man whose "situation is not one of ignorance, compromise, comedy and victimization but one where high principles and a degree of heroism may be attained" (*James Joyce and Sexuality*, p. 18).

13 A number of critics have defined the homoerotic attachment between Richard and Robert as an implicitly homosexual affiliation. According to Hélène Cixous, the "real couple" in the play "is formed by the two men, their relationship defined by analogy with that of Jesus and Judas." Robert, she observes, "is the reflection of Richard in a distorting mirror," and Richard "denounces his own Judas in order to assume the crown of thorns" (*The Exile of James Joyce*, pp. 539–41). Bertha is reduced to a figurative sexual mediator, "the nebulous matter in which the two men wander, . . . the *vas naturale*, . . . the means of sexual communication" (ibid., p. 538). It is interesting, however, that Bertha and Beatrice are brought together in a similar homoerotic configuration later in the play, when Bertha is moved spontaneously to befriend Beatrice and to acknowledge her as an *alter ego*. She admires the other woman's "lovely long eyelashes" and sad, myopic eyes. The two are united in their shared rejection by Richard. When Bertha boldly accuses her husband of egotistically manipulating them both, she offers an impassioned defense of Beatrice, whom Richard "made unhappy as you have made me and as you made your dead mother unhappy and killed her" (*E* 103). Beatrice, she ingenuously declares, "is a fine and high character. I like her. She is everything I am not – in birth and education" (*E* 103).

14 The idea of molding a woman in his own artistic image evidently appealed to Joyce, who saw a precedent for his relationship with Nora

in William Blake's choice of a marriage partner. Joyce declared in his 1912 essay on William Blake: "Like many other men of great genius, Blake was not attracted to cultured and refined women. Either he preferred to drawingroom graces . . . the simple woman, of hazy and sensual mentality, or, in his unlimited egoism, he wanted the soul of his beloved to be entirely a slow and painful creation of his own" (*CW* 217).

15 Nietzsche, *Joyful Wisdom*, p. 168. Most critics have identified Richard as a Joyce figure and Robert as his alter ego and mirror image – Stanislaus/Shaun/Bodkin/Gogarty/Kettle/Preziosi. Joyce's 1909 letters to Nora, however, reveal that the playwright has projected into the lascivious Robert many of his own complex and ambivalent attitudes towards sexuality. On 2 December 1909, Joyce wrote to Nora that "inside this spiritual love I have for you there is also a wild beast-like craving for every inch of your body, for every secret and shameful part of it, for every odour and act of it" (*SL* 181). The next day he was "still in a fever-fit of animal desire" and assured Nora of her Circean powers to "turn me into a beast" (*SL* 181–2). Addressing her as "my dirty little fuckbird," he praised her iteration of that *"one lovely word"* (*SL* 185). This four-letter monosyllable known to all men evidently refers to love as it dares not speak its name in *Exiles*.

16 Quoted in Robert Adams, "Light on Joyce's *Exiles*," p. 86. "I carried her away into exile," says Richard. "And now, after years, I carry her back again, remade in my own image" (ibid.).

17 Joyce's own notorious jealousy is documented in his letters of accusation to Nora at the time of the malicious hoax perpetrated in 1909 by Vincent Cosgrave. Fearing that Nora had "stepped out" with Cosgrave during their own 1904 courtship, Joyce wrote: "My eyes are full of tears, tears of sorrow and mortification. My heart is full of bitterness and despair. I can see nothing but your face as it was then raised to meet another's. O, Nora, pity me for what I suffer now. I shall cry for days. My faith in that face I loved is broken. . . . I cannot call you any dear name because tonight I have learnt that the only being I believed in was not loyal to me" (*SL* 158).

18 In *Deceit, Desire and the Novel*, René Girard describes, in a different literary context, the kind of triangulated desire characteristic of Richard's self-deceptive strategy: "The hero seems to offer the beloved wife freely to the mediator, as a believer would offer a sacrifice to his god. But the believer offers the object in order that the god might enjoy it, whereas the hero of internal mediation offers his sacrifice to the god in order that he might not enjoy it. He pushes the loved woman into the mediator's arms in order to arouse his desire and then triumph over the rival desire" (p. 50). In an unpublished fragment, Richard insists that he "remade" Bertha in his own image for the sake of Robert, who "risked nothing and lived prudently" (Robert Adams, "Light on Joyce's *Exiles*," p. 87). Robert retorts: "It is a queer kind of present, Richard, like the giver. You see of course that I have no intention of

accepting it. No, you have made her new and strange. She is yours. Keep her'' (ibid.).

19 Joyce observes in his notes for *Exiles* that since "the publication of the lost pages of *Madame Bovary* the centre of sympathy appears to have been esthetically shifted from the lover or fancyman to the husband or cuckold. . . . This change is utilized in *Exiles* although the union of Richard and Bertha is irregular to the extent that the spiritual revolt of Richard . . . can enter into combat with Robert's decrepit prudence'' (*E* 115 – 16). As Richard Brown points out, Rowan's own definition of "love" is elevated and highly mystical: "Love, for all Joyce's desire to replace romantic mystifications with biological certainties, is not solely represented as sexual passion. Indeed Robert is the apologist for nature's law of passion and Richard (and by implication Joyce too) condemns such a law as mere possessiveness, . . . saying that love is 'To wish her well' '' (*James Joyce and Sexuality*, p. 34).

20 Richard Ellmann tells us that "some of the wording and all the ambiguity'' of Robert Hand's article can be traced back to Thomas Kettle's review of Joyce's *Chamber Music* in the *Freeman's Journal* 1 June 1907. Although Kettle describes Joyce as "a lover of elfin paradoxes'' and the "very embodiment of the literary spirit,'' he also complains that he can find "no traces of the folklore, folk dialect, or even the national feeling'' of Ireland in Joyce's collection of verses, whose melodies he compares "with harps, with wood birds, with Paul Verlaine'' (*JJ* 261). According to Robert Adams, original fragments of the *Exiles* manuscript suggest that "Bertha's innocence and girlishness, associated with the naïveté of Irish political life and the naturalness of Irish rural existence, were to appear within the play as memories of childhood scenes. Bertha was evidently to be a character deeply rooted in the Irish soil'' ("Light on Joyce's *Exiles*,'' p. 98).

21 As Ruth Bauerle points out, Bertha exhibits in this scene "a fundamental integrity of character which brings fulfillment. She manifests not only honesty and truthfulness, but also a profound personal wholeness of being. . . . Bertha, exiled, lonely, and manipulated, shows the greatest faith of all, that of the mistress in the lover who has betrayed her and may do so again'' ("Bertha's Role in *Exiles*,'' pp. 123–4). This scene represents one of the few examples in Joyce's canon of one woman befriending another. Bernard Benstock observes that Bertha's "moment of defiance is capped with an offer of friendship with her presumed rival, an allegiance that transcends their rivalry for Richard. . . . The gesture of feminine solidarity consolidates Bertha's position as she returns her focus to the men who have viewed her as their domesticated mouse'' ("*Exiles*,'' p. 374).

22 See John Keats, "Ode to a Nightingale,'' l. 79; and "Ode on a Grecian Urn,'' ll. 17–20, 25–30, 49–50:

> Bold lover, never, never canst thou kiss,
> Though winning near the goal – yet do not grieve;

She cannot fade, though thou hast not thy bliss,
Forever wilt thou live, and she be fair!
        . . . .
More happy love! More happy, happy love!
    Forever warm and still to be enjoyed,
    Forever panting, and forever young;
All breathing human passion far above,
    That leaves a heart high-sorrowful and cloyed,
    A burning forehead, and a parching tongue.
        . . . .
"Beauty is truth, truth beauty," – that is all
Ye know on earth, and all ye need to know.

Sheldon Brivic, in *Joyce Between Freud and Jung*, makes a connection between Keats's theory of "negative capability" and Richard Rowan's obsessional desire for a creative, "wounding doubt." Brivic cites Keats's famous letter of 21 December 1817 defining "negative capability" as a state of mind in which "a man is capable of being in uncertainties, mysteries, doubts, without any irritable reaching after fact and reason" (p. 122).

23 Joyce offered this description of doubt in answer to a question which he posed, rhetorically, to Arthur Laubenstein: "Which would you say was the greater power in holding people together, complete faith or doubt?" (*JJ* 557). When Laubenstein guessed "faith," Joyce corrected him: "No, doubt is the thing" (*JJ* 557). As Simon Evans explains, *Exiles* "is deliberate in its withholding, for its audience as well as for its characters, the conditions of faith, knowledge, certainty, and belief" (*The Penetration of Exiles*, p. 36). John MacNicholas concludes that the final effect of *Exiles* "is anti-cathartic, which is to say that it is complex, impossible to categorize comfortably, vexing, arresting in the impenetrability of its doubt" ("Joyce's *Exiles*: The Argument for Doubt," p. 39).

24 Still another explanation of the ambiguous ending might be found in Joyce's rather clinical analysis of sexual possibilities in the play: "Bertha is reluctant to give the hospitality of her womb to Robert's seed . . . and for her the supreme concession is what the fathers of the church call *emissio seminis inter vas naturale*. As for the accomplishment of the act otherwise externally, by friction, or in the mouth, the question needs to be scrutinized still more. Would she allow her lust to carry her so far as to receive his emission of seed in any other opening of the body where it could not be acted upon, when once emitted, by the forces of her secret flesh?" (*E* 124). Richard Brown points out that here "the investigation of Bertha's feelings also involves a kind of inversion of the Catholic hierarchy of sins since, for her, in the modern situation of an adulteress, a 'lustful', 'perverse', 'onanistic' or non-reproductive sexual act is less of a 'concession' than a more conventionally legitimate one." In *Exiles*, Joyce "achieved his most striking dramatic

effects precisely by leaving unstated and mysterious the nature of Robert's and Bertha's desires and acts" (*James Joyce and Sexuality*, p. 57).

25 Compare Joyce's somewhat paranoid query to Nora in his letter dated 7 August 1909: "Is Georgie my son? The first night I slept with you in Zurich was October 11th and he was born July 27th. That is nine months and 16 days. I remember that there was very little blood that night. Were you fucked by anyone before you came to me?" (*SL* 158). "I have been a fool. . . . In Dublin here the rumor here is circulated that I have taken the leavings of others. Perhaps they laugh when they see me parading '*my*' son in the streets" (*SL* 159). The "demonic voices," according to Robert Adams, might well be another vestigial remnant of *Robert le Diable* ("Light on Joyce's *Exiles*," p. 101).

26 As Anika Lemaire explains, every desire "is a desire to have oneself recognized by the other . . . and a desire to impose oneself in some way upon the other" (*Jacques Lacan*, p. 174). "Like the Forbidden, the Sacrifice manifests the rupture through which the symbolic establishes itself as an order distinct from the natural or profane material given" (ibid., p. 62). "Subjects in language," writes Jacqueline Rose, "persist in their belief that somewhere there is a point of certainty, of knowledge and of truth. When the subject addresses its demand outside itself to another, this other becomes the fantasied place of just such a knowledge or certainty. Lacan calls this the Other – the side of language to which the speaking subject necessarily refers. The Other appears to hold the 'truth' of the subject and the power to make good its loss. But this is the ultimate fantasy" (*Sexuality*, pp. 55–6). Lacan insists that the "gap in this enigma betrays what determines it, conveyed at its simplest in this formula: that for each partner in the relation, the subject and the Other, it is not enough to be the subjects of need, nor the objects of love, but they must stand as the cause of desire . . . and to disguise this gap by relying on the virtue of the 'genital' to resolve it through the maturation of tenderness (that is by a recourse to the Other solely as reality), however piously intended, is none the less a fraud" (*Feminine Sexuality*, p. 81).

27 In *The Penetration of Exiles*, Simon Evans offers a fascinating discussion of Richard's wound by exploring the etymology of the verb "to exile," which he translates as "to wound," from the Latin *ex-ilia*, "out of – entrails"; or, alternatively, "to leap out," from the Latin *ex-salire*. "*Exiles*," he observes, "is contained within the space vacated by those two derivations, between the resonances of a symbolic wound that may refer either to a fatality or to the triumph of a resurrection" (p. 41).

28 Compare Stephen Dedalus's aesthetic theory in "Scylla and Charybdis" and my own analysis in *Joyce's Moraculous Sindbook*, pp. 65–73.

29 Ruth Bauerle concludes in "Bertha's Role in *Exiles*" that Bertha has emerged triumphant, "revealing to Hand courage and honor; to Beatrice, friendship; and to Rowan, compassion and the knowledge

that he cannot, finally, know. Having once made Rowan a man, she now makes him human. It has been Bertha's night" (p. 128). Celeste Loughman, in a note on "Bertha, Victress," suggests that Bertha proves to be "feminist in the best sense. She knows what she is and what she wants" and "seeks energetically to recapture an ideal relationship" (p. 72).

30 I use the term "imaginary" in the Lacanian sense, defined by Alan Sheridan as "the world, the register, the dimension of images, conscious or unconscious, perceived or imagined. In this respect, 'imaginary' is not simply the opposite of 'real' " (Lacan, *Ecrits: A Selection*, p. ix). Jacqueline Rose explains: "Lacan termed the order of language the symbolic, that of the ego and its identifications the imaginary (the stress, therefore, is quite deliberately on symbol and image, the idea of something which 'stands in'). The real was then his term for the moment of impossibility onto which both are grafted, the point of that moment's endless return" (*Sexuality*, p. 54).

31 Although Hugh Kenner was the first to point out Bertha's prelapsarian yearnings (*Dublin's Joyce*, p. 89), Simon Evans offers a corrective: "It is not simply the first Adam that she misses. The meaning of her 'again' is that she sues for the second greater man as well" (*The Penetration of Exiles*, p. 38). Simon Evans and John MacNicholas have both pointed out the similarity between the erotic discourse of *Exiles* and the "reverential concupiscence" of Joyce's earlier manuscript, *Giacomo Joyce*. Compare, for instance, the textual notes in *Exiles* with the following description: "Grey twilight moulds softly the slim and shapely haunches, the meek supple tendonous neck, the fineboned skull. Eve, peace, the dusk of wonder" (*GJ* 3). See John MacNicholas, *A Textual Companion*, p. 13; and Simon Evans, *The Penetration of Exiles*, p. 22. According to Robert Adams, prudence and justice give way, in the final benediction of *Exiles*, to "a darker, more passionate relation, that between the artist and his creation." Bertha, having made Richard a man, "must now cherish him as a child; having created his work of art, the artist must now suffer it to create him" ("Light on Joyce's *Exiles*," pp. 103–4).

4: UNCOUPLING *ULYSSES*

1 See Jane Gallop, *Feminism and Psychoanalysis*, p. 27. Gallop cites Michele Montrelay's Freudian critique that the "unbearably intense immediacy of the 'odor di femina' produces anxiety, a state totally threatening to the stability of the psychic economy . . . because it threatens to undo the achievements of repression and sublimation, threatens to return the subject to the powerlessness, intensity and anxiety of an immediate, unmediated connection with the body of the mother" (ibid.)

2 As Wendy Steiner notes, "Bloom watches Gerty seated on the beach; Gerty watches Bloom watching her. . . . Each creates the other by creating the other's response, inducing him or her to display and to desire. Thus, Gerty, totally engrossed in her role as Bloom's voyeuristic object, imagines herself in the third person and composes Bloom's response to that objectified self. . . . Each character projects a fantasy of the other in the course of this subject-object interplay – Gerty through the fallen romance clichés of ladies' journals, Bloom through the primordial symbolism of femininity and the homely wisdom of his own experience. . . . Gerty and Bloom here demonstrate the problem of intersubjectivity through the model of vision common to painting and romance – the temporary appropriation of another solely by looking" ("There Was Meaning in His Look," p. 98). I have discussed Gerty more extensively in "Gerty MacDowell: Joyce's Sentimental Heroine."

3 In *Joyce's Anatomy of Culture*, Cheryl Herr offers a convincing interpretation of "Circe" as a "Joycean pantomime which plays out the confusing implications of how culture not only determines gender traits but also shapes concepts of selfhood," so that "sexual identity is largely a cultural or even a theatrical phenomenon" (pp. 152–3). "In *Ulysses*, there is . . . no 'fully human' androgyny; there is only a perpetual rising to textual consciousness of gender traits that became rigidly entrapping labels, packages, and norms reflecting the culture's characteristic mechanism of binary encoding (male vs. female)" (p. 154). Although Herr and I both start from similar premisses concerning the cultural construction of gender, we arrive at somewhat different conclusions about Joyce's trans-sexual play in "Circe."

4 Shoshana Felman, "Rereading Femininity," p. 42.

5 ibid., p. 31. It is not surprising that Joyce chose a brothel as the setting for the "Circe" episode of *Ulysses*, since, as Michel Foucault points out, the brothel and the mental hospital were two places which escaped the nineteenth-century injunction to silence that surrounded sexual discourse beyond the boundaries of the nuclear family. "If it was truly necessary to make room for illegitimate sexualities, it was reasoned, let them take their infernal mischief elsewhere: to a place where they could be reintegrated, if not in the circuits of production, at least in those of profit. The brothel and the mental hospital would be those places of tolerance. . . . Words and gestures, quietly authorized, could be exchanged there at the going rate. Only in those places would untrammeled sex have a right to (safely insularized) forms of reality, and only to clandestine, circumscribed, and coded types of discourse" (*The History of Sexuality*, p. 4).

6 Daniel Ferrer, "Circe, Regret and Regression," p. 136. In an interview with Frank Budgen, Joyce acknowledged "an undercurrent of homosexuality in Bloom as well as his loneliness as a Jew" (Budgen, *James Joyce and the Making of "Ulysses,"* p. 315).

7 Gilles Deleuze and Félix Guattari, *Anti-Oedipus*, pp. 51, 67. In his persona as Henry Flower, Bloom illustrates what Deleuze and Guattari

celebrate as a Proustian "vegetal theme," the "innocence of flowers," which "brings us yet another message and another code: everyone is bisexual, everyone has two sexes, but partitioned, noncommunicating; the man is merely the one in whom the male part, and the woman the one in whom the female part, dominates statistically. . . . Here all guilt ceases, for it cannot cling to such flowers as these" (p. 69).

8 For an informative discussion of Bloom's role as Levitican holocaust, see Beryl Schlossman, *Joyce's Catholic Comedy of Language*, Chapter 2, "Love's Bitter Mystery: *Blumenlied*." "The concept of the phallus and the castration complex," writes Jacqueline Rose, "testify above all to the problematic nature of the subject's insertion into his or her sexual identity" (*Sexuality*, p. 64). "The subject has to recognise that there is a desire, or lack in the place of the Other, that there is no ultimate certainty or truth, and that the status of the phallus is a fraud" (ibid.).

9 Richard Ellmann points out a number of similarities between the "Circe" episode and Leopold von Sacher-Masoch's *Venus in Furs*, which "tells of a young man named Severin who so abases himself before his mistress, a wealthy woman named Wanda, . . . that she becomes increasingly tyrannical, makes him a servile go-between, and . . . turns him over to her most recent lover for a whipping" (*JJ* 369). "Bloom's daymares of self-reproach," observes Stanley Sultan, "draw again and again upon Sacher-Masoch's book. . . . Bloom . . . conforms to the pattern of the hero of *Venus in Furs*, the desire to be made to suffer by a woman to whose service he is dedicated . . . because of his sense of guilt for failing to be that woman's true husband" (*The Argument of "Ulysses,"* pp. 315–16). Sultan notes, furthermore, that Krafft-Ebing, in *Psychopathia Sexualis*, "delineates a classic development of male perversion from passivity to masochism to feminization" (p. 317). For a provocative discussion of Circean masochism from a Deleuzian perspective, see Frances L. Restuccia, "Molly in Furs." For *fin-de-siècle* sources of the Bella-Bloom encounter, see my earlier articles on "James Joyce and Joris-Karl Huysmans" and "James Joyce and Krafft-Ebing."

10 As Catherine Clément suggests in "The Guilty One," the scenario of the circus depends on the "institutionalization of hysteria. . . . The history of the sorceress and the hysteric rejoins the history of spectacles: *the fusion of public child's play with private sexual scenes*" (Cixous and Clément, *The Newly Born Woman*, p. 13). According to Cheryl Herr, "*Ulysses* argues that sexuality is sheer theater, at least on the social stage on which we dramatically construct the selves we play. . . . 'Circe' provides evidence that to change Bloom we would have to change his culture and to alter the structure of terms in which individuality is positioned" (*Joyce's Anatomy of Culture*, pp. 154–5).

11 In the Oedipal schema attacked by Deleuze and Guattari in *Anti-Oedipus*, "the libido as energy of selection and detachment is converted into the phallus as detached object, the latter existing only in the transcendent form of stock and lack" (p. 73). "Lack (*manque*) is,"

244

furthermore, "created, planned, and organized in and through social production" (p. 28). "Castration as a practical operation on the unconscious is achieved when the thousand break-flows of desiring machines . . . are projected into the same mythical space, the unitary stroke of the signifier" (p. 61).

12 Julia Kristeva, *Desire in Language*, pp. 78–9. For a discussion of Joyce and the carnivalesque, see Patrick Parrinder, *James Joyce*; and Elliott B. Gose, Jr, *The Transformation Process in Joyce's "Ulysses,"* Chapter 9, "Comedy in 'Circe.'"

13 For an analysis of Bloom's purgings and bestial transmogrifications, see Gose, *The Transformation Process*, Chapter 10, "The Grotesque in 'Circe.'"

14 As Luce Irigaray declares in *This Sex Which Is Not One*, "femininity" is itself "a role, an image, a value, imposed upon women by male systems of representation. In this masquerade of femininity, the woman loses herself, and loses herself by playing on her femininity. . . . In our social order, women are 'products' used and exchanged by men. Their status is that of merchandise, 'commodities.'" (pp. 84–5).

15 In *James Joyce and Sexuality*, Richard Brown explains why Molly Bloom's malapropism "coronado" should actually read "cornuto" (p. 19).

16 Sigmund Freud notes in *Beyond the Pleasure Principle* that such "punishment dreams" tend to "replace the forbidden wish-fulfillment by the appropriate punishment for it; that is to say, they fulfill the wish of the sense of guilt which is the reaction to the repudiated impulse" (p. 61). The first German edition of this work was published in 1920; the first English translation, by C. J. M. Hubback, in 1922. Either could have been known to Joyce.

17 The strategies of Bloom's unconscious are similar to those employed by the child initiating the *Fort/Da* game analyzed by Freud as a paradigm for the compensations offered the psyche at play. Children tend to repeat in play anything that makes a strong impression on them in real life, and "in doing so they abreact the strength of the impression and . . . make themselves master of the situation" (*Beyond the Pleasure Principle*, p. 36). Thus the child who symbolically casts away a spool at the end of a string, only to draw it back with exclamations of delight, enacts a pantomime of "instinctual renunciation," compensating for his mother's absence "by himself staging the disappearance and return of the objects within his reach. . . . At the outset he was in a *passive* situation – he was overpowered by the experience; but, by repeating it, unpleasurable though it was, as a game, he took on an *active* part. These efforts might be put down to an instinct for mastery that was acting independently of whether the memory was in itself pleasurable or not" (pp. 34–5). "Finally, a reminder may be added that the artistic play and artistic imitation carried out by adults . . . do not spare the spectators . . . the most painful experiences and can yet be felt by them as highly enjoyable" (p. 37). For a discussion of "scopophilia," see Chapter 2, note 30.

18 Hélène Cixous, "Sorties," in Cixous and Clément, *The Newly Born Woman*, p. 84.

19 Most psychoanalytic readings of "Circe" agree that Stephen and Bloom are, to some extent, cognizant of the dramatic events enacted on Joyce's textual stage and are psychologically transformed by their confrontation with specters from the past. In *Joyce in Nighttown*, Mark Shechner analyzes the drama by drawing on Joyce's own biographical obsessions and interprets "Circe" as an extensive desublimation of Bloom's (and Joyce's) fantasy life. "The comedy," he tells us, "will be most hilarious wherever the fantasy is most revealing" (p. 151). Sheldon Brivic, in *Joyce Between Freud and Jung*, is somewhat pessimistic about the cathartic effects of Joyce's comedy and sees little hope for spiritual deliverance. In contrast, Elliott B. Gose, Jr, in *The Transformation Process of Joyce's Ulysses*, describes "Circe" as a "dialectic of purging. Both Bloom and Stephen have projected their deepest fears and desires into hallucinations which we share with them," and both are "cured" of neuroses by the end of the episode. Bloom "emerges as a more integrated and authoritative person after experiencing his worst transformation" (pp. 128, 162). See also my own discussion of "Circe" as psychoanalytic transformation in *Joyce's Moraculous Sindbook*, Chapter 9. Contemporary post-structuralist critics tend to assess "Circe" as static rather than kinetic – either a mock pantomime or a carnivalesque play of linguistic *différance*. In *The Book as World*, Marilyn French tells us that "Bloom and Stephen are not hallucinating. The hallucinations are hypostatizations of their hidden feelings . . . production numbers staged by the author for the audience. . . . Circe is a nightmare sent by god-Joyce to the reader" (p. 187). According to Hugh Kenner, the chapter contains a "plethora of episodes that resemble hallucinations, . . . but are, in fact, either dramatized metaphors, . . . or else expressionistic equivalents of states of feeling" ("Circe," p. 352). Nonetheless, Kenner describes "Circe" as "a nearly accidental psychoanalysis, wholly lacking an analyst" and believes that both Stephen and Bloom are "at least temporarily" changed (ibid., pp. 359–60). Cheryl Herr observes that the chapter "shows us that we cannot burrow under a character's clothes to any essential nature, to any undiluted and potent identity, sexual or otherwise" (*Joyce's Anatomy of Culture*, p. 153). "Bloom's playing Bloom in 'Circe' describes his continuous adoption of one role or another, to the extent that we cannot distinguish character from role" (ibid., p. 155). My analysis of the episode in this chapter attempts to incorporate elements from both psychoanalytic and post-structuralist camps and, in so doing, swerves from the earlier psychoanalytic standpoint of *Joyce's Moraculous Sindbook*.

20 I use the term "abjection" both in the sense suggested by Julia Kristeva in *Powers of Horror* to connote the physical excrescences of the female body that tend to incite horror in the male imagination and in the psychoanalytic sense of an imaginative projection of the self/ego as an "abjected," cast off, and rejected product of the maternal body that

serves, in fantasy, as an imaginary matrix of wholeness and cohesion. In "A Clown's Inquest into Paternity," Jean-Michel Rabaté suggests that in "Lacanian terms, Stephen is the phallus for Bloom even more than for Molly, the phallus as a signifier of absence; this representation triggers the movement of ellipse back to mother" (p. 91). Immediately before this book went to press, I discovered that Kristeva's theory of abjection had led Patrick McGee to some similar (and dissimilar) conclusions about "Circe" in Chapter 4 of his recent study *Paperspace* (pp. 115–49).

21 Herr, *Joyce's Anatomy of Culture*, p. 176. For a discussion of Rudy's appearance in terms of the "Grand Transformation" scene of theatrical pantomine, see ibid., pp. 173–9.

22 In the "Scylla and Charybdis" episode, Stephen thinks: "Love, yes. Word known to all men" (*U* 9: 429–30). These crucial lines were restored to the text in Hans Walter Gabler's 1984 edition of *Ulysses* and are discussed by Richard Ellmann in his introduction to the 1986 Random House publication of the Gabler text (*U* p. xii). See also my own commentary "Reconstructing *Ulysses* in a Deconstructive Mode." For "love" as a four-letter word known to all men, see *SL* 185. The dead mother has become for Stephen what little Rudy has long been for Bloom – an always-already absent object of desire, forever cast in a mold of paralyzed bereavement. As in Freudian dreamscapes, the child psychologically changes places with the dead or absent or spiritually defeated parent; psychic energies are constantly mobile because perpetually transferable. Identifying with the "lost one," the subject confuses guilt with grieving, consequence with cause. Stephen cannot forgive himself for a filial rebellion he associates with his mother's death, just as Bloom mourns for Rudolph the elder, for a dead son he could not succeed magically in keeping alive, and for his own diminished generative powers. For further discussion of the encrypted *imago* of the lost one, see Jacques Derrida, "Fors."

23 Hélène Cixous, "Sorties," in Cixous and Clément, *The Newly Born Woman*, pp. 65–6.

24 According to Christine van Boheemen, "*Ulysses* is a deconstruction of the family romance, a decreation that seems to suggest that epigenetic models are based on preconceptions of patriarchal presence" (*The Novel as Family Romance*, p. 171).

25 As Boheemen observes, Joyce self-consciously "refused to follow the tradition of clear-cut resolution, of recovery of origin, identity, or title. Leopold Bloom's return to the bed of his wife Molly is not a climactic *coniunctio*; the meeting of Bloom and Stephen is unconvincing as an emblem of permanent bonding. . . . With the characters in the fiction, the reader is denied the *catharsis* of a totalizing perspective. There is no closure, no resolution of contradictions" (ibid., p. 133). "Whatever *Ulysses* presents, creates, or constructs is immediately deprived of full self-presence and put 'under erasure' " (ibid., p. 146).

26 Jane Gallop, *Reading Lacan*, pp. 147, 150.

27 According to Sheldon Brivic, Bloom has placed Molly in "the role of nursing mother. . . . The situation of nursing is evoked by the infantile orality of this scene. . . . In making a God of woman, Bloom is really putting her in the place of the father. He continually plays a submissive, filial role with Molly" (*Joyce Between Freud and Jung*, pp. 137–8). In contrast, Richard Ellmann describes this memory as "an epithalamium; love is its cause of motion. The spirit is liberated from its bonds through a eucharistic occasion. . . . Though such occasions are as rare as miracles, they are permanently sustaining" (*JJ* 379).

28 Christine van Boheemen, *The Novel as Family Romance*, p. 158. Although her book was published after the completion of this chapter, I have tried to acknowledge the similarity of our enterprises (triangulated by Deleuze and Guattari, *Anti-Oedipus*) by both incorporating and responding to Boheemen's analysis.

5: MOLLY BLOOM

1 As Bonnie Scott points out, readers have faced "the dilemma of whether to assign Molly to a realistic or a symbolic category, and then the decision of whether to exalt or denigrate her" (*Joyce and Feminism*, p. 157). Mark Shechner notes that "most of her interpreters have staked out positions in either of two opposed camps: the 'earth-mother' camp and the more modern and ever-more-popular 'satanic mistress' or 'thirty-shilling whore camp' " (*Joyce in Nighttown*, p. 197). Leading the cast of harsh Penelopean critics is Joyce's friend Mary Colum, who declared in "The Confessions of James Joyce" that Molly exhibits "the mind of a female gorilla who has been corrupted by contact with humans" (*The Critical Heritage*, vol. 1, p. 233). "She is a dirty joke," writes J. Mitchell Morse in "Molly Bloom Revisited." "No one regards her as anything but a whore" (p. 140). Robert Adams is equally severe in his indictment of Molly as "a slut, a sloven, and a voracious sexual animal" (*Common Sense and Beyond*, p. 166). Hugh Kenner calls her a "Satanic mistress" (*Dublin's Joyce*, p. 262). And Darcy O'Brien conceives of Molly as a *vagina dentata* who "would devour any man": "for all her fleshly charms and engaging bravado, she is at heart a thirty-shilling whore" (*Conscience*, p. 211). On the opposite side of this debate, S. L. Goldberg portrays Molly as the "mystery of Animate Flesh" whose vital potentiality remains couched in a "simple, shrewd, elemental" form (*Classical Temper*, pp. 293–5); and Marilyn French defines her as the "mythic, the archetypal other" (*The Book as World*, p. 259). As David Hayman reminds us in "The Empirical Molly," Joyce's Penelope tends to reflect the various "attitudes we accumulate toward her" (p. 111).

2 In "Molly in Furs," Frances L. Restuccia observes that "Joyce positions himself to write bisexually, to oscillate constantly throughout *Ulysses* between the (phallic) referential and (feminine) non-referential,

and ultimately to disseminate linguistic play" (p. 115). Daniel Schwarz believes that "Molly's obsessive sexuality is an expression of Joyce's conception of Nora. . . . As artistic 'father' of her uninhibited sexual energy – in the sense of creator – Joyce thus has a kind of control over the physiological life of Molly-Nora that, we know from his letters, he feared he might lose in life" (*Reading Joyce's "Ulysses,"* p. 268).

3 Elaine Unkeless, "The Conventional Molly Bloom," p. 159.

4 Darcy O'Brien, *Conscience*, pp. 204, 202. In his introductory lecture "On Narcissism," Sigmund Freud uses the term "to denote the attitude of a person who treats his own body in the same way as otherwise the body of a sexual object is treated; that is to say, he experiences sexual pleasure in gazing at, caressing, and fondling his body, till complete gratification ensues upon these activities. Developed to this degree, narcissism has the significance of a perversion, which has absorbed the whole sexual life of the subject" (*A General Selection*, p. 104). In his essay on "Femininity," Freud arbitrarily attributes "a larger amount of narcissism to femininity, which also affects women's choice of object, so that to be loved is a stronger need for them than to love" (*New Introductory Lectures*, p. 132).

5 *Joyce's "Ulysses" Notesheets*, ed. Phillip F. Herring, p. 498. In his Zurich notebook VIII.A.5, Joyce asked: "What kind of child can much fucked whore have?" – a question evidently intended for the mind of Leopold Bloom (*Joyce's Notes and Early Drafts for "Ulysses,"* ed. Phillip F. Herring, p. 17).

6 Julia Kristeva declares in *Powers of Horror*: "It is with Joyce that we shall discover that the feminine body, the maternal body, in its most unsignifiable, un-symbolizable aspect, shores up, in the individual, the fantasy of the loss in which he is engulfed or becomes inebriated, for want of the ability to name an object of desire" (p. 20). "Far from preserving us from the abject, Joyce causes it to break out in what he sees as a prototype of literary utterance: Molly's monologue. If that monologue spreads out the abject, it is not because there is a woman speaking. But because, from *afar*, the writer approaches the hysterical body so that it might speak, so that he might speak, using it as a springboard, of what eludes speech and turns out to be the hand to hand struggle of one woman with another, her mother of course, the absolute because primeval seat of the impossible – of the excluded, the outside-of-meaning, the abject" (ibid., p. 22). Kristeva and I both arrived independently at a similar assessment of Molly's response to mother-loss, though Kristeva mentions her hypothesis only as a critical aside. For further discussion of the term "abjection," see above, Chapter 2, note 18, and Chapter 4, note 20.

7 See Ruth von Phul's speculative re-creation of the military career of Major Brian Cooper Tweedy and his romance with Lunita Laredo in "'Major' Tweedy and His Daughter." Von Phul points out that Molly, as the daughter of a Jewish mother, "was technically Jewish herself, but her maternal relatives seem to have repudiated her." Molly apparently "remembers nothing about her mother, . . . so we can assume that she

died or decamped very early, and Molly's belittling remark reveals the resentment of a child who has lost a parent whether by death or desertion" (p. 345). In *Joyce's Uncertainty Principle*, Phillip Herring offers a fascinating reconstruction of the historical Molly Bloom and her maternal lineage. "There are both Christian and Jewish Laredos," he explains, "but those in Morocco and Gibraltar are Jewish" (p. 129). Are we to assume that Joyce knew this? Did he expect his reader to have access to such sociological information? Both Herring and von Phul believe that Lunita was Jewish, as she might well have been. But the question remains moot. Joyce piques our curiosity by having Molly describe Lunita as "jewess looking" in an ambivalent attribution which suggests either that Lunita *looked* like a Jew because she *was* one, or that her dark Spanish features gave her a mysteriously exotic, Oriental and Sephardic appearance. Similarly, Herring observes that "Molly's circumstances and actions strongly hint that she is illegitimate" (ibid., p. 134) and that Lunita was, or became, a courtesan. Although Joyce refers to Lunita in his notes as a "much fucked whore," all we know about her from the text is that she "simply disappeared after giving birth to Molly" (ibid., p. 136). The one other critic to have emphasized the profound impact of maternal loss on Molly's psychological development is Jan Good in "Behind Taittering Lips: Molly Bloom's Losses and Sexual Guilt." "Molly's psyche," Good tells us, "must protest that the mother, Lunita Laredo, was driven away not by Molly's powerful longing for closeness and affection with the father, but rather by Major Tweedy's own great love for his daughter" (p. 3).

8 How, one might wonder, does Molly know that she has Lunita's "eyes and figure"? Does she remember her mother as a physical presence? Has she seen a photograph? Has Tweedy compared her to Lunita in moments of nostalgic reminiscence? This is one of the titillating gaps in Joyce's text. In *The Reproduction of Mothering*, Nancy Chodorow speculates that women who experience an infantile "disruption in mother-child empathy" may, as adults, suffer from severe "ego and body-ego" distortions and find that their relation to reality is, "like an infant's, mediated by their mother as external ego." According to Chodorow, the "mother remains a primary internal object to the girl, so that heterosexual relationships are on the model of a nonexclusive, second relationship for her" (pp. 100-1, 198). Molly Bloom's complex, often contradictory, intra-psychic life seems to hinge on infantile emotional needs frustrated by the truncated drama of pre-Oedipal attachment – a developmental stage that largely determines the female child's "subsequent oedipal attachment to her father and her later relationship to men in general" (ibid., p. 96).

9 Luce Irigaray, *Speculum of the Other Woman*, p. 43. Irigaray does not apply this theory directly to Joyce, but I have found her psychoanalytic description of female desire highly provocative and useful in my own interpretation of Molly Bloom's psychological subject-position. According to classical myth, Persephone was raped by Hades/Pluto and

abducted to the underworld against her will. A legendary victim of male lust and innocent of primordial transgression, she (like Molly) was not responsible for mother/daughter separation, though her tasting of the pomegranate had dire and wintry consequences in terms of the seasonal absence of Demeter/Ceres.

10 Luce Irigaray, *Speculum of the Other Woman*, p. 50. Jacques Lacan writes: "I would say that it is in order to be the phallus, that is to say, the signifier of the desire of the Other, that the woman will reject an essential part of her femininity, notably all its attributes through masquerade. It is for what she is not that she expects to be desired as well as loved. But she finds the signifier of her own desire in the body of the one to whom she addresses her demand for love" (*Feminine Sexuality*, p. 84).

11 Luce Irigaray, *Speculum of the Other Woman*, p. 69. In his essay on "Anxiety and Instinctual Life," Freud posits the theory that an obsessive fear of loss of love in adult life may be "a later prolongation of the infant's anxiety if it finds its mother absent. . . . If a mother is absent or has withdrawn her love from her child, it is no longer sure of the satisfaction of its needs and is perhaps exposed to the most distressing feelings of tension" (*New Introductory Lectures*, p. 87). "The reproach against the mother which goes back furthest is that she gave the child too little milk – which is construed against her as lack of love. . . . It seems . . . that the child's avidity for its earliest nourishment is altogether insatiable, that it never gets over the pain of losing its mother's breast" (ibid., p. 122).

12 Sigmund Freud, "Mourning and Melancholia," in *A General Selection*, p. 134.

13 Luce Irigaray, *Speculum of the Other Woman*, pp. 78, 76.

14 ibid., p. 87.

15 Jane Gallop, *Feminism and Psychoanalysis*, pp. 70–1. It is interesting that Leopold and Molly both share similar histories in terms of mother-loss. Ellen Higgins Bloom, the Protestant spouse of Rudolph Virag Bloom, died at some unspecified point in Bloom's youth, and her husband, isolated and debt-ridden, committed suicide because he was unable to overcome feelings of bereavement after his wife's death. Ellen Bloom occupies surprisingly little space in Bloom's interior monologue. She appears in the "Circe" episode in a pantomimic guise that suggests cross-dressing and theatrical transvestism: she wears "*pantomime dame's stringed mobcap, widow Twankey's crinoline and bustle, blouse with muttonleg sleeves buttoned behind, grey mittens and cameo brooch, her plaited hair in a crispine net*" (*U* 15: 283–5). In *Joyce's Anatomy of Culture*, Cheryl Herr characterizes Ellen as Aladdin's "slapstick, widowed mother" in a popular Dublin pantomime and explains that the role was usually played by a male dame in drag: "Ellen's wearing of a male version of female apparel" subtly suggests that the reader's "notion of Bloom's character has to include a sense that his maternal image shows some gender confusion" (p. 145).

16 Freud notes in *Beyond the Pleasure Principle* that the subject of a repetition compulsion is "obliged to *repeat* the repressed material as a contemporary experience instead of . . . *remembering* it as something belonging to the past. These reproductions . . . always have as their subject some portion of infantile sexual life – of the Oedipus complex, that is, and its derivatives; and they are invariably acted out in . . . transference" (p. 39).

17 In *Nora: The Real Life of Molly Bloom*, Brenda Maddox draws a correlation between Molly Bloom's childhood in Gibraltar and Nora Barnacle's in Galway. As a young girl, "Nora was sent to live with her maternal grandmother, Catherine Mortimer Healy. This was Nora's first exile and the one that most shaped her personality. . . . Nora never forgave her mother for shutting her out. . . . Being sent to be fostered, common as that practice was, broke Nora's bond with her mother" (p. 12). Maddox concludes that for both Nora Barnacle and Molly Bloom, "maternal deprivation led to coquettish ways. . . . The maternal qualities that Nora saw in Joyce are the same that Molly saw in Bloom. By making Molly a motherless girl who had been reared by a man and who turned early to pleasing the opposite sex in search of affection, Joyce shows that he understood why Nora was the way she was, even though it drove him to frenzies of jealousy" (p. 203).

18 Nancy Chodorow, *The Reproduction of Mothering*, p. 194.

19 In *This Sex Which Is Not One*, Luce Irigaray calls attention to Jeanne Lampl de Groot's hypothesis concerning a *"girl's negative Oedipus*. Before arriving at a 'positive' desire for the father, which implies the advent of receptive 'passivity,' the girl wishes to possess the mother and supplant the father, and this wish operates in the 'active' and/or 'phallic' mode" (p. 58). This kind of "negative Oedipus" seems operative in Molly's adult sexual economy.

20 For further discussion of this aspect of Bloom's sexuality, see my essay entitled "Joyce's Bloom: Beyond Sexual Possessiveness."

21 According to Robert Boyle, "Bloom, who worships woman particularly in her life-giving and generative role, is here ritually approaching the source of human life." Boyle reminds us that the figure eight lying on its side (lemniscate) can be interpreted as a symbol of infinity ("Penelope," p. 412).

22 In *This Sex Which Is Not One*, Luce Irigaray observes about the representation of feminine desire in the dominant discourse of contemporary culture: "Woman, in this sexual imaginary, is only a more or less obliging prop for the enactment of man's fantasies. That she may find pleasure there in that role, by proxy, is possible, even certain. But such pleasure is above all a masochistic prostitution of her body to a desire that is not her own, and it leaves her in a familiar state of dependency upon man" (p. 25).

23 During the composition of "Penelope," Joyce asked Frank Budgen to send him "Fanny Hill *Memoirs* (unexpurgated)" (*Letters* I, 171). Molly's apparent fascination with penile size may derive intertextually from

Cleland's *Fanny Hill*, where the proportions of a man's "machine" are always obsessively detailed by the heroine/protagonist. Such concerns, however, are a staple of pornography (both classical and contemporary) and tend to reflect masculine fantasies about female pleasure rather than woman's own polymorphous desire.

24 J. Mitchell Morse has proposed the curious theory that Molly "can achieve orgasm only by masturbation or by the friction of her partner's finger" ("Molly Bloom Revisited," p. 142). In *Joyce and Feminism*, Bonnie Scott offers a feminist rejoinder: "Molly's description of vaginal orgasm . . . and her admiration of Boylan's organ for making her feel 'full up' . . . are questionable as female perceptions of coitus, though they reflect male and Freudian fallacies, uncorrected in an era preceding Masters and Johnson" (p. 172).

25 Sheldon Brivic, *Joyce Between Freud and Jung*, p. 194.

26 For an excellent discussion of Molly as a "counterprinciple" to male social and cultural values in *Ulysses*, see Bonnie Scott, *Joyce and Feminism*, Chapter 8.

27 Bonnie Scott relates Molly's "troubles" to Irish political history and offers a provocative assessment of her feminist propensities (*Joyce and Feminism*, pp. 174–6).

28 Charles Peake makes a strong case for an interpretation of Molly's attitudes as those of a 1904 protofeminist: "Women, she thinks, besides being more sensible and prudent than men, are also more sensitive . . . and more beautiful, . . . but they are the oppressed and under-privileged sex, burdened by nature and deprived in their social and personal relationships. Molly is no more consistent about this than about any other subject . . . but, in general, she asserts the physical and moral superiority of women, and, even in her most outspoken attack on the behavior of her own sex, explains it as due to all that women have to put up with" (*James Joyce: The Citizen and the Artist*, pp. 303–4).

29 Jane Gallop observes in *Feminism and Psychoanalysis* that in "Lacan's mirror-stage the infant is fixed, constrained in a representation which the infant believes to be the Other's, the mother's, image of her. The representation freezes the nameless flow. . . . Yet without representation there is only infantile passivity, powerlessness, and anxiety" (p. 121).

30 See Jan Good, "Behind Taittering Lips."

31 According to Brenda Maddox, Joyce and Nora had a similar experience when they first "stepped out" on 16 June 1904. Joyce took Nora to Ringsend where, with few preliminaries, this semi-experienced young woman "unbuttoned his trousers, slipped in her hand, pushed his shirt aside and, acting with some skill (according to his later account), made him a man" (*Nora: The Real Life of Molly Bloom*, p. 27).

32 Whether or not Molly has committed adultery with any of the suitors before Boylan has long been a heated issue of Joycean critical debate. Whereas early readers of *Ulysses* tended to interpret the Ithacan list of

Molly's "lovers" literally, critics since the early 1960s, perusing "Penelope" somewhat more judiciously, have concluded that few of the males in the catalogue could have actually enjoyed physical coition. Richard Ellmann announced in his biography of Joyce that the "two lovers Molly has had since her marriage are Bartell D'Arcy and Boylan, and only Boylan has fully consummated the sexual act" (*JJ* 377). Robert Adams, Stanley Sultan, and David Hayman all defend Molly's sexual fidelity to Bloom before the liaison with Boylan and support the "single lover" theory. See Robert Adams, *Surface and Symbol*, pp. 35–43; Stanley Sultan, *The Argument of "Ulysses,"* pp. 431–44; and David Hayman, "The Empirical Molly." As Hugh Kenner notes, "by post-1959 consensus the number of Molly's lovers other than Boylan swings between 0 and 1" – hardly the record of a hardened adulteress (*Ulysses*, p. 145 n).

33 Hugh Kenner, *Ulysses*, p. 143.

34 Although Joyce refers to the clitoris in the "Circe" episode of *Ulysses* as the "bachelor's button discovered by Rualdus Columbus" (*U* 15: 2341–2), he seems, like most men and women of his generation, to have sustained an entrenched Freudian faith in myths about vaginal orgasm. As I have pointed out elsewhere, Pygmalion authors have traditionally castrated the Galateas they create by excising the clitoris from their textual/sexual productions. And Molly Bloom, as a creation of male authorial fantasy, seems to be no exception, despite her popular reputation for sexual voracity. For further discussion of the issue of fictional "clitoridectomy," see Robert Scholes, "Uncoding Mama," in *Semiotics and Interpretation* and my own article on "Sexuality and Silence in Women's Literature."

35 David Hayman was the first critic to point out that the Ithacan allusion to a "period of 10 years, 5 months and 18 days during which carnal intercourse had been incomplete, without ejaculation of semen within the natural female organ" (*U* 17: 2282–4) does not preclude the possibility that Molly and Leopold practice "coitus interruptus, cunnilingus, or manual stimulation" ("The Empirical Molly," p. 115). In *James Joyce and Sexuality*, Richard Brown proposes the hypothesis that the Blooms' "estrangement" may simply refer to their reliance on birth control – either *coitus interruptus* or the use of condoms. He concludes that the Ithacan citation of a Catholic formulaic code for non-reproductive sexuality may be a "way of describing a contraceptive sexual relationship rather than sexual abstinence. Used with all the rigour, though none of the moral outrage, of the Jesuit theologians, it hardly entitles us to assume, as most critics of *Ulysses* do, that their marriage is an especially unhappy one" (p. 67). As I have suggested elsewhere, Bloom apparently suffers from what psychologists term "secondary impotence," the inability to complete sexual intercourse for reasons of anxiety or trauma – evidently, in this case, the trauma precipitated by the death of his infant son Rudy. I have used the term "impotence" to refer to the syndrome of secondary impotence, though

Bloom clearly retains the ability to experience both erection and ejaculation. Bloom's usual practice seems to be to kiss Molly's bottom, then to bring himself to orgasm on her backside. Whether or not this polymorphously perverse ritual changes on 17 June 1904 is beyond the scope of critical inquiry, though many readers have wished it so and have insisted that the Blooms do resume "normal" heterosexual practice at the conclusion (or, more precisely, beyond the ending) of the novel.

36 Nancy Chodorow, *The Reproduction of Mothering*, p. 90.
37 For a discussion of Molly Bloom's monologue as paschal canticle, see Beryl Schlossman, *Joyce's Catholic Comedy of Language*. According to Schlossman, "Molly's monologue is the word that Joyce brings into the world through a feminine mouth. . . . In the dis-graceful enunciation attributed to Molly (orality, narcissism, desire, betrayal), the vampire-like figure of femininity seems to shrink and disappear. Joyce overturns the prayer for the dying, replacing it with the joyous canticle of the quasi-virginal Molly remembering her first time with Bloom among the *roses* (rhododendrons or, etymologically, rose-trees) of Howth" (p. 63).
38 Sigmund Freud, "Anxiety and the Instinctual Life," in *New Introductory Lectures*, p. 101.
39 Jacques Lacan, "God and the Jouissance of The Woman," in *Feminine Sexuality*, pp. 144–5. For Joyce, as for Lacan, woman embodies the *pas-tout*, the "not everything" or "not-all" that refuses summation and defies the boundaries of logocentric discourse. Joyce, however, is describing a psychological gap; Lacan, an essentialist fallacy.
40 "Lacan used the word *lalangue* to describe elemental language and to imply its thing- or objectlike quality. This is a language with particular ambiguities and special patterns of internal resonance and multiple meanings" (Ragland-Sullivan, *Jacques Lacan and the Philosophy of Psychoanalysis*, p. 206).
41 Deleuze and Guattari, *Anti-Oedipus*, p. 67.
42 ibid., p. 69.

6: READING *FINNEGANS WAKE*

1 In *Joyce's Book of the Dark*, John Bishop explains this phenomenon as the mimetically morbid state of an unconscious sleeper inhabiting a mysterious, surrealistic night-world of darkness and dream. For a lucid discussion of the "clearobscure" dimensions of the *Wake*'s unique approach to night and sleep, see Bishop's introduction and Chapter One, "Reading the Evening World" (pp. 3–41).
2 Characters in the *Wake*, says Margot Norris, "are fluid and interchangeable, melting easily into their landscapes to become river and land, tree and stone, Howth Castle and Environs, or HCE. We find in the *Wake* not characters as such but ciphers, in formal relationship to each other" (*The Decentered Universe*, p. 4). In "*Finnegans Wake*":

A Plot Summary, John Gordon seeks "to extract a coherent narrative from this least reducible of masterpieces" (p. 8). Danis Rose and John O'Hanlon undertake a similar project in *Understanding "Finnegans Wake,"* as do Joseph Campbell and Henry Robinson in *A Skeleton Key to "Finnegans Wake."* In contrast, post-structuralist critics like Jacques Lacan and Jacques Derrida have celebrated Joyce's deconstructive "free play" with language for its unique qualities of indeterminacy and unlimited semiosis. In an essay entitled "Two Words for Joyce," Derrida compares the *Wake* to a "1000th generation computer" and confesses that "every time I write, and even in the most academic pieces of work, Joyce's ghost is always coming on board" (pp. 147–9). He cites, for example, Joyce's influence on *Dissemination, La Pharmacie de Platon, Scribble, La Carte postale,* and *Envois.*

3 In his study of *Joyce's Politics*, Dominic Manganiello repeatedly emphasizes Joyce's lifelong commitment to pacifism. The artist apparently took as his political models "Tolstoy, Proudhon and Benjamin Tucker" (p. 72). As early as 1898, Joyce somberly declared in an essay on "Force" that "all subjugation by force, if carried out and prosecuted by force is only so far successful in breaking men's spirits and aspirations" (*CW* 17). As a neutral citizen harbored in Switzerland during World War One, he gave parodic expression to his pacifist sentiments in the verse pastiche "Dooleysprudence" (*CW* 246–8). Mr Dooley, the "gentleman who won't salute the State" is an anarchist who remains contemptuous of both British and German military authorities. He observes that "Poor Europe ambles/Like sheep to shambles," goaded on by a Church that worships a Jingo Jesus and by ministers who sadistically "taught their flocks the only way to save all human souls/Was piercing human bodies through with dumdum bulletholes" (*CW* 247–8). Dooley notes skeptically that both sides are "out to collar/The dime and dollar," as they sacrifice citizens to martial slaughter. Refusing to collaborate with either faction, the defiant Dooley reserves the right "To paddle down the stream of life his personal canoe" (*CW* 246–8).

4 According to Campbell and Robinson, the jinnies may be seen both as "a couple of young mares on the battlefield" and "a pair of Napoleonic *filles du régiment.* These polymorphous beings correspond to the two temptresses of the Park episode" (*A Skeleton Key to "Finnegans Wake,"* p. 41, n. 7). Patrick Parrinder, in *James Joyce*, identifies the jinnies as those two nightingales, "Florence Nightingale of Crimean War fame and Jenny Lind." He sees the female figures as ironic reminders of the "infantile sexual content" in Joyce's wordplay with "Waterloo" as a "place for urinating" and for the titillating thrill of voyeuristically observing female micturition in a "game of textual hide-and-seek" (pp. 224–5). John Gordon reminds us that HCE in his mimetic Dublin incarnation is the pub-keeping Porter and ingeniously traces the Waterloo battle-scene to a calendar in the jakes of the Porter establishment in Chapelizod (*A Plot Summary*, p. 16).

5 For an excellent cartography of "Novo Nilbud by Swamplight" (*FW* 24.1), see John Bishop's illustration in *Joyce's Book of the Dark*, pp. 34–5. HCE's guilt remains perpetually mysterious and amorphous: "It was in Phoenix Park . . . that he committed an indecorous impropriety which now dogs him to the end of his life-nightmare. Briefly, he was caught peeping at or exhibiting himself to a couple of girls in Phoenix Park. The indiscretion was witnessed by three drunken soldiers, who could never be quite certain of what they had seen. . . . Earwicker himself is troubled by a passion, compounded of illicit and aspirational desires, for his own daughter, Isabel, whom he identifies with Tristram's Iseult, and who is the sweet little reincarnation of his wife" (Campbell and Robinson, *A Skeleton Key to "Finnegans Wake,"* pp. 7–8).

6 Cf. Dublin's motto, *Obedientia Civium Urbis Felicitas*. The story of the Prankquean has always remained a controversial riddle. William Tindall believes that the Prankquean is victorious: "Mother and daughter, ganging up – as composite 'duppy' – on father, defeat him. He falls to the sound of thunder, and from what remains of him a city arises" (*A Reader's Guide to "Finnegans Wake,"* p. 48). Margaret Solomon, in contrast, concludes that "the Prankquean's wetting was, in repetitious effect, the *reine* bringing the reign to the Jarl, thereby giving him the royal rein" (*Eternal Geomater*, p. 15). In "A Clown's Inquest into Paternity," Jean-Michel Rabaté offers still another perspective when he declares that the "incestuous position of the Emancipator/Immense pater is blatant: he emancipates his doubled daughter (or his wife plus his daughter) just to abuse them, and he conversely castrates the sons who are mere 'geldings'. . . . Women, spurned or raped, are the only fixed or stable points of reference in this reversible universe: but they are merely exchanged, taken as a pretext of the perverse male struggle for power" (pp. 103, 105). For an extensive analysis of the Prankquean's riddle, see Patrick A. McCarthy, *The Riddles of "Finnegans Wake,"* pp. 104–35. McCarthy concludes that the narrative of van Hoother and the Prankquean "stands as an emblem for the eternal male-female struggle that characterizes human life" and offers a temporary "synthesis of opposing principles" that merely "begins a new cycle of conflict and reconciliation" (pp. 106, 116).

7 Patrick Parrinder notes that the washerwomen's "interest in the act of conception, prurient though it may sometimes seem, is an interest in origins and thus an example of the fundamental historical impulse; and it is the root of all literature, being the basis of our quickened attention when we hear the basis of a tale" (*James Joyce*, p. 235). John Gordon proposes that the "Anna Livia Plurabelle" chapter, "always taken as the dialogue of two washerwomen," is actually the murmurings of Kate the Slop, "the dream-mediated record of her talking to herself while going about her chores" (*A Plot Summary*, pp. 71–2). John Bishop believes that the fluid language of this river-chapter simulates the sleeping hero's unconscious awareness of the torrential sensation evoked by the circulation of his own blood, "arteries and vessels of running water" that

reflect "the vitality of [the body's] own bloodstream" (*Joyce's Book of the Dark*, p. 342).

8 John Gordon claims that HCE has literally "branded" ALP as his conjugal possession. "There is a weird kind of Wakean logic to the idea that a man who has begotten three children should be envisioned as having three penises, and to the idea that from this oddity should derive . . . the three horizontal lines of the capital E which is his siglum. That brand (it is, after all, a fire-iron) is what he used to mark ALP as his own" (*A Plot Summary*, p. 23).

9 For further discussion of the *Wake*'s Egyptian sources, see John Bishop, *Joyce's Book of the Dark*, Chapter 4; Danis Rose, *Chapters of Coming Forth by Day*; Mark L. Troy, *Mummeries of Resurrection*; and my own article "James Joyce East and Middle East."

10 Roland McHugh tells us that "Simba" in Kiswahili is "lion" and that "oga" means "to bathe." "Siva the Slayer," furthermore, is a Hindu god of destruction, and "oga" is the Old English word for "fear" (*Annotations*, p. 203). Joyce's syntax in this passage suggests a double negative – perhaps implying that the lion slayer of Michael's fear is both "lewd" and slain" and that, as a result, his erotic passions undergo a phoenix-like resurrection.

11 The French verb *souffler* means "to blow, breathe, utter, or pant." The noun *sécheresse* implies drought, dryness, harshness, or a lack of feeling. A possible exegesis of this passage, then, would suggest that "while you would parch your dryness" (slake your thirst?), she "held her breath"; or, alternatively, "held herself panting." John Gordon ingeniously suggests that "alongside the obvious water-passage is a backwards account of a fire-making. . . . As remembered on other occasions, the Liffey is being set afire" (*A Plot Summary*, pp. 166–7).

12 Roland McHugh reminds us that the word "Dublin" originally meant "black pool" (*Annotations*, p. 204).

13 See Adaline Glasheen, *Third Census of "Finnegans Wake,"* pp. xlv–xlvi. I disagree with Glasheen's analogy of ALP's gift-giving with the release of evils from Pandora's box, since Anna's presents appear to be either beneficent or punitive, according to the "potluck" of their recipients. John Gordon summarizes the contents of the sack as "the raw material of all story-telling. Each of ALP's gifts is an individual destiny, a novel in miniature, some of them familiar to *Wake* readers" (*A Plot Summary*, p. 167).

14 Roland McHugh confirms the idiosyncratic nature of this saint's hagiography when he notes that St Margaret Mary Alacoque distinguished herself as a "visionary who preferred drinking water in which laundry had been washed" (*Annotations*, p. 214). She seems, then, an appropriate saint to be invoked by washerwomen. Her vision was of the Sacred Heart of Jesus, in whose honor she inaugurated the Eucharistic celebration of the nine first Fridays. As a saint associated with self-sacrifice and protracted martyrdom, she reminds us of Eveline's emotional sacrifice in *Dubliners*, as well as of ALP's

responsibilities as all-giving wife, mother, and family cook.

15 Danis Rose and John O'Hanlon point out that there are, in addition to the mamafesta version, "six principal forms of the Boston Letter cited in the *Wake*," beginning 11. 22, 116. 19, 280. 09, 301. 05, 369. 30, and 617. 20 (*Understanding "Finnegans Wake*," pp. 86–7).

16 As Patrick McCarthy observes, the letter, modeled on such texts as "*The Book of Kells*, Swift's *Drapier's Letters*, Parnell's letters (both his love letters to Kitty O'Shea and the phony letters forged by Richard Piggott), the forged bordereau used to convict Dreyfus, and Documents No. 1 and 2 (the 1922 treaty of Irish partition and Eamon de Valera's proposed alternative)," tends to appropriate "all documents, and its subject matter is human life on all its levels" ("The Structures and Meanings of *Finnegans Wake*," p. 576). In *Structure and Motif in "Finnegans Wake*," Clive Hart adds Frances Sheehy-Skeffington's 1908 *Michael Davitt* to the list of sources (in a pen/revolver/letter connection) and observes that Anna Livia Plurabelle "is physically identified with the Letter, and hence with the whole 'riverrun' of *Finnegans Wake*" (pp. 201–2).

17 Roland McHugh glosses the phrase as "simple as ABC," since the Hebrew letter Aleph means "ox," Beth means "house," and Gimel means "camel" (*Annotations*, p. 107).

18 The Shaun-like professor who subjects the letter to scholarly exegesis is an insufferable pedant, later identified as the infamous Professor Jones (*FW* 149), a parody of that "mucksrat" literary enemy, Wyndham Lewis, who condemned Joyce for his time-minded propensities in *Time and Western Man*. (Hence the time/space, dime/cash problem that besets those twin antagonists, Shem and Shaun.) "The lecturer's manner . . . varies from the formidably abstract to the breezily colloquial. . . . By turns he employs the methods of textual critics, contextual critics, biographers, paleographers, political and psychoanalytic critics. He examines the handwriting, the state of the paper, the punctuation (if any), each letter, sign, and word. In short, he is exhaustive; but what his exhausting analysis amounts to is an unintended criticism of criticism by an intending master of burlesque" (Tindall, *A Reader's Guide to "Finnegans Wake*," p. 100).

19 Anna's "cunniform letters," says John Bishop, "take the 'form' of the 'cunny,' purveying sense subsemantically, in the same way that the sound of arteries of water and 'meusic' do: hence the many 'warbly sangs' (200. 11–12) that Anna sings throughout 'Anna Livia' " (*Joyce's Book of the Dark*, p. 362). The language of the *Wake* is Anna's: "it argues the power not of phallogocentric structures but of utero-illogico-eccentric ones (like children and dreams)" (ibid., p. 383).

20 Shari Benstock, "Nightletters: Woman's Writing in the *Wake*," pp. 229–30.

21 John Bishop reminds us that "the Greek *to hen* signifies, in philosophy, 'that One' out of which the phenomenal world splinters, 'ab ove' (154. 35 [L. *ab ova*, 'from the egg'])" (*Joyce's Book of the Dark*, p. 376).

22 The "aggressive 'hun' who is the incubating subject of this construction becomes everywhere linked with a feminine 'hen' and 'her (Da. *hun*) with whom, bonded in 'original sin,' . . . he is latently 'co-erogenous' " (Bishop, *Joyce's Book of the Dark*, p. 379).

23 John Bishop gives an excellent description of Joyce's process of "scotography" or night/not/*nat*-writing, an elaborate "not language" which he "devised in order to represent the *nat* (Da. 'night')." This " 'nat language' now generates as a totality a kind of portraiture opposite in every particular from that afforded by the photograph and related forms of representation: antonymically inverting the sense of 'photography' (Gr. *phōtographia*, 'light-writing'), Joyce's sleep-descriptive 'scotography' (Gr. *skotos*, 'darkness') makes for a kind of 'darkness-writing' whose developed product, the inversion of a well-articulated positive print, is a 'partly obliterated negative' that captures the 'Real Absence' of an extremely 'Black Prince'. . . . Where the photograph, taken through the open-eyed lens of the camera lucida (171. 32), seeks to freeze the plenitude of the present in all its fleeting detail, the Wakean 'scotograph,' taken through 'blackeye lenses' (183. 17) kept as firmly 'SHUT' beneath 'a blind of black sailcloth' (182. 32–3) as those of the eyes in sleep, seeks to capture only the absent" (*Joyce's Book of the Dark*, pp. 51–2).

24 Patrick McCarthy explains that the letter ends with the traditional Irish ejaculation *Slainte* or "Health," usually associated with a drinking salute. "The *slain/slainte* pun, suggesting the death and resurrection of the hero-god, encapsulates not only the subject matter of the book, but also its circular structure" ("The Structures and Meaning of *Finnegans Wake*," p. 577).

25 There has been a great deal of argument about the symbolic import of the tea-stain at the end of the letter, which Clive Hart associates with Joyce's scatological/urinary obsession. The *Wake*, Hart tells us, "identifies urine with another symbol of fertility – strong Irish tea – and even with the communion wine itself." The letter, in its various incarnations, "usually ends with an act of micturition, a 'pee ess' (111. 18)," and the "post-script is a flow of urine: 'amber too' " (*Structure and Motif*, p. 206). Tindall euphemistically identifies the letter's tea-stain as "family tea" associated with marriage, the Prankquean's tea, and the Boston tea-party (*A Reader's Guide to "Finnegans Wake*," p. 103). It seems evident, however, that the stain carries pornographic, as well as scatological associations, and that the stain suggests genital excrescences, ambiguously male or female. (In a long-censored letter, Joyce implored Nora to send him a note inscribed with her own sweet vaginal fluids.)

26 Patrick McCarthy, "The Structures and Meanings of *Finnegans Wake*," p. 597.

27 Shari Benstock, "Nightletters," p. 231. Because of the parameters of my argument, I have chosen to talk almost exclusively about Anna Livia and to treat her daughter Issy as a rivulet-extension of the

mother/mater/river, "dadad's lottiest daughterpearl and brooder's cissiest auntybride" (*FW* 561. 15–16). For excellent discussions of Issy, see Bonnie Scott, *Joyce and Feminism*, pp. 184–200; and Shari Benstock, "The Genuine Christine: Psychodynamics of Issy." John Gordon believes that "Issy is the *Wake*'s occasion, theme, reason for existence, prime mover – the one for whom and because of whom the dream is dreamed" (*A Plot Summary*, p. 76). "The Original Sin of *Finnegans Wake* is the act of intercourse which produced Lucia Joyce. . . . Specifically, it is the marital copulation at which Issy was conceived, as witnessed by the boys" (ibid., pp. 81–2).

28 In *A Reader's Guide to "Finnegans Wake,"* William Tindall also contrasts Joyce's satirical portrait of wedlock with Lawrence's romantic notions of mystical marriage. For Joyce, sexual love is spirited and ludic, a laughable game that "Lawrence, despite his gamekeeper, would have abhorred" (ibid., p. 285). Tindall believes that Book III, Chapter Four, may be Joyce's "realistic rejoinder" to *Lady Chatterley's Lover*. For an ingenious description of the Porter pub and lodgings in the *Wake*, see John Gordon, *A Plot Summary*, pp. 9–36. One of the interesting aspects of Joyce's satirical portrait of married love is that its narrative presentation in Book III is both dramatic and voyeuristic. The Porters' deflated coupling is reported by Mamalujo, the four gospelers who double as the four bedposts of the Porter matrimonial bed and salaciously relish "every single ingle" of the couple's connubial activity in much the same way that the prurient nymph in *Ulysses* witnessed the conjugal couplings of the Blooms. As Rose and O'Hanlon observe, the bedroom is "treated as a stage set and the occupants as actors" (*Understanding "Finnegans Wake,"* p. 266). Moreover, HCE and ALP "are portrayed as two chess pieces, the king and queen, that are moving across a board (the floor of the bedroom)" (ibid., p. 286).

29 According to Lacan, Freud stresses the thematic affinity of the father and death and links "the appearance of the signifier of the Father, as author of the Law, with death, even to the murder of the Father – thus showing that if this murder is the fruitful moment of debt through which the subject binds himself for life to the Law, the symbolic Father is, in so far as he signifies this Law, the dead Father" (*Ecrits, A Selection*, p. 199).

30 As to the "legal entitlement" of the Catholic husband to access to his partner's body, see Ruth Bauerle's speculations about the likelihood of "mate rape" in the unhappy but prolific marriage of James Joyce's parents ("Date Rape, Mate Rape").

31 In *James Joyce and Sexuality*, Richard Brown offers a fascinating discussion of the way in which Joyce gives us, in the trial of Honuphrius and Anita, a comic parody of the kind of matrimonial casuistry that pre-occupied nineteenth-century Catholic theologians. He cites, in particular, M. M. Matharan's book *Casus de Matrimonio Fere Quingenti*, published in 1892: "For Matharan the sexual act is understood as a rendering of the conjugal debt incurred in the marriage contract and the

validity of specific acts is established or challenged in such terms. . . . The *Wake*'s English is no easier to unravel than Matharan's clerical Latin, but basically the case discusses the rights of Honuphrius (HCE) to exact the conjugal debt from Anita (ALP)'' (pp. 45–6). William Tindall observes: "This mishmash of incest, buggery, incestuous buggery, and, if possible, worse, is as intricate as a Restoration play and nastier than anything by a declining, or even a falling, Roman. The characters, who take their names from the Imperial City, are all the people of the *Wake*, and the scene of this Roman shocker is Chapelizod. Honophrius is H.C.E., Anita is A.L.P., Eugenius and Jeremias are the twins, and Felicia is Isabel" (*A Reader's Guide to "Finnegans Wake,"* p. 292). Rose and O'Hanlon set forth, as laconically as possible, the plot of this bizarre melodrama of sexual intrigue: "Honuphrius (H.C.E.), it goes, is imputed with the commission of incest with his virgin daughter, Felicia (Issy); with the seduction of his sons Eugenius (Shaun) and Jeremias (Shem); with voluntary self-chastisement (flagellism); and with the attempted prostitution of his spouse, Anita (A.L.P.). Anita, who has herself been guilty of adultery with Father Michael (a curate who wishes to seduce Eugenius), wishes to save the virginity of Felicia for Magravius (Magrath), who is urged by Mauritius (Sigurdsen) acting on the instructions of Honuphrius his master, to solicit the chastity of Anita after the death of his schismatical wife Gillia. . . . Magravius threatens to have Anita molested by Sulla, the leader of a band of thugs called the Sullivani (the Twelve) who (Sulla) wishes to procure Felicia for Gregorius, Leo, Vitellius, and Macdugalius (the Four) if she (Anita) will not submit to him and render Honuphrius conjugal duty" (*Understanding "Finnegans Wake,"* pp. 277–8).

32 John Gordon and Patrick Parrinder both interpret this chapter as a fairy-tale narrative of the Freudian primal scene, with the child(ren) witnessing the parents' copulation. (*A Plot Summary*, p. 254.; *James Joyce*, pp. 214–15). Gordon, in fact, hypothesizes that the "date of *Finnegans Wake* is Monday, the twenty-first of March, 1938, and the early morning of Tuesday the twenty-second" (*A Plot Summary*, p. 37). III. 4, he believes, recounts a scene of marital love-making that transpires once a year and provides the occasion for the conception of Issy-Lucia, born "at or around the time of a festival of light in the dark dead of winter, nine months later" (p. 38). He notes that "Nora Joyce became fifty-four on 21 March 1938," and that ALP's agnomen is LIV, the Roman numeral for fifty-four (p. 40). The "'allpurgers' night" (*FW* 556. 28) recounted in III. 4 unfolds as "the final occurrence of the primal scene, of young self spying on old self" (p. 259). But the chapter also celebrates the fulfillment, however temporary, of sexual desire and marital affection, the joys of that sexual/textual game of love played with farraginous gusto throughout the Joycean canon. As Robert Wilson observes, "we habitually play not only with words but also with toys, fantasies, ideas, possibilities, signs, signification, other people and playmates. . . . Any activity or thing can be playful, and

anything, even a game, can be converted into a plaything. . . . Play
is making and it is teasing: it is a constructive activity and a
deconstructive activity, pointed in opposite ways yet interbound" ("In
Palamedes' Shadow," p. 196). Joyce often used to compare his
aesthetic project with child's play, observing that children might just as
well play as not, since the ogre of death will come in any case. "I am
highly sheshe sherious," claims the narrator of the *Wake* (*FW* 570. 25).

33 Patrick Parrinder identifies "Saint Kevin, Hydrophilos" (*FW* 606.
4–5) as a Shaun figure based on Stanislaus Joyce. "He is connected
with the rite of baptism and . . . is a politician aspiring to be the new
broom to sweep up now that HCE is gone. Shem (James Joyce) is a
portrait of the artist as polluter and pornographer" (*James Joyce*,
p. 226).

34 In "Anna Livia Plurabelle: The Dream Woman," Margot Norris
judges HCE "an elderly invalid, a convalescent, probably a stroke
victim." Anna's paradoxical portrait, she feels, is "filtered through the
imagination of a dying old man who dreams of virile conquests and
senile passions, domestic life, humiliating dependencies, and of the
river and woman he has known in beauty, ugliness, youth, and age"
(pp. 199–200).

35 John Gordon describes this section as a "deathbed–like sequence of
flashbacks from their past lives, real or imagined" (*A Plot Summary*,
p. 275). For Rose and O'Hanlon, this peripatetic monologue is a
"walk down memory lane," a "sentimental journey." "But her
memory is weakening. She senses death and knows her riverwater is
mixing with the sea. . . . Coldly now she looks on life as she looks on
death" (*Understanding "Finnegans Wake,"* p. 319). For Tindall, ALP the
river-woman, "taking a mazy course from Chapelizod to Dublin Bay,
flows through memories of her family to acceptance of age and death"
(*A Reader's Guide to "Finnegans Wake,"* p. 324).

36 Clive Hart observes that whereas "anal-eroticism is unmistakeably
present in all of Joyce's works," it is particularly obvious in Joyce's
delineation of the fluid river-woman, "where head and buttocks are
once more united in a 'crosscomplimentary' group" (*Structure and Motif*,
p. 206). Thus Anna's metaphoric mouth or delta suggests at least three
physiological orifices – oral, genital, and anal. Margot Norris interprets this particular scene in the *Wake* as a violent, even sadistic, rape
and concludes that "old ALP, in her farewell speech to HCE, seems
able to forgive violent fellatio and beatings as though they were only
a cruel wind whipping over the river" ("Anna Livia Plurabelle: The
Dream Woman," p. 204).

37 "It is sorrowful, Lacan has said, that the loved person onto whom one
projects Desire and narcissism serves to give proof of the image and
pathos of existence. The other reveals the gap of human Desire, but
cannot permanently close it. . . . In love relations this imbalance
prevents a perfect coincidence between Desire and the object supposed
to provide sexual and psychic closure. The idealized harmony of

Romantic love belongs to the myth of the androgyn" (Ragland-Sullivan, *Jacques Lacan and the Philosophy of Psychoanalysis*, p. 81).

38 Joyce explained to Louis Gillet: "In *Ulysses*, . . . I had sought to end with the least forceful word I could possibly find. I had found the word 'yes', which is barely pronounced, which denotes acquiescence, self-abandon, relaxation, the end of all resistance. In *Work in Progress* I've tried to do better if I could. This time, I found the word which is the most slippery, the least accented, the weakest word in English, a word which is not even a word, which is scarcely sounded between the teeth, a breath, a nothing, the article *the*" (Louis Gillet, *Claybook*, p. 111).

RICORSO: ANNA LIVIA PLURABELLE AND *ECRITURE FEMININE*

1 Philippe Sollers, "Political Perspectives," p. 107.
2 Philippe Sollers, "Joyce and Co." pp. 108, 114.
3 Margot Norris, *The Decentered Universe*, pp. 54–61 and *passim*; Colin MacCabe, *James Joyce and the Revolution of the Word*, p. 146.
4 Gilbert and Gubar, *No Man's Land*, p. 232. "Whether like Joyce's fluidly fluent Anna Livia Plurabelle, woman ceaselessly burbles and babbles on her way to her 'cold mad feary father,' or whether like his fluently fluid Molly Bloom, she dribbles and drivels as she dreams of male jinglings, her artless jingles are secondary and asyntactic" (ibid.).
5 ibid., pp. 260–1.
6 Marks and Courtivron, *New French Feminisms*, p. 32.
7 Julia Kristeva, *Desire in Language*, pp. 133–6. "This *heterogeneousness*, detected genetically in the first echolalias of infants as rhythms and intonations anterior to the first phonemes, morphemes, lexemes and sentences; this heterogeneousness, which is later reactivated as rhythms, intonations, glossalalias in psychotic discourse, . . . this hetero-geneousness to signification operates through, despite, and in excess of it and produces in poetic language 'musical' but also nonsense effects that destroy not only accepted beliefs and significations, but, in radical experiments, syntax itself, that guarantee of thetic consciousness" (p. 133).
8 ibid., pp. 174, 191.
9 Julia Kristeva, *Revolution in Poetic Language*, pp. 36, 47.
10 Hélène Cixous, "Sorties," pp. 87–8.
11 ibid., pp. 90–1.

BIBLIOGRAPHY

Adams, Robert Martin. *Common Sense and Beyond*. New York: Random House, 1966.
—— "'Light on Joyce's *Exiles*?' A New MS, a Curious Analogue, and Some Speculations." *Studies in Bibliography*, 17 (1964): 83–105.
—— *Surface and Symbol*. New York: Oxford University Press, 1962.
Anderson, Chester. "Baby Tuckoo: Joyce's 'Features of Infancy.'" In *Approaches to Joyce's "Portrait": Ten Essays*, ed. Thomas F. Staley and Bernard Benstock, 135–69.
Attridge, Derek. *Peculiar Language*. London: Methuen, 1988.
Attridge, Derek and Ferrer, Daniel, eds. *Post-Structuralist Joyce: Essays from the French*. Cambridge: Cambridge University Press, 1984.
Atherton, J. S. *The Books at the Wake: A Study of Literary Allusions in James Joyce's "Finnegans Wake."* New York: Viking Press, 1960.
Aubert, Jacques. "Riverrun." In *Post-Structuralist Joyce: Essays from the French*, ed. Derek Attridge and Daniel Ferrer, 69–78.
Aubert, Jacques and Jolas, Maria, eds. *Joyce & Paris: 1902 . . . 1920–1940 . . . 1975*. 2 vols. Paris: Editions du CNRS, 1979.
Barthes, Roland. *S/Z*, trans. Richard Miller. New York: Hill & Wang, 1974.
Bauerle, Ruth. "Bertha's Role in *Exiles*." In *Women in Joyce*, ed. Suzette Henke and Elaine Unkeless, 108–31.
—— "Date Rape, Mate Rape: A Liturgical Interpretation of 'The Dead.'" In *New Alliances in Joyce Studies*, ed. Bonnie Kime Scott, 113–25.
Beauvoir, Simone de. *The Second Sex*, trans. and ed. H.M. Parshley. 1949; rpt New York: Bantam, 1952.
Benhabib, Seyla and Cornell, Drucilla, eds. *Feminism As Critique: On the Politics of Gender*. Minneapolis: University of Minnesota Press, 1987.
Beckett, Samuel *et al. Our Exagmination Round His Factification For Incamination of Work in Progress*. 1929; rpt London: Faber & Faber, 1961.
Begnal, Michael H. and Eckley, Grace. *Narrator and Character in "Finnegans Wake."* Lewisburg, Pa.: Bucknell University Press, 1975.
Begnal, Michael H. and Senn, Fritz, eds. *A Conceptual Guide to "Finnegans Wake."* University Park: Pennsylvania State University Press, 1974.

Beja, Morris. *Epiphany in the Modern Novel.* Seattle: University of Washington Press, 1971.

Beja, Morris *et al.*, eds. *James Joyce: The Centennial Symposium.* Urbana: University of Illinois Press, 1986.

Benstock, Bernard. *"Exiles."* In *A Companion to Joyce Studies,* ed. Zack Bowen and James F. Carens, 361–86.

—— *James Joyce: The Undiscover'd Country.* New York: Barnes & Noble, 1977.

—— *Joyce-Again's Wake.* Seattle: University of Washington Press, 1965.

—— "The Kenner Conundrum." *JJQ,* 13 (1976): 428–35.

—— "L. Boom as Dreamer in *Finnegans Wake.*" *PMLA,* 82 (1967): 91–7.

—— ed. *Critical Essays on James Joyce.* Boston: G.K. Hall, 1985.

—— ed. *The Seventh of Joyce.* Bloomington: University of Indiana Press, 1982.

Benstock, Shari. "Nightletters: Woman's Writing in the *Wake.*" In *Critical Essays on James Joyce,* ed. Bernard Benstock, 221–33.

—— "The Genuine Christine: Psychodynamics of Issy." In *Women in Joyce,* ed. Suzette Henke and Elaine Unkeless, 169–96.

Bishop, John. *Joyce's Book of the Dark: "Finnegans Wake."* Madison: University of Wisconsin Press, 1986.

Boheemen, Christine van. *The Novel as Family Romance.* Ithaca: Cornell University Press, 1987.

Bonheim, Helmut. *A Lexicon of the German in "Finnegans Wake."* Berkeley: University of California Press, 1967.

Bowen, Zack. "Joyce's Prophylactic Paralysis: Exposure in *Dubliners.*" *JJQ,* 19 (1982): 257–73.

Bowen, Zack and Carens, James F., eds. *A Companion to Joyce Studies.* Westport, Conn.: Greenwood Press, 1984.

Boyle, Robert. "Penelope." In *James Joyce's "Ulysses": Critical Essays,* ed. Clive Hart and David Hayman, 407–33.

Brandabur, Edward. *A Scrupulous Meanness.* Urbana: University of Illinois Press, 1971.

Bremen, Brian A. "'He Was Too Scrupulous Always': A Re-examination of Joyce's 'The Sisters.'" *JJQ,* 22 (1984): 55–66.

Brivic, Sheldon. *Joyce Between Freud and Jung.* Port Washington, NY: Kennikat Press, 1980.

—— "Joyce in Progress: A Freudian View." *JJQ,* 13 (1976): 306–27.

—— *Joyce the Creator.* Madison: University of Wisconsin Press, 1985.

—— "The Mind Factory: Kabbalah in *Finnegans Wake.*" *JJQ,* 21 (1983): 7–30.

Brown, Carole and Knuth, Leo. "James Joyce's *Exiles*: The Ordeal of Richard Rowan." *JJQ,* 17 (1979): 7–21.

Brown, Richard. *James Joyce and Sexuality.* Cambridge: Cambridge University Press, 1985.

Budgen, Frank. *James Joyce and the Making of "Ulysses."* Bloomington: Indiana University Press, 1967.

Burgess, Anthony. *Joysprick: An Introduction to the Language of James Joyce.*

New York: Harcourt Brace, 1973.
—— *ReJoyce*. New York: Norton, 1965.
Buttigieg, Joseph A. *A Portrait of the Artist in Different Perspective*. Athens, Ohio: Ohio University Press, 1987.
Campbell, Joseph and Robinson, Henry Morton. *A Skeleton Key to "Finnegans Wake."* New York: Harcourt, Brace, 1944.
Card, James Van Dyck. *An Anatomy of "Penelope."* Rutherford, NJ: Fairleigh Dickinson University Press, 1984.
Cheng, Vincent John. *Shakespeare and Joyce: A Study of "Finnegans Wake."* University Park: Pennsylvania State University Press, 1984.
Chodorow, Nancy. *The Reproduction of Mothering*. Berkeley: University of California Press, 1978.
Cixous, Hélène. *The Exile of James Joyce*, trans. Sally A. J. Purcell. New York: David Lewis, 1972.
—— "Joyce: The (R)use of Writing." In *Post-Structuralist Joyce: Essays from the French*, ed. Derek Attridge and Daniel Ferrer, 15–30.
—— "The Laugh of the Medusa." *Signs*, 1 (1976): 875–93; rpt in *New French Feminisms*, ed. Elaine Marks and Isabelle de Courtivron, 245–64.
—— "Sorties." In *The Newly Born Woman*, Hélène Cixous and Catherine Clément, 63–132.
Cixous, Hélène and Clément, Catherine, *The Newly Born Woman*, trans. Betsy Wing. Minneapolis: University of Minnesota Press, 1985.
Clément, Catherine. "The Guilty One." In *The Newly Born Woman*, Hélène Cixous and Catherine Clément, 1–59.
Colum, Mary. "The Confessions of James Joyce." In *James Joyce: The Critical Heritage*, ed. Robert H. Deming, vol. 1, 231–4.
Con Davis, Robert, ed. *The Fictional Father*. Amherst: University of Massachusetts Press, 1981.
Connolly, Thomas E. *James Joyce's Scribbledehobble*. Evanston, Ill.: Northwestern University Press, 1961.
Cornillon, Susan Koppelman, ed. *Images of Women in Fiction: Feminist Perspectives*. Bowling Green, Ohio: Bowling Green Popular Press, 1972.
Culler, Jonathan. *On Deconstruction: Theory and Criticism after Structuralism*. Ithaca: Cornell University Press, 1982.
Day, Robert Adams. "The Villanelle Perplex: Reading Joyce." *JJQ*, 25 (1987): 69–86.
Deleuze, Gilles and Guattari, Félix. *Anti-Oedipus: Capitalism and Schizophrenia*, trans. Robert Hurley, Mark Seem, and Helen R. Lane. Minneapolis: University of Minnesota Press, 1983.
Deming, Robert H. *James Joyce: The Critical Heritage*. 2 vols. London: Routledge, 1970.
Derrida, Jacques. *Dissemination*, trans. Barbara Johnson. Chicago: University of Chicago Press, 1981.
—— "Fors." *Georgia Review*, 31 (1977): 64–116.
—— *Margins of Philosophy*, trans. Alan Bass. Chicago: University of

Chicago Press, 1982.
—— *Of Grammatology*, trans. Gayatri Chakravorty Spivak. Baltimore: Johns Hopkins University Press, 1976.
—— *Positions*, trans. Alan Bass. Chicago: University of Chicago Press, 1981.
—— *Speech and Phenomena*, trans. David B. Allison. Evanston, Ill.: Northwestern University Press, 1973.
—— *Spurs/Eperons*, trans. Barbara Harlow. Chicago: University of Chicago Press, 1979.
—— "Two Words for Joyce." In *Post-Structuralist Joyce: Essays from the French*, ed. Derek Attridge and Daniel Ferrer, 145–59.
—— *Writing and Difference*, trans. Alan Bass. Chicago: University of Chicago Press, 1978.
Dinnerstein, Dorothy. *The Mermaid and the Minotaur: Sexual Arrangements and Human Malaise*. New York: Harper & Row, 1976.
Dombrowski, Theo. "Joyce's *Exiles*: The Problem of Love." *JJQ*, 15 (1978): 118–27.
Donovan, Josephine, ed. *Feminist Literary Criticism*. Lexington: University Press of Kentucky, 1975.
Eagleton, Terry. *Literary Theory: An Introduction*. Minneapolis: University of Minnesota Press, 1983.
Edwards, Lee and Diamond, Arlyn, eds. *The Authority of Experience*. Amherst: University of Massachusetts Press, 1977.
Eggers, Tilly. "What Is a Woman . . . a Symbol Of?" *JJQ*, 18 (1981): 379–95.
Ellmann, Maud. "Disremembering Dedalus: 'A Portrait of the Artist as a Young Man.'" In *Untying the Text*, ed. Robert Young, 189–206.
—— "Polytropic Man: Paternity, Identity and Naming in *The Odyssey* and *A Portrait of the Artist as a Young Man*." In *James Joyce: New Perspectives*, ed. Colin MacCabe, 73–104.
Ellmann, Mary. *Thinking about Women*. New York: Harcourt Brace, 1968.
Ellmann, Richard. *The Consciousness of Joyce*. Toronto and New York: Oxford University Press, 1977.
—— *James Joyce*; 1959; rpt New York: Oxford University Press, 1982.
—— *Ulysses on the Liffey*. London: Faber & Faber, 1972.
Epstein, Edmund L. *The Ordeal of Stephen Dedalus*. Carbondale: Southern Illinois University Press, 1971.
—— *A Starchamber Quiry*. New York: Methuen, 1982.
Evans, Simon. *The Penetration of "Exiles."* Colchester: A Wake Newslitter Press, 1984.
Felman, Shoshana. "Rereading Femininity." *Yale French Studies*, 62 (1981): 19–44.
Ferrer, Daniel. "Circe, Regret and Regression." In *Post-Structuralist Joyce*, ed. Derek Attridge and Daniel Ferrer, 127–44.
Fetterley, Judith. *The Resisting Reader: A Feminist Approach to American Fiction*. Bloomington: Indiana University Press, 1978.
Firestone, Shulamith. *The Dialectics of Sex*. New York: Bantam Books, 1971.

Fitch, Noel Riley. *Sylvia Beach and the Lost Generation*. New York: Norton, 1983.

Foucault, Michel. *Discipline and Punish*, trans. Alan Sheridan. 1975; rpt New York: Random House, 1979.

—— *The History of Sexuality: Volume I: An Introduction*, trans. Robert Hurley. New York: Penguin, 1978.

French, Marilyn. *The Book as World: James Joyce's "Ulysses."* Cambridge, Mass.: Harvard University Press, 1976.

Freud, Sigmund. *Beyond the Pleasure Principle*, trans. and ed. James Strachey. 1950; rpt New York: Bantam Books, 1959.

—— *Complete Psychological Works*, ed. James Strachey. 24 vols. London: Hogarth Press, 1953–74.

—— *A General Selection from the Works of Sigmund Freud*, ed. John Rickman. Garden City: Doubleday, 1957.

—— *The Interpretation of Dreams*, trans. James Strachey, ed. Angela Richards. Harmondsworth: Penguin, 1976.

—— *New Introductory Lectures on Psychoanalysis*, trans. and ed. James Strachey. 1933; rpt New York: Norton, 1965.

Friedman, Alan Warren, ed. *Forms of Modern British Fiction*. Austin: University of Texas Press, 1975.

Fuger, Wilhelm. "'Epistlemadethemology' (*FW* 374. 17): ALP's Letter and the Tradition of Interpolated Letters." *JJQ*, 19 (1982): 405–13.

Gabler, Hans Walter. "The Seven Lost Years of *A Portrait of the Artist as a Young Man*." In *Approaches to Joyce's "Portrait,"* ed. Thomas F. Staley and Bernard Benstock, 25–60.

Gaiser, Gottlieb, ed. *International Perspectives on James Joyce*. Troy, NY: Whitston, 1986.

Gallop, Jane. *Feminism and Psychoanalysis: The Daughter's Seduction*. London: Macmillan, 1982.

—— *Reading Lacan*. Ithaca: Cornell University Press, 1985.

Garner, Shirley Nelson, Kahane, Claire, and Sprengnether, Madelon, eds. *The M(other) Tongue: Essays in Feminist Psychoanalytic Interpretation*. Ithaca: Cornell University Press, 1985.

Genova, Judith, ed. *Power, Gender, Values*. Edmonton, Alberta: Academic Printing and Publishing, 1987.

Gifford, Don. *Notes for Joyce*. New York: E.P. Dutton, 1967.

Gifford, Don and Seidman, Robert J. *Notes for Joyce: An Annotation of James Joyce's "Ulysses."* New York: E.P. Dutton, 1974.

Gilbert, Sandra M. and Gubar, Susan. *No Man's Land: The Place of the Woman Writer in the Twentieth Century: Volume I: The War of the Words*. New Haven and London: Yale University Press, 1987.

Gilbert, Stuart. *James Joyce's "Ulysses."* New York: Random House, 1952.

Gillespie, Michael Patrick. *Inverted Volumes Improperly Arranged: James Joyce and His Trieste Library*. Ann Arbor: UMI Research Press, 1983.

Gillet, Louis. *Claybook for James Joyce*, trans. Georges Markow-Totevy. London and New York: Abelard-Schuman, 1958.

Gilligan, Carol. *In A Different Voice*. Cambridge, Mass.: Harvard University Press, 1982.

Girard,René. *Deceit, Desire and the Novel*, trans. Yvonne Freccero. Baltimore: Johns Hopkins University Press, 1965.

Givens, Seon, ed. *James Joyce: Two Decades of Criticism*. 2nd edn. 1948; rpt New York: Vanguard Press, 1963.

Glasheen, Adaline. *Third Census of "Finnegans Wake."* Berkeley: University of California Press, 1977.

Goldberg, S. L. *The Classical Temper*. London: Chatto & Windus, 1961.

Goldman, Arnold. *The Joyce Paradox: Form and Freedom in his Fiction*. London: Routledge, 1966.

Good, Jan. "Behind Taittering Lips: Molly Bloom's Losses and Sexual Guilt." *Literature and Psychology*, 33 (1987): 1–11.

Gordon, John. *"Finnegans Wake": A Plot Summary*. Syracuse: Syracuse University Press, 1986.

Gose, Elliott B., Jr. *The Transformation Process of Joyce's "Ulysses."* Toronto: University of Toronto Press, 1980.

Gottfried, Roy K. *The Art of Joyce's Syntax in "Ulysses."* Athens, Georgia: University of Georgia Press, 1980.

Groden, Michael. *"Ulysses" in Progress*. Princeton, NJ: Princeton University Press, 1977.

Groden, Michael *et al*. *The James Joyce Archive*. 63 vols. New York: Garland, 1978.

Harkness, Marguerite. *The Aesthetics of Dedalus and Bloom*. London and Toronto: Associated University Presses, 1984.

Hart, Clive. *A Concordance to "Finnegans Wake."* Minneapolis: University of Minnesota Press, 1963.

—— "The Elephant in the Belly: Exegesis of *Finnegans Wake*." In *A Wake Digest*, ed. Clive Hart and Fritz Senn, 3–12.

—— ed. *James Joyce's "Dubliners": Critical Essays*. New York: Viking, 1969.

—— *James Joyce's "Ulysses."* Sydney: Sydney University Press, 1968.

—— *Structure and Motif in "Finnegans Wake."* Evanston, Ill.: Northwestern University Press, 1962.

Hart, Clive and Hayman, David, eds. *James Joyce's "Ulysses": Critical Essays*. Berkeley: University of California Press, 1974.

Hart, Clive and Senn, Fritz, eds. *A Wake Digest*. Sydney: Sydney University Press, 1968.

Hayman, David. "The Empirical Molly." In *Approaches to "Ulysses,"* ed. Thomas F. Staley and Bernard Benstock, 103–35.

—— *A First-Draft Version of "Finnegans Wake."* Austin: University of Texas Press, 1963.

—— *Ulysses: The Mechanics of Meaning*. 2nd edn. Madison: University of Wisconsin Press, 1982.

Hayman, David and Anderson, Elliot, eds. *In the Wake of the "Wake."* Madison: University of Wisconsin Press, 1978.

Heath, Stephen. "Ambiviolences." *Tel Quel*, 50 (1972): 22–43, and 51

(1972): 64–76; rpt *Post-Structuralist Joyce: Essays from the French*, ed. Derek Attridge and Daniel Ferrer, 31–68.

—— "Joyce in Language." In *James Joyce: New Perspectives*, ed. Colin MacCabe, 129–48.

—— "Trames de lecture," *Tel Quel*, 54 (1973): 4–15.

Hedberg, Johannes. "Some Notes on Language and Atmosphere in *Dubliners.*" *Moderna Språk*, 75 (1981): 113–32.

Heilbrun, Carolyn. "Afterword." In *Women in Joyce*, ed. Suzette Henke and Elaine Unkeless, 215–16.

Heidegger, Martin. *Being and Time*, trans. John Macquarrie and Edward Robinson. 1926; rpt New York: Harper & Row, 1962.

Henke, Suzette A. "Gerty MacDowell: Joyce's Sentimental Heroine." In *Women in Joyce*, ed. Suzette Henke and Elaine Unkeless, 132–49.

—— "James Joyce and Joris-Karl Huysmans." In *James Joyce: New Glances*, ed. Edward A. Kopper, Jr, 68–72.

—— "James Joyce and Krafft-Ebing." *JJQ*, 17 (1979): 84–60.

—— "James Joyce and Women: The Matriarchal Muse." In *Work in Progress: Joyce Centenary Essays*, ed. Richard F. Peterson, Alan M. Cohn, and Edmund L. Epstein, 117–31.

—— "James Joyce East and Middle East: Literary Resonances of Judaism, Egyptology, and Indian Myth." *Journal of Modern Literature*, 13 (1986): 307–19.

—— "Joyce's Bloom: Beyond Sexual Possessiveness." *American Imago*, 32 (1975): 329–34.

—— *Joyce's Moraculous Sindbook: A Study of "Ulysses."* Columbus: Ohio State University Press, 1978.

—— "Reconstructing *Ulysses* in a Deconstructive Mode." In *Assessing the 1984 "Ulysses,"* ed. C. George Sandulescu and Clive Hart, 86–91.

—— "Sexuality and Silence in Women's Literature." In *Power, Gender, Values*, ed. Judith Genova, 45–62.

—— "Speculum of the Other Molly: A Feminist/Psychoanalytic Inquiry into James Joyce's Politics of Desire." *Mosaic*, 21/2–3 (1988): 149–64.

—— "Stephen Dedalus and Women: A Portrait of the Artist as a Young Misogynist." In *Women in Joyce*, ed. Suzette Henke and Elaine Unkeless, 82–107.

—— "Through a Cracked Looking-glass: Sex-role Stereotypes in *Dubliners.*" In *International Perspectives on James Joyce*, ed. Gottlieb Gaiser, 2–31.

Henke, Suzette and Unkeless, Elaine, eds. *Women in Joyce*. Urbana: University of Illinois Press, 1982.

Herr, Cheryl. *Joyce's Anatomy of Culture*. Urbana: University of Illinois Press, 1986.

Herring, Phillip F., ed. *Joyce's Notes and Early Drafts for "Ulysses."* Charlottesville: University of Virginia Press, 1977.

—— ed. *Joyce's "Ulysses" Notesheets in the British Museum*. Charlottesville: University of Virginia Press, 1972.

271

—— *Joyce's Uncertainty Principle*. Princeton, NJ: Princeton University Press, 1987.

—— "Toward an Historical Molly Bloom." *English Literary History*, 45 (1978): 501–21.

—— "Structure and Meaning in Joyce's 'The Sisters.'" In *The Seventh of Joyce*, ed. Bernard Benstock, 131–44.

Honton, Margaret. "Molly's Mistressstroke." *JJQ*, 14 (1976): 25–30.

Horney, Karen. *Feminine Psychology*, ed. Harold Kelman. New York: Norton, 1967.

Howe, Florence. "Feminism and Literature." In *Images of Women in Fiction: Feminist Perspectives*, ed. Susan Koppelman Cornillon, 253–77.

Hyman, Suzanne Katz. "'A Painful Case': The Movement of a Story through a Shift in Voice." *JJQ*, 19 (1982): 11–18.

Irigaray, Luce. *Speculum of the Other Woman*, trans. Gillian C. Gill. Ithaca: Cornell University Press, 1985.

—— *This Sex Which Is Not One*, trans. Catherine Porter with Carolyn Burke. Ithaca: Cornell University Press, 1985.

Jardine, Alice. *Gynesis: Configurations of Woman and Modernity*. Ithaca: Cornell University Press, 1985.

Jones, Ann Rosalind. "Writing the Body: Toward an Understanding of *l'Ecriture féminine.*" In *The New Feminist Criticism*, ed. Elaine Showalter, 361–77.

Joyce, James. *The Critical Writings of James Joyce*, ed. Ellsworth Mason and Richard Ellmann. New York: Viking Press, 1959.

—— *Dubliners: Text, Criticism and Notes*, ed. Robert Scholes and A. Walton Litz. 1914; rpt New York: Viking Press, 1969.

—— *Exiles*. 1918; rpt New York: Viking Press, 1951.

—— *Finnegans Wake*. New York: Viking Press, 1939; London: Faber & Faber, 1939.

—— *Giacomo Joyce*, ed. Richard Ellmann. New York: Viking Press, 1968.

—— *The James Joyce Archive*, ed. Michael Groden *et al.* New York and London: Garland, 1978.

—— *Letters of James Joyce*. Vol. I, ed. Stuart Gilbert. New York: Viking Press, 1957; reissued with corrections 1966. Vols II and III, ed. Richard Ellmann. New York: Viking Press, 1966.

—— *A Portrait of the Artist as a Young Man: Text, Criticism and Notes*, ed. Chester G. Anderson. 1916; rpt New York: Viking Press, 1968.

—— *Stephen Hero*, ed. John J. Slocum and Herbert Cahoon. New York: New Directions, 1944, 1963.

—— *Selected Letters of James Joyce*, ed. Richard Ellmann. New York: Viking Press, 1975.

—— *Ulysses*, ed. Hans Walter Gabler *et al.* 1922; rpt New York and London: Garland, 1984; rpt New York and Harmondsworth: Random House and Penguin, 1986.

Joyce, Stanislaus. *The Complete Dublin Diary of Stanislaus Joyce*, ed. George Harris Healey. Ithaca: Cornell University Press, 1962.

Kenner, Hugh. "Circe." In *James Joyce's "Ulysses": Critical Essays*, ed. Clive Hart and David Hayman, 341–62.

—— *Dublin's Joyce*. Boston: Beacon Press, 1962.

—— "Joyce's *Exiles*." *Hudson Review*, 5 (1952): 389–403.

—— *Joyce's Voices*. Berkeley and Los Angeles: University of California Press, 1978.

—— "Molly's Masterstroke." *JJQ*, 10 (1972): 19–28.

—— *The Pound Era*. Berkeley and Los Angeles: University of California Press, 1978.

—— *Ulysses*. 1980; rpt Baltimore and London: Johns Hopkins University Press, 1987.

—— "The Rhetoric of Silence." *JJQ*, 14 (1977): 382–94.

—— "Signs on a White Field." In *James Joyce: The Centennial Symposium*, ed. Morris Beja *et al.*, 209–19.

Kershner, R.B. *Joyce, Bakhtin, and Popular Literature: Chronicles of Disorder*. Chapel Hill and London: University of North Carolina Press, 1989.

Kimball, Jean. "Freud, Leonardo, and Joyce: The Dimensions of a Childhood Memory." *JJQ*, 17 (1980): 165–82.

Kofman, Sarah. *The Enigma of Woman: Woman in Freud's Writings*, trans. Catherine Porter. Ithaca: Cornell University Press, 1985.

Kopper, Edward A., Jr., ed. *James Joyce: New Glances*. Butler, Pa.: Modern British Literature Monograph Series, 1980.

Kristeva, Julia. *Desire in Language: A Semiotic Approach to Literature and Art*, ed. Leon S. Roudiez, trans. Thomas Gora, Alice Jardine, and Leon S. Roudiez. New York: Columbia University Press, 1980.

—— *Polylogue*. Paris: Editions de Seuil, 1977.

—— *Powers of Horror: An Essay on Abjection*, trans. Leon S. Roudiez. New York: Columbia University Press, 1982.

—— *Revolution in Poetic Language*, trans. Margaret Waller. New York: Columbia University Press, 1984.

Lacan, Jacques. *Ecrits*. Paris: Editions de Seuil, 1966.

—— *Ecrits* I. Paris: Editions de Seuil, 1970.

—— *Ecrits* II. Paris: Editions de Seuil, 1971.

—— *Ecrits: A Selection*, trans. Alan Sheridan. New York: Norton, 1977.

—— *The Four Fundamental Concepts of Psychoanalysis*, ed. Jacques-Alain Miller, trans. Alan Sheridan. New York: Norton, 1978.

—— *Feminine Sexuality: Jacques Lacan and the école freudienne*, ed. Juliet Mitchell and Jacqueline Rose, trans. Jacqueline Rose. New York: Norton, 1982.

—— "Joyce le symptôme," in *Joyce & Paris*, ed. Jacques Aubert and Maria Jolas, vol. 1, 13–17.

—— *Le Séminaire XX: Encore*. Paris: Editions de Seuil, 1975.

Lawrence, Karen. *The Odyssey of Style in "Ulysses."* Princeton, NJ: Princeton University Press, 1981.

Lemaire, Anika. *Jacques Lacan*, trans. David Macey. London: Routledge, 1977.

Leonard, Garry. "What is a Woman . . . a Symbol of?: A Lacanian Reading of Joyce's 'The Dead.' " *Mosaic* CONTEXTS Conference,

Winnipeg, Manitoba. May 15, 1987.

Loughman, Celeste. "Bertha, Victress, in Joyce's *Exiles.*" *JJQ*, 19 (1981): 69–72.

Lyons, J. B. *James Joyce and Medicine.* New York: Humanities Press, 1974.

MacCabe, Colin. *James Joyce and the Revolution of the Word.* London: Macmillan, 1978.

—— ed. *James Joyce: New Perspectives.* Bloomington: Indiana University Press, 1982.

MacNicholas, John. *James Joyce's "Exiles": A Textual Companion.* New York: Garland, 1979.

—— "Joyce's *Exiles*: The Argument for Doubt." *JJQ*, 11 (1973): 33–40.

—— "The Stage History of *Exiles.*" *JJQ*, 19 (1981): 9–26.

Maddox, Brenda. *Nora: The Real Life of Molly Bloom.* Boston: Houghton Mifflin, 1988.

Maddox, James H., Jr. *Joyce's "Ulysses" and the Assault upon Character.* New Brunswick, NJ: Rutgers University Press, 1978.

Magalaner, Marvin, ed. *A James Joyce Miscellany: Second Series.* Carbondale: Southern Illinois University Press, 1959.

Magalaner, Marvin and Kain, Richard M. *Joyce: The Man, the Work and the Reputation.* 1956; rpt New York: Collier Books, 1962.

Manganiello, Dominic. *Joyce's Politics.* London: Routledge & Kegan Paul, 1980.

Marks, Elaine and de Courtivron, Isabelle, eds. *New French Feminisms.* Amherst: University of Massachusetts Press, 1980.

McCarthy, Patrick A. *The Riddles of "Finnegans Wake."* London and Toronto: Associated University Presses, 1980.

—— "The Structures and Meanings of *Finnegans Wake.*" In *A Companion to Joyce Studies*, ed. Zack Bowen and James F. Carens, 559–632.

McConnell-Ginet, Sally, Borker, Ruth, and Furman, Nelly. *Women and Language in Literature and Society.* New York: Praeger, 1980.

McCormick, W. J. and Stead, Alistair, eds. *James Joyce and Modern Literature.* London: Routledge, 1982.

McGee, Patrick. *Paperspace: Style as Literary Ideology in Joyce's "Ulysses."* Lincoln and London: University of Nebraska Press, 1988.

McHugh, Roland. *Annotations to "Finnegans Wake."* Baltimore and London: Johns Hopkins University Press, 1980.

—— *The Sigla of "Finnegans Wake."* Austin: University of Texas Press, 1976.

McKnight, Jeanne. "Unlocking the Word-Hoard: Madness, Identity and Creativity in James Joyce." *JJQ*, 14 (1977): 420–35.

Millett, Kate. *Sexual Politics.* New York: Doubleday, 1970.

Mitchell, Juliet. *Psychoanalysis and Feminism.* London: Pantheon, 1974.

Mink, Louis O. *A "Finnegans Wake" Gazetteer.* Bloomington: Indiana University Press, 1978.

Modern Fiction Studies: James Joyce Number 4 (1958).

Modern Fiction Studies: James Joyce Number 15 (1969).

Moi, Toril. *Sexual/Textual Politics.* London and New York: Methuen, 1985.

Morrissey, L. J. "Joyce's Revision of 'The Sisters': From Epicleti to Modern Fiction." *JJQ*, 24 (1986): 33–54.

Morse, J. Mitchell. "Molly Bloom Revisited." In *A James Joyce Miscellany: Second Series*, ed. Marvin Magalaner, 139–49.

Naremore, James. "Consciousness and Society." In *Approaches to Joyce's "Portrait": Ten Essays*, ed. Thomas F. Staley and Bernard Benstock, 113–34.

Nietzsche, Friedrich. *The Joyful Wisdom*, trans. Thomas Common. 1882; rpt New York: Russell & Russell, 1964.

Noon, William. *Joyce and Aquinas*. New Haven: Yale University Press, 1957.

Norris, Margot. "Anna Livia Plurabelle: The Dream Woman." In *Women in Joyce*, ed. Suzette Henke and Elaine Unkeless, 197–213.

—— *The Decentered Universe of "Finnegans Wake."* Baltimore: Johns Hopkins University Press, 1976.

O'Brien, Darcy. *The Conscience of James Joyce*. Princeton, NJ: Princeton University Press, 1968.

—— "Some Determinants of Molly Bloom." In *Approaches to "Ulysses,"* ed. Thomas F. Staley and Bernard Benstock, 137–55.

O'Hehir, Brendan. *A Gaelic Lexicon for "Finnegans Wake."* Berkeley: University of California Press, 1967.

O'Hehir, Brendan and Dillon, John M. *A Classical Lexicon for "Finnegans Wake."* Berkeley: University of California Press, 1977.

Osteen, Mark. "Gabriel's Sarcasm: A Lost Line in 'The Dead.'" *JJQ*, 25 (1988): 259–61.

Owen, Rodney Wilson. *James Joyce and the Beginnings of "Ulysses."* Ann Arbor, Michigan: UMI Research Press, 1983.

Parrinder, Patrick. *James Joyce*. Cambridge: Cambridge University Press, 1984.

Peake, C. H. *James Joyce: The Citizen and the Artist*. Stanford: Stanford University Press, 1977.

Pecora, Vincent. "'The Dead' and the Generosity of the Word." *PMLA*, 101 (1986): 233–45.

Perreault, Jeanne. "Male Maternity in *Ulysses.*" *English Studies in Canada*, 13 (1987): 304–14.

Peterson, Richard F., Cohn, Alan M., and Epstein, Edmund L. *Work in Progress: Joyce Centenary Essays*. Carbondale: Southern Illinois University Press, 1982.

Phul, Ruth von. "'Major' Tweedy and His Daughter." *JJQ*, 19 (1982): 341–8.

Power, Arthur. *Conversations with James Joyce*, ed. Clive Hart. New York: Harper & Row, 1974.

Rabaté, Jean-Michel. "A Clown's Inquest into Paternity." In *The Fictional Father*, ed. Robert Con Davis, 73–114.

—— "Silence in *Dubliners.*" In *James Joyce: New Perspectives*, ed. Colin MacCabe, 45–72.

Radford, F.L. "Daedalus and the Bird Girl: Classical Text and Celtic

Subtext in *A Portrait.*" *JJQ*, 24 (1987): 253–74.

Ragland-Sullivan, Ellie. *Jacques Lacan and the Philosophy of Psychoanalysis.* Urbana: University of Illinois Press, 1986.

Raynaud, Claudine. "Woman, the Letter Writer; Man, the Writing Master." *JJQ*, 23 (1986): 299–324.

Register, Cheri. "American Feminist Literary Criticism: A Bibliographical Introduction." In *Feminist Literary Criticism*, ed. Josephine Donovan, 1–28.

Restuccia, Frances L. "Molly in Furs." *Novel*, 18 (1985): 101–16.

Reynolds, Mary. "The Dantean Design of Joyce's *Dubliners.*" In *The Seventh of Joyce*, ed. Bernard Benstock, 124–30.

—— *Joyce and Dante: The Shaping Imagination.* Princeton, NJ: Princeton University Press, 1981.

Roche, Anthony. "'The Strange Light of Some New World': Stephen's Vision in 'A Portrait.'" *JJQ*, 25 (1988): 323–32.

Rose, Danis. *Chapters of Coming Forth by Day.* Colchester: A Wake Newslitter Press, 1982.

Rose, Danis and O'Hanlon, John. *Understanding "Finnegans Wake": A Guide to the Narrative of James Joyce's Masterpiece.* New York and London: Garland, 1982.

Rose, Jacqueline. *Sexuality in the Field of Vision.* London: Verso Press, 1986.

Rossman, Charles. "Stephen Dedalus and the Spiritual-Heroic Refrigerating Apparatus: Art and Life in Joyce's *Portrait.*" In *Forms of Modern British Fiction*, ed. Alan Warren Friedman, 101–31.

Ryan, Michael. *Marxism and Deconstruction.* Baltimore: Johns Hopkins University Press, 1982.

Said, Edward. *Beginnings: Intention and Method.* New York: Basic Books, 1975.

Sandulescu, C. George and Hart, Clive, eds. *Assessing the 1984 "Ulysses."* Totowa, NJ: Barnes & Noble, 1986.

Sartre, Jean-Paul. *Being and Nothingness*, trans. Hazel E. Barnes. New York: Philosophical Library, 1956.

Schlossman, Beryl. *Joyce's Catholic Comedy of Language.* Madison: The University of Wisconsin Press, 1985.

Scholes, Robert. *Semiotics and Interpretation.* New Haven: Yale University Press, 1982.

—— "Stephen Dedalus: Poet or Esthete?" In James Joyce, *A Portrait of the Artist as a Young Man: Text, Criticism and Notes*, ed. Chester G. Anderson, 468–80.

Scholes, Robert and Kain, Richard M., eds. *The Workshop of Daedalus: James Joyce and the Raw Materials for "A Portrait of the Artist as a Young Man."* Evanston: Northwestern University Press, 1965.

Schutte, William M. *Twentieth Century Interpretations of "A Portrait of the Artist as a Young Man."* Englewood Cliffs, NJ: Prentice-Hall, 1968.

Schwarz, Daniel. *Reading Joyce's "Ulysses."* New York: St. Martin's Press, 1987.

Scott, Bonnie Kime. *James Joyce.* Brighton: Harvester Press, 1987.

—— *Joyce and Feminism.* Bloomington: Indiana University Press, 1984.

—— ed. *New Alliances in Joyce Studies*. Newark: University of Delaware Press, 1988.

Senn, Fritz. "'The Boarding House' Seen as a Tale of Misdirection." *JJQ*, 23 (1986): 405–13.

—— *Joyce's Dislocutions: Essays on Reading as Translation*, ed. John Paul Riquelme. Baltimore: Johns Hopkins University Press, 1984.

Seward, Barbara. "The Artist and the Rose." 1947; rpt in *Twentieth Century Interpretations of "A Portrait of the Artist as a Young Man,"* ed. William M. Schutte, 53–63.

Shechner, Mark. *Joyce in Nighttown*. Berkeley: University of California Press, 1974.

—— "The Song of the Wandering Aengus: James Joyce and His Mother." In *"Ulysses": Fifty Years*, ed. Thomas F. Staley, 72–89.

Showalter, Elaine, ed. *The New Feminist Criticism*. New York: Pantheon Books, 1985.

Slater, Philip E. *The Glory of Hera*. 1968; rpt Boston: Beacon Press, 1971.

Smith, Joseph H. and Kerrigan, William, eds. *Interpreting Lacan*. New Haven: Yale University Press, 1983.

Snitow, Ann, Stansell, Christine, and Thompson, Sharon, eds. *The Powers of Desire*. New York: Monthly Review Press, 1983.

Sollers, Philippe. "Joyce and Co." In *In the Wake of the "Wake,"* ed. David Hayman and Elliott Anderson, 107–21.

—— "Political Perspectives on Joyce's Work." In *Joyce & Paris*, ed. Jacques Aubert and Maria Jolas, vol. 2, 101–23.

Solomon, Margaret. *Eternal Geomater: The Sexual Universe of "Finnegans Wake."* Carbondale: Southern Illinois University Press, 1969.

Sosnoski, James. "Reading Acts and Reading Warrants: Some Implications of Readers Responding to Joyce's Portrait of Stephen." *JJQ*, 16 (1978/9): 42–63.

Spivak, Gayatri Chakravorty. "French Feminism in an International Frame." *Yale French Studies*, 62 (1981): 154–84.

Spoo, Robert. "'Una Piccola Nuvoletta': Ferrero's *Young Europe* and Joyce's Mature *Dubliners* Stories." *JJQ*, 24 (1987): 401–10.

Staley, Thomas F. "A Beginning: Signification, Story and Discourse in Joyce's 'The Sisters.'" In *Critical Essays on James Joyce*, ed. Bernard Benstock, 176–90.

—— ed. *"Ulysses": Fifty Years*. Bloomington: Indiana University Press, 1974.

Staley, Thomas F. and Benstock, Bernard, eds. *Approaches to Joyce's "Portrait": Ten Essays*. Pittsburgh: University of Pittsburgh Press, 1976.

—— *Approaches to "Ulysses."* Pittsburgh: University of Pittsburgh Press, 1970.

Steinberg, Erwin R. *The Stream of Consciousness and Beyond in "Ulysses."* Pittsburgh: University of Pittsburgh Press, 1973.

Steiner, Wendy. "'There Was Meaning in His Look': The Meeting of Pictorial Models in Joyce's 'Nausicaa.'" *University of Hartford Studies in Literature*, 16 (1984): 90–103.

Sultan, Stanley. *The Argument of "Ulysses."* Columbus: Ohio State University Press, 1958.

Thornton, Weldon. *Allusions in "Ulysses."* Chapel Hill: University of North Carolina Press, 1968.

Tindall, William York. *James Joyce: His Way of Interpreting the Modern World.* New York: Scribner's, 1950.

—— *A Reader's Guide to "Finnegans Wake."* New York: Farrar, Straus & Giroux, 1969.

—— *A Reader's Guide to James Joyce.* New York: Farrar, Straus & Giroux, 1959.

Torchiana, Donald. *Backgrounds for Joyce's "Dubliners."* Boston: Allen & Unwin, 1986.

Toynbee, Philip. "A Study of James Joyce's *Ulysses.*" In *James Joyce: Two Decades of Criticism,* ed. Seon Givens, 243–84.

Troy, Mark. *Mummeries of Resurrection: The Cycle of Osiris in "Finnegans Wake."* Uppsala: Acta Universitatis Upsaliensis, 1976.

Tucker, Lindsey. *Stephen and Bloom at Life's Feast: Alimentary Symbolism and the Creative Process in James Joyce's "Ulysses."* Columbus: Ohio State University Press, 1984.

Unkeless, Elaine. "Bats and Sanguivorous Bugaboos." *JJQ,* 15 (1978): 128–33.

—— "Leopold Bloom as a Womanly Man." *Modernist Studies,* 2 (1976): 35–44.

—— "The Conventional Molly Bloom." In *Women in Joyce,* ed. Suzette Henke and Elaine Unkeless, 150–68.

Vico, Giambattista. *The New Science of Giambattista Vico.* Abridged Translation of the Third Edition (1744), trans. and ed. Thomas Goddard Bergin and Max Harold Fisch. Ithaca: Cornell University Press, 1970.

Voelker, Joseph. "Molly Bloom and the Rhetorical Tradition." *Comparative Literature Studies,* 16 (1979): 146–64.

Waisbren, Burton A. and Walzl, Florence L. "Paresis and the Priest: James Joyce's Symbolic Use of Syphilis in 'The Sisters.' " *Annals of Internal Medicine,* 80 (1974): 758–62.

Walzl, Florence. "A Book of Signs and Symbols." In *The Seventh of Joyce,* ed. Bernard Benstock, 117–23.

—— "*Dubliners*: Women in Irish Society." In *Women in Joyce,* ed. Suzette Henke and Elaine Unkeless, 31–56.

—— "Gabriel and Michael: The Conclusion of 'The Dead.' " *JJQ,* 4 (1966): 17–31.

Walkley, R. Barrie. "The Bloom of Motherhood: Couvade as a Structural Device in *Ulysses.*" *JJQ,* 18 (1980): 55–67.

White, David A. *The Grand Continuum: Reflections on Joyce and Metaphysics.* Pittsburgh: University of Pittsburgh Press, 1983.

Wilson, Robert Rawdon. "In Palamedes' Shadow: Game and Play Concepts Today." *Canadian Review of Comparative Literature,* 12 (1985): 177–99.

Wright, David. *Characters of Joyce.* Totowa, NJ: Barnes & Noble, 1983.

Young, Robert, ed. *Untying the Text.* Boston: Routledge, 1981.

INDEX

Note: As Catholicism and Ireland are pervasive themes in Joyce's work they have not been exhaustively indexed. Abbreviations are as in the text.

279